Tibetan Logic

Tibetan Logic

Katherine Manchester Rogers

Snow Lion Publications
Ithaca, New York

Snow Lion Publications
P.O. Box 6483
Ithaca, NY 14851 USA
(607) 273-8519
www.snowlionpub.com

Printed in USA on acid-free recycled paper.

ISBN-10: 1-55939-315-7
ISBN-13: 978-1-55939-315-7

Library of Congress Cataloging-in-Publication Data

Rogers, Katherine, 1952-
  Tibetan logic / Katherine Manchester Rogers.
      p. cm.
  Includes bibliographical references and index.
  ISBN-13: 978-1-55939-315-7 (alk. paper)
  ISBN-10: 1-55939-315-7 (alk. paper)
  1. Phur-bu-lcog Byams-pa-rgya-mtsho, 1825-1901. Tshad ma'i gźuṅ don 'byed pa'i bsdus grwa'i rnam bźag rigs lam 'phrul gyi lde mig. 2. Buddhist logic. 3. Debates and debating--Religious aspects--Buddhism. I. Phur-bu-lcog Byams-pa-rgya-mtsho, 1825-1901. Tshad ma'i gźuṅ don 'byed pa'i bsdus grwa'i rnam bźag rigs lam 'phrul gyi lde mig. English. II. Title.
  BC25.P463R65 2008
  160.88'2943--dc22
                        2008042192

To my parents, Julia and Henry Rogers,
and to my grandparents, Iris and Wayne White

Contents (For a more detailed outline see p. 487)

TECHNICAL NOTE

In this work, the transliteration of Tibetan follows the system formulated by Turrell Wylie.[1] The names of Tibetan authors and orders are given in "essay phonetics" for the sake of easy pronunciation.

At the first occurrence of important technical terms, Tibetan equivalents are given, accompanied by the Sanskrit when available. These terms appear together in the Glossary, in English alphabetical order. Sanskrit terms that have been constructed from the Tibetan are indicated by an asterisk.

PART ONE:
ESSENTIALS OF REASONING

Introduction

PURPOSE AND METHOD

This book is an attempt to explain introductory Tibetan logic as it is studied and practiced in the monastic universities of the Ge-luk-pa order of Tibetan Buddhism. Since its founding by Tsong-kha-pa in the late fourteenth and early fifteenth centuries, the Ge-luk-pa order has created a system of education and a curriculum designed to enable the student to develop a "path of reasoning." A path of reasoning is a consciousness that has been trained in reasoned analysis until it can use analysis to realize, first, the meaning of religious texts and, eventually, the true nature of reality.

This work is primarily exegetical, explaining the vocabulary, concepts, and principles of Ge-luk-pa logic as it is taught today. However, there is no monolithic Ge-luk-pa presentation of logic; there is no definitive and unchallenged point of view on all topics. Any given monastic college will have its own emphasis and favorite texts; and even within one monastic college, different scholars will have different opinions on the issues that arise in the study of introductory logic. There is thus no single, unquestioned point of view. Rather, Ge-luk-pa logic today presents a fascinating nexus of opinions and counteropinions, of complications and contradictions. My purpose is to draw out of this nexus a general appreciation of the Ge-luk-pa approach to logic and its place in the religious life.

As the basis for this study, I have translated an introductory logic manual on *Signs and Reasonings* by Pur-bu-jok,[a] the Thirteenth Dalai Lama's philosophy tutor. I use this text as the framework of an attempt to articulate a "Ge-luk-pa presentation" of the subject. It is one way of ordering the sometimes bewildering complexity and richness of the Ge-luk-pa tradition. Where there is consensus, I explain it as fully as

---

[a] Pur-bu-jok's full name is Pur-bu-jok Jam-pa-gya-tso (*phur bu lcog byams ba rgya mtsho*, 1825-1901). *Signs and Reasonings* is a title given to a genre of works dealing with introductory logic. The full name of Pur-bu-jok's work on *Signs and Reasonings* is *The Topic of Signs and Reasonings from the "Great Path of Reasoning" in the Magic Key to the Path of Reasoning, Explanation of the Collected Topics Revealing the Meaning of the Texts on Prime Cognition* (Buxador: 1965). This textbook is used as part of the curriculum at the Jay (*byes*) College of Se-ra (*se rwa*) Monastic University and the Jang-tsay (*byang rtsɛ*) College of Gan-den (*dga' ldan*) Monastic University.

possible, drawing on a number of sources. Where there is difference of opinion, I similarly explain that. In this way I hope to sketch the essentials and the lively diversity of the Ge-luk-pa system of logic as it is being transmitted today in the monastic universities.

I have incorporated into my explanation material from: (1) other Ge-luk-pa texts, some on logic and some on related topics, and (2) commentary I have received from eminent Ge-luk-pa scholars.

I. *Ge-luk-pa texts*

(a) Commentaries on Dharmakīrti's *Commentary on (Dignāga's) "Compilation of Prime Cognition"* [a]
    (1) Gyel-tsap's *Revealer of the Path of Liberation* [2]
    (2) The First Dalai Lama's *Ornament of Reasoning on Prime Cognition* [3]
    (3) Paṇ-chen Sö-nam-drak-pa's *Illumination of the Thought* [4]
(b) Introductory logic manuals
    (1) Ge-shay Tsül-trim-nam-gyel's *Signs and Reasonings* [5]
    (2) Jam-yang-shay-pa's *Signs and Reasonings* [6]

(c) Other introductory manuals
    (1) Pur-bu-jok's *Collected Topics* [b]
    (2) Ge-shay Jam-pel-sam-pel's *Awareness and Knowledge* [7]

II. *4*

I received commentary on the texts listed above from numerous teachers; those from whom I received extensive commentary are:

(1) Lati Rin-po-che, former abbot of Shar-tsay College of Gan-den Monastic University.
(2) Ken-sur Ye-shay-tup-ten, former abbot of Lo-sel-ling College of

---

[a] Dharmakīrti (*chos kyi grags pa*, 600-660), *Commentary on (Dignāga's) "Compilation of Prime Cognition,"* P5709, vol. 130. This text is the main root text used by Ge-luk-pa monasteries in their study of the topics of "Prime Cognition," for which the manuals on *Signs and Reasonings* serve as an introduction.

[b] Pur-bu-jok, *The Presentation of the Collected Topics Revealing the Meaning of the Texts on Prime Cognition, Magic Key to the Path of Reasoning* (Buxa: n.p., 1965). This work is made up of three parts: "The Greater Path of Reasoning," "The Introductory Path of Reasoning," and "The Middling Path of Reasoning." The "Greater Path of Reasoning" contains his works on "Awareness and Knowledge" and "*Signs and Reasonings,*" as well as other introductory topics. For a complete list of the contents of each of the three parts of Pur-bu-jok's *Collected Topics*, see Daniel Perdue's *Debate in Tibetan Buddhism* (Ithaca, New York: Snow Lion Publications, 1992), pp. xvi-xvii.

Dre-pung Monastic University.

(3) Ge-shay Ge-dün-lo-drö, of Go-mang College of Dre-pung Monastic University.

(4) Ge-shay Pel-den-drak-pa, of Lo-sel-ling.

(5) Ge-shay Lob-sang-gya-tso, of Lo-sel-ling.

(6) Ge-shay Sang-gyay-sam-drup (Georges Dreyfus), who was the first Westerner to receive the ge-shay degree in 1985 after having studied at the Buddhist School of Dialectics in Dharamsala and all three Ge-luk-pa monastic universities in South India.

The texts listed above span six centuries, from the fifteenth through the twentieth, but this study is not a historical analysis. I am not comparing Ge-luk-pa logic texts over time nor tracing the development of Ge-luk-pa ideas. I also am not tracing the development of Ge-luk-pa logic from its roots in the works of Dignāga and Dharmakīrti nor comparing the Ge-luk-pa logic manuals with pre-Ge-luk-pa forerunners (e.g., logic works of the Sa-kya order, such as Sa-kya Paṇḍita's *Treasury of Reasoning*).[8] And I am not comparing the introductory logic manuals used today in Ge-luk-pa monasteries with earlier versions, such as the well-known Ra-tö (*rwa stod*) manual of *Signs and Reasonings* by Jam-yang-chok-hla-ö-ser.[9]

The Ge-luk-pa order has several competing monastic colleges, following various oral traditions. My exposition illustrates the diversity of these traditions by citing and comparing the points of view of scholars from Gan-den Shar-tsay, Lo-sel-ling, and Go-mang Colleges. The organization is around issues, and thus the reader should not expect a systematic comparison of Ge-luk-pa logic of the various monastic universities, nor a historical account of the development of their various oral traditions. This is a general presentation of Ge-luk-pa logic as explained in Ge-luk-pa monasteries today. By putting this diversity into an order based on Pur-bu-jok's text, I highlight conflicting points of view and avoid oversimplification. I hope to show the general nature of Ge-luk-pa thought without imposing on it an artificial "unity."

To add depth to this presentation, I compare the current Ge-luk-pa treatment of key issues with the corresponding treatment in a source outside of the sect, an eleventh-century logic text by the Indian Buddhist logician Mokṣākaragupta.[10] I do this for two reasons: to show that many aspects of the Ge-luk-pa system of logic are not innovations but part of an even older tradition and to highlight features of various issues that may be unique to the Ge-luk-pa point of view.

Tibetan logic manuals are extremely terse and concise. Rather like a teacher's notes, they are not meant to be the complete exposition;

discussion and debate fill out the topic. In explaining the topics of introductory logic, I present Pur-bu-jok's manual in its entirety and incorporate passages from other Ge-luk-pa logic texts, as well as the commentary of Ge-luk-pa scholars.

Pur-bu-jok's text is in the usual shorthand style, not readily understandable outside the tradition. The ideas are fleshed out by teachers in the classroom and more advanced students in the debate courtyard, along generally accepted lines. An occasional statement is so brief as to be ambiguous, however. To illustrate this, as well as the variety of responses of Ge-luk-pa scholars, I will cite a passage from Pur-bu-jok's explanation of correct nature signs. The highly technical aspects of this topic are explained in my chapter on "The Pervasions"; here I present it only briefly.

Correct reasons, or signs (the terms are equivalent in this context), are reasons that are capable of generating new understanding of a thesis in the mind of an appropriate person. In the syllogism, "The subject, sound, is impermanent because of being a product," the sign is "product," and that which is being proved (the probandum) is that sound is impermanent. A person who has understood that sound is a product and is wondering whether sound is impermanent or not is said to be *ready* to understand that sound is impermanent; and that understanding can be precipitated by this reasoning.

In this syllogism, "product" is a nature sign. Correct signs can be categorized in several ways, but the primary division is into three: effect signs, nature signs, and nonobservation signs. Pur-bu-jok's definition of something's being a correct nature sign is:

> (1) It (x) is a correct sign in the proof of something and (2) it is posited from the point of view that whatever is held as the explicit predicate of the probandum in the proof of that by the sign x must be of one nature with x.[11]

This is all; he goes on to discuss the division of nature signs into two types and to give illustrations.

From the above definition alone, one learns that the sign must be correct and the predicate (impermanent) must be of one nature with the sign (product). If that were an adequate characterization of nature signs, then any correct sign involving a predicate of the same nature as the sign would be a correct nature sign—which is not the case.

Ge-luk-pa scholars agree in amplifying Pur-bu-jok's points to mean that a nature sign must be (1) a correct sign *of (that is, proving) a positive phenomenon* and (2) *related to* the predicate in a strictly defined "*relationship of sameness of nature.*" Neither of these requirements is clear in Pur-bu-jok's definition, although both can be understood through study of (a) other parts of Pur-bu-jok's text, (b) the commentary of Ge-luk-pa scholars, and (c) the treatment of this topic in other Ge-luk-pa logic texts.

I. The first issue: a nature sign must be a "correct sign of *a positive phenomenon.*" For most colleges this means that the predicate of the probandum *itself* must be a positive phenomenon. Lati Rin-po-che reflects this point of view when he says,

> The first two types, correct effect and nature signs, are called correct signs of a positive phenomenon because the predicate of the probandum is a positive phenomenon; that is, that which is held as the explicit predicate of the probandum is a positive phenomenon.[12]

In the syllogism, "The subject, sound, is impermanent because of being a product," "product" is a correct nature sign, and (according to most colleges) "impermanent" is a positive phenomenon.[a] Scholars of the Go-mang College of Dre-pung Monastic University have a different view. Ge-shay Pel-den-drak-pa explains,

> According to Go-mang College, [in the case of nature signs] the predicate of the probandum does not [itself] have to be a positive phenomenon; it is sufficient that the sign be proving a positive phenomenon.[13]

Go-mang scholars agree that a nature sign proves a positive phenomenon, but teach that the predicate *itself* may be a negative phenomenon.[b]

Despite their differences about the predicate, all the colleges agree that a nature sign must be a sign of a positive phenomenon. Pur-bu-jok's definition omits this point, however, specifying only that it must

---

[a] "Impermanent" is defined as meaning "momentary" and is a positive phenomenon, according to most colleges.

[b] According to Go-mang scholars, "impermanent" is a negative phenomenon. They agree that product is a nature sign in the proof of sound as impermanent, but disagree about whether impermanent is a positive or negative phenomenon. Regarding another syllogism—"the subject, sound, is opposite from nonimpermanent because of being a product"—there is complete agreement that the predicate is a negative phenomenon. Most colleges, however, call product in this case a nonobservation sign, because (for them) any proof involving the proof of a negative phenomenon is necessarily a nonobservation sign. For Go-mang, however, product is a nature sign in this proof because in that school a nature sign may have as predicate a negative phenomenon.

be a correct sign. It is interesting to note how different scholars respond to this omission. Ge-shay Lob-sang-gya-tso says that there is no flaw in the text; the meaning is intended, though not fully expressed in the definition, and one has only to bring material from elsewhere to fill in the meaning. He cites Pur-bu-jok's own statement, elsewhere in his text, that "whatever is either a correct effect sign or a correct nature sign is necessarily a correct sign of a *positive phenomenon*."[14]

An interesting fact that emerges from this study is that Ge-luk-pa scholars do not consider ambiguity to be a flaw in a text, and even sometimes explain it as a way to provoke debate. This may of course be an apologetic on the part of the scholars, a way of glossing over mistakes in the texts; however, some express the view that there may be a pedagogical purpose in apparent mistakes, especially in introductory manuals. Ge-shay Ge-dün-lo-drö supports this approach, saying, in a different, but similar, context, "There is no flaw in the text; it is written this way to provoke debate." And Lati Rin-po-che comments, "It's as if Pur-bu-jok were making trouble—to provoke debate." Seeming inconsistencies can inspire analysis and careful scrutiny. These are held to be very important, because the purpose of the study of logic goes beyond gaining familiarity with the logic texts; it is meant to be a tool to develop a path of reason—to become able to confront, creatively and with enthusiasm, the contradictions that arise in study and in meditation on a broad range of topics.

Other scholars cope with Pur-bu-jok's definition by suggesting changes. After pointing out, as a problem with the definition, that one could posit examples that satisfy it but are not actually correct nature signs, Ge-shay Pel-den-drak-pa says,

> One should add to the definition the requirement that whatever is held as the explicit predicate of the probandum in that proof is necessarily a positive phenomenon or the requirement that the sign must be a sign of a positive phenomenon.[15]

II. The second issue: a correct nature sign "must be *related* to the predicate in *a relationship of sameness of nature*." This is more precise and more subtle than Pur-bu-jok's "must be of one nature." There must be a special relationship between the sign and the predicate, which involves more than being merely of one nature. To characterize the special relationship between the sign and the predicate, teachers explain that (1) the predicate must be the same nature as the sign and (2) the predicate must pervade the sign. The first alone is not enough, because the predicate must pervade the sign, whereas the sign need not pervade the predicate. In this respect, Pur-bu-jok's definition is incomplete and could be misleading. Students will learn the technical requirements and subtleties of a relationship of sameness of nature later in their monastic studies, but Pur-bu-jok could easily have made his definition more precise.

Here is the First Dalai Lama's definition of correct nature sign:

> 1) It is a correct sign of a positive phenomenon in the proof of that and (2) whatever is the explicit predicate of the probandum in the proof of that is necessarily a pervader that is the same nature as it.[16]

The first part states the "positive phenomenon" requirement, which is not expressed explicitly by Pur-bu-jok; and the second part expresses the second criterion of nature signs more accurately and completely than does Pur-bu-jok. The First Dalai Lama's definition was well known, but Pur-bu-jok chose to provide a different definition that could be misleading. Is it a casual mistake, to be corrected, or a teaching device, to be used for debate? Pur-bu-jok's text contains other passages of ambiguous brevity, which I will explore in detail as they appear.

In this book, my purpose is to explain all the topics covered in Pur-bu-jok's manual, *Signs and Reasonings*. Explanation is necessary: like other texts used in the Ge-luk-pa curriculum, it is written in a terse and turgid style. It is not intended that the manual be used by a solitary student; it is always studied under the guidance of a teacher, and the study is enhanced by many hours of intense and lively debate.

My further purpose is to set Pur-bu-jok's topics in context, showing how his manual is used in the Ge-luk-pa curriculum. That text is not intended to cover the whole of Tibetan logic. It serves as an introduction to the more complex topics of valid cognition by giving a beginner the vocabulary and conceptual framework needed for such studies.

CONTEXT OF THE CULTIVATION OF A "PATH OF REASONING"

A fundamental teaching of Buddhism is that, under analysis, ordinary life is found to be a state of suffering. Roughly speaking, beings who suffer (sentient beings) are caught in a cycle of birth, death, and rebirth; and this cycle is set in motion and powered by a cause that abides in their own minds—ignorance. This root of suffering is a specific and fundamental ignorance: ignorance of the true nature of reality. Sentient beings misunderstand the way things (that is, themselves and the phenomena around them) exist.

The various tenet systems of Buddhism are said to explain this fundamental misconception with varying degrees of subtlety. The Prāsaṅgika-Madhyamaka tenet system—which seemingly all schools of Tibetan Buddhism agree to be the highest (most subtle)—identifies this root ignorance as the conception that phenomena are inherently existent. More fully phrased, sentient beings innately conceive of themselves and phenomena as existing inherently, concretely, "from their own side"; this misconception draws them into mistaken and afflicted states of mind (such as desire and hatred); afflicted states draw them into nonvirtuous activities; these activities bring harm and suffering to themselves and others; and the process continues until the sentient beings replace root ignorance by wisdom.

Anyone who wishes to break this cycle of suffering must develop "wisdom understanding the true nature of reality." The stated goal of religious practice in Tibetan Buddhism is not only to liberate oneself from the suffering of cyclic existence but also, and more importantly, to liberate others.

Tsong-kha-pa summarizes the aspects of the path to enlightenment as three: renunciation, *bodhicitta*, and the correct view of emptiness. Renunciation means having seen that the true character of cyclic existence is suffering and renounced all attachment to it; the more clearly one regards cyclic existence the less enticement it holds except as an opportunity for engaging in religious practice. *Bodhicitta* is induced by great compassion; it is a mind that cherishes all sentient beings and one-pointedly seeks highest enlightenment, not for one's own sake but to free sentient beings from suffering and from the causes of suffering. The correct view of emptiness is the wisdom realizing the emptiness of inherent existence of persons and phenomena.

To attain wisdom, one must cultivate valid knowledge; wisdom is valid knowledge regarding the nature of oneself and of phenomena. One cultivates valid knowledge in order to transform oneself: to become a person who can help others effectively—to develop the compassion and wisdom of a Buddha.

In the context of meditative practice, experience of the Madhyamaka view is acquired by meditation on emptiness, as set forth in the Madhyamaka system of tenets. This emptiness is not nonexistence, obliteration, or negation of existence; it is the negation of a certain quality or characteristic of existence—a quality (inherent existence) that untrained persons attribute automatically to themselves and, by extension, to all phenomena.

The root cause of cyclic existence is in oneself (in one's own mental continuum). It is described in various phrases: "the conception of inherent existence," "the mind conceiving inherent existence," or "the innate consciousness conceiving 'I.'"

According to the Ge-luk-pa system, as a beginner in meditation on emptiness one undertakes an extensive, analytically demanding, deeply probing examination into one's own self, into how one perceives oneself and the world—how one experiences life. The effort requires a capable mind and the persistence to make it a strong mind—a strong "path of reasoning" (a mind trained in valid knowledge), focused and fortified by years of training. The training involves a ruthless pursuit of falsity, of mistakes in one's thought, in one's mind, in one's attitudes and views. Extreme discipline is needed, first, because the meditations are intellectually demanding and, second, because the technique involves generating strong emotion and then analyzing the root of that emotion, to get at the underlying misconception that is its source.

Thus, the student needs a strong "path of reasoning" to pursue not only the academic path (the requirements of the Ge-shay degree are rigorous) but also the path of meditation and self-transformation. This "path of reasoning" refers to a mind that is trained, powerful, flexible, and able to approach an idea from numerous points of view, to discern the logical consequences of any view, and to express the consequences succinctly and clearly, so as to guide others to see mistakes in their views. This skill begins in the classroom with the first introductory topics and is perfected in the debate courtyard. When it is applied in meditation on emptiness, it is a powerful tool for self-transformation.

The curriculum of the monastic universities covers five core topics:

(1) The Perfection of Wisdom,
(2) Madhyamaka Philosophy,
(3) Phenomenology,
(4) Discipline, and
(5) Valid Cognition.

Before students begin the study of the core topics, however, they give considerable attention to introductory topics, which focus on three main subjects: (1) *Collected Topics* (*bsdus grva*), (2) *Awareness and Knowledge* (*blo rig*), and (3) *Signs and Reasonings* (*rtags rigs*). In working to develop a path of reasoning, Ge-luk-pa students devote their first few years to the study of introductory topics. These present the basic vocabulary and concepts that they will need in the more complex core studies to follow.

In the *Collected Topics*,[17] the beginner will learn about such concepts as established bases, existents, impermanent phenomena, and permanent phenomena; and will study generality and particularity and the relationship between a generality and the particularities subsumed in it. As in any discipline, there is a vocabulary to be learned. "Isolate" is an example: the isolate of a pencil is the pencil itself, in isolation from all other phenomena; only the pencil itself is "one with the pencil," the isolate of the pencil. These concepts will be essential in future study of the topics of valid cognition and Madhyamaka philosophy.

After a year, the student begins "Awareness and Knowledge," the study of types of consciousnesses, such as direct perception and inference. In the following year the student takes up *Signs and Reasonings,* the introduction to logic. This includes the mechanics of reasoning, syllogisms and their parts, and the correct reasons and signs and how they come to be correct—that is, able to induce in the debater or meditator new knowledge about something not formerly understood.

The Ge-luk-pa student is seeking to develop a mind capable of subtle and clear understanding—capable of penetrating the truth, of discerning phenomena as they are. The truth is not held to be something that one can be told; the crucial element is that the student must find it alone and afresh. Thus, the Buddha emphasized the need for the student to analyze well his words:

> Monks, my words are to be accepted by scholars
> Not [merely] out of respect
> But upon having analyzed them, just as
> Gold is accepted after scorching, cutting, rubbing.[18]

Phenomena appear in one way but exist in another. That is, according to Buddhism, we do not see things as they ultimately exist; there is a discrepancy between the true nature of a phenomenon and our perception of it. The mind that can perceive the true nature of phenomena is a "wisdom-consciousness." Such a mind is described as valid[a]—as incontrovertible in its perception of that true nature.

Such a valid mind can be conceptual or nonconceptual. In fact, it is important to note in the Ge-luk-pa system the importance placed on conceptual, analytical thought. There are two valid modes of knowledge: direct valid cognition and inferential valid cognition. Direct ways of perceiving are nonconceptual, unaccompanied by conceptual

---

[a] From the Latin *validus* (strong), "valid" carries the sense of being sound, able to stand examination. Validity is soundness—the strength that comes from being supported by fact.

thought in any form. Inference is an indirect way of perceiving, because it is conceptual—its functioning is based on mental images (conceptual constructs). Inference is not, however, to be rejected or undervalued. An essential point in the Ge-luk-pa system is that inference—even though it is indirect—is incontrovertible, in the sense that it does bring valid knowledge concerning the object on which it is focused. This point (that inference can enable one truly to grasp the object under consideration) is extremely important and justifies the tremendous emphasis put on mental training and discipline in this system.

The mind sought is a completely nonmistaken mind perceiving truth—a direct valid perceiver. The development of such a mind depends on and must be preceded by development of an indirect, conceptual understanding of emptiness. In this system, inference is viewed as a necessary interim stage between wrong understanding and direct valid cognition. Inference is indeed mistaken, but in only one sense: that what appears to it is not an object's true nature. What appears to the well-trained mind (the good "path of reasoning") is still a mental construct, but it is utterly correct and a true reflection of the phenomenon, and thus it enables one to experience that phenomenon's true nature. A person who has developed a good path of reasoning can attain clear knowledge of all phenomena.

In the language of the basic logic texts, it is said that "in dependence on the presentation of *Signs and Reasonings* the mode of abiding of all phenomena can be seen clearly, as if in a mirror"; the claim is that when one knows well the presentation of *Signs and Reasonings*, one can attain clear knowledge of all phenomena. By means of this strong path of reasoning, valid knowledge is attained—wisdom penetrating the true nature of phenomena, their mode of abiding, just as they are. For this reason, the study of *Signs and Reasonings* is said to be a key unlocking the door to the profound treatises on valid cognition.

Validity does not arise of itself; a mind incontrovertible in its perception of the true nature of phenomena must be generated. The Buddha is said to have become valid; that is, he generated validity in himself in order to help others. This is reflected in the opening stanzas of one of the main texts on valid cognition, Dignāga's *Compilation of Prime Cognition:*

> Homage to the one
> Who has become valid,
> Who has assumed the task of helping transmigrators,

The Teacher, Sugata and Protector.[a]

Commenting on this verse, Pur-bu-jok writes:

> The words "has assumed the task of helping transmigrators" indicate that [a Buddha] comes into being in dependence on his causes, the fulfillment of contemplation and application.
>   What qualities does our teacher possess? The expression "Sugata and Protector" indicates that he is an unsurpassed protector because of possessing both the fulfillment of abandonment for one's own sake and the fulfillment of realization for the sake of others' welfare.[19]

Minds are not automatically capable of penetrating the truth; this skill must be developed. A mind that has this skill—trained in the topics of valid knowledge and *Signs and Reasonings*—is called a "path of reasoning." Ultimately the student seeks to understand the true nature of all phenomena. Dharmakīrti says of the Buddha, "He has cleared away the net of conceptuality." Conceptuality is always in relation to something, to some object. Its two parts—conception of self of phenomena and self of persons—are like nets or traps, which have to be cleared away.

It is not contradictory for a mental training manual, devoted to aiding a student in the rigorous channeling of *conceptual* thought and the development of *conceptual* power, to praise the one who has "cleared away the net of conceptuality."[b] On the contrary, this clearing away is the ultimate goal of the mental discipline.

And what is the object toward which this correct thought (valid consciousness) is directed? It is the true nature of reality, emptiness, as it is taught in the Prāsaṅgika-Madhyamaka system of tenets. Thus, the Ge-luk-pa student is attempting to develop true (strong, valid) knowledge of phenomena, which requires the elimination of wrong ideas. As

---

[a]   The Sanskrit for this passage is:

pramāṇa-bhūtāya jagad-dhitaiṣiṇe
praṇamya śāstre sugatāya tāyine
pramāṇa-siddhyai sva-matāt samuccayaḥ
kariṣyate viprasṛtād ihaikataḥ

Masaaki Hattori, translator and annotator, *Dignāga on Perception, being the Pratyakṣapariccheda of Dignāga's Pramāṇasamuccaya from the Sanskrit fragments and the Tibetan version* (Cambridge, Massachusetts: Harvard University Press, 1968), p. 73.

[b]   A passage from the salutation at the beginning of Dharmakīrti's *Commentary on (Dignāga's) Compilation of Prime Cognition*, cited by Pur-bu-jok in *Signs and Reasonings*, p. 1a.4.

Mahāyāna beginners, seeking understanding of ultimate truth, Ge-luk-pa students recognize that their perception of the nature of reality is mistaken, that phenomena are overlaid with mental superimpositions that prevent one's grasping their true nature. The mental training is only partly aimed at eliminating misconceptions in regard to the topics studied. Its more important purpose is to eliminate one's misconceptions concerning people and phenomena.

The study of Madhyamaka is preceded by years of experience in debate and logic. Study of valid cognition pervades the whole curriculum in that, beginning with *Signs and Reasonings,* the topics of valid cognition are generally studied for two months of every year. It is thus a unifying thread of the curriculum.

The study of valid cognition encompasses eight topics, as set forth in the commentaries on the *Pramāṇavarttika,*[a] but the introductory logic manuals deal with only two of these: correct inference and [incorrect] quasi-inference. The student's concern at this stage is to understand inference: its generation, its process (how it is developed), and its basis (correct signs).

SOME VOCABULARY USED IN *SIGNS AND REASONINGS*

A sign (*rtags*) is a reason (*gtan tshigs*)—the terms are synonymous—used in a syllogism to prove a particular thesis. Reasoning is a broad, general term for the application of the rules of logic. Reasoning encompasses not only signs, but also syllogisms (*sbyor ba*), proof statements (*sgrub ngag*), and consequences (*thal 'gyur*)—in fact, everything involved in establishing the validity of a thesis.

Pur-bu-jok posits as the definition of "sign": "that which is set as a sign."[20] Lati Rin-po-che explains this definition to mean "that which is taken to mind as a sign."[21] Pur-bu-jok goes on to say, however,

> Whatever is either an existent or a nonexistent is necessarily a sign in the proof of something because whatever is either an existent or a nonexistent is necessarily set as a sign in the proof of that. This is because "horn of a rabbit" is set as the sign in "Such-and-such a subject is impermanent because of being the horn of a rabbit."[22]

Clearly, anything may be taken to mind as a sign, however absurd it

---

[a] These eight "categories of logic" are correct direct perception and quasi-direct perception, correct inference and quasi-inference, correct proof statements and quasi-proof statements, correct refutations and quasi refutations.

may be. What is set as a sign is not necessarily a "correct sign" (*rtags yang dag*).

Correct signs can lead to valid knowledge concerning phenomena that would otherwise remain hidden and inaccessible. Reasoning is the means of developing incontrovertible knowledge of, and experience of, phenomena that are currently hidden, and it is the means of eliminating ignorance—that is, such misconceptions as attributing inherent existence to phenomena and persons.

Sentient beings are considered to have mistaken views about many things. If we attribute the quality x to an object that does not in fact have that quality, then, in Ge-luk-pa phraseology, x is nonexistent in relation to that object. For example, a person with emphysema may have every right to a parking spot reserved for the handicapped and yet, appearing to be able bodied, may be unfairly criticized. The critic attributes physical strength to the person on the basis of appearance, but strength is in fact nonexistent in relation to that person. The attribution is false, and all judgments of the person based on it are false.

The beginners' manuals of logic provide a way to develop valid knowledge regarding hidden phenomena—those that are not accessible to direct perception. Hidden phenomena include subtle impermanence and emptiness, and knowledge of these is developed—initially—only through reasoning. Furthermore, according to the basic principles set forth in the logic manuals, a reason can be the basis of correct inferential knowledge only if it is a correct reason. Not every reason, or sign, is correct. A correct sign is defined as "that which is the three modes"[23] (see p. 399).

The three modes (*tshul gsum*) are the three characteristics that a sign must have in order to be correct; they are criteria for establishing the validity of the sign. The modes refer to the relationships that must exist in a syllogism between the subject (*chos can*), the predicate of the probandum (*bsgrub bya'i chos*), and the sign if the sign is to cause inferential understanding of the thesis. These three modes are: (1) the property of the subject (*phyogs chos*), (2) the forward pervasion (*rjes khyab*), and (3) the counterpervasion (*ldog khyab*).

To help students grasp these ideas, Ge-luk-pa teachers discuss them in terms of specific syllogisms. They have several "model" syllogisms that are used over and over again.

The model syllogism. Let us examine a traditional syllogism and its two proof statements. In the syllogism, "The subject, sound, is impermanent because of being a product":

- The subject is "sound."
- The thesis (that which is to be proved, the "probandum") is "sound is impermanent."
- The predicate of the probandum is "impermanent."
- The sign is "product."

This syllogism has two proof statements:

- Positive: "Whatever is a product is necessarily impermanent, as is the case with pot; sound also is a product."
- Negative: "Whatever is permanent is necessarily a nonproduct, as is the case with uncompounded space; sound, however, is a product."

Each of the two proof statements explicitly expresses the three modes. "Sound also [or 'however'] is a product" states the first mode (the property of the subject) in stating that the sign "product" is a property of the subject "sound." The positive and negative statements of pervasion ("whatever is a product is necessarily impermanent" and "whatever is permanent is necessarily a nonproduct") state the two aspects of the relationship between the sign and the predicate that constitute the second mode (forward pervasion) and the third mode (counterpervasion). The syllogism summarizes the three modes and states the conclusion (the thesis being proved).

The consequence. Another basis of inference is the consequence, a statement of the logical extension of an idea. If someone holds that sound is permanent, for example, the "consequence" statement is: "It follows that sound is not a product, because of being permanent." In other words, if sound is permanent, it follows that it is not a product.

Western students are unlikely to argue that sound is permanent, but, according to Buddhists, many Hindu students—raised on the doctrinal statement that the sound of the Vedas lasts forever—have had an unexamined idea of sound as permanent. To state the consequence that sound must therefore be a nonproduct leads to a logical examination of such an idea.

Syllogisms and consequences have the function of precipitating new understanding in a "correct opponent"—a person who is *ready*. The readiness of a person is an essential point in Tibetan logic. If a person has taken something for granted, and if that idea is not valid, then a clear statement of the logical consequences of the idea can cause intellectual effort and lead to understanding. If there has been an unconscious emotional and psychological attachment to the invalid idea, the effort may be startling or even frightening.

If a "consequence" is to help someone generate a new understanding—of impermanence, for example—it must be relevant to that person. Mountains might be an example: many people find psychological security in the concept of permanence, and mountains are symbols of permanence in many traditions. Logic can weaken attachment to this particular concept of permanence. The consequence is stated: "It follows that a mountain is a nonproduct because of being permanent." But a mountain is a product—geologists have studied mountain-building and made the process a part of conventional knowledge. Stating the consequence explicitly can weaken adherence to the view of mountains as permanent.

The concept of impermanence is considered important in general, and it is thoroughly studied in the Ge-luk-pa system. The impermanence that is easily recognized is said to be coarse impermanence—the fact that objects disintegrate over time, break, lose their form, die. But the impermanence being sought through reasoning is the subtle impermanence. This is the object's momentary nature, its nature of forming, disintegrating, and reforming moment by moment.

Given twenty-first-century physics and chemistry, well-read people are not shocked by the statement that a porcelain bowl is changing every moment; the concept of atoms and subatomic particles swirling in patterns is a familiar and comfortable mental perspective. But it is an ivory-tower perspective, usually kept separate from the mental perspective one uses for daily living. The real understanding of impermanence involves deep analysis of phenomena, eventually to the point of being able to see directly the fleeting disintegration of the bowl.

In the tenet system of the Prāsaṅgika-Madhyamaka, the mere statement of the consequence of an unexamined belief (that a mountain is a nonproduct) is enough to induce, in the student who is ready, the inferential cognition realizing the impermanence of mountains. This is not the case in every tenet system, however. The system of Sautrāntika Following Reason, for example, holds that the statement of a consequence will not in itself generate inferential understanding of a thesis. For example, the mere statement of a consequence ("It follows that a mountain is a nonproduct because of being permanent") will not in itself generate inferential understanding of the thesis (that a mountain is impermanent). It will, however, weaken adherence to the idea of the mountain's permanence. Then the positive and negative proof statements are used to summarize the three modes of the sign. The positive proof statement is: "Whatever is a product is necessarily impermanent, as is the case with pot; mountain also is a product." The negative is, "Whatever is permanent is necessarily a nonproduct, as is the case with uncompounded space; mountain, however, is a product." Finally the syllogism is stated ("The subject, mountain, is impermanent because of being a product")—and it is this statement, at this point, that precipitates inferential understanding of the thesis (mountain is impermanent) in the mind of the "correct opponent."

The teachings encompassed in the topic of valid cognition reflect the viewpoint of the tenet system of the Sautrāntika Following Reason. This means that while the Ge-luk-pa order, like all Tibetan Buddhist orders, adheres to the Madhyamaka system, some aspects of its studies are expressed from the viewpoint of, and in the vocabulary of, lesser tenet systems. The basic principles of logic taught in the Ge-luk-pa monasteries accord with the Sautrāntika system. The purpose of the teaching, however, transcends the limits of the Sautrāntika system, in that the student will eventually use this very system of logic to develop understanding of the subtle Madhyamaka view.

VALIDITY

An important feature of Tibetan logic is that it is used to acquire new and valid understanding about oneself and the world. Valid knowledge is considered to be irrefutable, unshakable; it is authentic, true, and certain. Western logic is fundamentally different from Tibetan logic. In the Western system, a sharp distinction is made between empirical knowledge and knowledge acquired through application of the rules of formal logic. Empirical knowledge depends on experience and observation and is considered to be necessarily contingent, indefinite, conjectural; it is not discernable as definitely and irrefutably true. Only in mathematics and formal logic can there be certainty; all other knowledge must remain conjectural. This point of view is reflected clearly in the words of the Western logician Karl Popper,

> In the empirical sciences, which alone can furnish us with information about the world we live in, proofs do not occur, if we mean by "proof" an argument that establishes once and forever the truth of a theory. On the other hand, pure mathematics and logic, which permit of proofs, give us no information about the world, but only develop the means of describing it.[24]

This points to a fundamental difference between Western and Tibetan logic. In the point of view of some Western logicians, no new knowledge about the world is possible through logic; it is not the purpose of

logic to produce new knowledge. The aim of logic is strictly propositional, in that it depends strictly on the form of propositions for its validity. In Western logic, validity attaches to the proper logical form of
an argument. A Western logician, Stephen Barker, explains,

> In logic, we are mainly interested in considering arguments
> whose validity depends on their logical forms. ... When the
> premises of an argument are linked to the conclusion in the
> right sort of way, the argument is called valid.[25]

In the Ge-luk-pa system of education, the purpose of logic is to generate new knowledge, not about propositions, but about phenomena; that
is, about oneself and the world. Logic is used to develop a path of reasoning, in order to acquire valid knowledge. Tibetan logic is transfor-
mational, in that it is intended to bring new and valid knowledge that
changes one's relationship with the world and brings one closer to the
truth and to enlightenment—closer to the truth, in that one's understanding of the world is more accurate and one's relationships with
people are based on true understanding of the nature of reality rather
than on illusion and ignorance.

GENESIS OF THIS STUDY

The beginnings of this project go back to 1976, when Lati Rin-po-che
came to the University of Virginia as a visiting lecturer and taught the
three introductory topics of the Ge-luk-pa curriculum, *Collected Topics*,
Awareness and Knowledge, and *Signs and Reasonings*. Under his guidance,
our class studied the whole of the introductory logic manual on *Signs
and Reasonings* by Ge-shay Tsül-trim-nam-gyel, and part of the manual
written by Pur-bu-jok. Lati Rin-po-che's commentary was translated by
Jeffrey Hopkins and transcribed by class members. Subsequently, I
translated the whole of Pur-bu-jok's *Signs and Reasonings* (that translation is included in this book). I also received commentary on Pur-bu-
jok's *Signs and Reasonings* from Ge-shay Ge-dün-lo-drö in 1979, when he
was a visiting scholar at the University of Virginia.

   Later, in India on an American Institute of Indian Studies fellow-
ship, I received commentary on it from Ge-shay Pel-den-drak-pa, at
that time the resident scholar at Tibet House in New Delhi, and from
Ge-shay Lob-sang-gya-tso, a scholar of Lo-sel-ling College of Dre-pung
Monastic University in South India. I recorded and transcribed all
commentary received from these teachers.

While in Northern India, I attended the Buddhist School of Dialectics in Dharamsala, joining a class on the *Collected Topics* for one full school year in 1983 and again for two months in 1984. I attended classes and debated with my classmates, in two sessions daily—morning and evening. During that time, I also attended classes on "Awareness and Knowledge" and on "Valid Cognition"; the latter dealt specifically with the relationship between the sign and the predicate in a valid proof. The text used in that class was Paṇ-chen Sö-nam-drak-pa's *Illumination of the Thought*, of which I translated the portion studied in that class.

I also met with advanced students to discuss both the introductory topics of *Signs and Reasonings* and topics of "Valid Cognition." In the study of valid cognition, the most important root texts are Dignāga's *Compendium on Prime Cognition* and Dharmakīrti's commentary on it. There are numerous Ge-luk-pa commentaries on these; one that is widely used is by Gyel-tsap (his *Revealer of the Path of Liberation*), of which I translated one section, on the topic of the relationship between sign and predicate. While in Dharamsala, I received extensive commentary on this section of Gyel-tsap's text from Ge-shay Sang-gyay-sam-drup (Professor Georges Dreyfus). I also attended classes on this topic at the Buddhist School of Dialectics and met with students to discuss and debate related issues.

In 1983 and 1984, I spent a total of five months at Lo-sel-ling College. There I joined a class on *Signs and Reasonings* and received individual instruction on the topic from Ge-shay Lob-sang-gya-tso. I also met with other students to debate topics of logic.

I would like to express my thanks to all of these scholars, and to the teachers and students at the Buddhist School of Dialectics, who were extremely kind and encouraging during my period of study there. Special thanks go also to Georges Dreyfus, who has helped me many times and been generous with his expertise in the topic of valid cognition.

I am deeply grateful to my family for their patience and encouragement, and their many, many hours at the word processor, helping to bring this project to completion.

Finally, my thanks go to Jeffrey Hopkins for his immeasurable help.

PREVIEW

My first three chapters deal with the criteria of a correct sign—the necessary relationship between the subject, predicate, and reason in a valid syllogism. To be valid, the proof must be able to generate, in the mind of an appropriate person, a new valid understanding of the thesis.

There are criteria of validity: the reason must be the three modes, explained in these chapters.

Chapters four through seven cover the different types of correct signs. The main division of correct signs is into three: correct effect, nature, and nonobservation signs. This division is made depending on two criteria: the type of relationship between the sign and the predicate, and whether the predicate is a positive or a negative phenomenon.

Chapter eight is on other ways of dividing correct signs. These do not contradict the main division; they are ways to highlight certain important issues. One division, for example, depends on whether the predicate is a definition or the thing defined (definiendum); study of this topic requires careful consideration of such related issues as the order in which definitions and definiendums are ascertained. Another division highlights the difference between very hidden phenomena and slightly hidden phenomena. Study of correct signs from the point of view of the nature of the predicate of the probandum brings up such issues as the different types of inferential valid cognition and the kind of reasoning each type depends on.

Chapter nine is on quasi-signs—those that do not fulfill the requirements of correct signs.

Chapter ten is an attempt at a concise summation of all the important topics contained in Pur-bu-jok's text.

1. The Property of the Subject

In order for a sign to be correct in a particular proof, it must satisfy the criteria for a correct sign. It must "be the three modes" (must be ascertained as being each of the three modes) in that particular proof. For example, in the proof of sound as impermanent, one must first take to mind a reason, a sign, such as product. One can then consider whether product is a correct sign; does it irrefutably prove the thesis that sound is impermanent? If product is to be a correct sign in the proof of sound as impermanent, product must be established as the three modes in that proof; "to establish the sign as the three modes" means to prove the sign.

The first mode is the property of the subject. "The property of the subject" refers to the relationship between the subject and the sign in a syllogism. The sign must be the property of the subject; it must be present in the subject; it must exist in relation to the subject. The meaning of these phrases becomes clear with analysis of the two criteria that a sign must fulfill in order to be the property of the subject in a given proof. These are expressed clearly in Pur-bu-jok's definition of "something's [x's] being the property of the subject in the proof of sound as impermanent":

> (1) Sound is the flawless subject sought to be known (*shes' dod chos can skyon med*) in the proof of sound as impermanent by the sign x; (2) x is ascertained by valid cognition as only existing, in accordance with the mode of statement, with sound in the manner of mutual difference with sound.[26]

Pur-bu-jok posits product as an illustration (*mtshan gzhi*) of the property of the subject in the proof of sound as impermanent; he writes,

> Product is the property of the subject, as well as the forward pervasion and counterpervasion in the proof of sound as impermanent by the sign, product.[27]

In order for a sign to be the property of the subject in the proof of sound as impermanent, it must fulfill these two criteria: the subject in that proof (sound) must be a flawless subject, and the sign must be established in relation to the subject. In other words, sound must be a product. Before analyzing each part of Pur-bu-jok's definition, it is necessary to understand the significance of the term "flawless subject."

FLAWLESS SUBJECT

Pur-bu-jok specifies that the flawless subject is "the basis of relation" (*ltos gzhi*) of the property of the subject.[a] The flawless subject is called the basis of relation of the property of the subject because that property (product) is established in relation to that subject. Lati Rin-po-che explains,

> The flawless subject is the ground or basis for establishing the property of the subject because in order to establish the property of the subject one must depend on the subject; for example, sound in the proof of sound as impermanent by the sign, product.
>
> Sound is the substratum with respect to which one is ascertaining "productness"; therefore it is called "the basis of relation" of the property of the subject. When the property of the subject is established in the proof of sound as impermanent by the sign, product, one has ascertained the "productness" of sound. One takes sound as the substratum and by valid cognition ascertains its being a product.[28]

Sound is thus the point of reference in the proof of—or in the establishing of—the property of the subject in the proof of sound as impermanent by the sign, product.

The flawless subject is also referred to as the basis of debate (*rtsod gzhi*) and the basis of inference (*dpag gzhi*; **anumāna-āśraya*). It is the basis of debate because it is the basis in regard to which there is debate; it is the basis of inference because it is the basis in regard to which inference is generated. The terms "subject sought to be known" (*shes 'dod chos can,* also translated "subject of inquiry"), "flawless subject" (*chos can skyon med*), "flawless subject sought to be known" (*shes 'dod chos can skyon med*), "basis of debate"(*rtsod gzhi*), and "basis of inference" (*dpag gzhi*) are said by Ge-luk-pa scholars, such as Lati Rin-po-che and Ge-shay Pel-den-drak-pa and others, to be equivalent (*don gcig*) in this context.[b]

---

[a] Pur-bu-jok's explanation of "the basis of relation of the property of the subject" has three parts: "definition of a subject sought to be known, an illustration, and, ancillarily, identification of the predicate of the probandum" (ibid., p. 3b.4). The definition and illustration follow immediately; Pur-bu-jok's explanation of the predicate of the probandum is in the section by that title, below.

[b] A complication in translation is that the subject and the sign in a correct syllogism are described in different Tibetan terms (*dpag gzhi* and *dpag rten*), both of which may be

If the sign, product, is to perform its function as proof of the impermanence of the subject, sound, sound must first of all be a flawless subject. A subject is flawless when it is both (1) the basis of debate and (2) appropriate to the understanding of the opponent (the person considering the question).

The logic manuals state these requirements very carefully. Pur-bu-jok states the definition of something's "being a flawless subject" sought to be known in the proof of sound as impermanent by the sign, product, thus:

> That observed as a common locus of (1) being held as a basis of debate in the proof of sound as impermanent by the sign, product, and of (2) there existing a person who, having ascertained that it (sound) is a product, is engaged in wanting to know whether or not it is impermanent.[29]

Pur-bu-jok then posits an illustration of flawless subject (or subject sought to be known):

> Sound is the subject sought to be known in the proof of sound as impermanent by the sign, product. Whatever is the subject sought to be known in the proof of sound as impermanent by the sign, product, is necessarily one with sound (*sgra dang gcig*).[30]

The syllogism under consideration is, "The subject, sound, is impermanent because of being a product." Sound is the subject and, furthermore, is said to be the "flawless subject" in that syllogism because it satisfies the requirements set forth in the definition of something's being a flawless subject in the proof of sound as impermanent by the sign, product. Pur-bu-jok writes,

> It follows that the subject, sound, is the flawless subject sought to be known in the proof of sound as impermanent by the sign, product, because it [sound] is held as the basis of debate in the proof of sound as impermanent by the sign, product, and because there exists a person who, having ascertained it [sound] by valid cognition as a product, is engaged in wanting to know

---

translated into English as "basis of inference." The subject is the basis or locus of inference (*dpag gzhi*) in the sense that the new understanding being generated is centered on it. The sign is called the basis of inference (*dpag rten*) from the point of view that it serves as a cause of inference; the inference is generated in dependence on a correct sign.

whether or not it is impermanent.[31]

Pur-bu-jok then goes on to explain briefly how sound satisfies each of the two criteria set forth in the definition. He writes,

> It follows [that the subject, sound, is held as the basis of debate in the proof of sound as impermanent by the sign, product,] because there exists the syllogism "The subject, sound, is impermanent because of being a product."[32]

The subject of any given syllogism is "that which is held as the basis of debate" in that syllogism. Pur-bu-jok continues,

> It follows [that there exists a person who, having ascertained by valid cognition that sound is a product, is engaged in wanting to know whether or not it is impermanent] because there exists a person who has not already ascertained by valid cognition that sound is impermanent.[33]

Here, Pur-bu-jok is proving the existence of someone who wants to know whether sound is impermanent by reason of the existence of "a person who has not already ascertained that sound is impermanent." The pervasion in Pur-bu-jok's reasoning is: "If there exists a person who has not already ascertained by valid cognition that sound is impermanent, there necessarily exists a person wondering whether sound is impermanent or not."

Although Pur-bu-jok seems to be saying that anyone who has not already realized that sound is impermanent is necessarily wanting to know whether sound is impermanent, that is not his meaning here, according to Ge-luk-pa scholars. Lati Rin-po-che makes this point clearly when he says,

> The mere existence of a person who has ascertained that sound is a product but not that sound is impermanent[a] does not necessarily entail that there exists a person who wants to know whether sound is impermanent. That is not the pervasion here. But once there are people who have ascertained that sound is a product but not that sound is impermanent, there will necessarily be some among that group who want to know [whether

---

[a]   Pur-bu-jok's reason is "because there exists a person who has not already ascertained that sound is impermanent." Lati Rin-po-che understands this to mean "because there exists a person who has ascertained that sound is a product but has not ascertained that sound is impermanent" (commentary on *Signs and Reasonings,* vol. 1, Feb. 14, 1977, p. 3).

the thesis—that sound is impermanent—is true].[34]

The subject, sound, is a flawless subject in the proof of sound as impermanent only if the opponent for whom the reasoning is employed is a person who has not already ascertained by valid cognition that sound is a product.

This brief explanation by Pur-bu-jok of the two criteria of a flawless subject will not alone produce understanding—and is not expected to. Ge-luk-pa students do not rely solely on a text; it is amplified by their teachers, and their understanding develops as they study and debate the topic. Memorizing Pur-bu-jok's words provides a nucleus around which understanding may develop.

SUBJECT AS BASIS OF DEBATE

To "establish the property of the subject" of a syllogism is to prove the sign in relation to a specific subject—to prove that the sign, product, is the property of the subject, sound, for example. In Tibetan logic, a proof cannot be general or abstract, separated from a specific base. As Ge-shay Pel-den-drak-pa says,

> There is no correct sign without a subject because there would be no way to understand the sign in a proof unless it were related to a subject; for example, there would be no way to understand product as a correct sign in the proof of impermanent [without specifying any subject].[35]

The proof of a reasoning always relates to the specific subject under analysis. There must always be a subject, a basis, with regard to which inference is cultivated.

This requirement that there be a specific subject that is the basis of debate becomes especially important when students begin to apply the principles of logic to meditation on the emptiness of inherent existence of phenomena. Emptiness is always proved in relation to a specific subject; it is not an abstraction that one may ponder on per se. Emptiness can only be known in relation to a specific phenomenon, such as a table, or tree, or one's own mind.

The reasoning employed in the proof of emptiness is also summarized in syllogisms. Several sample syllogisms from Madhyamaka are:

- "The subject, the person (*gang zag*), is empty of inherent existence (*rang bzhin gyis stong pa*) because of being a dependent-arising (*rten 'byung*; *pratītya-samutpāda*)."

- "The subject, the mind (*sems*), is empty of inherent existence because of being a dependent-arising."
- "The subject, the 'I' (*nga*), is not established from its own side (*rang ngos nas ma sgrub pa*), because of not being established from its own side as either one with the aggregates or different from the aggregates."

In all these cases, there is a specific subject—the person, mind, or "I"—to which the reasoning applies.

When one understands, for example, that the mind is empty of inherent existence because it is a dependent-arising, that subject, the mind, is the phenomenon that is the substratum, the basis, of that emptiness being understood. Emptiness is not being understood in isolation, as mere nothingness; rather, it is specifically the mind's emptiness of inherent existence that the student is realizing. Similarly, when one understands that a particular subject, such as sound, is impermanent because it is a product, the subject *sound* is then the substratum or basis of the new inference, in that impermanence is being realized specifically in relation to sound.

SUBJECT AS APPROPRIATE TO THE OPPONENT

A flawless subject is not flawless because of its own characteristics only; flawlessness depends on the subject and person together. The flawless subject is being held as the basis or locus of debate by someone who is newly developing understanding of the thesis. This is someone who has not previously understood the thesis but, having thought about it, is wondering if it is correct. For example, with regard to the syllogism, "The subject, sound, is impermanent because of being a product," the subject in that proof, sound, is only "flawless" if the person (for whom the proof is being employed) is someone who has developed ascertainment of each of the three modes of the sign, and is now wondering whether the thesis is correct or not. This person, having ascertained that sound is a product, is now wondering whether sound is impermanent or not. As Lati Rin-po-che says,

> The one for whom this sign—[product in the syllogism,] "The subject, sound, is impermanent because of being a product"—is stated, has to be someone who has realized that sound is a product, but not realized that sound is impermanent. Having ascertained that sound is a product, one will have doubt, wondering, "Is sound permanent or impermanent? It is probably

impermanent," and thus one becomes engaged in wanting to know [the thesis].[a]

If the opponent for whom the sign is being employed is not someone who has a desire to know whether the thesis is correct or not, then there is not a flawless subject and the reasoning becomes invalid. Lati Rin-po-che explains,

> If there is not a person who is engaged in wanting to know whether or not sound is impermanent, it (sound) cannot be a flawless subject. For instance, if you state, "The subject, un-compounded space (*'dus ma byas kyi nam mkha'*), is impermanent because of being a product," the basis of debate in that syllogism is uncompounded space; however, there is no person who has ascertained with valid cognition that uncompounded space is a product and, therefore, it is not a flawless subject.[36]

Uncompounded space is said to be permanent and therefore there cannot exist a person who has ascertained by valid cognition that uncompounded space is a product.

The opponent for whom the sign, product, serves as a correct sign in the proof of sound as impermanent is someone who has not yet understood that sound is impermanent, but is ready to. Such a person (ready to understand the thesis) must be one for whom the sign is established as a correct sign, and therefore it must be someone who has understood all three modes of the sign. He or she has ascertained that sound is a product (understanding acquired in establishing the first mode—the property of the subject) and has ascertained that product is impermanent and that whatever is a product is impermanent (understandings acquired in establishing the second and third modes—the pervasions). As Lati Rin-po-che says,

> Stating product as the reason in the proof of sound as impermanent is not correct if the opponent is someone who has not

---

[a] The person for whom a correct proof is being employed must be someone who is wondering whether the thesis is true or not. Ge-luk-pa scholars explain that there must be a desire to know whether the thesis is true; that wish to know does not have to be doubt (*the tshom*), it may also be assumption (*yid dpyod*). Lati Rin-po-che says, "This desire to know is either doubt tending to the factual, or assumption" (commentary on *Signs and Reasonings*, vol. 1, p. 36). And Ge-shay Pel-den-drak-pa says, "This person does not know whether sound is impermanent. There does not have to be doubt specifically; there may be assumption, but it is not known. There must, in any case, be a desire to know" (commentary on *Signs and Reasonings*, vol. 1, p. 9).

> realized that a product is impermanent...The one for whom this
> reason is stated has to be a someone who has realized that
> sound is a product but not that sound is impermanent. And he
> has to have realized that product is impermanent; and he must
> have ascertained that whatever is a product is impermanent. It
> is only for such an opponent that this would be a correct sign.[37]

This person is ready to understand the thesis and is thus a correct or
prepared opponent (*phyi rgol yang dag; samyak-pūrva-pakṣa*). The correct
opponent for whom the reasoning is being employed may be external
(a partner in debate) or internal (oneself in meditation).[a]

VALIDITY

The requirement of a correct opponent is important, for it illuminates
the Tibetan (and Indian) Buddhist view of validity. In this view, validity
is always relative; no proof is absolutely correct or correct in all instances. Product is a valid reason, in the proof of the impermanence of
sound, only for someone who has already understood that sound is a
product and is now actively seeking to learn whether sound is impermanent or not. For someone who already knows that sound is impermanent, product cannot be a correct sign in that proof ("proving" the
known is of benefit to no one). And for someone who does not yet understand that sound is a product, product cannot be a correct sign in
that proof (the idea is premature).

The linkage of flawless subject and correct opponent reflects the
subjective aspect of validity. In this system, logic does not function in
the abstract. Logic is tied to a specific understanding—the mind of the
individual debater or meditator. In this sense, no syllogism is true at all
times and in relation to every mind. As Lati Rin-po-che says,

> Whether something is a correct sign or not in a certain proof
> depends on the specific disputant involved.[38]

In a general way, product can be said to be a correct sign in the syllogism, "The subject, sound, is impermanent because of being a product."
More precisely, however, product is only potentially a correct sign—
given the right opponent, it may induce a new understanding of the
thesis. The person for whom the sign has been stated must be someone
who has not yet understood the thesis; there must be a desire to know

---

[a] This is discussed in greater detail in the topic "the division of correct signs by way of
the opponent" in chapter eight.

the thesis on the part of the opponent.

Similarly, in a general way, "momentary" (the definition of impermanent) is considered to be potentially a correct sign in the proof of sound as impermanent.[a] This means that momentary may serve—for the appropriate opponent—as the cause for new understanding of the thesis that sound is impermanent. However, as Lati Rin-po-che points out,

> For someone who has not realized that sound is momentary, momentary would not be a correct sign in the proof of sound as impermanent. For someone who *has* realized that sound is momentary and who has not forgotten it, momentary would be a correct sign in the proof of sound as impermanent; that proof would be stated: "The subject, sound, is impermanent because of being momentary."[39]

Tibetan Buddhists are not interested in building up a logical system of static and abstract validity. The correctness of reasoning in the Ge-luk-pa system is always in relation to the understanding of a particular person at a particular time. This is a very specific meaning of validity.

The subjective aspect of validity does not mean that truth is fluid and changeable, however. What is established *by valid cognition* as existent by one person will never be established by valid cognition as nonexistent by another person. Valid cognition is always correct, irrefutable, incontrovertible.[b]

ESTABLISHING THE PROPERTY OF THE SUBJECT

DEFINITION

To establish the property of the subject, one must understand its criteria. Pur-bu-jok's explanation of the property of the subject has three

---

[a] "Momentary," being the definition of "impermanent," may, in the right circumstances, serve as a correct sign in the proof of sound as impermanent. However, according to Buddhist logic, "impermanent" cannot serve as a correct sign in the proof of sound as "momentary" because momentary must be ascertained before impermanent. This is discussed in greater detail in the section "the division of correct signs by way of the modes of proof," in chapter eight.

[b] A Ge-luk-pa definition of valid cognition is "a new and incontrovertible knower." Thus, according to Ge-luk-pa systems, whatever is established by valid cognition must be correct and incontrovertible. See Lati Rin-po-che's discussion of this topic in *Mind in Tibetan Buddhism* (London: Rider, 1980; Ithaca, New York: Snow Lion Publications, 1980), pp 116-120.

parts; as he indicates,

> Each of the three modes has its own definition, illustration, and mode of proof.[40]

To repeat Pur-bu-jok's definition of something's being the property of the subject in the proof of sound as impermanent:

> Sound is the flawless subject sought to be known in the proof of sound as impermanent by the sign, x; x is ascertained by valid cognition as only existing, in accordance with the mode of statement, with sound in the manner of mutual difference with sound."[41]

This formal statement of the two criteria is precise but complicated. More simply, the definition of property of the subject in the proof of something is:

> That ascertained by valid cognition as only existing in accordance with the mode of statement, with the flawless subject sought to be known in the proof of that.[42]

Pur-bu-jok also provides simple definitions of the other two modes of a correct sign, the forward pervasion and the counterpervasion (see the appropriate sections of chapter three). He then explains that these definitions are intended only as a general guide and are not meant to be definitive. He writes,

> These [brief] definitions are formulated mainly for the sake of understanding; there is no definiteness with regard to them.[43]

Pur-bu-jok explains that these definitions are not definitive because "although sound is [that is, fulfills the requirements of] those three definitions in the proof of sound as impermanent, [sound] is not their definiendum."[44]

Ge-luk-pa scholars agree that these definitions are problematic—but not necessarily for that reason.[a] These brief definitions are posited,

---

[a] Lati Rin-po-che questions whether sound does satisfy the requirements of the definition of all three modes in the proof of sound as impermanent, arguing that it probably does not fulfill the requirements of the first mode, property of the subject, in that proof. He says, "It is questionable to say that sound is ascertained as only existing with sound [the subject] in accordance with the mode of statement. If [sound] is ascertained by valid cognition as only existing with itself, it would have to be different from itself. This would contradict the statement in the *Collected Topics* that whatever is an established base is one with itself." On the other hand, in support of the opposite point of

as Pur-bu-jok notes, "for the sake of understanding"; thus, they are meant to be helpful; they may bring a rough understanding of the general criteria of the three modes, but they are not accurate and will not withstand careful analysis; under analysis they will be found to be faulty. According to Lati Rin-po-che, these are posited by Pur-bu-jok to make students think, to provoke questions and qualms.[a]

ILLUSTRATION

As an illustration of "property of the subject," Pur-bu-jok posits product in the proof of sound as impermanent. It should be noted that, although the "property of the subject" refers to the relationship between the sign and the subject in a correct proof, if one is asked to posit the property of the subject in the proof of sound as impermanent, the response is just "product." Product is an illustration of a correct sign in the proof of sound as impermanent, and it is thus something that *is* itself those three modes in that proof. Lati Rin-po-che makes this point clearly:

> Only that which is the three modes is a correct sign. If one is asked to posit the property of the subject in the proof of sound as impermanent by the sign, product, one cannot posit anything other than "product."[45]

One might think that the property of the subject is "that sound is a product," but clearly that is not the case.

METHOD OF PROOF

Pur-bu-jok then explains briefly the "reasoning proving that product is the property of the subject in the proof of sound as impermanent":

> It follows that the subject, product, is the property of the subject in the proof of sound as impermanent because of being [that is, satisfying] that definition.[46]

That is—if we substitute product for x in Pur-bu-jok's definition[b]—

---

view, Lati Rin-po-che points out that "in the Sautrāntika system, sound has to exist objectively; therefore, it exists with itself (*sgra sgra'i steng du yod*)." Commentary on *Signs and Reasonings,* vol. 2, Feb. 9, 1977, p. 4.

[a] Ibid., p. 5. See the section below on "complications and sample debates" for examples of problems that arise from the use of these definitions.

[b] The definition of something's being the property of the subject in the proof of sound as impermanent is at the beginning of this section.

because (first root reason) sound is the flawless subject sought to be known in the proof of sound as impermanent by the sign, product [x], and (second root reason) product [x] is ascertained by valid cognition as only existing, in accordance with the mode of statement, with sound in the manner of mutual difference with sound.

In order for product to be a correct sign in the proof of sound as impermanent, the first root reason is that the subject is flawless, that is, is both held as the basis of debate and appropriate to the opponent.[a]

The second part of Pur-bu-jok's definition specifies that the sign must be established (that is, proved) in relation to the subject. In proving this part of the definition, he writes,

> If someone says that the second root reason [that is, "x is ascertained by valid cognition as only existing, in accordance with the mode of statement, with sound in the manner of mutual difference with sound"] is not established, [then the response is,] "It follows that the subject, product, is ascertained by valid cognition as only existing, in accordance with the mode of statement, with sound in the manner of mutual difference with sound because it [product] (1) is mutually different from sound and (2) is ascertained by valid cognition as only existing, in accordance with the mode of statement, with sound.
>
> The [first point] is easy [to prove because product is different from sound and sound is different from product]. [As to the second point,] it follows that the subject, product, is ascertained by valid cognition as only existing, in accordance with the mode of statement, with sound because (1) the mode of statement in the proof of that [that is, the proof of sound as impermanent] by the sign of it [product] is an "is" statement [rather than an "exists" statement], (2) sound is it [product], and (3) it [product] is with the subject, sound [that is, product is a quality of sound]. These reasons are easy [to prove].[47]

To clarify this requires analysis of Pur-bu-jok's four points: that the sign must (1) exist with sound *in accordance with the mode of statement*; (2) *only* exist with sound; (3) be *ascertained* in relation to the subject; and (4) be different from sound.

---

[a]   Pur-bu-jok's brief discussion of this first root reason was cited in the section on "the flawless subject," at the beginning of this chapter.

Mode of Statement: "Be" and "Exist"

Product must be ascertained as only existing with sound *in accordance with the mode of statement.* There are two modes or ways of stating a syllogism, the copular and the ontological. The copular mode is an "is" statement using the linking verb "to be," and the ontological mode is an "exists" statement using the verb "to exist." The familiar syllogism, "The subject, sound, *is* impermanent because of being a product" is in the copular mode. Another syllogism often found in the logic manuals is expressed in the ontological mode: "With respect to the subject, on a smoky pass, fire exists, because smoke exists." In the copular mode, sound must be ascertained as *being* a product; in the ontological mode, smoke must be ascertained as *existing* in the place specified by the subject, a smoky pass.

Pur-bu-jok's definition of something's being the property of the subject in the proof of sound as impermanent is complicated because it is intended as a "universal" model. It is phrased in such a way as to be applicable to other syllogisms, such as: "With respect to the subject, on a smoky pass, fire exists because smoke exists." When it is applied to this syllogism, the definition becomes:

> The definition of something's being the property of the subject in the proof of fire as existing on a smoky pass by the sign, smoke, is: smoky pass is a flawless subject in the proof of fire as existing on a smoky pass by the sign x; and x is ascertained by valid cognition as only existing, in accordance with the mode of statement, with smoky pass, in the manner of mutual difference with smoky pass.

Smoke will function as a correct sign in this syllogism because smoke exists with the subject in accordance with the mode of statement; that is, because smoke *exists* on the smoky pass. That smoke exists with smoky pass in accordance with the mode of statement does not mean that smoky pass *is* itself smoke, but that in relation to smoky pass, smoke *exists.*

Pur-bu-jok explains that product exists with sound *in accordance with the mode of statement* in this way:

> It follows that product is ascertained by valid cognition as only existing in accordance with the mode of statement with sound because: (1) the mode of statement in the proof of that [that is, of sound as impermanent] by the sign of it [product] is an "is" statement; (2) that [sound] *is* it [product]; and (3) it [product] is

with that [sound].⁴⁸

The mode of statement in this syllogism is copular; therefore sound must *be* a product. Saying that product "exists with" sound here means that sound is a product. Product's being "with" sound means that product is a quality or a feature (*khyad chos*) of sound.⁴⁹

For product to be a correct sign, it must "exist with" sound. This criterion makes it impossible to posit as correct signs in that proof any phenomena that do not "exist with" sound, such as "object of apprehension of an eye consciousness," "color," and "shape"; none of these exists with sound, in accordance with the mode of statement, because none of these is a quality or feature of sound.

If someone posits the syllogism, "The subject, sound, is impermanent because of being an object of apprehension of an eye consciousness," that sign cannot be the property of the subject in this proof because "being an object of apprehension of an eye consciousness" does not exist with sound; that is, it cannot be a property of sound. Sound is an object of apprehension of an ear consciousness, not of an eye consciousness, and "object of apprehension of an eye consciousness" is not a quality or property of sound. The signs, color and shape, are similarly eliminated as property of the subject in the proof of sound as impermanent.

Thus, phenomenon x does not "exist with" sound if sound is not x and x is not a quality of sound. Sound is not a shape, and "shape" is not a quality of sound. Product, on the other hand, does exist with sound, because sound is a product and "product" is a quality or property of sound.

"Only Exist"

According to Pur-bu-jok's definition of something's being the property of the subject in the proof of sound as impermanent, a sign must not merely "exist with" sound but "*only exist* with" sound. This means with sound as a whole; there can be no case of its not existing with sound. The sign x cannot exist in relation to some sounds and not to others. A phenomenon, x, that is ascertained as merely "existing with sound in accordance with the mode of statement" may not actually be the property of the subject in that proof. Merely existing with sound is not enough to enable x to be the property of the subject; the sign must *only exist* with sound. Thus, all sounds are products; there is no case in which a sound is not a product.

This criterion of "only existing" makes it impossible to posit as a correct sign in the proof of sound as impermanent any phenomenon that exists with sound but does not only exist with sound. For example, someone might posit the syllogism: "The subject, sound, is impermanent because of being arisen from exertion."[a] It is true that "arisen from exertion" exists with sound, in that many sounds arise from (a person's) exertion. But "arisen from exertion" cannot be the property of the subject in that proof because it does not only exist with sound. Lati Rin-po-che explains,

> Being arisen from exertion does exist among sounds; this is because there are sounds that do arise from exertion. However, "arisen from exertion" does not only exist with sounds. This is because it does not exist with regard to *all* sounds. Whatever is a sound is not necessarily arisen from exertion. Among sounds, there are both those arisen from exertion and those not arisen from exertion.[50]

If "arisen from exertion" only existed with sound, then there would be no case of its not existing with sound—there would be no sound that is not arisen from (a person's) exertion; all sounds would have to be generated by people. That is not the case, of course; the sound of the wind does not arise from exertion.

Thus the criterion that x must only exist with sound means both (1) that sound is x and x is a feature of sound and (2) that each and every sound must be x; there are no sounds that are not x.

To grasp this thoroughly, students investigate the following questions: First, what are the possibilities (*mu*) between (a) only existing with sound (*sgra la yod pa kho na*) and (b) existing with sound (*sgra la yod pa*), and second, what are the possibilities between (a) only existing with sound (*sgra la yod pa kho na*) and (b) existing with only sound (*sgra kho na la yod pa*)?[51]

If we consider the first question, between only existing with sound and existing with sound, there are three possibilities:

1. That which is the first but not the second: whatever only exists with sound necessarily exists with sound, but whatever exists with sound does not necessarily only exist with sound. Arisen from exertion, for example, exists with sound because some sounds are arisen from (a person's) exertion; but it does not only exist with sound because it does not exist with all sounds—not all sounds are arisen

---

[a] "Arisen from exertion" means arisen from the exertion of a person (*gang zag*); "person" refers to any sentient being.

from exertion.

2. That which is both: object of comprehension (*gzhal bya, prameya*). Object of comprehension exists with sound because sound is an object of comprehension. It only exists with sound because it exists with all sounds; all sounds are objects of comprehension.

3. That which is neither: shape. A shape neither exists with sound nor only exists with sound. Shape is not a quality of sound; there is no sound that is a shape.

If we consider the second question, between only existing with sound and existing with only sound there are four possibilities:

1. Something that only exists with sound but does not exist only with sound is "object of knowledge" (*shes bya; jñeya*). Object of knowledge only exists with sound because it exists with all sounds; but it does not exist with only sound because it exists with phenomena other than sound; for example, the permanent (*rtag pa*). Object of knowledge exists with the permanent because the permanent is an object of knowledge.

2. Something that exists with only sound but does not only exist with sound is the sound of a conch. This exists with only sound because of (a) existing with sound (the sound of a conch is a sound) and (b) not existing with phenomena other than sound. It does not only exist with sound because it does not exist with all sounds.

3. Something that both exists only with sound and only exists with sound is "object of hearing." This only exists with sound because it exists with all sounds; it exists with only sound because it (a) exists with sound and (b) does not exist with other phenomena.

4. Something that is neither: a shape.

It is clear that the position of the word "only" is important in the definition of property of the subject, even though it makes a rather awkward English sentence. An English modifier normally limits the word that follows it. In Tibetan (as in French), the modifier limits or describes the word before it. If the "only" were put before "exists" in Tibetan, it would be following the sign, x, meaning that "only x exists with sound." The "only" is put where it is in "only exists with sound" in order to eliminate the possibility that "only object of hearing" could be the property of the subject in the proof of sound as impermanent.

If someone says, "The subject, sound, is impermanent because of being only an object of hearing," that reason cannot be the property of the subject in that proof because sound is not only an object of hearing; it is many other things: an existent, an object of knowledge, and so on.

Object of hearing only exists with sound—because all objects of hearing are sounds. But "only object of hearing" does not exist with sound, because other phenomena also exist with sound. Lati Rin-po-che grounds the point in an accessible example:

> What is eliminated by this placement of the word "just" (or "only")? For example, it is for the sake of eliminating that being only an object of hearing could be the property of the subject in the proof of sound as impermanent. Object of hearing only exists with sound, but not only object of hearing exists with sound; many things also exist with sound; object of comprehension also does, thing does, etc. For example, John is a student of this school but "only John" is not a student of this school; many others are also students of this school.[52]

"Difference"

In his definition, Pur-bu-jok specifies that the sign must exist in the manner of a "mutual difference with sound." The sign and subject must not be the same. One cannot posit sound itself as a correct sign in the proof of sound as impermanent. According to Lati Rin-po-che,

> Pur-bu-jok specifies that there must be mutual difference so as to eliminate the possibility of stating sound itself as the reason in the proof of sound as impermanent.[53]

"Ascertain"

Pur-bu-jok includes the word "ascertain" in his definition of property of the subject ("x is ascertained by valid cognition as only existing..."). This is because the criteria for the property of the subject must be "ascertained" in relation to the sign x if x is to be the property of the subject. The word "ascertain" insures that no debater will propose that "product" can be the property of the subject in the proof of sound as impermanent for an opponent who *doubts* whether sound is a product.

If someone posits the syllogism, "The subject, sound, is impermanent because of being a product," to a person who has doubt as to whether or not sound is a product, product cannot be the property of the subject in that proof because that person has not ascertained product as only existent with sound. As Lati Rin-po-che explains,

> For someone who has not realized that sound is a product, that is, for someone who still has doubts about whether or not

sound is a product—for such a person, product cannot be the property of the subject in the proof of sound as impermanent. This is because although product *does* exist in accordance with the mode of statement with sound, this person has not ascertained that it does so.[54]

In that proof and for that opponent, product cannot be the property of the subject. The opponent must first ascertain by valid cognition that sound is a product. Then that opponent begins to wonder whether the thesis is true or not, and the opponent who knows that sound is a product but is still unsure whether sound is impermanent becomes a "correct (or prepared) opponent."

According to some Ge-luk-pa scholars, a person who ascertains by valid cognition that sound is a product is someone for whom product "has become the property of the subject" (*phyogs chos can du song ba*). Lati Rin-po-che says,

A person who has ascertained by valid cognition that sound is a product is someone for whom product has become the property of the subject. These two, (1) the ascertainment that sound is a product and (2) product's becoming the property of the subject are simultaneous.[a]

Thus, for that person, ascertainment that product only exists with sound in accordance with the mode of statement and ascertaining that sound is a product are simultaneous. At that moment, product becomes the property of the subject for that person.[b]

But this is not the same as product's being established or proved as the property of the subject for that person.[c] Ascertaining that sound is

---

[a] Ibid., vol. 1, p. 33. This discussion arises in relation to the definition of property of the subject set forth by Ge-shay Tsül-trim-nam-gyel, author of the Lo-sel-ling textbook on *Signs and Reasonings*. His definition is discussed below.

[b] There is a disagreement among Ge-luk-pa scholars about what it means to say "product has become the property of the subject in the proof of sound as impermanent." Lati Rin-po-che says this means that "product [the sign] is ascertained by the opponent as just existing with sound [the subject], but the opponent is not necessarily wondering whether it is impermanent" (commentary on *Signs and Reasonings*, vol. 1, p. 29). Ge-shay Pel-den-drak-pa says this means that sound must be a flawless subject in that proof; that is, sound must be held as the basis of debate and the opponent must be a person who, having ascertained that sound is a product, is wondering if sound is impermanent (commentary on *Signs and Reasonings*, vol. 2, p. 2).

[c] According to Lati Rin-po-che, "The fact that [Tsül-trim-nam-gyel's] definition states that the sign has become the property of the subject does not mean that for this person

indeed a product is not enough to establish the first mode in the proof of sound as impermanent by the sign, product. The correct opponent must not only have ascertained that sound is a product, but also be actively wanting to know whether sound is impermanent or not. According to Lati Rin-po-che,

> In general, the measure of establishing the property of the subject includes the person's becoming involved in wanting to know whether or not sound is impermanent.[55]

To clarify the important features of the Ge-luk-pa view concerning the nature of the property of the subject in a correct proof, it will be helpful to compare their view with that of the early Buddhist logician Mokṣākaragupta. He explains the property of the subject in this way:

> Its [h's] definite (niścitam) presence in all [the members of the class of] the locus (p) of inference.[a]
>
> *Anumeya* here means the locus of inference (dharmin) such as a mountain etc. A logical mark must just (eva) subsist in it. This is one of the three characteristics [of a logical mark] and is named pakṣadharmatā [h's being a property of p].
>
> The word sattvam (presence) is employed to guard against the fallacy of an illegitimate h (asiddha). For instance, in the inference "Sound is impermanent because of invisibility," visibility (h) which means to be an object of the visual organ, does not truly exist in p or sound.
>
> By the particle eva the fallacy of h's nonexistence in part [that is, some members] of p is refuted. For instance, the Digambara Jaina formulates the syllogism "Trees have consciousness because they sleep." By sleeping here is meant the state of shriveled leaves; but this is not found in all trees.
>
> The word niścitam (definitely) is employed in order to reject the fallacy of h's dubious reality (saṃdigdhāsiddha). For instance, [the following inference is to be rejected:] "Here there is fire because of the existence of a mass of [smokelike] elements which, however, is suspected to be vapor."
>
> The significance of the word eva being placed [not before]

[the opponent] the sign has been established as the property of the subject. This person is still in the process of establishing the sign as such" (commentary on *Signs and Reasonings*, vol. 1, p. 29).

[a] This is from Kajiyama's translation of *The Tarkabhāṣā*. The letter "h" refers to the sign, and the "p" refers to the basis or locus of debate.

but after the word *sattvam* is to reject the fallacy of *h* subsisting only in *p* (*asādhāraṇa*). For instance, "Sound is impermanent because of its audibility" [is an inconclusive inference, because the *h*, audibility, is an exclusive property of sound].[56]

It is interesting to note that the Ge-luk-pa tradition has maintained, in both its oral and written traditions, many of the features of the explanation found in Mokṣākaragupta's text. The logic manual used at Lo-sel-ling College of Dre-pung Monastic University contains an explanation of the property of the subject that is similar to that of Mokṣākaragupta. The author of the Lo-sel-ling textbook, Ge-shay Tsül-trim-nam-gyel, posits this definition of something's (x's) being the property of the subject in the proof of sound as impermanent:

> By a person for whom x has become the property of the subject in the proof of sound as impermanent, x is ascertained as just existent—in accordance with the mode of proof—with sound.[a]

The ge-shay then follows the same format used by Mokṣākaragupta in explaining the definition of the property of the subject. This approach is summarized by Lati Rin-po-che as,

> There are four [aspects of the definition] that are eliminating four things; these are "existent" (*yod pa, sat*), "just" (or "only"—*nyid, eva*), "ascertain" (*nges pa, niścitam*), and the fact that "just" is placed before "existent" and not after. Thus the definition of property of the subject eliminates four things and establishes four things.[57]

Mokṣākaragupta's statement (quoted above) of the definition of the property of the subject reads: "The word *sattvam* (presence) is employed to guard against the fallacy of an illegitimate *h* (*asiddha*). For instance, in the inference 'Sound is impermanent because of visibility,' visibility (*h*), which means to be an object of the visual organ, does not truly exist in *p* or sound." Ge-shay Tsül-trim-nam-gyel begins his explanation with almost the same words,

> There is a purpose for stating the word "existent" (*yod pa, sat-tva*) as part of this definition; it is for the sake of eliminating [the possibility] that object of apprehension of an eye consciousness is the property of the subject in the proof of sound

---

[a]   Ge-shay Tsül-trim-nam-gyel, *Signs and Reasonings*, p. 4a.1-2. In this context, "mode of proof" is said to have the same meaning as "mode of statement."

as impermanent. This is because, in dependence on this word ["existent"], that [object of apprehension of an eye consciousness is the property of the subject in the proof of sound as impermanent] is refuted, because object of apprehension of an eye consciousness does not exist with sound. This is because sound is not an object of apprehension of an eye consciousness.[58]

Pur-bu-jok's explanation does not mirror the reasoning of Mokṣākaragupta and Ge-shay Tsül-trim-nam-gyel explicitly and provides no example; however, it does provide the same fundamental information. As Pur-bu-jok puts it:

It follows that the subject, product, is ascertained by valid cognition as only existing, in accordance with the mode of statement, with sound, because (1) the mode of statement in the proof of that by the sign of it is an "is" statement, (2) sound is it [that is, product], and (3) it is with the subject, sound [that is, product is a quality of sound].[59]

In commentary on Pur-bu-jok's explanation, Ge-luk-pa teachers routinely use as an example the object of apprehension of an eye consciousness, because it is so obviously something that does not exist with sound. "Object of apprehension of an eye consciousness" cannot be the property of the subject in the proof of sound as impermanent because object of apprehension of an eye consciousness does not exist with the subject of that proof, sound. If something exists with sound in accordance with the mode of statement (that is, in this context, an "is" statement), then it is necessarily a quality of sound. As Ge-shay Pel-den-drak-pa says,

To say that the sign just exists with the subject, sound, means that, in relation to or with that subject, sound, the sign is seen to just exist.[60]

Next, Mokṣākaragupta's explanation for the presence of the term *eva* in the definition of property of the subject is: "By the particle *eva* the fallacy of *h*'s nonexistence in part [that is, in some members] of *p* is refuted. For instance, the Digambara Jaina formulates the syllogism 'Trees have consciousness because they sleep.' By sleeping here is meant the state of shriveled leaves; but this is not found in all trees." Ge-shay Tsül-trim-nam-gyel's explanation differs only in being expressed in greater detail:

There is a purpose for stating the word "just" (*nyid, eva*) because it is for the sake of eliminating folding its leaves at night
and sleeping as the property of the subject in the proof of trees
as sentient. This is because, in dependence on this word
["just"], that is refuted, because although sleeping at night with
folded leaves exists among trees, it does not *only* exist among
trees. This is because it does not exist among all trees. This, in
turn, is because whatever is a tree does not necessarily sleep at
night with folded leaves.[61]

For a sign (x) to be the property of the subject in the proof of sound as
impermanent, it must both exist with sound and must *only* exist with
sound. Another example of something that does not fulfill the requirement of just existing with the subject (and is thus eliminated as a correct sign) is "arisen from exertion" in the proof of sound as impermanent. Arisen from exertion cannot be the property of the subject in the
proof of sound as impermanent because although arisen from exertion
exists with sound, it does not only exist with sound. Lati Rin-po-che
comments,

Arisen from exertion does not *only exist* with sound because it
does not exist with all sounds; whatever is a sound is not necessarily arisen from exertion.[62]

Mokṣākaragupta's explanation for the position of the term *eva* is: "The
significance of the word *eva* being placed [not before] but after the
word *sattvam* is to reject the fallacy of *h* subsisting only in *p*
(*asādhāraṇa*). For instance, 'Sound is impermanent because of its audibility' [is an inconclusive inference, because the *h*, audibility, is an exclusive property of sound]." The equivalent statement in Ge-shay Tsül-
trim-nam-gyel's textbook is:

There is a purpose for stating the word "only" after "existent"
and not before, because it is for the sake of eliminating "only
object of hearing" as the property of the subject in the proof of
sound as impermanent. This is because in dependence on this
[placement of the word], that [the idea of "only an object of
hearing" being the property of the subject in that proof] is refuted, because although object of hearing is only existent
among sounds, only object of hearing does not exist among
sounds. This is because object of comprehension exists among
sounds.[63]

Although Pur-bu-jok does not specifically comment on the importance of the position of the term "just," its importance is impressed upon the Ge-luk-pa students by their teachers, as part of the study of the property of the subject. The explanations by Mokṣākaragupta and Ge-shay Tsül-trim-nam-gyel are also part of the oral tradition to which a Ge-luk-pa student is introduced—in classes and on the debate courtyard—by teachers and by more advanced students.

Returning to Mokṣākaragupta's explanation of property of the subject, we note that the Ge-luk-pa explanation of the term *niścitam* differs. Mokṣākaragupta's is: "The word *niścitam* is employed in order to reject the fallacy of *h*'s dubious reality (*saṃdigdhāsiddha*). For instance, [the following inference is to be rejected:] 'Here there is fire because of the existence of a mass of [smokelike] elements which, however, is suspected to be vapor.'" Here Ge-shay Tsül-trim-nam-gyel's explanation diverges from that of Mokṣākaragupta. The ge-shay writes,

> There is a purpose for stating the word "ascertain" (*nges pa*, *niścitam*) because it is for the sake of eliminating that product is the property of the subject in the proof of sound as impermanent for an opponent who has doubts concerning whether sound is a product.[64]

Kajiyama translates the term *niścitam* as "definite." It can also be translated as "ascertained."[a] Kajiyama's translation seems consistent, however, with Mokṣākaragupta's explanation of the importance of the term in the definition of property of the subject. Mokṣākaragupta explains that *niścitam* is included in the definition in order to eliminate, as a correct sign, any sign in a proof involving an unclear, indefinite, ambiguous situation. The example he posits is "a mass of [smokelike] elements, suspected to be vapor" as the sign in the proof of the existence of fire in a particular place. Something smokelike cannot serve as proof of the presence of fire. Mokṣākaragupta's example thus involves a situation in which there is a lack of certainty in regard to the nature of the object held as the sign; it may be smoke, but it may not be. The nature of the sign itself is not clearly discernable.

This emphasis on the uncertain nature of the sign makes it appropriate to translate *niścitam* in this context as either "definite" or "ascertained." In the example, the sign is not definite; and being indefinite, it cannot be ascertained. The sign itself (that is, the phenomenon set as the sign) is not ascertainable with any certainty and thus cannot serve as a correct sign.

---

[a] *Niścitam* is a past perfect participle and thus may be translated as "ascertained."

The Ge-luk-pas' explanation concerning the significance of *niścitam* differs from Mokṣākaragupta's. They emphasize that the term is included in the definition in order to eliminate, for example, the possibility that product could be a correct sign in the proof of sound as impermanent for a person who has not already understood that sound is a product. This is a very different situation from that in the example posited by Mokṣākaragupta. Product is not an unclear or ambiguous phenomenon, and product's existence with the subject, sound, is not generally indefinite.

By choosing this example, Ge-luk-pa scholars are emphasizing the consciousness of the opponent involved. "The mass of [smokelike] elements" can never serve as a correct sign of the existence of fire; but product may (or may not) serve as a correct sign of the impermanence of sound. Its correctness depends entirely on the consciousness of the opponent involved. The term "ascertain" thus specifies that the sign x must be *ascertained by the opponent* as existent with the subject. Lati Rinpo-che emphasizes the importance of the consciousness of the individual opponent:

> Even though the reason only exists with the subject, it may not be a correct sign; this person [that is, the correct opponent] has to ascertain it with valid cognition. It is not enough for the sign to definitely exist with the subject, it must also be ascertained as such by the opponent.[65]

In the Ge-luk-pa explanation, the term *niścitam* involves the opponent, who must have ascertained, for example, that sound is a product. For the Ge-luk-pa, the sign in the syllogism, "The subject, sound, is impermanent because of being a product," though it seems to satisfy the requirements in Mokṣākaragupta's definition, is not necessarily a correct sign. The property of the subject is not necessarily established in that proof: it is not enough for sound to be *definitely* a product. The opponent must also *ascertain* it as such. The Ge-luk-pa explanation shows a possible shift toward a greater emphasis on the consciousness of the individual debater. Further indication of this shift is the Ge-luk-pa's more complete definition of property of the subject, incorporating the explicit requirement that there be a flawless subject. Mokṣākaragupta does not specify the existence of the flawless subject. As Pur-bu-jok explains, being the flawless subject means not only that the subject is held as the basis of debate in a syllogism but also that there exists a person who is "engaged in wanting to know" whether or not the thesis is correct.

PREDICATE OF THE PROBANDUM

In his explanation of the basis of relation of the property of the subject, Pur-bu-jok includes the following explanation of the meaning of "predicate of the probandum":

> The definition of a predicate of the probandum is:
>
> that which is held as the predicate of the probandum.[a]
>
> Whatever is selfless is necessarily a predicate of the probandum because whatever is selfless is necessarily the predicate of the probandum in the proof of sound as it. Therefore, whatever is a predicate of a probandum (*sādhyadharma*) is not necessarily a phenomenon (*dharma*).[66]

The selfless encompasses both existents and nonexistents. Just as anything may be set as a sign, whether correct or not, so also anything, whether existent or nonexistent, may be held as the predicate of the probandum in a hypothetical proof, no matter how absurd it may be. For example, a horn of a rabbit is the predicate of the probandum in the syllogism, "The subject, sound, is a horn of a rabbit because of being a product." Thus, it is possible to posit an absurd proof containing a nonexistent as its predicate of the probandum. It is from this point of view that Pur-bu-jok asserts that "whatever is the predicate of the probandum is not necessarily a phenomenon."

However, in the case of a correct syllogism, by which something is actually being proved satisfactorily to the inferential valid cognition of a correct opponent, the predicate will always be a phenomenon, and never a nonexistent. It is from this point of view that Ge-shay Pel-den-drak-pa says, "One must say that whatever is a predicate of the probandum is necessarily a phenomenon."[67] This must be the case because whatever is realized by inferential valid cognition is necessarily an existent. In general, however, anything may be posited as predicate; and thus in general the predicate of the probandum need not be a phenomenon.

The explanation continues,

> The definition of the predicate of the probandum in the proof

---

[a] It may be argued that this definition is not the least bit helpful; in fact, some Ge-luk-pa scholars find fault with the use of such definitions. Ge-shay Pel-den-drak-pa says of this one, "Nothing can be understood by it; the purpose of definitions is to make something understandable" (commentary on *Signs and Reasonings*, vol. 1, p. 19).

of sound as impermanent is:

> that which is held as the predicate of the probandum in the proof of sound as impermanent.

If the predicates of the probandum in the proof of sound as impermanent are divided, they are of two types: the explicit and implicit predicates of the probandum in the proof of sound as impermanent. The definition of the explicit predicate of the probandum in the proof of sound as impermanent is:

> that which is held as the explicit predicate of the probandum in the proof of sound as impermanent.

The impermanent (*mi rtag pa*) is an illustration [of an explicit predicate of the probandum, as in "sound is impermanent because of being a product"].

The definition of the implicit predicate of the probandum in the proof of sound as impermanent is:

> that which is held as the implicit predicate of the probandum in the proof of sound as impermanent.

Opposite from not being impermanent (*mi rtag pa ma yin pa las log pa*) is an illustration [of an implicit predicate of the probandum, as in "sound is impermanent because of being a product"].[68]

When proving, with valid reasoning, that sound is impermanent, one is at the same time proving implicitly that sound is opposite from not being impermanent and that sound is not permanent. As Lati Rin-po-che says,

> When you state that sound is impermanent by the sign, product, you are explicitly proving sound's impermanence, and you are implicitly proving that sound is opposite from not being impermanent.[a]

This is also clear in the words of Ge-shay Pel-den-drak-pa:

> In the proof of sound as impermanent, nonpermanent is an implicit predicate of the probandum; that sound is nonpermanent is an implicit probandum.[69]

---

[a] Commentary on *Signs and Reasonings*, vol. 2, Jan. 28, 1977, p. 8. "Opposite from not *being* impermanent" is sometimes translated into English as "opposite from nonimpermanent."

Pur-bu-jok's discussion continues,

> Furthermore, [in the syllogism, "The subject, sound, is imper-
> manent because of being a product," two explicit and two im-
> plicit predicates of the probandum are posited]. The two, im-
> permanent and [its definition], momentary, are each the expli-
> cit predicate of the probandum in the proof of sound as imper-
> manent by the sign, product. The two, opposite from not being
> impermanent and opposite from not being momentary, are
> each the implicit predicate of the probandum in the proof of
> sound as impermanent by the sign, product.[70]

There is disagreement among Ge-luk-pa scholars concerning what may
be posited as the explicit and implicit predicates in a given proof. According to Lati Rin-po-che, "The difference between explicit and implicit has to do with whether the aspect of the object actually appears to
your mind or not."[71] Ge-luk-pa scholars agree that momentary is the
definition of impermanent and that the ascertainment of impermanent
must thus be preceded by ascertainment of momentary. It is agreed
that when impermanent is realized by valid cognition, momentary
must already have been realized; but does this mean that when impermanent appears to the mind, momentary must necessarily also appear?
This is where opinions differ.

Pur-bu-jok asserts that in the proof of sound as impermanent by
the sign, product, there are two explicit predicates, and thus two phenomena are being proved explicitly at the same time: impermanent and
momentary. For Lati Rin-po-che, in the same proof, momentary cannot
be an explicit predicate because only impermanent can be such; he
says,

> Whatever is the explicit predicate of the probandum in the
> proof of sound as impermanent is necessarily one with imper-
> manent.[72]

According to Lati Rin-po-che and Ge-shay Pel-den-drak-pa, to say that
momentary is an explicit predicate in the proof of sound as impermanent brings problems. In the ge-shay's opinion, if one says that momentary is the explicit predicate, then momentary and impermanent
necessarily appear together; if they do, when one realizes sound is
momentary, one necessarily also realizes sound is impermanent; if such
is the case, momentary could not serve as a correct sign of sound's

impermanence.[a]

Summing all this up, Pur-bu-jok says,

> In the statement, "The subject, sound, is impermanent because of being a product,"
>
> (1) The basis of debate in the proof of that is: sound.
> (2) The predicate of the probandum in the proof of that is: the impermanent.
> (3) The probandum is: that sound is impermanent.
> (4) The correct sign is: product.
> (5) The predicate of the negandum is: the permanent.
> (6) The negandum [that which is being negated] in the proof of that is: that sound is permanent.
>
> Extend this to others.[73]

When this is extended (for example) to the syllogism, "With respect to the subject, on a smoky pass, fire exists because smoke exists":

The basis of debate is: a smoky pass.
The predicate of the probandum is: fire (or the existence of fire).
The probandum is: that fire exists.
The correct sign is: smoke.
The predicate of the negandum is: fire does not exist.
The negandum is: that fire does not exist.

Pur-bu-jok continues,

> *Proofs:* The subject, impermanent, is the explicit predicate of the probandum in the proof of sound as impermanent because of being that which is held as the explicit predicate of the probandum in the proof of sound as impermanent.
>
> The subject, momentary, is not the explicit predicate of the probandum in the proof of sound as impermanent because of being a correct sign in that proof.[74]

Momentary is potentially a correct sign in the proof of sound as impermanent; but only if the opponent has not already ascertained sound

---

[a] Commentary on *Signs and Reasonings*, vol. 1, p. 20. This reasoning illustrates the problem: in Ge-luk-pa teaching, momentary is potentially a correct sign in the proof of sound as impermanent. Thus, there must exist a correct opponent who, having ascertained that sound is momentary, is wondering whether sound is impermanent or not. As the ge-shay points out, if momentary and impermanent are necessarily ascertained together, then there could be no such doubt in the mind of an opponent.

as impermanent. Lati Rin-po-che explains,

> That [momentary is a correct sign in the proof of sound as impermanent] is true in general. In actual application, however, whether something is a correct sign or not in a certain proof depends on the specific disputant involved.[75]

The opponent must be newly ascertaining the impermanence of sound by the sign, momentary. If momentary is the sign, it cannot be considered an explicit predicate. As Ge-shay Pel-den-drak-pa says, "In general, these [the subject, predicate, and sign] must be different."[76]

BRIEF ANALYSIS OF TERMS

It is necessary to understand the precise terms used in this study: property of the subject (*pakṣadharma, phyogs chos*) and predicate of the probandum (*sādhyadharma, bsgrub bya'i chos*).[a]

In its broadest meaning, *pakṣa* refers to the probandum, which is also what *sādhya* refers to, but these two terms, *pakṣadharma* and *sādhyadharma*, are not identical in meaning. In *pakṣadharma, pakṣa* refers to just the subject and not to the combination of subject and predicate (the probandum). *Dharma* here means feature or property (*khyad chos*). *Pakṣadharma* thus means the feature or property of the subject; this means that with (or in relation to) that subject, the sign is ascertained to just exist (that is, there is no instance of its not existing with the subject).[77] This refers to the presence of the sign in the subject.

In *sādhyadharma, sādhya* refers to the probandum, the subject and predicate together; *dharma* refers to the predicate. These terms will be discussed in detail in the next chapter.

COMPLICATIONS AND SAMPLE DEBATES

A major task of the Ge-luk-pa students as beginners is to develop a path of reasoning. Toward that end they are taught to analyze carefully the definitions they come across in their studies. To impress upon them the importance of the wording of definitions, teachers will engage them in debate and will play with the concepts involved, to bring more precise understanding.

---

[a] The Sanskrit is given first because the root text is in Sanskrit.

1. THE THREE MODES: IS/EXISTS

One complication arises from the definition of a correct sign: "that which is the three modes."[a] Typically, the Ge-luk-pa student memorizes this definition; the teacher might then say to the student, "It follows that in order for the sign to be correct in a given proof, the three modes must be present (*yod pa*) in that proof (in other words, that proof must have the three modes)." Knowing that there are indeed three modes, and that each one has to be established in order for a sign to be correct in a given proof, a student will say, "I accept" ('*dod*), meaning "I agree with your thesis that a correct proof must have the three modes." The teacher will continue, "It follows that if the three modes are present in a proof, then there is a correct sign in that proof." The student might say "'*dod*" to this as well, meaning, "I accept your thesis that if a proof has the three modes (if the three modes are present) then the sign in that proof is correct."

The teacher will then point out an unexpected consequence of that position by saying, "Then it follows that there exists a correct sign in the proof of sound as permanent." Surprised, the student answers, "Why?" (*ci'i phyir*), meaning, "Why? I do not accept the thesis."[b] The teacher answers, "Because the three modes—the property of the subject, the forward pervasion and the counterpervasion—exist (are present) in the proof of sound as permanent." If the student says, "The reason is not established," the teacher's response will be, "The reason is established (that is, the three modes exist in the proof of sound as permanent) because the property of the subject exists in the proof of sound as permanent by the sign, product, and because the forward pervasion and counterpervasion exist in the proof of sound as permanent by the sign, nonproduct."

This reason involves two separate signs—product and nonproduct. Now the student will say, "There is no pervasion," meaning that the reason does not prove the thesis that there exists a correct sign in the proof of sound as permanent. The teacher goes on, "It follows that if

---

[a]   See p. 399.

[b]   There are two possible responses to "Why?" One may posit (1) a reason proving one's thesis or (2) a consequence of the opponent's response. For example, if person *a* says to person *b*, "It follows that sound is permanent," *b* may say, "Why?", meaning, "I do not accept the thesis." Then, *a* may posit either (1) a reason for his or her own thesis: "because of being a common locus of phenomenon and the nonmomentary (to which *b* would say "the reason is not established"), or (2) a consequence of *b*'s position: "It follows that sound is not permanent" (to which *b* would say "I accept").

there exist the three modes in a particular proof, there is not necessarily a correct sign in that proof." The student responds, "I accept." Now the student is caught in a contradiction, having agreed that if the three modes are present in relation to a given proof, then there must be a correct sign in that proof. Now he or she understands that it is not enough to say that the three modes are present; they must also apply to one locus. The teacher then says, "*tshar*" ("finished"), meaning, "It's all over—you've contradicted yourself!"

Thus the student learns that it is not the same to say (1) *being* the modes (or that which is the three modes) and (2) the three modes *exist* (or are present). Lati Rin-po-che points out,

> This qualification [that a correct sign must be the three modes] is made in order to eliminate the idea that there exists a correct sign in the proof of sound as permanent. For, someone could debate that there does exist a correct sign in the proof of sound as permanent because these three—the property of the subject, the forward pervasion and the counterpervasion—exist in the proof of sound as permanent. When one says, "The subject, sound, is permanent because of being a product," "product" is [truly] the property of the subject. When one says, "The subject, sound, is permanent because of being a nonproduct," "nonproduct" is [truly] the forward pervasion and the counterpervasion. Thus, whereas the property of the subject applies to "product," the forward pervasion and counterpervasion apply to "nonproduct."[78]

Pur-bu-jok's definition of a correct sign is general; it does not specify the context in relation to which the sign is the three modes. In class and in the debate courtyard, the student learns that the sign must be the three modes in relation to one locus—the *same* correct sign must itself be all three modes. As Lati Rin-po-che puts it,

> There does not exist a correct sign in the proof of sound as permanent in which all three modes of proof apply to one specific phenomenon.
>
> The definition of a correct sign is stated in a general way for the sake of understanding. It actually applies only to proofs in which the three—the property of the subject, the forward pervasion and the counterpervasion—all apply to the same phenomenon. That is, the same correct sign must be all three modes.[79]

Through this type of debate, the student learns to pay close attention to the meaning of every word in a definition, at first so as to understand simple topics and to avoid being led into self-contradiction in debate. This precision in words and in reasoning will find fruition in identifying subtle points of reasoning on more profound topics, such as the emptiness of inherent existence of phenomena.

2. "CORRECT" SIGNS THAT DO NOT SATISFY THE REQUIREMENTS

It has been established that a correct sign must itself be all three modes in a given proof—but it is interesting to note that certain signs, viewed by the Ge-luk-pa tradition as "correct," do not in fact satisfy all the requirements of correct signs. Examples are the signs in the two syllogisms that follow.

(a) The subject, object of knowledge, is permanent because of being the common locus of phenomenon and the nonmomentary. This is generally considered to be a correct proof. But if so, then the sign (being the common locus of phenomenon and the nonmomentary) must satisfy the criteria of the property of the subject in that proof. The definition of property of the subject in any given proof specifies that it must be ascertained as only existing with the subject (in this case, object of knowledge). It has been shown that, in the Ge-luk-pa explanation, something (x) "only existing" with sound means that all sounds are x; there is no case in which a sound is not x.[80]

Applying the same principles to the example under consideration, it would have to be the case that all objects of knowledge are a common locus of phenomenon and the nonmomentary. Whatever is such a common locus would necessarily be permanent (this is because "common locus of phenomenon and the nonmomentary" is the definition of permanent). Therefore, all objects of knowledge would have to be permanent. However, this is clearly not the case. There are many phenomena that are not permanent: pot, mountain, tree, and so on.

(b) The subject, product, is a sign in the proof of sound as impermanent by the sign, product, because of being set as the sign in the proof of sound as impermanent by the sign, product. Pur-bu-jok's definition of "sign in the proof of sound as impermanent by the sign, product," is: "that which is set as the sign in the proof of sound as impermanent by the sign, product." This being the case, it is customary to consider the syllogism above to be valid.

A debate between a challenger (C) and a defender (D)[a] might proceed as follows:

C: It follows that "set as a sign in the proof of sound as impermanent by the sign, product," is a correct sign in the proof of product as a correct sign in the proof of sound as impermanent by the sign, product.

D: I accept.

C: It follows that the property of the subject is established in that proof.

D: I accept.

C: It follows that "set as a sign in the proof of sound as impermanent by the sign, product," is ascertained as only existing with product.

D: I accept.

C: It follows that all products are set as a sign in the proof of sound as impermanent by the sign, product.

D: I accept.

As Ge-shay Pel-den-drak-pa points out, if this is accepted, then it would follow that pot is set as the sign in the proof of sound as impermanent by the sign, product. The syllogism that would result is: "The subject, sound, is impermanent because of being a pot." This of course is absurd.[81]

The signs in these two syllogisms (a and b, above) are correct. But one must be aware that they do not satisfy the established criteria, the general rule concerning the nature of correct signs. Ge-shay Pel-den-drak-pa summarizes the issue this way: "The same problem exists in relation to these [two] signs; being correct signs they should exist with all instances of the subject, but they do not."[82] There are exceptions to the general rule. It is usually the case, in a correct proof, that the subject is general; for example, in the syllogism, "The subject, sound, is impermanent because of being a product," the subject is general in that "sound" refers not only to sound itself (that is, the self-isolate of sound) but also to instances of sound.[b] The fact that product is a correct sign in

---

[a] The challenger is the one who poses the problems, and the defender is the one who must respond to the challenge and then defend his positions. The challenger is usually referred to as the "former opponent" (*snga rgol*) and the defender as the "latter opponent" (*phyir rgol*), but not necessarily. See chapter eight for a discussion of the topic of the different types of opponents.

[b] It is important to note that although in this case the subject (sound) is general, it is best understood as singular. Impermanence is being proved in relation to a specific

this proof indicates both (1) that sound itself is a product and (2) that each and every sound—the sound of a conch, the sound of the wind, etc.—is also a product.

The syllogisms (a) and (b) above are two of a number of well-known exceptions to the established criteria. In these syllogisms, the subject is not general. The subject of the first, "object of knowledge," must be understood to refer only to object of knowledge itself (the self-isolate of object of knowledge) and not to instances of object of knowledge. Similarly, in the second, "product" refers only to the self-isolate of product and not to instances of product.

Ge-shay Pel-den-drak-pa emphasizes that it is important not only to understand well the definitions establishing the criteria of correct signs, but also to understand that there are correct signs that do not meet these criteria:

> If one holds strictly to [these criteria], then that eliminates many signs that we know have to be considered as correct signs.... There are always exceptions; one has to be aware of the problems and limitations of the definitions—knowing how to use them, but also knowing their limitations.[83]

3. *"Faulty" Definitions*

Pur-bu-jok gives a detailed definition of each of the three modes and then provides a more simple definition for each. The brief definition of "something's being the property of the subject in a given proof"[a] is,

> That ascertained by valid cognition as just existing—in accordance with the mode of statement—with the flawless subject sought to be known in the proof of that.[84]

It is held that this definition is not intended to be definitive. It is

---

impermanent basis, sound. It would be a mistake to consider the subject as "all sounds," because "all sounds" is not itself a basis with respect to which impermanence can be realized. Daniel Perdue discusses in detail the nature of the subject in Tibetan logic in *Debate in Tibetan Buddhism* (Ithaca, New York: Snow Lion Publications, 1992), especially in the sections on quantification (pp. 85-88) and copulative association (pp. 778-789). He emphasizes the singular nature of the subject: "In no case is there fault in taking the subject to be singular, and this is the intention of the system" (p. 785). Here, in the context of focus on the property of the subject, the discussion emphasizes the *general* nature of that singular subject.

[a] A literal translation is "something's being the property of the subject in the proof of that." The proof is not specified, because the definition is establishing a general rule concerning the property of the subject in any given proof.

intended to help bring understanding of the general idea involved, but is not intended to hold up to thorough analysis. As Lati Rin-po-che points out, if taken literally, it will be found to be faulty:

> The definition is worded in this general way because Pur-bu-jok wants to give an impression of what the property of the subject is, in general.... However, if you debated strictly on the topic using this definition, you would get into trouble. It is important to pay attention to whether [a definition] would withstand the thorough analysis of debate, to pay attention to whether or not the pervasion is established.[85]

The pervasion is "whatever is ascertained as just existing in accordance with the mode of statement with the flawless subject in the proof of that is necessarily the property of the subject in the proof of that."[a]

If this is accepted, it follows that whatever is ascertained as existing in accordance with the flawless subject in the proof of sound as impermanent is necessarily the property of the subject in the proof of sound as impermanent. If this too is accepted, then it follows that a common locus of phenomenon and the nonmomentary is the property of the subject in the proof of sound as impermanent. A debate on this point might proceed as follows:

C: It follows that "that which is ascertained by valid cognition as just existing—in accordance with the mode of statement—with the subject sought to be known in the proof of sound as impermanent" is the definition of the property of the subject in the proof of sound as impermanent.

D: I accept.

C: It follows that the subject, the common locus of being a phenomenon and not being momentary, is the property of the subject in the proof of sound as impermanent.

D: Why?

---

[a] A definition may be used as a sign proving that definition's definiendum; for example, "momentary" is the definition of "impermanent"; thus momentary may be used as a correct sign in the proof of the impermanent. Similarly, the definition of property of the subject ("that which is ascertained as just existing—in accordance with the mode of statement—with the flawless subject in the proof of that") should be a correct sign in the proof of something (x) as the property of the subject in the proof of that. Such a proof is: "The subject, x, is the property of the subject in the proof of that because of being that which is ascertained as just existing—in accordance with the mode of statement—with the flawless subject in the proof of that."

C: Because of being ascertained by valid cognition as only existing—in accordance with the mode of statement—with the flawless subject sought to be known in the proof of that.

D: The reason is not established.

The reason is, in fact, established—because "flawless subject" is itself
permanent. The defender is arguing that "the common locus of being a
phenomenon and not being momentary" is not ascertained as only existing with *sound*; however, it *is* ascertained as only existing with *flawless subject*. The common locus of phenomenon and the nonmomentary
exists with flawless subject because flawless subject is permanent, and
there does not exist an instance of a permanent phenomenon that is
not a common locus of phenomenon and the nonmomentary; this is
because the definition of the permanent is "a common locus of phenomenon and the nonmomentary."

In any particular correct proof, the sign (for example, product in
the proof of sound as impermanent) must be ascertained as only existing with the subject (that is, sound). Product does, in fact, only exist
with sound, because all sounds are products; however, product does not
exist with "the flawless subject" in that proof. Sound itself (sound's
self-isolate) is an impermanent phenomenon, an object of hearing, a
product. "Flawless subject" itself (that is, flawless subject's self-isolate)
is *not* impermanent, *not* an object of hearing, and *not* a product. Flawless subject itself is considered to be permanent. As Ge-shay Pel-den-
drak-pa says,

> The self-isolate of flawless subject is permanent. "Sign," "sub-
> ject," and so forth, are all considered to be imputations by
> thought and thus permanent.... When you say "subject," even if
> it refers to "sound," it is something that appears to be fabri-
> cated by thought; from among direct perception and [concep-
> tual] thought, it appears to be a phenomenon that is mainly po-
> sited by thought.[86]

Lati Rin-po-che explains that Pur-bu-jok probably included these
brief but problematic definitions in order to cause students to think, in
order to cause qualms; he says,

> It is as if Pur-bu-jok were purposely stating it in this general
> way to make trouble, so that you would think about where the
> pervasion is established and where it is not.[a]

---

[a]   Commentary on *Signs and Reasonings*, vol. 2, Feb. 9, 1977, pp. 4-5. (Of course, this may

4. SHIFTING THE REFERENT

Ge-shay Tsül-trim-nam-gyel, in his logic manual, specifies that whatever is set as a sign in the proof of sound as impermanent by the sign, product, must be one with product.[87] A playful debate arises on this topic. Here is the context: In class, Ge-luk-pa teachers routinely drill the students, asking them to posit definitions, divisions, and illustrations, and then going into debates to help them probe the meaning of these. For example, a teacher will say, "Posit the definition of a sign in the proof of sound as impermanent." The student's answer is: "That which is set as a sign in the proof of sound as impermanent." Then the teacher might say, "It follows that whatever is set as a sign in the proof of sound as impermanent by the sign, product, is necessarily one with product." The student responds: "I accept."

The teacher might then say, "Posit an illustration of a sign." The response might be, "The subject, product, at the time of stating, 'The subject, sound, is impermanent because of being a product.'" This is the usual way of positing a specific sign. The students are taught to respond in this way, stating first the sign and then specifying the context in which it is functioning as a sign. Asked to posit a correct nature sign, the student might respond, "The subject, product, at the time of stating, 'The subject, sound, is impermanent because of being a product.'" And if asked to posit a correct effect sign, he or she might respond, "The subject, smoke, at the time of stating, 'With respect to the subject, on a smoky pass, fire exists because smoke exists.'" Every Ge-luk-pa student is likely to encounter a debate that plays with this standard response.

> Teacher (T): It follows that whatever is set as the sign in the proof of sound as impermanent by the sign, product, is necessarily one with product.
>
> Student (S): I accept.
>
> T: Posit that which is set as the sign in the proof of sound as impermanent by the sign, product.
>
> S: The subject, product, at the time of stating, "The subject, sound, is impermanent because of being a product."
>
> T: It follows that "product at the time of stating, 'The subject, sound, is impermanent because of being a product'" is set as the sign in the proof of sound as impermanent by the sign, product.

S: I accept.

T: Then it follows that "product at the time of stating, 'The subject, sound, is impermanent because of being a product'" is one with product.

S: I accept.

A beginner might accept this, but "product at the time of stating, 'The subject, sound, is impermanent because of being a product'" is not one with product, is not the definition of created thing, and is not impermanent. "Product at the time of stating, 'The subject, sound, is impermanent because of being a product'" is itself a permanent phenomenon.

T: It follows that "product at the time of stating, 'The subject, sound, is impermanent because of being a product'" is the definiendum of created thing.

That which is set as the sign in the proof of sound as impermanent (that is, product) is necessarily one with product. But "product at the time of stating, 'The subject, sound, is impermanent because of being a product'" cannot be one with product. Only product itself (the self-isolate of product) is one with product. If *product at the time of stating, "The subject, sound, is impermanent because of being a product,"* were one with product, it would have to be the definiendum of created thing (the definition of product)—but only *product* is the definiendum of created thing.

S: Why?

T: It follows that there does not exist that which is set as a sign in the proof of sound as impermanent by the sign, product.

T: Then posit that which is set as the sign in the proof of sound as impermanent by the sign, product.

S: Product, at the time of stating, "The subject, sound, is impermanent because of being a product."

The student intends to posit just "product," but the teacher plays with this standard response, shifting the referent from the term "product" to the whole phrase. The referent of "product" is just the self-isolate of product; the referent of "product at the time of stating..." is not the self-isolate of product.

This is the kind of debate that can easily confuse a beginner.

5. Relationship between Definiendum and Definition

There is a reason why Pur-bu-jok's presentation of "flawless subject" (*chos can skyon med*) is phrased "*being* the flawless subject" (*chos can skyon med yin pa*). Without "being" (*yin pa*), the definition would be faulty.[a] This hinges on the nature of definienda and their definitions.

During their study of the *Collected Topics*, Ge-luk-pa students learn that between any phenomenon x and its definition y, there must be a certain relationship: it must be possible to ascertain y by valid cognition prior to ascertaining x by valid cognition, and between x (a definiendum) and y (a definition) eight pervasions must prevail. These pervasions are:

1)   whatever is x is necessarily y;
2)   whatever is y is necessarily x;
3)   whatever is not x is necessarily not y;
4)   whatever is not y is necessarily not x;
5)   wherever x exists, y necessarily exists;
6)   wherever y exists, x necessarily exists;
7)   wherever x does not exist, y necessarily does not exist;
8)   wherever y does not exist, x necessarily does not exist.

These can be summarized as the pervasions of being, of nonbeing, of existence, and of nonexistence.

If we omit "being" and consider the definiendum to be simply "flawless subject...," the pervasion of existence (number 5, above) would not prevail. This is because wherever there exists "*flawless subject* sought to be known in the proof of sound as impermanent by the sign, product" (the definiendum), it is not true that there *necessarily* exists the definition: "that which is observed as a common locus of (1) being held as the basis of debate in the proof of sound as impermanent by the sign, product, and of (2) there existing a person who, having ascertained that it (sound) is a product, is engaged in wanting to know whether or not it is impermanent."

This can be illustrated if we use "the permanent" as the subject. In the permanent (that is, in relation to the permanent), the faulty definiendum exists but the definition does not.

---

[a] Pur-bu-jok's definition at the beginning of this chapter is not a definition of "flawless subject" but of "*being* a flawless subject." The discussion here of the importance of the term "being" in this definition is based on the commentary on *Signs and Reasonings* by Ge-shay Lob-sang-gya-tso, vol. 1, p. 7

(a) To illustrate that the faulty *definiendum does exist in the permanent*, one might say, "With respect to the subject, permanent, there exists a flawless subject sought to be known in the proof of sound as impermanent by the sign, product." This statement is acceptable if one disregards the subject; the predicate of the probandum (there exists a flawless subject sought to be known in the proof of sound as impermanent by the sign, product) is understood to be complete in itself. The subject has, in effect, become superfluous. There does in fact exist a flawless subject sought to be known in the proof of sound as impermanent, and therefore (since the subject of the original syllogism has become superfluous) anything could be posited as that subject and the statement would still be acceptable.

(b) To illustrate that the *definition does not exist in the permanent*, one might say, "With respect to the subject, permanent, there exists that observed as a common locus of (1) being held as the basis of debate in the proof of sound as impermanent by the sign, product, and of (2) there existing a person who, having ascertained that it (sound) is a product, is engaged in wanting to know whether or not it is impermanent." This is unacceptable, because the permanent is not a common locus of those two. There does not exist a person who, having ascertained permanent as a product, is wondering whether permanent is impermanent or not. Permanent cannot be ascertained as a product by valid cognition, because it is a nonproduct.

This complication is avoided if the word "being" is included in the explanation of the definition of flawless subject. This is because wherever there exists "*being the flawless subject* sought to be known in the proof of sound as impermanent by the sign, product," it is true that there *necessarily* exists "that observed as a common locus of (1) being held as the basis of debate in the proof of sound as impermanent by the sign, product, and of (2) there existing a person who, having ascertained that it (sound) is a product, is engaged in wanting to know whether or not it is impermanent."

6. DEFINIENDUM AND DEFINITION: SHIFTING THE REFERENT

The relationship between a definiendum and its definition can give rise to another complication. Pur-bu-jok specifies that "whatever is the flawless subject sought to be known in the proof of sound as impermanent by the sign, product, is necessarily one with sound (*sgra dang gcig*)." A debate on this statement might run as follows:

C: It follows that "that observed as a common locus of (1) being

held as the basis of debate in the proof of sound as impermanent by the sign, product, and of (2) there existing a person
who, having ascertained that it (sound) is a product, is engaged
in wanting to know whether or not it is impermanent" is the
definition of being the flawless subject sought to be known in
the proof of sound as impermanent by the sign, product. [This
is true.]

D: I accept it.
C: It follows that the subject, "that observed as a common locus of
(1) being held as the basis of debate in the proof of sound as
impermanent by the sign, product, and of (2) there existing a
person who, having ascertained that it (sound) is a product, is
engaged in wanting to know whether or not it is impermanent," is the flawless subject sought to be known in the proof of
sound as impermanent by the sign, product.

D: Why?
C: Because it is the definition of being the flawless subject sought
to be known in the proof of sound as impermanent by the sign,
product.

D: I accept it.
C: It follows that "that observed as a common locus of (1) being
held as the basis of debate in the proof of sound as impermanent by the sign, product, and of (2) there existing a person
who, having ascertained that it (sound) is a product, is engaged
in wanting to know whether or not it is impermanent" is one
with sound.

D: Why?
C: Because of being the flawless subject sought to be known in the
proof of sound as impermanent by the sign, product.

At this point, the debate can go different ways. One is:

D: There is no entailment.
C: There is entailment because of Pur-bu-jok's statement, "Whatever is the flawless subject sought to be known in the proof of
sound as impermanent by the sign, product, is necessarily one
with sound."

An alternative course of debate might be:

D: The reason is not established.
C: It follows that whatever is the definition of being a flawless
subject is not necessarily a flawless subject.

D: I accept.

C: Then, it follows that whatever is the definition of thing is not necessarily a thing.

D: Why?

C: It follows that whatever is the definition of thing is necessarily a thing.

D: I accept.

C: Then, whatever is the definition of flawless subject sought to be known in the proof of sound as impermanent by the sign, product, is necessarily the flawless subject sought to be known in the proof of sound as impermanent by the sign, product.

D: Why?

C: Because whatever is the definition of thing is necessarily a thing and the situations are parallel.

D: I accept.

C: Then it follows that "that observed as a common locus of (1) being held as the basis of debate in the proof of sound as impermanent by the sign, product, and of (2) there existing a person who, having ascertained that it (sound) is a product, is engaged in wanting to know whether or not it is impermanent" is the flawless subject sought to be known in the proof of sound as impermanent by the sign, product.

D: Why?

C: Because it is the definition of flawless subject.

D: I accept.

C: It follows then that the definition of flawless subject in that proof is one with sound.

If the defender accepts that the definition of the flawless subject in that proof is the flawless subject in that proof, then these absurd consequences would follow:

(1) that the definition of flawless subject is one with sound;
(2) that the definition of flawless subject is a definiendum;
(3) that object of hearing is the definition of flawless subject.

It would then follow that the sound of a conch is the flawless subject in that proof. The defender is arguing that whatever is the definition of flawless subject has to *be* the flawless subject because whatever is the definition of thing is necessarily a thing and the situations are parallel.

Ge-luk-pa students confronted with such a debate have to work out for themselves whether the situations are in fact parallel. If they are, then it is true that whatever is the definition of flawless subject is necessarily the flawless subject itself; but such does not seem to be the case. If the situations are different, then in what way are they different, and why?

The students are required to consider very carefully the referent of every term used. This sixth complication centers on the fact that if *a* is the definition of *b*, the following two phrases:

(1) "Whatever is the definition of b"
(2) "Whatever is a"

have two different meanings—even though a is in fact the definition of b. The referent of the term "whatever" is different in these two statements. That which is the definition of b is just a; that which is a is whatever phenomenon is described by a. Thus:

- in (1) the referent of "whatever" is a;
- in (2) the referent of "whatever" is something (c) that satisfies the requirements of the definition, a.

To avoid such entanglements, the student must use words very carefully. To take a shortcut in debate and say "that definition" when one means a (the definition spelled out) is to walk into trouble.

7. ONLY THE SELF-ISOLATE OF X IS ONE WITH X

The seventh complication, like the sixth, centers on the statement by Pur-bu-jok, "Whatever is the flawless subject in the proof of sound as impermanent by the sign, product, must be one with sound." A challenger might begin a debate:

C: It follows that the subject, object of hearing, is one with sound.
D: Why?
C: Because of being the flawless subject sought to be known in the proof of sound as impermanent.
D: The reason is not established.
C: Because of being "that observed as a common locus of (1) being held as the basis of debate in the proof of sound as impermanent by the sign, product, and of (2) there existing a person who, having ascertained that it (sound) is a product, is engaged in wanting to know whether or not it is impermanent."
D: The first reason is not established.
C If object of hearing is not the basis of debate in that proof, then when one apprehends sound, does one not also apprehend object of hearing?

D: Yes, one does.

C: Then it follows that the opposite from not being sound is one with sound.

D: Why?

C: Because of being the flawless subject sought to be known in the proof of sound as impermanent.

Or, as Ge-shay Pel-den-drak-pa points out, the challenger could say, "It follows that the subject, sound, is one with *sgra* (the Tibetan equivalent of 'sound') because of being the basis of debate in the proof of sound as impermanent by the sign, product."[88] Such topics are debated.

Ge-luk-pa students encounter the concepts of sameness and difference in their study of the *Collected Topics,* and by the time they study *Signs and Reasonings* they are already familiar with what it means to be one with x (*dang gcig*) or different from x (*dang tha dad*). What is one with x is just x's self-isolate (*rang ldog*) and nothing else. There are a number of phenomena that are said to appear to the mind whenever the term "sound" appears to the mind; but these phenomena are *not* therefore one with sound. These are not also taken to be the basis of debate in the proof of sound as impermanent.

There is some justification, however, for thinking that such phenomena would be the basis of debate in the proof of sound as impermanent, along with sound. Pur-bu-jok explains that in the proof of sound as impermanent there are two explicit predicates of the probandum: impermanent and momentary. He considers momentary to be an explicit predicate of the probandum in that proof because whenever impermanent appears to the mind, momentary must also appear to the mind. Thus, one might argue that object of hearing is the basis of debate in the proof of sound as impermanent, because momentary is the explicit predicate of the probandum in the proof of sound as impermanent, and the situation is parallel.

Whatever is the flawless subject in the proof of sound as impermanent is necessarily one with sound (is necessarily the self-isolate of sound). Therefore "that observed as a common locus of (1) being held as the basis of debate in the proof of sound as impermanent by the sign, product, and of (2) there existing a person who, having ascertained that it (sound) is a product, is engaged in wanting to know whether or not it is impermanent" is not the subject because it is not the isolate of sound (is not one with sound). It is in fact mutually inclusive with the isolate of sound, but it is not itself the isolate of sound. Whatever is the flawless subject in that proof is the isolate of sound, and whatever is the isolate of sound is *it* (that which is the basis of debate, the flawless subject in that proof).

Whatever is the flawless subject in the proof of sound as impermanent is necessarily the self-isolate of sound; and the self-isolate of
sound is sound. *That which is* the flawless subject is thus impermanent,
but *flawless subject* itself is permanent. As mentioned earlier, "flawless
subject," "predicate," and "sign" are all permanent because of being
mental constructs.[a] Pur-bu-jok makes this point clearly when he writes,

> The three—the sign, predicate of the probandum, and basis of
> debate [or "flawless subject"]—in the proof of sound as imper-
> manent by the sign, product, are generally characterized phe-
> nomena merely designated by thought; however, whatever is
> any of the three—the sign, predicate of the probandum, and ba-
> sis of debate in the proof of that—must be a specifically charac-
> terized phenomenon. This is because whatever is [any of those
> three] must be a thing. This in turn is because whatever is the
> basis of debate in the proof of that must be sound, for
>
> (1) whatever is the basis of debate in the proof of that must be
>   one with sound;
> (2) whatever is the explicit predicate of the probandum must
>   be the impermanent; and
> (3) the sign must be just product.
>
> Therefore, it is said that the three (the sign, predicate of the
> probandum, and basis of debate in the proof of that) are not the
> three (the sign, predicate of the probandum, and basis of de-
> bate in the proof of that).[89]

Thus the flawless subject in the proof of sound as impermanent is not
the flawless subject in that proof, and the basis of debate is not the ba-
sis of debate. Sound is the basis of debate. That which is the basis of debate is the basis of debate, but "basis of debate" is not *itself* the basis of
debate. "Basis of debate" is a phrase referring to something else
(sound). The self-isolate of "basis of debate" is just—basis of debate.
This way of looking at the meaning and referent of every term is very
important in the beginner's attempt to master the logic and debate in
this system of education.

---

[a] This is explained by Ge-shay Pel-den-drak-pa above in the discussion of the third
complication, "faulty definitions."

2. Bases of Relation of the Pervasions: The Similar and Dissimilar Classes

The forward pervasion and counterpervasion in a particular proof refer to the relationship between the sign and the predicate of the probandum in that proof. In order for a sign to be correct in a given proof, it must be in a strictly defined logical relationship with the predicate of the probandum. In the proof of sound as impermanent by the sign, product, for example, there must be irrefutable entailment between the sign, product, and the predicate, impermanent. This entailment has two parts: the forward pervasion and the counterpervasion. Ascertainment of the forward pervasion involves ascertainment that whatever is a product is necessarily impermanent (the sign must entail the predicate); ascertainment of the counterpervasion involves ascertainment that whatever is permanent is necessarily a nonproduct (the opposite of the predicate, the predicate of the negandum, must entail the opposite of the sign).

A correct (prepared) opponent, having understood that sound is a product, is then wondering whether or not sound is impermanent. In order to ascertain that sound is impermanent, all possibility of its being permanent must be eliminated. This is another way of saying that there must be an irrefutable entailment between the sign, product, and the predicate, impermanent.

For something to be a correct sign in a particular proof, it must satisfy the criteria for the pervasions in that proof. Pur-bu-jok sets forth these criteria in the following definitions:

> Something (x) is the forward pervasion in the proof of sound as impermanent when:
>
> 1) There exists a correct similar example (*mthun dpe*, **sadṛṣṭānta*) that possesses both the sign and the predicate of the probandum, in the proof of sound as impermanent by the sign x;
> 2) x is related with impermanent; and
> 3) x is ascertained by valid cognition as just existing, in accordance with the mode of statement, in only the similar class (*mthun phyogs*, *sapakṣa*) in the proof of sound as impermanent.

Something (x) is the counterpervasion in the proof of sound as impermanent when:

1) There exists a correct dissimilar example (*mi mthun dpe, *vidṛṣṭānta*), which possesses neither the sign nor the predicate of the probandum, in the proof of sound as impermanent by the sign, x;
2) x is related with impermanent; and
3) x is ascertained by valid cognition as only nonexistent in the dissimilar class (*mi mthun phyogs, vipakṣa*) in the proof of sound as impermanent.[90]

These definitions precisely describe the relationship that must exist between the predicate and the sign if the sign is to be correct. In order to understand them, one must first understand the terms "similar class" and "dissimilar class."[a]

Just as the property of the subject has a "basis of relation" (the flawless subject), so do the pervasions. The basis of relation of the forward pervasion is the similar class, and the basis of relation of the counterpervasion is the dissimilar class.[b] For example, in the proof of sound as impermanent by the sign, product, the similar class is the base with respect to which one ascertains the pervasion that whatever is a product is necessarily impermanent (product is pervaded by impermanent); this base is *the impermanent*. The dissimilar class is the base with respect to which one ascertains the pervasion that whatever is a

---

[a]   The term here translated as "class" is the Tibetan *phyogs,* a translation of the Sanskrit term *pakṣa.* In *pakṣadharma,* translated as "property of the subject," *pakṣa* is translated as "subject." Four uses of the term *pakṣa* are discussed below.

[b]   Pur-bu-jok's explanation of the topic, "The bases of relation of the pervasions," is divided into two parts: "The actual explanation and, ancillarily, the explanation of the similar and dissimilar examples." He divides the actual explanation of the bases of relation of the pervasions into four parts, "Definitions, divisions, enumeration of the four possibilities (*mu*) between the etymology and the actual usage (including the meaning of the term *pakṣa*), and analysis of whether or not similar and dissimilar classes are explicitly contradictory." *Signs and Reasonings,* p. 3b.1-2. The discussion here does not follow Pur-bu-jok's organization. This chapter will be ordered as follows:

1) similar class: definition, enumeration of possibilities; discussion of the meanings of the term *pakṣa;*
2) dissimilar class: definition, divisions, enumeration of the possibilities between etymology and actual usage;
3) consideration of whether similar and dissimilar classes are explicitly contradictory; and
4) similar and dissimilar examples.

product is necessarily not nonimpermanent (product is pervaded by not being nonimpermanent); this base is *the nonimpermanent*.[a]

THE SIMILAR CLASS

Pur-bu-jok defines the similar class in the proof of sound as impermanent as:

> That which is not empty of impermanence, in accordance with the mode of proof, in the proof of sound as impermanent.[91]

That which is "not empty" of impermanence (or of the impermanent) is, of course, anything that *is* impermanent; this includes *the impermanent* itself (the self-isolate of impermanent), as well as all instances of impermanence. As Ge-shay Lob-sang-gya-tso says,

> Whatever is impermanent is necessarily not empty of impermanence in accordance with the mode of proof in the proof of sound as impermanent; and whatever is not impermanent is necessarily empty of impermanence in accordance with the mode of proof in the proof of sound as impermanent.[92]

According to Pur-bu-jok, "Similar class in the proof of that [that is, in the proof of sound as impermanent] and the impermanent are mutually inclusive (*yin khyab mnyam*)."[b] Thus, whatever is the similar class

---

[a] Lati Rin-po-che, commentary on *Signs and Reasonings*, vol. 1, p. 25. On page 1 of this chapter it was mentioned that ascertainment of the counterpervasion involves ascertaining that "whatever is permanent is necessarily a nonproduct." Here, the pervasion is stated as "whatever is a product is necessarily not nonimpermanent." It should be noted that in different contexts the term "counterpervasion" may have different referents:

1. In the context of discussing the relationship between the sign (product) and the predicate (impermanent) in the proof of sound as impermanent, it is said that ascertainment of the counterpervasion involves ascertainment that whatever is permanent is necessarily a nonproduct.
2. From another point of view, it is said that when one ascertains (1) the forward pervasion and (2) the counterpervasion in relation to the sign, product, one understands (1) that whatever is a product is impermanent and (2) that whatever is a product is not nonimpermanent. (These are discussed in chapter three, in the section on "relationship between sign and predicate.")

[b] *Signs and Reasonings*, p. 3b.3. Ge-shay Ge-dün-lo-drö explains: "'Similar class in the proof of sound as impermanent' and 'impermanent' are mutually inclusive; this means that (1) whatever is the similar class in the proof of sound as impermanent is necessarily impermanent and (2) whatever is impermanent is necessarily the similar class in the proof of sound as impermanent" (commentary on *Signs and Reasonings*, section 2, p. 2).

(that is, whatever is a member of the similar class) in the proof of sound as impermanent is necessarily impermanent, and whatever is impermanent is necessarily [a member of] the similar class in the proof of sound as impermanent.

There are two modes of proof, an "is" (copular) proof and an "exists" (ontological) proof.[93] The similar class must accord with whatever mode of proof is present in the syllogism. For example, in "The subject, sound, is impermanent because of being a product," the verb is the linking verb "is," so the mode of proof is copular. In this case, phenomena that are not empty of impermanence in accordance with the copular mode must themselves "be" impermanent. As Lati Rin-po-che says,

> The proof of sound as impermanent is an "is" proof. The definition [of similar class] specifies "...not empty of impermanence in accordance with the mode of proof"; this means "...not empty of *being* impermanent." If it were an "exists" proof, a proof of something as existing, it ["not empty of impermanence in accordance with the mode of proof"] would mean "not empty of the *existence* of impermanent" (or "impermanent [is] not empty of *existing*"—*mi rtag pa yod pas mi stong ba*).[a]

All impermanent phenomena accord with the mode of proof and are thus the similar class in the proof of sound as impermanent; all phenomena that are the similar class must be impermanent. Lati Rin-po-che adds,

> In order for something to be the similar class in the proof of sound as impermanent, it has to be the predicate of the probandum in the proof of sound as impermanent; that is, it has to be impermanent.[94]

The qualification "in accordance with the mode of proof" thus serves to eliminate from the similar class, in the proof of sound as impermanent, those phenomena that *exist in* the impermanent, but are themselves permanent, such as object of knowledge.

An "exists" proof would be: "The subject, sound, exists in the impermanent because of being a product." In this case, all phenomena that "exist in the impermanent" would compose the similar class. The

---

[a] Commentary on *Signs and Reasonings*, vol. 1, p. 23. Elsewhere (chapter three) the phrase here translated as "the existence of impermanent" (*mi rtag pa yod pa*) is understood by Lati Rin-po-che and other Ge-luk-pa scholars to mean "exists *in* the impermanent" (*mi rtag pa la yod pa*).

"exists" proof brings in a much larger class than the "is" proof (sound *is* impermanent), in which only impermanent phenomena compose the similar class. Phenomena that "exist in the impermanent" include—in addition to impermanent phenomena—all phenomena that refer to categories that contain impermanent phenomena but are not themselves impermanent.

For example, "object of knowledge" is itself permanent, but as a category it contains some objects of knowledge that are permanent and others that are impermanent. Because impermanent phenomena can be known, "object of knowledge" is said to "exist in" the impermanent.

"Particularity of product" is another example. This also is itself permanent; but (unlike object of knowledge, which encompasses both permanent and impermanent phenomena) particularity of product encompasses only impermanent phenomena—products. Although particularity of product is permanent, whatever *is* a particularity of product is necessarily impermanent; thus, particularity of product is said to exist in the impermanent.[a]

To sum up, in the syllogism, "the subject, sound, *is* impermanent because of being a product," the similar class is "the impermanent." Because this is a copular proof, whatever *is* impermanent is a member of the similar class in that proof. A hypothetical syllogism phrased in the "exists" mode is: "The subject, sound, *exists* in the impermanent because of being a product." In this case, too, the similar class is "the impermanent"; but, because this is an ontological proof, whatever *exists* in impermanent (that is, in the category of the impermanent) is a member of the similar class in that proof.

ETYMOLOGICAL EXPLANATION OF SIMILAR CLASS

A sign that exists in accordance with the etymological explanation (*sgra bshad du yod pa*) of similar class (in the proof of sound as impermanent, for example) must be similar to the subject (sound) in that proof in *being* the similar class (that is, in being impermanent). To satisfy the

---

[a] This discussion of phenomena which, although themselves permanent, nevertheless "exist in the impermanent" depends on commentary by Ge-shay Lob-sang-gya-tso. He says, "Whatever exists in impermanent is not necessarily impermanent; for example, object of knowledge. It is also the case that whatever is not impermanent does not necessarily not exist in impermanent; for example, object of knowledge. Object of knowledge is not impermanent, but does exist in impermanent. This category also includes isolate of pot, isolate of pillar, and particularity of product; these are not impermanent, but exist in impermanent" (commentary on *Signs and Reasonings*, vol. 2, p. 15).

etymology of similar class, there must be a similarity between the subject and the sign; this is called a qualitative similarity (*chos mthun pa*),
because it is the quality of the predicate (in this case, impermanent)
that they have in common.

THE MEANING OF SIMILAR AND DISSIMILAR CLASS

To clarify the meaning of "similar class" and "dissimilar class," Pur-bu-
jok considers four questions:

(1) Does whatever *is* [a member of] the similar class in the proof of
    something necessarily *exist* in accordance with the etymological
    explanation of similar class in the proof of that?
(2) Can something *exist* in accordance with the etymological explana-
    tion of similar class in a given proof but not *be* the similar class in
    that proof?
(3) If something *is* the class in the expression "similar class in the proof
    of something" (*de sgrub kyi mthun phyogs*), is it necessarily the pre-
    dicate of the probandum in that proof? and
(4) If something *exists* in accordance with the etymological explanation
    of dissimilar class in a given proof, *is* it necessarily the dissimilar
    class in that proof?

The first two questions (which concern the etymological meaning of
"similar class"—*mthun phyogs*) and the third (which concerns the meaning of the term here translated as "class"—*pakṣa*) will be considered in
this section. The fourth (which concerns the etymology of "dissimilar
class"—*mi mthun phyogs*) will be considered in the section "etymological
explanation of dissimilar class," below.

Pur-bu-jok takes up these questions in turn: First, does whatever *is*
the similar class in the proof of something necessarily *exist* in accordance with the etymological explanation of similar class in the proof of
that? His answer is:

> No. There are three possibilities (*mu*) between being the similar
> class in the proof of something and existing in accordance with
> the etymological explanation of similar class in the proof of
> that.[95]

In this general statement, Pur-bu-jok does not specify the context within which these three possibilities are being considered. As will be explained below, it is only by ignoring the context that one can posit
three possibilities (between being a member of the similar class and

existing in accordance with the etymological explanation of similar class). As Ge-shay Ge-dün-lo-drö says,

> This [statement by Pur-bu-jok] is true only in general, if there is no reference to any one specific proof. When one does consider a specific proof, however, there are not three possibilities. For example, there are not three possibilities between being a member of the similar class and existing in accordance with the etymological explanation of similar class in the proof of sound as impermanent.
>
> There are three possibilities only from the point of view of considering two proofs: both the proof of sound as impermanent and the proof of sound as permanent.
>
> Thus, in the following enumeration [by Pur-bu-jok] of the three possibilities, the first applies to the proof of sound as permanent and the other two apply to the proof of sound as impermanent.[96]

According to Pur-bu-jok, the three possibilities that can be posited are:

> (1) The possibility of being [a member of] the similar class in the proof of something but not existing in accordance with the etymological explanation of similar class in that proof. [For example,] uncompounded space is the similar class in the proof of sound as permanent but does not exist in accordance with the etymological explanation of similar class in the proof of sound as permanent.
>
> The proof of this example is: the subject, uncompounded space, is the similar class in the proof of sound as permanent because it is permanent. It does not exist in accordance with the etymological explanation of similar class in that proof because uncompounded space and sound are not qualitatively similar (*chos mi mthun pa*) in being permanent. [Uncompounded space is permanent, and sound is impermanent.][97]

In the proof of sound as permanent, the similar class is "the permanent." Using Pur-bu-jok's definition of similar class in the proof of sound as impermanent as a model, the definition of similar class in the proof of sound as permanent would be: that which is not empty of permanence (or the permanent, *rtag pa*) in accordance with the mode of proof in the proof of sound as permanent. The similar class in that proof thus includes whatever *is* permanent. Uncompounded space is permanent and therefore is the similar class in that proof.

Then, whatever exists in accordance with the etymological explanation of similar class in the proof of sound as permanent has to be qualitatively similar with the subject (sound) in being permanent. If this were true of uncompounded space, it and sound would both *be* permanent. This is not the case, because although uncompounded space is permanent, sound is impermanent.

Pur-bu-jok continues his enumeration of the three possibilities:

(2) The possibility of both being the similar class in the proof of something and existing in accordance with the etymological explanation of similar class in that proof. [For example,] pot both is the similar class in the proof of sound as impermanent and exists in accordance with the etymological explanation of similar class in the proof of sound as impermanent.

The proof of this example is: the subject, pot, is the similar class in the proof of sound as impermanent because it is impermanent. The subject, pot, exists in accordance with the etymological explanation of similar class in that proof because the two, pot and sound, are qualitatively similar in that both are impermanent.

(3) The possibility of neither being the similar class in the proof of something nor existing in accordance with the etymological explanation of similar class in that proof. [For example,] uncompounded space neither is the similar class in the proof of sound as impermanent nor exists in accordance with the etymological explanation of similar class in that proof.

The proof of this example is: the subject, uncompounded space, is not the similar class in the proof of sound as impermanent because it is not impermanent. The subject, uncompounded space, does not exist in accordance with the etymological explanation of similar class in the proof of sound as impermanent because it and sound are not qualitatively similar; [uncompounded space] is permanent and sound is impermanent.[98]

The reasoning used by Pur-bu-jok here in (2) and (3) is identical to that used above in (1). In the proof of sound as impermanent, the similar class is "the impermanent." Pur-bu-jok specifies that "similar class in the proof of sound as impermanent" and "the impermanent" are mutually inclusive.⁹⁹ Therefore, whatever is the similar class in that proof is necessarily impermanent and whatever is impermanent is necessarily the similar class. Thus, pot, being impermanent, must be the similar class in the proof of sound as impermanent. Uncompounded space, being permanent, is not the similar class.

Then, whatever exists in accordance with the etymological explanation of the similar class in the proof of sound as impermanent must be qualitatively similar with the subject (sound) in being impermanent. That is the case with pot, but not with uncompounded space.

In summary, in order for something (x) to be [a member of] the similar class in the proof of sound as impermanent, x must itself be impermanent. As Lati Rin-po-che says,

> If something is the similar class in the proof of sound as impermanent, it must have the quality that is the predicate of the probandum in the proof of sound as impermanent; that is, it must *be* impermanent.¹⁰⁰

In order for x to exist in accordance with the etymological explanation of similar class in the proof of sound as impermanent, it must not only be impermanent but also share that quality with the subject in that proof.

It is therefore clear that if only one proof—of sound as impermanent—is considered, we do not have Pur-bu-jok's three possibilities. According to Ge-shay Ge-dün-lo-drö,

> If two proofs are not considered, there are not three possibilities. There are not three possibilities between [being the] similar class and existing in accordance with the etymological explanation of similar class, because (1) whatever is the similar class in the proof of sound as impermanent necessarily exists in accordance with the etymological explanation of similar class in that proof; and (2) whatever exists in accordance with the etymological explanation of similar class in the proof of sound as impermanent necessarily is the similar class in that proof.¹⁰¹

Ge-shay Ge-dün-lo-drö is indicating that the two categories—(1) whatever is the similar class in the proof of sound as impermanent and (2) whatever exists in accordance with the etymological explanation of similar class in that proof—are equivalent. Whatever is one is necessarily the other. Whatever is the similar class in the proof of sound as impermanent must necessarily be impermanent. Furthermore, whatever exists in accordance with the etymological explanation of similar class in the proof of sound as impermanent must be qualitatively similar with sound in being impermanent. This means it must share with sound the quality of impermanence; thus it is clear that it also must *be* impermanent.

Nevertheless, it is not considered a fault to posit three possibilities, as Pur-bu-jok does. This serves a pedagogical purpose by giving rise to debate, as Ge-shay Ge-dün-lo-drö explains:

> There is no fault here in [Pur-bu-jok's] text; it is stated this way for the sake of debate. One can say that there are three possibilities only on the strength of using two separate reasonings, the proof of sound as impermanent and the proof of sound as permanent.[102]

Pur-bu-jok then considers the second question: Can something *exist* in accordance with the etymological explanation of similar class in a given proof, but not *be* [a member of] the similar class in that proof? He explains that it cannot:

> A possibility of existing in accordance with the etymological explanation of similar class in the proof of something, but not being the similar class in that proof does not exist. This is because whatever exists in accordance with the etymological explanation of similar class in the proof of something must be the similar class in the proof of that.[103]

Whatever "exists in accordance with the etymological explanation of the similar class" in the proof of sound as impermanent must be qualitatively similar to sound in being impermanent. The similar class in that proof is the impermanent. Whatever is qualitatively similar to sound in being impermanent must be a member of the similar class in that proof; if one looks for something that is similar to sound in being impermanent, but is not impermanent, one will not find anything.

Thus, the etymological explanation of similar class itself precludes the possibility of there being anything that exists in accordance with that explanation but is not the similar class. If the etymological explanation of similar class is satisfied in relation to a given proof, the sign and the subject in that proof must be similar in being members of the similar class; how could the sign then not be a member of the similar class? It is not possible.

Lati Rin-po-che comments that all impermanent phenomena—all things (*dngos po*)—are necessarily [members of] the similar class in the proof of sound as impermanent because they necessarily exist in accordance with the etymological explanation of similar class. He says,

> With regard to whatever is a thing, there is necessarily a simi-
> larity between its impermanence and sound's impermanence.[a]
> Therefore, whatever is a thing is necessarily the similar class in
> the proof of sound as impermanent.[104]

In summary, if something (x) *exists* in accordance with the etymological explanation of similar class in a particular proof, then x must be
similar with the subject in *being* the similar class in that proof. However, the fact that the subject in a proof has a qualitative similarity to x is
not enough to make x a correct sign in that proof. If this were enough,
then "teapot" would be a correct sign in the proof of sound as impermanent. The subject *sound* and the sign *teapot* are similar in their impermanence, but teapot is clearly not a correct sign in this instance.

On the other hand, it is interesting to note that in the Ge-luk-pa
school a sign may be a correct sign in a given proof and yet not necessarily exist in accordance with the etymological explanation of similar
class in that proof. For example, "particularity of product" (*byas pa'i bye
brag*) is considered to be a correct sign in the proof of sound as impermanent, but it is *not* qualitatively similar to sound in being the similar
class—impermanent. This is because particularity of product is permanent. Lati Rin-po-che points out,

> Particularity of product is a permanent phenomenon; this is
> because it only appears to the mind by way of the appearance
> of the generality, product. Particularity of product is not a phe-
> nomenon that can appear to the mind directly.[105]

Being permanent, particularity of product is a member not of the similar class (the impermanent) but of the dissimilar class (the nonimpermanent). However, even though it *is* a member of the dissimilar class, it
does not *exist* in the dissimilar class, because no instance of particularity of product is permanent. As specified in the definition of forward
pervasion, a correct sign must be existent in only the similar class.
What is existent in *only* the similar class cannot exist at all in the dissimilar class. Although particularity of product is itself permanent, it
does not exist in the dissimilar class (the permanent) because no instance of particularity of product is permanent.

---

[a] Because this qualitative similarity is the requirement of existing in accordance with
the etymological explanation of similar class, one may conclude that all *things* necessarily exist in accordance with the etymological explanation of similar class in the proof of
sound as impermanent.

Pur-bu-jok next considers the third question: If something *is* [a member of] the class in the expression "similar class in the proof of something," is it necessarily the predicate of the probandum in that proof? He comments:

> Whatever is the class in the expression "similar class in the proof of something" is *not* necessarily the predicate of the pro-bandum in the proof of that. This is because the two,
>
> (a) class (*phyogs*) in "is the similar class (*mthun phyogs*) in the proof of sound as impermanent" (*sgra mi rtag par sgrub kyi mthun phyogs*) and
> (b) class (*phyogs*) in "exists in the similar class (*mthun phyogs la yod pa*) in the proof of sound as impermanent" (*sgra mi rtag par sgrub kyi mthun phyogs la yod pa*)
>
> must be posited as dissimilar.[a]

The term "class" (*phyogs*) has a different referent in Pur-bu-jok's phrases (a) and (b). In phrase a ("is the similar class"), anything that is impermanent *is* the similar class in the proof of sound as impermanent, and this includes not only *the impermanent* itself but also any instance of impermanence—tree, pot, etc. However, the phrase b ("exists in the similar class") means specifically "exists in *the impermanent*"—not "exists in pot, tree, etc." In this second context, "class" refers only to the generality of that which is being held as the predicate of the proban-dum—impermanent. Lati Rin-po-che clarifies this point:

> In the phrase "similar class in the proof of sound as imperma-nent," the word "class" can refer to (1) the self-isolate of im-permanent, (2) the general-isolate of impermanent, and (3) any of the instances of impermanence. However, in the phrase "ex-ists in the similar class," "class" refers only to the generality of impermanence.[b]

Pur-bu-jok continues,

> The two, (a) class in "similar class in the proof of sound as im-permanent" and (b) class in "exists in the similar class in the

---

[a]   *Signs and Reasonings*, p. 4a.6-7. The Sanskrit *pakṣa* (Tibetan *phyogs*) can be translated, according to context, by the English words "class," "position," or "subject" (see discussion below).

[b]   Commentary on *Signs and Reasonings*, vol. 2, Feb. 2, 1977, p. 7. Note that "self-isolate" and "general-isolate" are said to be equivalent (*don gcig*) in meaning.

proof of sound as impermanent" must be posited as dissimilar because there are three usages of, or objects to be inferred by, the term *pakṣa* in the proof of sound as impermanent.[a]

In order for the forward pervasion to be established in the proof of sound as impermanent, the sign must be ascertained as "existing in only the similar class" in that proof; in order for the counterpervasion to be established, the sign must be ascertained as "just nonexistent in the dissimilar class." To understand the distinction between these two phrases, we must understand the precise meaning of "class."

THE MEANING OF "CLASS"

The English word "class" translates *phyogs*, a Tibetan translation of the Sanskrit term *pakṣa*. In *pakṣadharma*, translated as "property of the subject," *pakṣa* is translated not as "class" but as "subject." *Pakṣa* is put into English differently to convey its different uses.

1. *Pakṣa* (*phyogs*) *in its broadest meaning.* This refers to the "position" (also called the "actual position") in a proof—that which is being proved. In this sense, *pakṣa* refers to the subject and the predicate together. The "position" in the proof of sound as impermanent is that sound is impermanent (this is what is to be proved, the probandum). The whole probandum—called the "actual position" (*dngos phyogs*)—is made up of two components: the subject, sound, and the predicate of the probandum, impermanent. Each of these components, alone, is called an "imputed or designated position" (*btags phyogs*), but the "actual position" in that proof is the two together. As Lati Rin-po-che says,

    > The actual position and the probandum in the proof of sound as impermanent are the same: that sound is impermanent. Each of [its components] individually is an imputed position, not the actual position, whereas the composite of the two is the actual position in the proof of sound as impermanent.[106]

---

[a] *Signs and Reasonings*, p. 4a.7. Pur-bu-jok presents three uses of the term *pakṣa*; there is a fourth, not included by Pur-bu-jok, which Dharmakīrti identifies in the *Pramāṇa-vārttika* as the primary use of *pakṣa*. This is presented first in the section below on the meaning of "class"; Pur-bu-jok's three uses are numbered 2, 3, and 4. For a discussion of the primary use of *pakṣa*, see Mookerjee and Nagasaki's *The Pramāṇavārttikam of Dharmakīrti* (Nalanda, Patna: Nālandā Mahāvihāra, 1964), pp. 6-8.

2. *Pakṣa* as it is used in *pakṣadharma*, "property of the subject." In this
    case, *dharma* is translated "property," and *pakṣa* refers not to the
    whole actual position (probandum), but to its component, the sub-
    ject. The sign, product, is a property or quality of the imputed posi-
    tion—the subject, sound. *Pakṣa*, which standing alone is the name of
    the whole actual position, is in the compound *pakṣadharma* applied
    to only one of its imputed positions (the subject). Pur-bu-jok writes,

    > In "property of the subject (*pakṣadharma*) in the proof
    > of sound as impermanent," subject (*pakṣa*) refers to the
    > subject sought to be known in the proof of sound as
    > impermanent.[a]

3. *Pakṣa* (*phyogs*) in the expression *mthun phyogs la yod pa* ("exists in
    the similar class"). Here, *pakṣa* ("class") refers to the other imputed
    position, the predicate of the probandum (impermanent itself).
    That is, it refers to impermanent's self-isolate (*rang ldog*)—the op-
    posite of not being impermanent (*mi rtag pa ma yin pa les log pa*)—
    but not to other phenomena that are impermanent. To say that
    something exists in the similar class means that it exists in the im-
    permanent itself, not that it exists in the various instances of im-
    permanent—pot, tree, etc. Of this meaning of *pakṣa*, Pur-bu-jok
    notes,

    > The two—(a) *pakṣa* (*class*) in "exists or does not exist in
    > the similar class in the proof of sound as impermanent"
    > and (b) *pakṣa* (*position*) [or predicate], which is the ob-
    > ject of relation of the pervasion in the proof of that—
    > both refer to the general-isolate (*spyi ldog*) [or self-
    > isolate (*rang ldog*)] of the impermanent [that is to say,
    > *impermanence* itself], the predicate of the probandum in
    > the proof of sound as impermanent.[107]

The Tibetan *mthun phyogs la yod pa* means "exists in the similar class."
That which *exists* in the similar class intersects the similar class in various ways without necessarily being found only in the similar class. In
other words, that which *exists* in the similar class may not necessarily
be the similar class.

According to Lati Rin-po-che, there are three ways in which a phenomenon can exist in the similar class:

---

[a] *Signs and Reasonings*, p. 4a.7-4b.1. Because *pakṣa* in *pakṣadharma* refers to the subject
sought to be known, *pakṣadharma* is translated as property of the subject.

  a. "Pot" exists in the similar class in the proof of sound as impermanent because a pot is impermanent.
  b. "Object of knowledge" exists in the similar class in the proof of sound as impermanent because the impermanent (or impermanence) is itself an object of knowledge. However, object of knowledge cannot *be* a member of the similar class; it is a member of the dissimilar class because of being permanent.
  c. "Particularity of product," even though it itself is permanent, exists in the similar class in the proof of sound as impermanent because whatever is a particularity of product is necessarily impermanent. However, particularity of product is a member of the dissimilar class in that proof because of being permanent.[108]

4. *Pakṣa* in *mthun phyogs* (*sapakṣa*), "similar class." The term "class" in "similar class" in the proof of sound as impermanent refers not only to the self-isolate of impermanence but also to instances of the impermanent; it thus refers to members of the similar class, phenomena that are impermanent. Pur-bu-jok's statement is,

> Class (*pakṣa*) in "similar class in the proof of sound as impermanent" must be posited as the general-isolate (*spyi ldog*) of impermanent and as all basis-isolates (*gzhi ldog*) of impermanent [that is to say, all phenomena that are impermanent].[109]

Pur-bu-jok defined "similar class in the proof of sound as impermanent" as "that which is not empty of impermanence in that proof." Whatever is not empty of impermanence is therefore the similar class in that proof; this includes not only "impermanent" itself but also instances of it. Any phenomenon that is impermanent is a member of the similar class "impermanent."

THE DISSIMILAR CLASS

Pur-bu-jok's definition of dissimilar class in the proof of sound as impermanent is:

> That which is empty of impermanence in accordance with the mode of proof in the proof of sound as impermanent.[110]

That which is empty of impermanence (*mi rtag pas stong pa*) is the non-impermanent (*mi rtag pa ma yin pa*). As Ge-shay Lob-sang-gya-tso says,

> Whatever is not impermanent (or nonimpermanent) is neces-
> sarily empty of impermanence in accordance with the mode of
> proof in the proof of sound as impermanent.[111]

Furthermore, according to Pur-bu-jok, "nonimpermanent" and "dissimilar class"—in the proof of sound as impermanent—are mutually inclusive.[112] Thus, whatever is nonimpermanent is necessarily the dissimilar class in that proof, and whatever is the dissimilar class in that proof
is necessarily nonimpermanent.

In order for the counterpervasion to be established, the sign must
be "just *nonexistent*" in the dissimilar class; this means it cannot *exist* in
the dissimilar class. And, furthermore, the sign cannot *exist in the dissimilar class in accordance with the mode of statement*. Therefore, in the
proof of sound as impermanent, no instance of the sign can *be* a member of the dissimilar class; that is, no instance of the sign can *be* nonimpermanent.[a]

The dissimilar class in the proof of sound as impermanent is the
nonimpermanent. The nonimpermanent includes both nonexistents
and permanent phenomena; thus the dissimilar class in the proof of
sound as impermanent includes both nonexistents and permanent
phenomena. Furthermore, members of the dissimilar class that are
permanent fall into two categories: those that are "other than impermanent" (*mi rtag pa las gzhan pa*) and those that are "contradictory with
impermanent" (*mi rtag pa dang 'gal ba*). Pur-bu-jok tells us,

> There are three types of dissimilar class:
>
> 1) [A member of] the dissimilar class that is a nonexistent in
>   the proof of sound as impermanent: [for instance,] horn of
>   a rabbit.
> 2) The dissimilar class that is other [than impermanent] in the
>   proof of sound as impermanent: object of knowledge.
> 3) The dissimilar class that is contradictory [with the imper-
>   manent] in the proof of sound as impermanent: the perma-
>   nent.[113]

---

[a] This is a general rule, but there are exceptions. "Particularity of product" is in fact
nonimpermanent and yet is a correct sign in the proof of sound as impermanent. It
should be noted that the qualification "in accordance with the mode of statement" is
included in Pur-bu-jok's brief definition of counterpervasion (chapter three) but omitted from his longer definition (page 2 of this chapter).

DISSIMILAR CLASS THAT IS A NONEXISTENT

A nonexistent, like "horn of a rabbit," is the dissimilar class in the proof of sound as impermanent because it is empty of impermanence in accordance with the mode of proof (copular) in that proof. This is because horn of a rabbit, being nonexistent, is not impermanent. All other nonexistents are similarly considered to be members of the dissimilar class in the proof of sound as impermanent. Ge-shay Lob-sang-gya-tso explains,

> Anything that is not observed by valid cognition is [a member of] the dissimilar class that is nonexistent in the proof of sound as impermanent.[a]

DISSIMILAR CLASS THAT IS OTHER

The second type—the dissimilar class that is other [than impermanent]—is made up of permanent phenomena that are noncontradictory (mi 'gal pa) with impermanent. If something is a member of "the dissimilar class that is other" in the proof of sound as impermanent, it must meet these two criteria; Ge-shay Lob-sang-gya-tso continues,

> Something is the dissimilar class that is other [than impermanent] because (1) it is permanent and (2) there exists a common locus of it and the impermanent.[114]

There are many permanent phenomena that share a common locus with the impermanent, for example:

- "Definition" itself is considered to be a permanent phenomenon; but there exists a common locus of definition and the impermanent: "that which is able to perform a function" is both a definition (the definition of "thing") and impermanent.
- "Object of knowledge" is itself permanent, but there exists a common locus of object of knowledge and impermanent—"pot" is both an object of knowledge and impermanent.
- "Particularity of product" is itself permanent, but there exists a common locus of particularity of product and the impermanent— "pot" is both a particularity of product and impermanent.

These illustrate the dissimilar class that is other [than impermanent] in

---

[a] Commentary on Signs and Reasonings, vol. 1, p. 12. The definition of existent is: that which is observed by valid cognition (tshad mas dmigs pa), the definition of nonexistent is: that which is not observed by valid cognition (tshad mas ma dmigs pa).

the proof of sound as impermanent because of being noncontradictory with the impermanent.[a]

DISSIMILAR CLASS THAT IS CONTRADICTORY

If something (x) is a member of the dissimilar class that is "contradictory with impermanent" in the proof of sound as impermanent, it must meet two criteria. Ge-shay Lob-sang-gya-tso comments,

> Something is the dissimilar class that is contradictory [with impermanent] in the proof of sound as impermanent because (1) it is permanent and (2) there is no common locus of it and impermanent.[115]

This third category contains, for example, "permanent" and "uncompounded space." In fact, the ge-shay adds, any phenomenon that is explicitly contradictory (*dngos 'gal*) with the impermanent (that is, with impermanence) is this dissimilar class.[116]

Two phenomena are said to be explicitly contradictory if the ascertainment of one necessitates the elimination of the other. Ge-shay Lob-sang-gya-tso continues,

> The impermanent and the permanent are explicit contradictories; if impermanent is established as existing in relation to a phenomenon, then permanent is necessarily eliminated in relation to that phenomenon. Thus, permanent is the dissimilar class that is contradictory in the proof of sound as impermanent because of being a phenomenon that is explicitly contradictory with impermanent.[117]

---

[a]   It should be noted that not everything that is "other than impermanent" (*mi rtag pa las gzhan pa*) is necessarily the dissimilar class which is *other than impermanent* in the proof of sound as impermanent. The dissimilar class which is other than impermanent is made up only of permanent phenomena that are noncontradictory with impermanent. They are noncontradictory with impermanent because, although permanent themselves, they have a common locus with impermanent. "Uncompounded space," being contradictory with impermanent, is the dissimilar class which is contradictory and not the dissimilar class which is other.

Ge-shay Pel-den-drak-pa points out that if someone says horn of a rabbit is the dissimilar class which is other because it is other than impermanent, there is no pervasion. (That is, whatever is other than impermanent is not necessarily the dissimilar class which is other.) If horn of a rabbit were *noncontradictory* with impermanent, there would have to be a common locus of horn of a rabbit and impermanent. But such does not exist. (Commentary on *Signs and Reasonings*, vol. 1, p 11.)

In order for the sign, product, to be established as the counterpervasion in the proof of sound as impermanent, it must be ascertained as just nonexistent in the dissimilar class; product cannot *exist* in that class. No instance of product can exist in the nonimpermanent in accordance with the mode of proof—which means that no instance of product can *be* nonimpermanent (none can *be* permanent or nonexistent).

This type of dissimilar class (that which is contradictory) serves an important purpose: it shows the Ge-luk-pa students that in relation to a given proof, they must very precisely define the negandum—that which is being eliminated (*dgag bya*) by the reasoning. In establishing the pervasion in any proof it is essential to identify the object of negation correctly.

For example, in the syllogism, "The subject, sound, is impermanent because of being a product," the probandum (that which is to be proved) is *sound is impermanent* (*sgra mi rtag pa yin pa*). And one might think that the negandum (that which is being eliminated) is *sound is not impermanent* (*sgra mi rtag pa ma yin pa*)—in which case "not impermanent" (or nonimpermanent, *mi rtag pa ma yin pa*) would be the object negated. However, "not impermanent" is *not* the object negated in this reasoning. Only the nonimpermanent that are explicitly contradictory with impermanent are negated in this reasoning. Only phenomena that are *explicitly* contradictory with impermanent (and thus are members of the dissimilar class that is contradictory) are explicitly and irrefutably eliminated by the sign, product. In other words, the sign, product, eliminates all possibility of sound's being permanent, but it does not eliminate sound's being an object of knowledge; and object of knowledge, as we have seen, is a member of the dissimilar class that is other. Thus, the object of negation (the negandum or, more precisely, the predicate of the negandum) is not exactly the same as the dissimilar class. The negandum must be explicitly contradictory with the sign.

ETYMOLOGICAL EXPLANATION OF DISSIMILAR CLASS

Something that *exists* in accordance with the etymological explanation of dissimilar class (in the proof of sound as impermanent, for example) must be dissimilar to the subject (sound) in relation to the quality of impermanence. To satisfy the etymology of dissimilar class, there must be a dissimilarity between the subject and the sign; this is called a qualitative dissimilarity (*chos mi mthun pa*) because it is in relation to the quality of the predicate (in this case, impermanent) that they are dissimilar.

After describing the divisions of dissimilar class, Pur-bu-jok writes,

Question: Whatever exists in accordance with the etymological explanation of dissimilar class in the proof of something—must it necessarily *be* the dissimilar class in the proof of that?

Answer: No, there are three possibilities:

(1) "Uncompounded space" exists in accordance with the etymological explanation of dissimilar class in the proof of sound as permanent without being the dissimilar class in the proof of sound as permanent.[118]

Uncompounded space exists in accordance with the etymological explanation of dissimilar class in the proof of sound as *permanent*, because uncompounded space and sound are dissimilar in relation to permanence. Furthermore, uncompounded space is *not* the dissimilar class in the proof of sound as permanent. Lati Rin-po-che explains,

Uncompounded space exists in accordance with the etymological explanation of dissimilar class in the proof of sound as permanent. This is because uncompounded space and sound are not qualitatively similar in being permanent (*rtag pa yin par chos mthun gyi ma red*); the one is permanent, the other is impermanent.

But uncompounded space is not the dissimilar class in the proof of sound as permanent. This is because it is the *similar* class in the proof of sound as permanent. This, in turn, is because uncompounded space is permanent.[119]

Pur-bu-jok goes on,

(2) "Pot" neither [exists in accordance with the etymological explanation of dissimilar class nor is a member of the dissimilar class] in the proof of sound as impermanent.[120]

Lati Rin-po-che amplifies this, saying:

Pot does not exist in accordance with the etymological explanation of dissimilar class in the proof of sound as impermanent, because it exists in accordance with the etymological explanation of the *similar* class in the proof of sound as impermanent.

Pot is not the dissimilar class in the proof of sound as impermanent because of being the similar class in the proof of sound as impermanent.[121]

Pot exists in accordance with the etymological explanation of similar class in the proof of sound as impermanent because of sharing with sound the quality of impermanence. Pot is the similar class in that proof because of being impermanent.

Pur-bu-jok then gives the third possibility:

> (3) "Uncompounded space" exists in accordance with the etymological explanation of dissimilar class in the proof of sound as impermanent and also is the dissimilar class in the proof of sound as impermanent.[122]

Uncompounded space exists in accordance with the etymological explanation of dissimilar class in the proof of sound as impermanent because, as Lati Rin-po-che notes, "uncompounded space is qualitatively dissimilar with sound in regard to impermanence (*mi rtag pa yin par chos mi mthun*)."[123] Uncompounded space is permanent, while sound is impermanent. Furthermore, uncompounded space is the dissimilar class in the proof of sound as impermanent, because of being permanent.

Pur-bu-jok concludes this section:

> There is no [fourth] possibility of being the dissimilar class in the proof of something but not existing in accordance with the etymological explanation of dissimilar class in that proof. This is because whatever is the dissimilar class in the proof of something necessarily exists in accordance with the etymological explanation of dissimilar class in that proof.[124]

Whatever is the dissimilar class in the proof of sound as impermanent, for example, must necessarily *be* permanent. And whatever is permanent necessarily exists in accordance with the etymological explanation of dissimilar class in the proof of sound as impermanent, because whatever is permanent is qualitatively dissimilar with sound in relation to the quality of impermanence.

As Ge-shay Ge-dün-lo-drö points out, one can posit three possibilities between being the dissimilar class and existing in accordance with the etymological explanation of dissimilar class—but only if one is considering two proofs: of sound as impermanent and of sound as permanent, for example. In relation to one specific proof, there cannot be three possibilities.[a] In his words,

> There are not three possibilities between being [a member of]

---

the dissimilar class and existing in accordance with the etymological explanation of the dissimilar class in the proof of sound
as impermanent because (1) whatever is the dissimilar class in
the proof of sound as impermanent necessarily exists in accordance with the etymological explanation of dissimilar class in
that proof; and (2) whatever exists in accordance with the etymological explanation of dissimilar class is necessarily the dissimilar class in that proof.[125]

Whatever is [a member of] the dissimilar class in the proof of sound as
impermanent necessarily exists in accordance with the etymological
explanation of dissimilar class in that proof. Whatever is the dissimilar
class in the proof of sound as impermanent is necessarily nonimpermanent: if something (x) is nonimpermanent, x necessarily exists in
accordance with the etymological explanation of dissimilar class in the
proof of sound as impermanent, because x is necessarily dissimilar to
the subject, sound, in relation to the quality of impermanence (sound is
impermanent and x is permanent).

Conversely, whatever exists in accordance with the etymological
explanation of dissimilar class in the proof of sound as impermanent is
necessarily [a member of] the dissimilar class in that proof. This is because if something (x) satisfies the requirements of the etymological
explanation of dissimilar class, x must be dissimilar to the subject,
sound, in relation to the quality of impermanence. Since sound is impermanent, x must be nonimpermanent, and therefore a member of
the dissimilar class.

CONCLUDING TOPICS

Pur-bu-jok ends his discussion of the bases of relation of the pervasions
with a comment on two topics: (1) "whether or not similar and dissimilar classes are explicitly contradictory," and (2) "explanation of similar
and dissimilar examples."

WHETHER SIMILAR AND DISSIMILAR CLASSES ARE EXPLICITLY CONTRADICTORY

On this question, Pur-bu-jok writes,

Although similar class is explicitly contradictory with dissimilar class, dissimilar class is not explicitly contradictory with
similar class—because dissimilar class does not exist. This is because whatever is an established base is necessarily [a member

of] the similar class because whatever is an established base is necessarily [a member of] the similar class of a correct sign. This is because whatever is an established base is necessarily [a member of] the similar class of a correct sign in the proof of sound as an object of knowledge. [This in turn is true because whatever is an established base is an object of knowledge.][126]

In the proof of sound as an object of knowledge, the similar class is "object of knowledge"; whatever is an object of knowledge is thus a member of the similar class in that proof. Since all established bases are objects of knowledge, they are all members of the similar class.

Some Ge-luk-pa scholars go further, saying that whatever is selfless (*bdag med*) is necessarily a similar class, thus including both established bases and nonestablished bases. According to Ge-shay Ge-dün-lo-drö,

> There is [*in general*] no dissimilar class because whatever is selfless is a similar class; this is true because whatever is empty [of inherent existence] can be proved.[127]

Consider, for example, this proof: "The subject, the 'I,' is empty of inherent existence because of being a dependent-arising." Here the similar class (the empty of inherent existence) includes everything that is selfless, and thus includes both established bases and nonestablished bases, both existents and nonexistents.

This is the reasoning behind the statement that, in general, dissimilar class does not exist. It explains Pur-bu-jok's statement, quoted above, that dissimilar class is not explicitly contradictory with similar class, although similar class *is* explicitly contradictory with dissimilar class. A nonexistent cannot be contradictory with anything; whatever is contradictory is necessarily a phenomenon.[a]

Pur-bu-jok continues,

> *Objection:* It follows that dissimilar class does exist, because a dissimilar class in the proof of sound as impermanent exists, and because a correct proof statement using a qualitative dissimilarity [between the subject and an example] also exists.

---

[a] Pur-bu-jok's definition of contradictories is: "those observed as a common locus of (1) their being different (*tha dad*) and (2) something which is them both does not occur (*khyod yin pa mi srid pa*)." This definition is from his "Middling Path of Reasoning," in *Collected Topics*, p. 5a.4. As to the first part of this definition, whatever is different is necessarily a phenomenon—the definition of "different" is "phenomena which are separate (*so so ba'i chos*)." The second part of the definition specifies that there does not occur any phenomenon which is both.

Answer to the objection: [Although the reason is true,] it does not entail [that dissimilar class exists].[128]

By saying, "it does not entail that..." (or "there is no pervasion," *ma khyab*), one is implicitly accepting that the reason is true. Here Pur-bu-jok acknowledges that in relation to a *particular* proof (such as the proof of sound as impermanent) there can exist (1) a dissimilar class and (2) a correct statement of proof using an example that has qualitative dissimilarity (that is, a dissimilar example). In his opinion, however, the reason does not entail that dissimilar class exists *in general.*

This opinion stirs the Ge-luk-pa students to lively debate, centering on the question of whether it is reasonable to say that dissimilar class does not exist—and even on whether it is reasonable to say that a nonexistent does not exist. After all, there is widespread agreement that many nonexistents do exist; for example, the nonexistence of a pot on a bare table is said to exist, because that particular nonexistence can be ascertained by valid cognition. Similarly, the nonexistence of an inherently existent self is said to exist because it too is ascertainable by valid cognition.

There is similar opportunity for discussion in Pur-bu-jok's acknowledgement that a dissimilar example exists in relation to the proof of sound as impermanent. There are two types of proof statements, (1) those using a qualitative similarity between the subject and the example and (2) those using a qualitative dissimilarity between the subject and the example.

An example of the first type is: "Whatever is a product is necessarily impermanent, as is the case with pot; sound also is a product." Pot is a similar example in this proof statement because it is similar to the subject in possessing the two qualities represented by the predicate and the sign; it is impermanent and it is a product.

An example of the second type of proof statement is: "Whatever is permanent is necessarily not a product, as is the case with uncompounded space; sound, however, is a product." Uncompounded space is a dissimilar example because it is dissimilar to the subject; the subject has the two qualities (impermanent and product) referred to by the predicate and the sign, but the example does not.

Qualitative similarity and dissimilarity here refer specifically to similarity or dissimilarity between the subject of the syllogism and the example given in the proof statement. As Lati Rin-po-che says,

Qualitative similarity or dissimilarity applies to the basis of debate [the subject]; the question is whether something is qualitatively similar or dissimilar to the basis of debate. In the proof statement under consideration, pot is the similar example: pot, because it is a product, is impermanent; in just that way, sound, because it is a product, is impermanent. Both production [the sign] and impermanence [the predicate] are qualities (*khyad chos*) of a pot [the similar example], and both production and impermanence are qualities of sound [the basis of debate].

Thus, the qualitative similarity (*chos mthun pa*) here is the similarity of pot and sound in that each possesses both the predicate of the probandum and the sign. On the other hand, uncompounded space does not possess either; thus qualitative dissimilarity (*chos mi mthun pa*) is a dissimilarity [of the example] to the basis of debate [in regard to possessing the predicate and the sign].[a]

A proof statement, with its example, is an aid in understanding these two complementary pervasions: the pervasion of the sign by the predicate and the pervasion of the opposite of the predicate by the opposite of the sign. Pot is commonly referred to as the similar example and uncompounded space as the dissimilar example. "Dissimilar example," however, is subject to the same caveat as "dissimilar class." It is said to be nonexistent—in general—even though a particular dissimilar example exists in a particular proof statement.

EXPLANATION OF SIMILAR AND DISSIMILAR EXAMPLES

Similar Example

Pur-bu-jok goes on to define "similar example," "similar example in the proof of sound as impermanent," and "similar example in the proof of sound as impermanent by the sign, product." These definitions indicate primarily that anything whatsoever may be posited as a similar example in a given proof, regardless of validity. According to Pur-bu-jok,

The definition of a similar example is:

that [which is] held as a similar example. [Whatever

---

[a] Commentary on *Signs and Reasonings*, vol. 2, Feb. 4, 1977, pp. 4-5. Lati Rin-po-che goes on (p. 6) to explain that qualitative similarity or dissimilarity may be expressed through the use of either a proof statement (discussed here) or a syllogism. An example of a syllogism expressing a qualitative similarity is: "The subject, sound, is impermanent because of being a product, as is the case with pot."

someone posits as a similar example—whether right or wrong—is a similar example.]

Whatever is selfless is necessarily a similar example because whatever is an established base is necessarily a similar example and also whatever is not an established base is necessarily a similar example.[129]

Some Ge-luk-pa scholars question the usefulness of this very general comment on examples that provides no practical application. Ge-shay Pel-den-drak-pa comments,

If whatever is selfless is necessarily held as a similar example, it must be held as such by someone; by whom is it held? Must each and every existent and nonexistent be held as a similar example by someone?

There are many instances of the selfless that are not held as similar examples. If whatever is an established base is necessarily a correct similar example, then it follows that all phenomena without exception (*chos thams cad gcig ma lhag*) are correct similar examples; but whose similar examples could they be? Someone would have to realize all without exception (*gcig kyang ma lus*).[a]

Pur-bu-jok goes on,

[It follows that whatever is an established base is necessarily a similar example because] pot is a similar example and all [other established bases] are the same.

It follows that whatever is not an established base is necessarily a similar example because horn of a rabbit is a similar example and all [other nonestablished bases] are the same.

It follows that the subject, horn of a rabbit, is a similar example because of being held as a similar example in the proof of sound as impermanent. This is because there can exist a syllogism, "The subject, sound, is impermanent because of being a product, as is the case with it [horn of a rabbit]," and there can

---

[a] Commentary on *Signs and Reasonings*, vol. 2, p. 1. It should be noted that Pur-bu-jok does not specify that whatever is an established base is necessarily a *correct* similar example. "All phenomena" is itself considered to be an existent, so there would have to be someone holding it as a similar example. It is ascertained by valid cognition—but only by the valid cognition of a Buddha (a Buddha has no need for an example). Since only a Buddha can grasp it, "all phenomena" cannot actually be held as a similar example by an ordinary being.

also exist a proof statement, "Whatever is a product is necessarily impermanent, as is the case with it [horn of a rabbit]."[130]

In commentary on this passage, Lati Rin-po-che makes a clear distinction between "similar example" and "*correct* similar example":

Whatever is selfless is necessarily a similar example. If one
states, "The subject, sound, is impermanent because of being a
product, as is the case with the horn of a rabbit," horn of a rabbit is held as a similar example—it is not a correct similar example, but it is indeed held as a similar example. It *is* necessarily a similar example, but it is not a *correct* similar example. A
correct similar example must have the characteristics of a correct similar example.[a]

Pur-bu-jok concludes his explanation of similar examples,

The definition of a similar example in the proof of sound as impermanent is:

> that [which is] held as a similar example in the proof of
> sound as impermanent.

Whatever is selfless is necessarily a similar example in the
proof of sound as impermanent. Extend the reasoning [in the
same way as above, adding "in the proof of sound as impermanent": "Whatever is selfless is necessarily a similar example in
the proof of sound as impermanent because] whatever is an established base [is necessarily a similar example in the proof of
sound as impermanent, and also whatever is not an established
base is necessarily a similar example in the proof of sound as
impermanent." And so forth, through the rest of the sub-
proofs.]

The same [mode of progression] is also to be applied with
respect to [the proof of sound as impermanent by] the sign,
product: [The definition of similar example in the proof of
sound as impermanent by the sign, product, is: That held as the
similar example in the proof of sound as impermanent by the
sign, product, and so forth, through the sub-proofs.][b]

---

[a] Commentary on *Signs and Reasonings*, vol. 1, p. 13. The characteristics of a correct
similar example are explained in chapter three.

[b] *Signs and Reasonings*, p. 5a.5-6. Pur-bu-jok often gives full treatment to the first statement in a series and drastically abbreviates those that follow, expecting the teachers to
see that their students do the mental exercise. His actual words are:

In commentary on this passage, Ge-luk-pa scholars fill in the context and expand on the real function of examples as an aid in understanding the pervasions. Similar and dissimilar examples are used in debate in proof statements, to help generate understanding of the pervasions in the mind of a correct opponent.

Ge-shay Pel-den-drak-pa summarizes the function of examples in this way:

> How does a similar example function? Let us take as an example this proof: "The subject, sound, is impermanent because of being a product, as is the case with a pot." What is the mode of procedure (*'gro tshul*) here? [That is, how does the similar example work?] Before ascertaining the pervasion (whatever is a product is necessarily impermanent) in relation to the basis of debate (sound), [the opponent] ascertains it in relation to pot.[131]

Dissimilar Example

After his explanation of similar example Pur-bu-jok comments briefly on dissimilar example:

> That [which is] held as a dissimilar example is not the definition of dissimilar example. This is because dissimilar example does not exist, since whatever is an established base is necessarily a correct similar example. However, it has already been proved above that there exists a correct dissimilar example in the proof of sound as impermanent.[a]

In his discussion of similar example Pur-bu-jok asserted that whatever is selfless is necessarily (1) a similar example, (2) a similar example in the proof of sound as impermanent, and (3) a similar example in the proof of sound as impermanent by the sign, product. He makes the point that anything imaginable is potentially a similar example in a given proof, whether it is correct or not; and thus, in general, dissimilar

---

The definition of a similar example in the proof of sound as impermanent is: that held as a similar example in the proof of sound as impermanent. Whatever is selfless is necessarily that. Extend the reasoning...whatever is an established base, etc. The same is also to be applied with respect to the sign, product.

[a] *Signs and Reasonings*, p. 5a.6-7. This has not been proved explicitly in Pur-bu-jok's work, but it is implied in his acknowledgement, above (in the discussion of whether similar and dissimilar classes are explicitly contradictory), that there exists a correct proof statement using a qualitative dissimilarity in the proof of sound as impermanent.

example does not exist.

Pur-bu-jok's statement on examples does not explain the qualities of examples in actual application; it serves primarily to present the idea that anything imaginable is potentially a similar example. The context here is not that of validity. This section of Pur-bu-jok's text thus serves as a basis for debate and as a basis for the next topic—establishment of the pervasions—in which the context of validity is introduced.

3. Establishing the Forward Pervasion and the Counterpervasion

ESTABLISHING THE FORWARD PERVASION

In order for the forward pervasion (that is, the second mode) to be established in the proof of sound as impermanent by the sign, product, all of the criteria set forth in the definition of forward pervasion must be met. Pur-bu-jok's definition is:

> Something (x) is the forward pervasion in the proof of sound as impermanent because:
>
> (1) There exists a correct similar example (*mthun dpe*, **sadṛṣṭānta*) that possesses both the sign and the predicate of the probandum, in the proof of sound as impermanent by the sign x;
> (2) x is related with impermanent; and
> (3) x is ascertained by valid cognition as existing, in accordance with the mode of statement, in only the similar class in the proof of sound as impermanent.[a]

As an illustration of the forward pervasion in the proof of sound as impermanent, Pur-bu-jok posits product—just "product," not "whatever is a product is impermanent." He writes,

> It follows with respect to the subject, product, that it is the forward pervasion in the proof of sound as impermanent because of being [fulfilling] that definition.[132]

He takes up each of the three parts or "root reasons" of his definition in turn.

1. THERE EXISTS A CORRECT SIMILAR EXAMPLE

Pur-bu-jok writes,

---

[a] *Signs and Reasonings*, p. 5b.6-7. Pur-bu-jok also provides a short definition: forward pervasion is "that ascertained by valid cognition as existing in only the similar class in accordance with the mode of statement in the proof of that." (Ibid., p. 5b.2-3.) As explained in chapter one, "establishing the property of the subject," Pur-bu-jok provides brief definitions of each of the three modes, adding that these are not intended to be definitive.

The first root reason follows because pot is a correct similar example that possesses both the sign and the predicate of the
probandum, in the proof of sound as impermanent by the sign
of it [product]. If someone says that this reason is not established, [then the response is:] "It follows with respect to the
subject, pot, that it is a correct similar example that possesses
both the sign and the predicate in the proof of that by the sign,
product, because

(a) it is held as a similar example in the proof of that by the
    sign, product, and
(b) there exists a correct opponent in the proof of that who,
    before ascertaining by valid cognition that whatever is a
    product is necessarily impermanent—in terms of sound—
    ascertains by valid cognition that whatever is a product is
    necessarily impermanent—in terms of it [pot]. This is be-
    cause it [pot] is a particularity of product.[a]

To establish product as the forward pervasion in the proof of sound as
impermanent by the sign, product, one must first ascertain the pervasion "whatever is a product is impermanent" in relation to a correct
example. As Ge-shay Pel-den-drak-pa says, "If there is no similar example, then there is no way to establish the pervasion."[133]

Something, x, is said to be a correct similar example in a proof if x
is the basis with respect to which one ascertains the pervasion (that
whatever is a product is necessarily impermanent)—*prior to* ascertaining the same pervasion with respect to the basis of debate, sound. Ge-
shay Lob-sang-gya-tso explains that it is thus the example that makes
the establishment of the pervasion possible.[134] Pur-bu-jok specifies that
the correct similar example in the proof of sound as impermanent must
"possess both the sign and the predicate, in the proof of sound as impermanent." It must possess the qualities of that which is held as the
predicate (impermanent) and that which is held as the sign (product);
in other words, the correct similar example must be both impermanent
and a product.

---

[a] *Signs and Reasonings,* pp. 6a.7-b.3. According to Ge-shay Pel-den-drak-pa, there is no
pervasion with regard to the last statement. That is, if something is a particularity of
product, it is not necessarily a correct similar example in the proof of sound as impermanent. If there were such a pervasion, one could posit sound, or object of hearing, as a
correct similar example. These are particularities of product but are not similar examples in the proof of sound as impermanent. (Commentary on *Signs and Reasonings,* vol. 2,
p. 17.)

Pur-bu-jok continues,

> If someone says that the first reason [a: that pot is held as a similar example in the proof of that by the sign, product,] is not established, [then the response is:] "It follows with respect to the subject, pot, that it is held as a similar example in the proof of that by the sign, product, because there exists the syllogism, 'The subject, sound, is impermanent because of being a product, as is the case with pot.'"[135]

This is a syllogism using a qualitative similarity. As explained in chapter two,[a] the qualitative similarity between subject and example may be expressed through the use of either a syllogism or a proof statement.

Pur-bu-jok further comments,

> If someone says that the second reason [b: that there exists a correct opponent, etc.[b]] is not established, [then the response is:] "It follows with respect to the subject, object of knowledge, that there exists such a correct opponent because there exists a correct opponent in the proof of that who, before ascertaining by valid cognition that sound is impermanent, ascertains by valid cognition that pot is impermanent. This is because there exists a correct opponent in the proof of sound as impermanent. This [in turn] is because a correct opponent in the proof of sound as impermanent is [one who, before ascertaining by valid cognition that sound is impermanent, has ascertained by valid cognition that pot is impermanent]. And this is because the correct opponent in the proof of that is a person who has not ascertained by valid cognition that sound is impermanent, but who has ascertained by valid cognition that a pot is impermanent. These latter two signs are proven by the subject.[136]

That a correct opponent has *not* ascertained by valid cognition that sound is impermanent, but *has* ascertained by valid cognition that pot is impermanent, is established by the fact that he or she is a correct

---

[a] See the "concluding topics" section on "whether similar and dissimilar classes are explicitly contradictory."

[b] "The second reason" here means Pur-bu-jok's second point (b) in his statement of the first root reason. He means, "If someone says that there does not exist a correct opponent in the proof of that who, before ascertaining by valid cognition that whatever is a product is necessarily impermanent (in terms of sound), ascertains by valid cognition that whatever is a product is necessarily impermanent (in terms of pot)..."

opponent.[a] For the forward pervasion to be established, there must be a correct similar example; an example must be used. The correct opponent is someone who is ascertaining the pervasion in relation to an example like pot. Lati Rin-po-che elaborates,

> In what way is something held as a similar example? It is like "pot" when one states, "The subject, sound, is impermanent because of being a product, as is the case with pot." Pot is not always or necessarily a correct similar example. For someone who has not realized that sound is impermanent but has realized that pot is impermanent, it is a correct similar example in that proof; for someone who has not realized that pot is impermanent, it is not.[137]

If, before realizing with respect to sound that whatever is a product is impermanent, the opponent realizes with respect to pot that whatever is a product is impermanent, then pot will have the necessary characteristics to be a correct similar example for that person.

2. THE SIGN IS RELATED WITH IMPERMANENT

Pur-bu-jok continues the discussion of his definition of forward pervasion:

> The second root reason [why the sign must be related with impermanent] follows because it [product] is related as one entity with impermanent.[138]

For something, x, to be a correct sign in the proof of sound as impermanent, there must be a strictly defined logical relationship between x and the predicate, impermanent.[b] However, in the opinion of some Ge-

---

[a] Commentary on *Signs and Reasonings*, section 4, p. 8. He adds,

> The definition of a correct opponent is a person who, having ascertained the three modes by valid cognition, is engaged in wanting to understand the probandum. So this person knows:
>
> (1) that sound is a product,
> (2) that whatever is a product is necessarily impermanent, and
> (3) that whatever is not impermanent is necessarily not a product [understands the relationship between product and impermanent].
>
> Knowing all that, he is seeking to find out if sound is impermanent. Furthermore, although he does not realize that sound is impermanent, he does realize that pot is impermanent.

[b] The sign-predicate relationship is discussed by Pur-bu-jok in terms of the way the sign relates to the similar and dissimilar classes. It thus belongs to the discussion of the

luk-pa scholars, the second root reason (that x is related to impermanent) in Pur-bu-jok's definition does not refer primarily to this technical relationship between x and the predicate. According to Lati Rin-po-
che, the main purpose of the second root reason is to ensure that the
sign be a phenomenon that is other than the predicate. He says,

> The reason for including "it is related to impermanent" in the
> definition is to eliminate impermanent itself as a sign.[139]

The sign must be "related with" (*'brel ba*) the predicate; it must therefore be different from it. For any phenomenon to be related with
another, it must first of all be different from it.[a]

3. RELATIONSHIP BETWEEN SIGN AND SIMILAR CLASS

The final root reason why something (x) is the forward pervasion in the
proof of sound as impermanent is the most complicated of the three in
the definition of forward pervasion—though Pur-bu-jok's comments
are, as always, brief. The greater part of what follows is a summary of
the explanatory work of later Tibetan scholars. Pur-bu-jok says,

> The third root reason [that is, that the sign, product, is ascer-
> tained by valid cognition as existing, in accordance with the
> mode of statement, in only the similar class (the impermanent)
> in the proof of sound as impermanent] follows because:
>
> (1) the mode of statement in the proof of sound as imperma-
>   nent by the sign of it [product] is an "is" statement,
> (2) the mode of proof is an "is" proof,
> (3) [product] is impermanent, and
> (4) whatever is it [product] is necessarily impermanent.
>
> The first reason is easy [to understand because the *mode of
> statement* is copular: "The subject, sound, *is* impermanent

---

third part of the definition, relationship between sign and similar class, below.

[a] The definition of something (x) being related as one nature (or entity) with a phenomenon is: "X is different from that phenomenon, within being of the same nature,
and when that phenomenon is eliminated, x is also eliminated." Pur-bu-jok, *Collected
Topics* (*Middling Path of Reasoning, rigs lam 'bring*), p. 5b.2-3. This technical relationship is
described in greater detail in the section below on the relationship between sign and
predicate. Ge-luk-pa students do not confront all the details of Tibetan logic at once;
the work is spread out over a number of years. Analysis of the technical relationship
between the predicate and the sign is generally studied a year or two after the study of
Signs and Reasonings begins.

because of being a product"].

The second reason follows because (a) the *mode of proof* in the proof of sound as impermanent by the sign, product, can be only an "is" proof or an "exists" proof, and (b) it is not the latter. It follows [that the mode of proof in the proof of sound as impermanent by the sign, product, is either copular or ontological] because it is set as a sign in the proof of that.[a]

If a person says that the second reason [b, above] is not established [which is to say that the mode of proof is not copular but ontological—that is, the subject, sound, "exists" in or with the impermanent because of being a product], then the response is, "It follows [from that view] that product is a sign that relates as pervader to the similar class in the proof of sound as existing with [or in] the impermanent because [according to you] there exists a sign that relates to the similar class in the proof of that as a pervader."

If that is accepted, then it [absurdly] follows that the subject, object of knowledge, is a product because of existing [with or in] the impermanent.[b]

In a given proof, the predicate necessarily pervades any correct sign, but the sign may or may not pervade the predicate. There is general agreement among Ge-luk-pa scholars that, in the proof of sound as [being] impermanent, the sign, *product*, relates to the similar class (the impermanent) as pervader; that is, product pervades impermanent. Whatever *is* impermanent is necessarily a product.

If a person agrees that product relates to the similar class as pervader, but also asserts that the mode of proof is an "exists" proof, it

---

[a]   Pur-bu-jok posits two modes of proof: the "is" or copular and the "exists" or ontological. Any statement of proof must involve one or the other. Other Ge-luk-pa scholars refer to four modes of proof, but this is not a significant difference of opinion. Lati Rin-po-che, for example (in his commentary on *Signs and Reasonings*, vol. 1, p. 23), describes the affirmative and negative forms of the copular and ontological modes as distinct categories, thus positing these four modes of proof: "is" (*yin*), "is not" (*ma yin*), "exists" (*yod*), "does not exist" (*med*).

[b]   *Signs and Reasonings*, pp. 6b.6-7a.2. On page 7a.1, Pur-bu-jok refers to the predicate of the probandum in this ontological proof as "exists as (or with) the impermanent" (*mi rtag par yod pa*); on line 2 of that same page (when he has transferred the predicate of the probandum to the sign position of a new syllogism) he renders it as "impermanent exists" (*mi rtag pa yod pa*). Thus it is not clear which of these he intends. However, in this context, both Lati Rin-po-che and Ge-shay Ge-dün-lo-drö understand Pur-bu-jok to mean "exists in impermanent"—see next footnote.

would follow that product pervades, not "[being] impermanent" (*mi rtag pa yin pa*), but "exists in impermanent" (*mi rtag pa la yod pa*).[a] Lati Rin-po-che explains,

> Pur-bu-jok is pointing out that if this proof is made an "exists" proof, then the sign, product, [is no longer a sign that relates to the similar class as pervader, but rather] is a sign that relates to the similar class in two ways:
>
>> Whatever exists in impermanent is not necessarily a product and is not necessarily not a product.[140]

If the person asserts that product relates to the similar class as a pervader in the proof of sound as *existing* in impermanent, it follows that "whatever exists in impermanent must be a product." This is mistaken, because something can be posited that exists in impermanent but is not a product. For example, object of knowledge "exists in" impermanent, because impermanent phenomena are objects of knowledge; however, object of knowledge cannot *be* impermanent—because it is permanent.[141]

Pur-bu-jok concludes,

> With respect to the third reason, it follows [that product is impermanent] because of being a product. The fourth reason [whatever is a product is necessarily impermanent] is set aside.[142]

Ge-luk-pa Commentary on Similar Class

In commentary on the third part or "root reason" of the definition ["x is ascertained by valid cognition as existing, in accordance with the mode of statement, in only the similar class in the proof of sound as impermanent"], Ge-luk-pa scholars bring in much more detail than Pur-bu-jok provides. Their explanation of the requirements specified by the third root reason of Pur-bu-jok's definition of forward pervasion can best be summarized in four parts. The sign x:

---

[a] A strict rendering of the "exists" proof would state "impermanent exists" (*mi rtag ba yod pa*); however, some Ge-luk-pa scholars explain this to mean "exists *in* impermanent" (*mi rtag pa la yat pa*). Lati Rin-po-che does so (commentary on *Signs and Reasonings*, vol. 2, Feb. 18, 1977, p. 7), as does Ge-shay Ge-dün-lo-drö, who comments, "To say that this is an exists proof and that the sign relates to the predicate as pervader would mean that whatever exists in the impermanent must be a product. But this is not so." (Commentary on *Signs and Reasonings*, section 4, p. 8.)

(a) must exist in the similar class, in accordance with the mode of statement;[a]
(b) must exist in *only* the similar class;
(c) must exist in only the similar class, as opposed to *only existing* in the similar class (the position of "only" is important);
(d) must be *ascertained* as existent in only the similar class.

The sign must exist in the similar class

To be the forward pervasion in the proof of sound as impermanent, the sign (x) must exist in the similar class (that is, in the impermanent).[b] Furthermore, it must exist in the impermanent in accordance with the mode of statement. The mode of statement in the syllogism is copular; therefore x must *be* impermanent. Something that is not impermanent (nonproduct space, for example) does not exist in the similar class in accordance with the mode of statement. Something that does not exist in the similar class in the proof of sound as impermanent cannot be the forward pervasion in that proof.

The sign must exist in only the similar class

If x is a correct sign in a given proof, it must exist in only the similar class in that proof—not in both the similar and the dissimilar classes.[c]

---

[a] This part (a) includes the whole of Pur-bu-jok's discussion of the third root reason; he does not address the other three directly. However, the scholars' parts (b) through (d) have become part of the oral tradition and are routinely discussed in commentary on Pur-bu-jok's text. This format, which involves discussing the definition in four parts, is followed by Mokṣākaragupta in his *Tarkabhāṣā* (translated by Kajiyama in his *An Introduction to Buddhist Philosophy*, pp 67-69). It is also followed by Ge-shay Tsül-trim-nam-gyel in his *Signs and Reasonings* (the logic manual used at Lo-sel-ling College), p. 4b.4-5b.1.

[b] The explanation provided in the Lo-sel-ling logic manual is: "There is a purpose for stating 'exists' as part of that [definition] because it is for the sake of eliminating product as being the forward pervasion in the proof of sound as permanent. In dependence on this word ['exists'], that [product is the forward pervasion in the proof of sound as permanent] is refuted, because product does not exist in the similar class in the proof of sound as permanent." Ge-shay Tsül-trim-nam-gyel, *Signs and Reasonings*, pp. 4b.4-5a.2.

[c] The explanation in the Lo-sel-ling manual is: "There is a purpose for stating 'only' because it is for the sake of eliminating object of comprehension as the forward pervasion in the proof of sound as impermanent. In dependence on this word ["only"], that [object of comprehension] is refuted because object of comprehension does not exist in only the similar class in the proof of sound as impermanent. This is because [object of

This is specified so that no one will posit such phenomena as "object of knowledge" or "object of comprehension" as the forward pervasion in the proof of sound as impermanent. Object of comprehension does exist in the similar class in the proof of sound as impermanent, in that some objects of comprehension are impermanent. However, it also exists in the dissimilar class: some are not impermanent; objects of comprehension may be either impermanent or permanent. It does not exist *only* in the similar class and therefore cannot be the forward pervasion in that proof.[143]

The position of "only"

There is a reason for specifying that x must "exist in (or among) only" (*kho na la yod pa*) the similar class, instead of must "only exist" (*yod pa kho na*) in the similar class. The placement of the word "only" is important. If, in the Tibetan, "only" had been placed after "exist" it would modify "exist," indicating that x *only exists* in the similar class—that is, exists in all of that class. The correct Tibetan phrase becomes the English: "exist in only." To say that x exists in only the similar class means that all x is the similar class (x does not exist in the dissimilar class), and some (but not necessarily all) of the similar class is x. To say that x only exists in the similar class means that all of the similar class is x. This last statement is not true of all correct signs. In the case of the similar class—the impermanent—it is true, for example, of the sign "product" (all impermanent phenomena are products) but not of the sign "arisen from [a person's] exertion" (all impermanent phenomena are not arisen from a person's exertion).

Arisen from exertion "exists in only" the similar class in the proof of the sound of a conch as impermanent, because all things arisen from exertion are impermanent. Arisen from exertion does not "only exist" in impermanent; if one said so, it would mean that all impermanent phenomena arise from (a person's) exertion—but many impermanent phenomena do not. As Ge-shay Lob-sang-gya-tso says,

> "Arisen from exertion" is the forward pervasion in the proof of sound as impermanent because it exists in only the similar class in the proof of sound as impermanent. Although "arisen from exertion" exists in only impermanent, it does not only exist in the similar class; this is because it does not exist in *all* the

---

comprehension] exists in both the similar class and the dissimilar class in the proof of that. Ge-shay Tsul-trim-nam-gyal, *Signs and Reasonings*, p. 5a.2-3.

similar class—it does not exist with rocky cliff. Arisen from exertion exists in only the impermanent. Why? Because it exists
among the impermanent and it does not exist among phenomena other than the impermanent.[a]

Thus it is clear that there are some correct signs of which it can be said
that although the sign exists in only the similar class, it does not only
exist in the similar class. This is why the general definition must contain the correct specification—to include all examples of correct signs.
Arisen from exertion is said to exist in (or among) the impermanent
because *some* (but not all) impermanent phenomena are arisen from
exertion.

In contrast, all impermanent phenomena *are* products; thus, product is a correct sign that exists in all instances of the similar class in the
syllogism, "The subject, sound, is impermanent because of being a
product." It would not be incorrect to state "product only exists in the
similar class."

These two illustrations make an important point: a correct sign
need not exist in all members of the similar class in order to function as
a correct sign; it may exist in only some. It *must* exist in the similar
class (and it must not exist at all in the dissimilar class), but it *need not*
only exist in the similar class.[b] Expressing the definition as "exists in
only" enables "arisen from (a person's) exertion" to be the forward
pervasion in the proof of the sound of a conch as impermanent.

The sign must be ascertained

The scholars have a reason for specifying that the sign's existence in
only the similar class must be *ascertained*. This makes it impossible for
product to be the forward pervasion in the proof of sound as impermanent—for a person who is not *sure* that product exists in only the similar class. A person who has doubt (about whether product is impermanent or not) does not have full ascertainment, and thus product cannot
be the forward pervasion in that proof. It is true that careful analysis
will show that product exists in only the impermanent; but if a particular person has not ascertained that, then for him or her it is not

---

[a] Commentary on *Signs and Reasonings*, vol. 2, p. 7. The Lo-sel-ling text provides a similar explanation (pp. 5a.3-5b.1).

[b] It is also interesting to note that while a correct sign must exist in only the similar
class, it need not *be* the similar class. For example, particularity of product is not the
similar class in the proof of sound as impermanent, but it exists in only the similar class
and is considered to be a correct sign.

established as the forward pervasion. As Lati Rin-po-che notes,

> Someone who has doubt about whether product is imperma-
> nent or not does not have the full qualifications of ascertain-
> ment; thus [for that person] product cannot be the forward
> pervasion in the proof of sound as impermanent.[144]

The forward pervasion is established with the help of a proof statement
using a similar example. That is, a person who has not ascertained the
point will first realize the pervasion "whatever is a product is necessarily impermanent" in relation to an example, such as "pot." This
means one understands that pot is a product and that it is impermanent.[a] When one actually establishes the forward pervasion in the proof
of sound as impermanent, one understands it in relation to product.
This means that one is focused on product; one is understanding that
product is impermanent; and that product is existent in only impermanent.

In considering the validity of a proof, the Ge-luk-pa apparently
place a great emphasis on the consciousness of the person involved.
This may be a point of contrast with earlier scholars, such as the eleventh-century Buddhist logician Mokṣākaragupta. If we compare the
Ge-luk-pa explanation of the Tibetan *nges pa* in the definition of forward pervasion with Mokṣākaragupta's explanation of the equivalent
Sanskrit *niścitam,* a difference, at least of emphasis, is discernable. As
was explained in the chapter one discussion of "ascertain," the two
terms are sometimes translated as "definite" and sometimes as "ascertained."

Mokṣākaragupta's explanation of the definition of forward pervasion is in four parts, and these four are mirrored in the text of Ge-shay
Tsül-trim-nam-gyel of Lo-sel-ling. Although Pur-bu-jok does not follow
this format in his text, the information included in Mokṣākaragupta's
text and that of Lo-sel-ling are now part of the oral tradition of the

---

[a] It is generally agreed among Ge-luk-pa scholars that an example is needed for establishment of the pervasions. Lati Rin-po-che comments that in the case of the proof of
sound as impermanent, "pot is a correct similar example only in the context of [the
opponent's] already having realized that pot is impermanent." (Commentary on *Signs
and Reasonings,* vol. 1, p. 13.) But what about the context of proving impermanence to an
opponent who has never before ascertained impermanence—how can there be a similar
example? In that case, the similar example is a phenomenon such as the last moment of
a flame, an instance of coarse impermanence, which generally can be ascertained directly by ordinary beings (ibid., p. 14). The issue of how the similar example functions
in the context of newly establishing impermanence—the focal point of considerable
debate—is beyond the scope of this book.

Ge-luk-pa and emerge in the course of study. There is no significant difference in the first three:

(1) the significance of "exists in the similar class,"
(2) the significance of "exists in only the similar class," and
(3) the significance of the position of "only."

In the fourth part, a possible difference between the Ge-luk-pa teaching and Mokṣākaragupta's is seen in the explanation of the term translated as "ascertained" (*nges pa, niścitam*). The Ge-luk-pa stress the consciousness of the opponent in determining the validity of a proof. This validity depends only partially on the relationship between the parts of the syllogism (the subject, the predicate, and the sign); it depends even more on the consciousness of the opponent.

This is illustrated by a comparison of Mokṣākaragupta's explanation of the Sanskrit *niścitam* and the Ge-luk-pa explanation of the equivalent Tibetan *nges pa*. Mokṣākaragupta begins his explanation of the forward pervasion (the second mode) with these words:

> [The second characteristic is] defined as follows:
>
> > Its definite presence only in things similar to *p* [*sapakṣa*, that is, the members of the class of *s*].[a]

He then explains the significance of the term "definite" (*niścitam*) in his definition of forward pervasion:

> The employment of the word "definite" is to preclude a dubious *anvaya* [forward pervasion], as in the following inference: "This man is not omniscient because he speaks as any other person does." For we never know whether, in any person as a member of the class of *s*, "speakerness" is pervaded by nonomniscience or not.[b]

The logic manual written by Ge-shay Tsül-trim-nam-gyal contains the Lo-sel-ling explanation of the term *nges pa*, the Tibetan equivalent of *niścitam*:

---

[a] Kajiyama, *An Introduction to Buddhist Philosophy*, p. 67. On page 69 Kajiyama explains that *s* refers to the predicate of the probandum. "Second characteristic" is Kajiyama's phrase for "second mode." This quotation is Kajiyama's translation of *sapakṣa eva sattvam niścitam* (lit: "that which is ascertained (or definite) as only existing in the similar class").

[b] Ibid., p. 69. It is not clear from Mokṣākaragupta's explanation whether the term *niścitam* should be translated as "ascertained" or "definite"; Kajiyama translates it as "definite." It is clear that in Ge-luk-pa discussions the term means "ascertain."

> [In the definition of the forward pervasion,] there is a purpose
> for stating "ascertain," because it is for the sake of eliminating
> "uttering speech" as a positive pervasion in the proof that the
> person over there uttering speech is omniscient.[145]

The syllogism under consideration is, "The subject, that being over
there uttering speech, is omniscient because of uttering speech"; as Lati
Rin-po-che points out, "[The syllogism] could equally well have been,
'The subject, that being over there uttering speech, is *not* omniscient
because of uttering speech.'"[146] The similar class in the first is "the omniscient" and in the second, "the nonomniscient." An ordinary being
for whom omniscience is a supersensory object will not be able to ascertain by valid cognition whether speaking exists *only* among the nonomniscient. This cannot be known by an ordinary being, who has no
way of knowing with valid cognition whether the omniscient speak or
not. Lati Rin-po-che adds,

> These positions [omniscient or nonomniscient because of utter-
> ing speech] are held by some non-Buddhists. In these proofs
> the forward pervasion is not established. Why? Because it is not
> ascertained whether uttering speech does or does not exist
> among the omniscient...These non-Buddhists have doubt about
> whether omniscience exists or not. One who does not ascertain
> omniscience cannot ascertain whether uttering speech exists
> or not among the omniscient.[a]

A person who has no experience or specific knowledge of omniscience
cannot ascertain whether the sign exists in *only* the similar class (whichever the similar class may be—the omniscient or the nonomniscient).

   The Ge-luk-pa explanation of forward pervasion takes into account
the example posited by Mokṣākaragupta, eliminating uttering speech
as a correct sign in the proof of a person uttering speech as not omniscient. (And, as Lati Rin-po-che notes, it also eliminates it as the forward
pervasion in the proof of a person as omniscient.) Although this example is mentioned, it is not considered to indicate clearly the main purpose for including the term "ascertain" in the definition of forward
pervasion. According to Lati Rin-po-che, that purpose is easier to
understand in relation to another example, the proof of sound as

---

[a] Commentary on *Signs and Reasonings,* vol. 1, p. 43. Lati Rin-po-che continues, "The
Nirgranthas [the Jains] say, 'The subject, that person over there, is not omniscient because of uttering speech.' This is because they say one who utters speech must have
motivation or a wish, and anyone who has motivation or a wish is not omniscient."

impermanent. He explains,

> The definition states, "The sign is ascertained as existing in only the similar class." Someone who has doubt about whether product is impermanent does not have the full qualifications of ascertainment, and thus product cannot be the forward pervasion in the proof of sound as impermanent. Product does in fact exist in only the impermanent [there is nothing indefinite about the status of product in relation to impermanent], but the person is not ascertaining that it exists in only the impermanent. Thus for him [or her], product is not established as the forward pervasion.[147]

For the forward pervasion to be established, the opponent must understand the relationship between the predicate and the sign—must thus understand by valid cognition that product is impermanent. If the opponent does not know this, then the pervasion cannot be established for that person.

The Ge-luk-pa example has an emphasis on the consciousness of the person involved. Thus, in explaining the purpose for the term *niścitam* in the definition, the emphasis in the Ge-luk-pa presentation is on eliminating product as a sign in the proof of sound as impermanent for one who does not know that product is impermanent. For someone who has not ascertained that product is impermanent, product cannot be a correct sign—cannot be the forward pervasion. And someone who has ascertained that product is impermanent is not necessarily a correct opponent. Though there appears to be a difference of emphasis between the presentations of Mokṣākaragupta and of the Ge-luk-pa, it should be noted that no information is available on the way Mokṣākaragupta's explanation was used by scholars of his time—that is, we lack the accompanying commentary.

ESTABLISHING THE COUNTERPERVASION

Pur-bu-jok's definition is:

> Something (x) is the counterpervasion in the proof of sound as impermanent because:

> (1) There exists a correct dissimilar example (*mi mthun dpe*, **vidṛṣṭānta*), which possesses neither the sign nor the predicate of the probandum, in the proof of sound as impermanent by the sign x;

(2) x is related to impermanent; and
(3) x is ascertained by valid cognition as only nonexistent in
     the dissimilar class in the proof of sound as impermanent.[a]

As an illustration of the counterpervasion in the proof of sound as impermanent, Pur-bu-jok posits *product* (just "product," not "whatever is permanent is necessarily not a product"). He continues,

> It follows that the subject, product, is the counterpervasion in
> the proof of sound as impermanent because of being [fulfilling]
> this definition.[148]

Pur-bu-jok's discussion of the three root reasons in his definition of the counterpervasion follows the general pattern of his previous discussion of establishing the forward pervasion. It is shorter, because the course of reasoning has already been established.

1. THERE EXISTS A DISSIMILAR EXAMPLE

As was the case with the forward pervasion, one must first ascertain the counterpervasion in relation to a correct example. Pur-bu-jok writes,

> The first root reason [that is, that there exists a correct dissimi-
> lar example that does not possess either the sign or the predi-
> cate in the proof of sound as impermanent by the sign, *product*]
> is established because uncompounded space is [a dissimilar ex-
> ample that fulfills the definition].[149]

To establish product as the counterpervasion in the proof of sound as impermanent, one must first ascertain the pervasion "whatever is

---

[a] *Signs and Reasonings*, pp. 5b.7-6a.2. Pur-bu-jok also posits a short definition of counterpervasion: "That ascertained by valid cognition as only nonexistent in the dissimilar class, in accordance with the mode of statement, in the proof of that by the power of [the sign's] relation with the meaning-isolate of the explicit predicate of the probandum in the proof of that." (Ibid., p. 5b.3-4.) He does not comment on this definition except to say that it is "formulated mainly for the sake of understanding" and is not definitive.

Lati Rin-po-che comments, "The explicit predicate of the probandum is 'impermanent,' and the meaning-isolate of impermanent is its definition—momentary. Because product is related with momentary, productness is only nonexistent in the permanent." (Commentary on *Signs and Reasonings*, vol. 2, Feb. 9, 1977, p. 4.) However, according to Ge-shay Pel-den-drak-pa, the "meaning-isolate" of the explicit predicate of the probandum (impermanent) probably refers in this context to "impermanent" itself. (Commentary on *Signs and Reasonings*, vol. 2, p. 12.)

permanent is necessarily *not a product*" in relation to a correct example. It is referred to as a "dissimilar example" because it does not possess the qualities of either the predicate or the sign. As Ge-shay Lob-sang-gya-tso says,

> "The subject, sound, is impermanent because of being a prod-uct—for example, uncompounded space"—in that syllogism, the dissimilar example, uncompounded space, does not possess [that is, is not qualified by] the sign or the predicate of the pro-bandum. What is the sign that is the nonpossessed sign? Prod-uct. And what is the predicate that is the nonpossessed predi-cate? Impermanent.[150]

2. THE SIGN IS RELATED WITH IMPERMANENT

Pur-bu-jok's discussion continues,

> The second root reason [that is, that x is related to imperma-nent] has already been established.[151]

The relationship between a correct sign and the predicate of the pro-bandum is discussed briefly above in the section on the forward perva-sion. There it is explained that, according to Ge-luk-pa scholars, Pur-bu-jok's main purpose in specifying that the sign must be related with impermanent is to indicate that a correct sign in any given proof must be different from the predicate.

3. RELATIONSHIP BETWEEN SIGN AND DISSIMILAR CLASS

Pur-bu-jok goes on,

> The third root reason [that product is ascertained by valid cog-nition as only nonexistent in the dissimilar class in the proof of sound as impermanent] is established because product does not exist among the nonimpermanent.[152]

The dissimilar class in the proof of sound as impermanent is the non-impermanent. Product is only nonexistent in the dissimilar class in that proof and thus does not exist at all—that is, is not found at all—in the nonimpermanent.

This very brief explanation provided by Pur-bu-jok is not by itself enough to bring thorough understanding of the topic, but it is the basis for more detailed information provided by teachers. The detailed ex-planation of the relationship between sign and dissimilar class that emerges in commentary can be summarized in four parts. The sign x:

(a) must be nonexistent in the dissimilar class;
(b) must be *only* nonexistent in the dissimilar class;
(c) must be only nonexistent in the dissimilar class, as opposed to being *nonexistent in only* the dissimilar class (the position of "only" is important);
(d) must be *ascertained* as only nonexistent in the dissimilar class.

The sign must be nonexistent in the dissimilar class

To be the counterpervasion in the proof of sound as impermanent, the sign, product, must not exist in the dissimilar class. This is specified in order to eliminate, for example, "nonproduct" as the counterpervasion in that proof. Nonproduct is not "nonexistent in the dissimilar class" in that proof—it does exist in the dissimilar class, because it is permanent. Lati Rin-po-che comments:

> Why is nonproduct not the counterpervasion in the proof of sound as impermanent? Because nonproduct is not nonexistent in the dissimilar class in that proof; it exists in the dissimilar class. The phrase "must be nonexistent" in that definition eliminates such signs as "nonproduct," "generally characterized phenomenon," and "phenomenon that is a nonthing" as the counterpervasion in that proof. These are not nonexistent in the dissimilar class in the proof of sound as impermanent; all [are permanent and therefore] exist in the dissimilar class.[153]

The sign must be only nonexistent in the dissimilar class

The requirement that the sign x must be "only" [or "just"] nonexistent in the dissimilar class indicates that x must be nonexistent in *all* members of the dissimilar class. This eliminates, for example, impermanent as the counterpervasion in the proof of the sound of a conch as arisen from (a person's) exertion. Impermanent cannot be the counterpervasion, because it is both nonexistent and existent in the dissimilar class in that proof. Whatever is the dissimilar class in that proof is not necessarily impermanent and is not necessarily not impermanent. The dissimilar class—that is, whatever is *not* arisen from exertion—contains both impermanent and permanent phenomena. Lati Rin-po-che makes this clear when he says,

Impermanent does exist in the dissimilar class in the proof of the sound of a conch as arisen from exertion, and thus is not *just* nonexistent in the dissimilar class. This is because impermanent is not nonexistent in [or with] all the dissimilar class in the proof of the sound of a conch as arisen from exertion. It exists with some members of the nonarisen from exertion; lightning is [a member of] the dissimilar class in that proof and is impermanent. Nonproduct space is also a member of the dissimilar class, but is permanent.[a]

Thus, the impermanent is not nonexistent in (or with) *all* members of the dissimilar class in that proof.

The position of "only"

It is important to state that the sign "must be only nonexistent" in the dissimilar class, because this enables the sign "arisen from exertion" to be the counterpervasion in the proof of the sound of a conch as impermanent. It is true that "arisen from exertion" is *only nonexistent* (*med pa kho na*) in the dissimilar class in the proof of the sound of a conch as impermanent. If the "only" were moved, the statement would be incorrect. "Arisen from exertion" is not "nonexistent in *only*" (*kho na la med pa*) the dissimilar class; it is also nonexistent in the similar class. Lati Rin-po-che gives an example:

> If the word *just* were placed before "nonexistent" [in the Tibetan], one could not understand that arisen from exertion is the counterpervasion in the proof of the sound [of a conch] as impermanent. Since it is placed after "nonexistent," one can understand it. This is because although arisen from exertion is only nonexistent in the dissimilar class in the proof of the sound of a conch as impermanent, it is not nonexistent in only the dissimilar class. Being arisen from exertion also is nonexistent in some members of the similar class, such as "mountain"; [mountain is not arisen from (a person's) exertion and is impermanent].[154]

---

[a] Ibid., vol. 1, p. 47. The Lo-sel-ling logic manual by Ge-shay Tsül-trim-nam-gyel makes the same point with the same examples (pp. 5b.3-6a.1), and although these specifics are not included in Pur-bu-jok's text, they are included in the oral commentary given by the Ge-luk-pa teachers.

The sign must be ascertained

Ge-luk-pa scholars assert that the sign must be *ascertained* as only non-existent in the dissimilar class. Their reason is the same as that given in the discussion of the forward pervasion—there must be a correct opponent.

Here it may be helpful to discuss briefly the Ge-luk-pa explanation of the term "ascertain" in the definition of counterpervasion and to review the comparison of the Ge-luk-pa approach with that of Mokṣākaragupta. His definition of counterpervasion is,

> Its definite, absolute absence in the anti-*pakṣa* [*vipakṣa*—that is, any member of the class incompatible with *s*].[a]

Mokṣākaragupta explains the use of *niścitam* as follows,

> The employment of the word "definite" is to preclude the fallacious *hetu* [reason] whose nonoccurrence in the *vipakṣa* is doubtful (*saṃdigdhavipakṣavyāvṛttika*). [This fallacy] may be illustrated in the following: "This man is not free from desire, because he speaks, as a man on the highway"; for all the cases in which "being not free from desire" is absent are the cases in which "speakerness" is also absent, like a piece of rock. [This inference is wrong, because] though both the qualities are excluded from a piece of stone, yet we do not know whether speakerness is absent from a piece of stone due to the absence of the state of being free from desire, or it is so simply by nature. Thus, this is a case of inconclusiveness (*anaikāntika*) due to a dubious negative pervasion.[b]

Freedom from desire, like omniscience, is a supersensory object for ordinary beings; thus an ordinary being cannot know either the specific features of it or the specific occurrences of it. And just as an ordinary being cannot know the specific occurrences of omniscience, so he or she also cannot know the specific occurrences of the absence of desire.

Ge-shay Tsül-trim-nam-gyel presents an example that is similar in that it involves a supersensory object, omniscience:

> There is a purpose for stating "ascertain"; it is for the sake of

---

[a] This is Kajiyama's translation of *asapakṣe ca sattvam eva niścitam*; literally (and in accordance with the Ge-luk-pa point of view), "that ascertained as just nonexistent in the dissimilar class." (*An Introduction to Buddhist Philosophy*, p. 69.)

[b] Ibid., p. 70.

eliminating "uttering speech" as the forward pervasion in the proof that "the person over there uttering speech is omniscient."[155]

Lati Rin-po-che comments on this example,

> The reason for specifying ascertainment [in this definition of counterpervasion] is the same as in the definition of forward pervasion. For example, when one states, "The subject, that being over there [who is] uttering speech, is not omniscient because of uttering speech," the opponent cannot ascertain with valid cognition whether or not the uttering of speech exists in the similar class—the not omniscient. The opponent also cannot ascertain whether or not uttering speech is nonexistent among the omniscient. A person who does not know whether omniscience exists cannot possibly know whether omniscient persons utter speech.[156]

It is interesting to note that the definitions presented by Mokṣākaragupta do not specify that there must exist a similar example in the first case (the forward pervasion) and a dissimilar example in the second (the counterpervasion). From the Ge-luk-pa point of view this would make these definitions faulty and indefinite (just as Pur-bu-jok's own short definitions, as he says himself, are indefinite and included only to give a rough understanding of the general principles involved).[157]

This is not a point of conflict between the two presentations, however. The Ge-luk-pa definitions state the requirement for correct similar and dissimilar examples explicitly. Mokṣākaragupta posits such examples in his text, although he never specifies the need for them. He posits as a syllogism involving a qualitative similarity,

> A syllogism by the method of agreement formulated with a logical mark of causality is next illustrated: "Wherever there is smoke there is fire, as in a kitchen; here there is smoke [therefore here there is fire]."[158]

And as a syllogism involving a qualitative dissimilarity,

> Where there is no fire there is no smoke, as in a great tank [of water]; however, here there is smoke [therefore here there is fire].[159]

THE RELATIONSHIP BETWEEN SIGN AND PREDICATE

In order for the pervasions to be established in a particular proof, the sign in that proof must be in a strictly defined logical relationship with the predicate of the probandum. Furthermore, this precise relationship must be ascertained before ascertainment of the pervasions. For example, before ascertaining the pervasions in the proof of sound as impermanent by the sign, product, one must ascertain the relationship between product (the sign) and impermanent (the predicate of the probandum).

Something (a) is, by definition, related to something else (b) because:

(1) a is different from b, and
(2) by the force of the elimination of b, a is also eliminated.[160]

In the proof of sound as impermanent by the sign, product, if the pervasions are to be established, the sign (product) must be related with the predicate of the probandum (impermanent) in accordance with points (1) and (2). Thus, product is related to impermanent because (1) product is different from impermanent and (2) by the force of the elimination of the impermanent, product is also eliminated.

THE THREE VALID COGNITIONS

An explanation of how the pervasions are established in the proof of sound as impermanent by the sign, product, is provided by Gyel-tsap. He explains that ascertainment of the pervasions must be preceded by ascertainment of the relationship between the predicate and the sign.[161] If the predicate and the sign are not in the strictly defined logical relationship, then the pervasions cannot be established.

How does one prove irrefutably that the predicate of the probandum follows from the sign? One might think that it is by nonobservation of counterexamples. But that alone cannot irrefutably prove it; as an ordinary being, one could never be sure that one has eliminated *all* possibilities. The pervasion is established irrefutably not by nonobservation of counterexamples but by ascertainment of the relationship between the sign and the predicate of the probandum.[162] Part of understanding this relationship involves understanding that product exists in only impermanent (or applies to only impermanent). Of this, Gyel-tsap writes,

In order to ascertain that product applies to only the impermanent, three valid cognitions are needed; beyond these more are not needed:

(1) the valid cognition that ascertains permanent [the predicate of the negandum] and impermanent [the predicate of the probandum] as direct contradictories;
(2) the valid cognition that ascertains the illustration [of the sign]—product;
(3) the valid cognition that eliminates product in permanent.[a]

The first valid cognition required is the one ascertaining the direct contradictories. In order for product to be a correct sign in the proof of sound as impermanent, it must be related with the impermanent; this means that "by force of the elimination of impermanent, product is also eliminated." This means that on the basis or locus of elimination of the impermanent, product must also be eliminated.[163] The basis or locus of elimination of impermanent is the permanent, and the locus of elimination of the permanent is the impermanent; these are explicit contradictories. If one is present, the other is necessarily absent. In the proof of sound as impermanent, impermanent is the predicate of the probandum, and that which is explicitly contradictory with it, permanent, is the predicate of the negandum. The predicate of the probandum in any proof explicitly eliminates its opposite, the predicate of the negandum.

Gyel-tsap explains that in order to ascertain product as the forward pervasion in the proof of sound as impermanent, one must first know that impermanent and permanent are explicit contradictories. This is true of any proof: the predicate of the probandum and the predicate of the negandum must be ascertained as explicit contradictories. This is the first necessary valid cognition.

The second valid cognition is that which ascertains the illustration of the sign. If product is to be established as the forward pervasion and counterpervasion in the proof of sound as impermanent, it must be taken to mind as the sign in that proof. Taking it to mind means that one must consider product in relation to the subject (sound), while keeping one's mind focused on product as the sign. While establishing the pervasion, the focus or substratum of one's mind is the sign,

---

[a] *Revealer of the Path of Liberation*, pp. 36.20-37.3. The Tibetan for these is: (1) *rtag mi rtag dngos 'gal du nges pa'i tshad ma*; (2) *tshan gzhi byas pa nges byed gyi tshad ma*; (3) *rtag pa la byas pa 'gog pa'i tshad ma*.

product, in its function as a sign in that particular proof. This second requirement specifies the context of the establishment of the pervasion. That establishment must be in relation to product (that is, product is the substratum or focus); but, in order for the pervasion to be established, the opponent must be not only taking product as substratum but also explicitly holding product as the sign in the proof of sound as impermanent. This means the opponent is keeping the context vividly in mind—the context being the proof of sound as impermanent. As Geshay Sang-gyay-sam-drup says,

> Holding the illustration of the sign [product] as a basis means not just holding product as the basis [or substratum—*khyad gzhi*], it also means holding product as being a reason proving that sound is impermanent.[164]

The third valid cognition required for ascertaining that product applies to only the impermanent is the valid cognition that eliminates the sign (in the proof under consideration) in the predicate of the negandum. This valid cognition ascertains that product does not exist in the permanent. Such ascertainment does not represent full understanding of the relationship between product and impermanent. This relationship has two aspects to be understood. One is that product is empty of permanent (*byas pa rtag stong*), and the other that permanent is empty of product (*rtag pa byas stong*). Paṇ-chen Sö-nam-drak-pa explains that when one establishes (or understands) the two aspects of this relationship, two sets of four valid cognitions occur simultaneously. One set is that:

(1) product is different from impermanent and by force of eliminating impermanent, product is also eliminated;
(2) in the permanent, product does not exist (permanent is empty of product);
(3) permanent and product are without common locus; and
(4) whatever is permanent is necessarily a nonproduct.

The second set of simultaneous cognitions is that:

(1) permanent is different from nonproduct and by force of eliminating nonproduct, permanent is also eliminated;
(2) in product, permanent does not exist (product is empty of permanent);
(3) product and permanent are without common locus; and

(4) whatever is a product is necessarily impermanent.[a]

To summarize: to ascertain the pervasions in the proof of sound as impermanent by the sign, product, one must first ascertain the relationship between product and impermanent; and to ascertain that relationship one must ascertain its two aspects (that product is empty of permanent and permanent is empty of product).

PROOF STATEMENTS

The two aspects of the relationship between product and impermanent are expressed in the two proof statements (positive and negative) that accompany the syllogism, "The subject, sound, is impermanent because of being a product." The positive proof statement (that is, the proof statement using a qualitative similarity between the example and the subject—*chos mthun sbyor gyi sgrub ngag*) is:

> Whatever is a product is necessarily impermanent, as is the case with pot; sound also is a product.

The negative proof statement (that is, using a qualitative dissimilarity between the example and the subject—*chos mi thun sbyor gyi sgrub ngag*) is:

> Whatever is permanent is necessarily a nonproduct, as is the case with uncompounded space; sound, however, is a product.

The positive proof statement includes a similar example, and the negative a dissimilar example.

The similar example is that phenomenon with respect to which the pervasion, "whatever is a product is necessarily impermanent," is first ascertained. The dissimilar example is that phenomenon with respect to which the pervasion, "whatever is permanent is necessarily a nonproduct," is first ascertained. It is important to note that the pervasions that are realized in relation to the examples are not, strictly speaking, the forward pervasion and counterpervasion. The forward pervasion and counterpervasion must be ascertained *in relation to the sign—* product. According to Ge-shay Lob-sang-gya-tso,

---

[a] This explanation is based on instructions from Ge-shay Sang-gyay-sam-drup (commentary on *Revealer of the Path of Liberation*, vol. 1, May 25, 1983, p. 10). The ge-shay goes on to explain that the four valid cognitions in each set are simultaneous; the eight are not simultaneous.

When one speaks of establishing the forward pervasion in relation to the example, pot, that forward pervasion has a [corresponding] proof statement; that proof statement includes [the statement of] a pervasion: "whatever is a product is necessarily impermanent." That pervasion is established in relation to the similar example, pot—which is a step toward establishing the forward pervasion, but it is not itself the forward pervasion.[165]

In other words, when one has understood the pervasion, "whatever is a product is necessarily impermanent," in relation to pot, one's mind is focused on the example, pot; one has not thereby ascertained the forward pervasion.

To ascertain the forward pervasion, one must ascertain the pervasion, "whatever is a product is necessarily impermanent," in relation to product—that is, with the mind focused on product itself, not on any example.

In the course of establishing the forward pervasion and counterpervasion, one must first understand the two aspects of the relationship between product (sign) and impermanent (predicate).[a] The similar and dissimilar examples are used to facilitate understanding of those two aspects. This means that the pervasion, "whatever is a product is necessarily impermanent," is first realized *in relation to the similar example;* at that time, the example is the substratum, the focus, of the understanding. However, when the forward pervasion is realized, it is in relation not to the example but *to the sign;* at that time, the sign is the substratum. The forward pervasion and counterpervasion are established in relation to the basis of illustration of the sign.[b]

When, having taken *product*—the illustration of the sign—as basis, one realizes the relationship between product and impermanent, one has realized the forward pervasion and counterpervasion. To put it another way, when one has ascertained the two aspects of the relationship (that product is empty of permanent and that permanent is empty of product) in the context of having taken product as the illustration of the sign, then one has established the pervasions.[166] Gyel-tsap sums up the topic in this way:

The forward pervasion and counterpervasion are: having taken, as basis, an illustration of the sign, such as "product," the ascer-

---

[a] The two aspects of the relationship are that product is empty of permanent and that permanent is empty of product. (See "the third valid cognition," above.)
[b] This is the second of Gyel-tsap's three necessary valid cognitions (above).

tainment that it exists in only the similar class and the ascertainment that it is only nonexistent in the dissimilar class. These [ascertainments] must be preceded by ascertainment of the meaning-isolate of the relationship.[a]

It is apparent that in the process of developing ascertainment of the three modes there is a shift in the focal point of the mind. When the property of the subject is established, the mind is focused on the subject, and when the pervasions are established, it is focused on the sign. Ascertainment of the three modes then serves as cause of ascertainment of the thesis. When the pervasions are ascertained *in relation to the subject,* the thesis is understood.[167]

Pur-bu-jok makes it clear that the proof statements that accompany a given syllogism, such as "The subject, sound, is impermanent because of being a product," express not only the relationship between the sign and the predicate of the probandum, but also the full three modes. He writes,

> In general, a correct proof statement must indicate the three modes as well as an example, without anything extra or anything missing. To give a mere illustration of this, having stated, "The subject, sound, is impermanent because of being a product," one states, "Whatever is a product is necessarily impermanent, as is the case with pot; sound also is a product." [In that statement, the words] "whatever is a product is necessarily impermanent," explicitly express the forward pervasion and implicitly imply the counterpervasion. [The words] "sound also is a product" explicitly express the property of the subject [that is, position] in the sense of subject. [The words] "as is the case with pot" explicitly express a similar example.
>
> With respect to explicitly expressing the property of the subject and the counterpervasion and implicitly indicating the forward pervasion, [there is, for instance,] the statement, "Whatever is permanent is necessarily not a product [or "is necessarily a nonproduct"], as is the case with space; sound, however, is a product."[168]

---

[a] Gyel-tsap, *Revealer of the Path of Liberation*, p. 39.15-18. The self-isolate of the relationship (*'brel ba'i rang ldog*) is: "a relationship exists between product and impermanent;" and the meaning-isolate of the relationship (*'brel ba'i don ldog*) is: "[product] is different from impermanent and by the force of the elimination of impermanent, product is eliminated." (Ge-shay Sang-gyay-sam-drup, commentary on *Revealer of the Path of Liberation*, vol. 1, May 25, 1983, p. 4.)

Thus, the phrase, "whatever is a product is necessarily impermanent," explicitly *expresses* the forward pervasion and the phrase, "whatever is permanent is necessarily not a product," explicitly *expresses* the counterpervasion in the proof of sound as impermanent. However, it is important to remember that only "product" itself *is* the forward pervasion and counterpervasion in that proof. Pur-bu-jok makes this clear when he says:

> However, the two, "whatever is a product is necessarily impermanent" and "whatever is permanent is necessarily not a product," are not the forward pervasion and the counterpervasion of the syllogism ["The subject, sound, is impermanent because of being a product"]. On the contrary, product alone is the forward pervasion and the counterpervasion, as well as the property of the subject of that [syllogism] because of being the three modes in that.[169]

"SIMULTANEOUS" REALIZATION

It is said that the forward pervasion and counterpervasion are realized simultaneously (when one is realized explicitly, the other is realized implicitly). However, this does not apply to proof statements. It does *not* mean that when one realizes the positive proof statement, "whatever is a product is necessarily impermanent," one simultaneously realizes the negative proof statement, "whatever is permanent is necessarily a nonproduct." That is not the case.[a] The pervasions expressed in the proof statements are not the same as the pervasions (the forward pervasion and counterpervasion) themselves.

The pervasions in the positive and negative proof statements are said to express explicitly the forward pervasion and the counterpervasion, respectively. As phrased in the proof statements, the two pervasions have different focal points: product in the positive (whatever is a product is necessarily impermanent), and permanent in the negative (whatever is permanent is necessarily a nonproduct). However, there is general agreement among Ge-luk-pa scholars that when the forward pervasion and counterpervasion are ascertained, they are ascertained simultaneously, and that during this ascertainment the mind is necessarily focused on the same phenomenon—product.

---

[a] Ge-shay Sang-gyay-sam-drup, commentary on *Revealer of the Path of Liberation*, vol. 1, June 3, 1983, p. 3. There are variations in Ge-luk-pa explanations of this point, which are beyond the scope of this book.

Gyel-tsap points out that there is a difference between the expression of the pervasion (in the proof statement) and the realization of the pervasion:

> The mode of engagement of a prime cognition and the mode of expression are not the same.[170]

Ge-shay Sang-gyay-sam-drup puts this more plainly:

> Although the *statement* of the counterpervasion is "whatever is permanent is necessarily a nonproduct," what actually appears to the mind is "whatever is a product is necessarily not permanent."[171]

Therefore, when Ge-luk-pa scholars say that the forward pervasion and counterpervasion appear simultaneously to the mind, they are referring to the simultaneous understanding of these pervasions: "whatever is a product is necessarily impermanent" and "whatever is a product is necessarily not nonimpermanent (or not permanent)." Ge-shay Sang-gyay-sam-drup explains,

> The real forward pervasion is "product" and the real counterpervasion is "product," but this is not what is meant when one speaks of explicit and implicit realization of the pervasions. When [scholars] say the pervasions are realized [together], one explicitly and one implicitly, they refer to realization of "whatever is a product is necessarily impermanent" (*byas na mi rtag pas khyab*) and "whatever is a product is necessarily not permanent" (*byas na rtag pa ma yin pas khyab*).
>
> There are people who say the two pervasions are "whatever is a product is necessarily impermanent" and "whatever is permanent is necessarily not a product." But this is not the case, because the two pervasions must be established on the same subject [that is, the focus of the mind, the substratum—*khyad gzhi*—must be the same for each].[172]

SUMMARY

In order for the pervasions to be established in a particular proof, the sign must be in a strictly defined logical relationship with the predicate of the probandum. In the introductory logic manuals, this relationship is explained in stages: first the forward pervasion in terms of the way the sign relates to the similar class in that proof; and then the counterpervasion in terms of the way it relates to the dissimilar class.

In later studies on the topic of valid cognition, the student approaches the relationship of sign and predicate through analysis of the precise meaning of relationship: a is related to b only if a is different from b and if by the force of the elimination of b, a is also eliminated. Because product and impermanent are related in the strictly defined sense, product is existent in only the similar class (the impermanent) and is only nonexistent in the dissimilar class (the nonimpermanent). The introductory manuals describe the similar and dissimilar classes as the basis of relation of the forward pervasion and counterpervasion, respectively.

To ascertain that product exists in only the similar class in the proof of sound as impermanent requires understanding the two parts of the relationship between product and impermanent—that product is empty of permanent and that permanent is empty of product. These two aspect of the relationship are expressed by the proof statements.

The proof statements are an aid in understanding the forward pervasion and counterpervasion. The pervasions as expressed in the proof statements are ascertained first in relation to examples. That is, when one first understands that whatever is a product is impermanent (or the equivalent: product is empty of permanent), this understanding is in relation to an example, such as pot. And when one first understands that whatever is permanent is necessarily a nonproduct (or the equivalent: permanent is empty of product), this understanding is in relation to an example, such as uncompounded space. However, the pervasions that are ascertained *by means of* the proof statements (that is, the forward pervasion and counterpervasion) are ascertained in relation to the sign, product. The pervasions ascertained by means of the proof statements are "whatever is a product is necessarily impermanent" and "whatever is a product is necessarily not nonimpermanent."

The proof statements not only express the two aspects of the relationship between product and impermanent, they also express the three modes of the sign in the proof of sound as impermanent. The syllogism summarizes the three modes and the conclusion—that sound is impermanent.

When the property of the subject is ascertained, the substratum or focus of the mind is the subject, sound. When the pervasions are established, the substratum is the sign, product. When the thesis is finally realized, the substratum is once again the subject. When one ascertains the pervasions *in relation to the subject*, then one has realized the thesis. In order to do so, one must have understood the three modes of the sign. Ge-shay Kön-chok-tse-ring says of the steps in realizing the three modes:

> First, one thinks about "whatever is a product is necessarily impermanent" in relation to [the similar example] pot; and about "whatever is permanent is necessarily not a product" in relation to [the dissimilar example] uncompounded space.
>
> Then one thinks about these pervasions in relation to [the sign] product. [It has already been shown that in doing so, one ascertains "whatever is a product is necessarily impermanent" and "whatever is a product is necessarily not nonimpermanent."]
>
> Finally, when the pervasions are established in relation to [the subject] sound, the probandum is established.[173]

That is, with the mind focused on sound, one ascertains that whatever is a product is necessarily impermanent and whatever is a product is necessarily not nonimpermanent.

Each of the three modes is ascertained by inferential valid cognition. After the ascertainment of the three modes separately by valid cognition, there is generated an understanding of the three modes together. This is not a prime cognition; it is a subsequent cognition called a simultaneous recollection of the three modes. As Ge-shay Sang-gyay-sam-drup explains, it is called "simultaneous," but that does not mean all three are present in a single cognition; it means that one is able to recollect them in quick succession. From this recollection of the three modes is generated the new valid inferential cognition of the thesis, that sound is impermanent.[174]

COMPLICATIONS

WHETHER THERE CAN BE DOUBT AFTER PERVASIONS ARE ESTABLISHED

The most interesting and difficult of the complications that arise in the study of the pervasions centers on this issue: Having ascertained the pervasions in the proof of sound as impermanent, can one still be in doubt about whether sound is impermanent? Whichever way this is answered, there are problems to be confronted.

What is realized when one realizes the pervasions? First of all it must be understood clearly that, with product as the substratum of one's mind, one realizes the relationship between product and impermanent. To ascertain this relationship, one must ascertain both that product is empty of permanent and that permanent is empty of product. Having thus ascertained the relationship between product and impermanent, one can have no doubt concerning the irrefutable entailment: product eliminates the permanent.

Having ascertained that permanent is empty of product and that whatever is a product is necessarily impermanent, how can one possibly doubt whether a *particular* instance of product is impermanent? How can one be certain that product is empty of permanent if one still doubts whether a particular instance of product, sound, is permanent or not? But if there is *no* doubt, then when the pervasion is established, the probandum would also be established for the opponent—and the definition of a correct proof makes this impossible.[a]

If there is no doubt after establishing the pervasions, then the probandum must be established at the same time as the pervasions. If that is so, then product cannot be a correct sign in that proof.

If there is still doubt about whether one particular instance of product is impermanent, then how could the pervasions ever be established? A full discussion of this problem is beyond the scope of this book, but an overview of the issues may suggest what the advanced students will pursue in detail.

Tsong-kha-pa makes an interesting statement, which is used as a focal point for much of the debate on this topic:

> The thought that realizes that the son of a barren woman does not exist does not simultaneously realize that the hand of the son of a barren woman does not exist. However, it is able to eliminate superimposition (*sgro 'dogs chod nus*) [holding that hand to exist].[b]

Ge-shay Sang-gyay-sam-drup comments:

> One can interpret this to mean that although [the thought] is *able* to eliminate superimpositions, it does not do so.[175]

---

[a] As was explained earlier, a correct opponent is someone who, having ascertained the three modes, is *ready* to ascertain the thesis. Ascertainment of the thesis must follow ascertainment of the three modes and cannot be simultaneous with ascertainment of any of the three modes. If understanding of the pervasion brought automatic understanding of the thesis, that would not be a valid reasoning. For example, "sound is impermanent because of being an object of hearing" is considered to be invalid, because there is no possibility of ascertaining the impermanence of object of hearing without simultaneously understanding the impermanence of sound.

[b] This could be translated "...it is able to eliminate the mental superimposition (or attribution) of existence to that hand." Cited by Ge-shay Sang-gyay-sam-drup, commentary on *Revealer of the Path of Liberation*, vol 1, May 27, 1983, p. 4.

Ge-luk-pa scholars disagree about whether superimpositions are eliminated. In any case, eliminating attributions regarding the probandum does not mean there is necessarily realization of the probandum.

When correct opponents realize the pervasions in the proof of sound as impermanent by the sign, product, they have thoroughly eliminated all possibility of superimposing permanence on sound (of attributing permanence to sound, conceiving sound to be permanent), but they do not yet *realize* that sound is impermanent until they turn their minds to it. They have now only to turn their attention specifically to sound, and then they will ascertain the absence of permanence in relation to it as well.[176]

It should be remembered that when one ascertains the forward pervasion, one realizes "whatever is a product is necessarily impermanent"—eliminating all possibility of any instance of product being permanent. However, one does not ascertain the lack of permanence in relation to *every* product; one must turn one's mind to the individual product before the realization can be achieved.

Those who hold that there *is* elimination of superimposition [of permanence] must hold it in such a way that there still remains doubt in the mind of the opponent in regard to the probandum. According to Gyel-tsap, the establishment of the pervasions does bring ascertainment of (a) the absence of product in all instances of permanent and (b) the absence of permanent in all instances of product, but it does *not* bring refutation of the negandum or establishment of the probandum. Why not? Because the ascertainment of the absence of product in all instances of permanent and the ascertainment of the absence of permanent in all instances of product are in relation to *product*, not in relation to *sound*. Gyel-tsap writes,

> The valid cognition ascertaining the forward pervasion establishes the emptiness of the permanence of sound on the basis, product, but does not eliminate [the superimposition of] permanence within having taken sound as the basis.[a]

---

[a]   *Revealer of the Path of Liberation*, pp. 41.19-42.1. In this text, Gyel-tsap asserts the view that the superimpositions are eliminated. On page 40.16-18 he writes:

> ...then, this valid cognition [ascertaining that whatever is arisen from exertion is necessarily impermanent, as part of ascertaining the forward pervasion in the proof of sound arisen from exertion as impermanent by the sign, arisen from exertion] must eliminate superimpositions of permanence also with respect to the sound arisen from exertion. [It follows that] the valid cognition ascertaining the forward pervasion [whatever is arisen from exertion

Although ascertainment of the forward pervasion brings ascertainment of sound as empty of permanence, this ascertainment is only on the basis of product and not on the basis of sound. And thus the probandum is not ascertained.

Ge-luk-pa scholars might accept the following way to bypass terminological disputes about whether the superimpositions are eliminated regarding the probandum. When one ascertains the pervasion, one eliminates all possibility of attributing permanence to sound, but one does not actually ascertain that sound is impermanent. Now one must turn one's mind to sound and (holding it as the substratum) apply the realization that whatever is a product is necessarily impermanent and is necessarily not nonimpermanent. When those pervasions are ascertained in relation to sound (as the focus), then one has realized the thesis.

According to this concept, realizing the pervasions does not entail realization of the thesis. The two realizations must be achieved in separate steps if the reasoning is to be valid—is actually to bring inferential valid cognition of the thesis.

Through establishing the three modes, one eliminates all possibility of conceiving sound to be permanent; but one does not explicitly eliminate the conception of sound as permanent. The realization that sound is impermanent is made virtually inevitable, but it is not simultaneous. Ge-shay Sang-gyay-sam-drup comments:

> When you have valid cognition realizing the pervasion, what is still missing; why do you not already and simultaneously realize the thesis; what more do you need to do? The mind is not turned toward the subject; is not directed toward the subject; thus there is not yet realization of that pervasion *in relation to the subject.*[177]

Coping with this particular complication shows something about the Ge-luk-pa view of how the mind works. It clarifies one's understanding of the basis—the substratum or focus of the mind. The change of focus may be so quick as to appear instantaneous; but some Ge-luk-pa scholars assert that it is not instantaneous; that is, realization of the thesis is not simultaneous with realization of the three modes.[a]

---

is necessarily impermanent] would eliminate superimpositions [that is, attributions of permanence] in regard to the probandum. If someone says this, I am in full agreement.

[a] Laṭi Rin-po-che points out that in the case of someone newly establishing impermanence, there are differences of opinion concerning whether realization of the thesis is

Beginners in the study of logic, those studying the topic of *Signs and Reasonings,* do not confront this complication in any detail; it depends on material not generally covered in the study of Pur-bu-jok's text. These students are laying the foundation for dealing with the subtleties of this problem later.

IMPERMANENT AND SIMILAR CLASS ARE MUTUALLY PERVASIVE, BUT...

Pur-bu-jok specifies that, in the proof of sound as impermanent, the similar class and the impermanent are mutually pervasive. Whatever is the similar class is necessarily impermanent, and whatever is impermanent is necessarily the similar class. Two complications arise in this regard.

1. Some debaters may express the view that the similar class in this proof cannot contain *all* impermanent phenomena, because it cannot contain the two specific phenomena that have been placed as the subject (sound) and the sign (product) in that proof.

If such an opponent says, "It follows that the subject, sound, is not a member of the similar class in the proof of sound as impermanent because it is the basis of debate in that proof," the response is, "Although the reason (in that syllogistic statement) is true, it does not entail that sound is not a member of the similar class in that proof."[a]

Similarly, if an opponent says, "It follows that the subject, product, is not a member of the similar class in the proof of sound as impermanent because it is the sign in that proof," the response is, "Although the reason is true, it does not entail that sound is not a member of the similar class in that proof."[b]

---

simultaneous with realization of the three modes (commentary on *Signs and Reasonings,* vol. 1, p. 15). This issue is beyond the scope of this book.

[a] Lati Rin-po-che explains that, in the proof of sound as impermanent, there are three possibilities between being the basis of debate and being a member of the similar class:

(1) it is possible to be both (for example, sound);
(2) whatever is held as the basis of debate in that proof is necessarily a member of the similar class, but whatever is a member of the similar class is not necessarily held as the basis of debate (for example, pot);
(3) it is possible to be neither (for example, the permanent). (Commentary on *Signs and Reasonings,* vol. 2, Feb. 2, 1977, p. 3.)

[b] In the proof of sound as impermanent, there are four possibilities between being a correct sign and being a member of the similar class. It is possible to be:

(1) both (for example, product);
(2) a member of the similar class but not a correct sign in that proof (for example, sound);

2. Pur-bu-jok's statement that similar class and the impermanent are mutually pervasive gives rise to another complication. A challenger might say, "It follows that the subject, not being permanent, is impermanent."

Defender: Why?
C: Because of being the similar class in the proof of sound as impermanent.
D: The reason is not established.
C: It follows that "not being permanent" is the dissimilar class.
D: I accept.

Ge-shay Pel-den-drak-pa comments,

· "Not being permanent" is itself permanent. From that point of view, it is the dissimilar class. "Not being *impermanent*" is also the dissimilar class.[178]

The same reasoning applies to such phenomena as "opposite from nonimpermanent" and "isolate of impermanent." Although these point to the impermanent, they are themselves permanent and therefore are the dissimilar class in the proof of sound as impermanent.

The referent of all these phenomena is the impermanent, in that only the impermanent is opposite from nonimpermanent and is the isolate of impermanent. However, opposite from nonimpermanent and isolate of impermanent are themselves permanent and therefore are not the similar class in that proof.

BEING THE SIMILAR CLASS VS. EXISTING IN THE SIMILAR CLASS

What are the possibilities between *being* the similar class and *existing* in the similar class in the proof of sound as impermanent—in other words, between being impermanent and existing in the impermanent?[a] Two complications arise when this question is asked.

---

(3)   a correct sign but not a member of the similar class (particularity of product);
(4)   neither (uncompounded space). (Lati Rin-po-che, commentary on *Signs and Reasonings*, vol. 2, Feb. 2, 1977, pp. 3-4.)
[a]   Pur-bu-jok explains that existing in the similar class means existing in the impermanent—"impermanent" here referring specifically to the self-isolate of impermanent, that is, impermanent itself. In other words, existing in impermanent does not mean existing in all instances of impermanent—it just means existing in "impermanent." See chapter two, in his discussion of the third question under "the meaning of similar and dissimilar class."

1. It has been established that whatever is impermanent is necessarily the similar class, but does it necessarily exist in the similar class? Debate on this subject might run:

C: If something is impermanent, does it necessarily exist in impermanent?

D: Yes.

C: The three spheres (*'khor gsum*)![a] It follows that the subject, cause of impermanent, exists in impermanent.

D: Why?

C: Because of being impermanent.

D: I accept.

C: It follows that the cause of smoke exists with smoke.

D: Why?

C: It follows that the cause of smoke does not exist with smoke.

D: I accept.

C: Explain why.

D: Because of preceding smoke.

C: Then, [applying the same reasoning to the earlier issue,] it follows that the cause of impermanent does not exist with impermanent because of preceding impermanent.

The challenger is arguing that these are parallel situations. Ge-shay Lob-sang-gya-tso comments,

> Why is it that the cause of smoke does not exist with smoke? If you say because it must precede smoke, or because at the time of smoke it does not exist, then it must follow that the cause of impermanent does not exist with impermanent for the same reasons—because it precedes impermanent and because at the time of impermanent, it does not exist.[179]

It is generally held by Ge-luk-pa scholars that the cause of something (x) must precede x. They do not occur together, and thus there cannot be a common locus of x and its cause. Therefore it cannot be said that the cause of impermanent exists with impermanent.[b] This is problematic, however: isn't cause of impermanent itself impermanent?[c] If so,

---

[a]   This comment is explained in the third of the debates that conclude chapter eight.

[b]   Ge-shay Pel-den-drak-pa explains the meaning of the phrase "exists with" in this way: "Object of comprehension exists with sound. What does this mean? It means that there is a common locus of object of comprehension and sound." (Commentary on *Signs and Reasonings*, vol. 2, p. 9.)

[c]   Reminder: Causes are impermanent; cause, effect, impermanent, thing—these are

then there does occur a common locus of impermanent and cause of impermanent. But if cause of impermanent must precede impermanent, how could such a common locus occur?

2. Is whatever exists in impermanent necessarily impermanent? There are a number of phenomena that, although permanent, exist in the impermanent—such as object of knowledge, isolate of pot, and particularity of product.[180] A complication arises:

C: It follows that particularity of product exists in (or with) impermanent.
D: I accept.
C: It follows that in impermanent, permanent exists.
D: Why?
C: Because particularity of product is permanent and exists in impermanent.
D: There is no pervasion.

Although particularity of product is permanent and exists in impermanent, this does not entail that permanent exists in impermanent. Geshay Lob-sang-gya-tso explains,

> The challenger has argued that in impermanent, permanent exists (*mi rtag pa la rtag pa yod*), because particularity of product is permanent and exists in impermanent. But this is like arguing that in object of knowledge, tail exists [which could also be translated as "object of knowledge has a tail"] because tail is an object of knowledge and exists in object of knowledge. There is no pervasion.[181]

The order of the words is significant here. It is true that tail is an object of knowledge and that tail exists in object of knowledge, but it does not follow that in object of knowledge, tail exists. Tail, pot, pillar, etc., are said to exist in object of knowledge, but in object of knowledge, none of these exists. Ge-shay Lob-sang-gya-tso says,

> Pot exists in object of knowledge (*bum pa shes bya la yod*), but in object of knowledge, pot does not exist (*shes bya la bum pa med*).[182]

---

equivalent.

COMPLICATIONS HINGING ON THE WORD "ONLY (JUST)"

Product is a correct sign in the proof of sound as impermanent; therefore product exists in *only* the similar class (the impermanent) and is *just* nonexistent in the dissimilar class (the nonimpermanent). A complication arises:

> C: It follows that product is just nonexistent in the dissimilar class [in the proof of sound as impermanent].
>
> D: I accept.
>
> C: It follows that product must be nonexistent in all [three types of] the dissimilar class.
>
> D: I accept.
>
> C: It follows that product does not exist in the dissimilar class that is other [than impermanent—the predicate of the probandum].
>
> D: I accept.
>
> C: It follows that product does not exist in object of knowledge.
>
> D: Why?
>
> C: Because of not existing in the dissimilar class that is other.

Here the challenger is trying to talk the defender into equating "not existing in the dissimilar class that is other" with "not existing in *an instance of* the dissimilar class that is other." However, product does exist in particularity of product, in object of knowledge, and in many other phenomena that are themselves permanent.

Pur-bu-jok explains that "impermanent" in "exists in the impermanent" refers to the self-isolate of impermanent and not to the instances of impermanent.[a] It is apparent that, in a similar way, "nonimpermanent" in "not existent in nonimpermanent" refers to the self-isolate of nonimpermanent and not to the instances of nonimpermanent. Product does not exist in "nonimpermanent"; but product is not necessarily nonexistent in any given instance of nonimpermanent. Product is nonexistent in some instances of the nonimpermanent—uncompounded space, horn of a rabbit, etc. But product is existent in others—object of knowledge, particularity of product, self-isolate of product, etc.

Object of knowledge, particularity of product, and isolate of product are themselves permanent and thus the dissimilar class in the proof of sound as impermanent. Although each of these is the dissimilar class, and product exists in each of them, product does *not* exist in the

---

[a] Pur-bu-jok's discussion of this point is in chapter two, in his third question under "the meaning of similar and dissimilar class."

dissimilar class.

THE DISSIMILAR CLASS THAT IS NONEXISTENT—DOES IT EXIST?

Also debated is whether the dissimilar class that is a nonexistent exists or not. A debater might say that if it does not exist, then there is no way to realize it (that is, it is unrealizable in a given proof); but it is realizable, because an instance can be posited— "horn of a rabbit." Or one might say that dissimilar class that is nonexistent does exist, because horn of a rabbit is such a class and is realizable. Then it follows that a nonexistent exists, because horn of a rabbit is a nonexistent and is realizable.

The same kinds of problem arise if one debates whether nonexistents exist or not. According to Ge-shay Pel-den-drak-pa, both points of view present problems.[a] One might argue that nonexistent exists because horn of a rabbit is nonexistent and is realizable. Some hold that the dissimilar class that is a nonexistent is not realizable, some that it is. The latter assert that one can take an instance to mind: one can realize "horn of a rabbit" as an instance of dissimilar class that is a nonexistent. They agree that one is not realizing horn of a rabbit—how can one realize a nonexistent when the definition of existent is "that realized by valid cognition"? If something is realizable by valid cognition, then it must exist. If something is not realizable by valid cognition, then it must not exist. All agree that the horn of a rabbit does not exist, but does an instance of dissimilar class that is a nonexistent exist?

---

[a] This discussion is based on the explanation of Ge-shay Pel-den-drak-pa, commentary on *Signs and Reasonings*, vol. 1, pp. 11-12.

4. The Main Division of Correct Signs

A thorough analysis of correct signs involves approaching them from a number of perspectives, reflected in six ways of dividing correct signs. Pur-bu-jok writes,

> The divisions of correct signs are of six types: divisions by way of (1) the entity, (2) the predicate of the probandum, (3) the mode of proof, (4) the probandum, (5) the mode of relating to the similar class, and (6) the opponent.[183]

DIVISION BY WAY OF THE ENTITY

The first of these is considered to be the main division; its discussion here occupies chapters four through seven. Chapter eight discusses the other five ways of examining correct signs. From the point of view of the first division, by way of entity (*ngo bo*), analysis centers on the relationship between the predicate of the probandum and the sign. Depending on their relationship, they are either one entity (*ngo bo gcig*) or separate entities (*ngo bo tha dad*).[a]

In a particular proof, a sign is considered to be a correct sign (and thus effective in generating ascertainment of the thesis in the mind of a correct opponent) only if it is related with the predicate of the probandum in accordance with the following definition:

> Something (a) is related with another thing (b) because a is different from b and because by force of the elimination of b, a is also eliminated.

Ge-luk-pa students learn from their study of the *Collected Topics* that such a relationship can be of two types: relationship of provenance (*de byung 'brel, tadutpatti-saṃbandha*) and relationship of sameness of nature (*bdag gcig 'brel; tadātmya-saṃbandha*). Thus, the sign in a correct proof must be related to the predicate of the probandum in a

---

[a] This is not the only criterion for this main division of correct signs; as will be explained, this is combined with another criterion—whether the predicate is a positive or a negative phenomenon—to arrive at the division into effect, nature, and nonobservation signs. Ge-shay Pel-den-drak-pa expresses qualms about calling this a division "from the point of view of entity"; he says, "A division from the point of view of the entity of the sign really only yields two types, correct effect and nature signs, depending on whether the entity of the sign is the effect of or the same nature as the entity of the predicate of the probandum." (*Commentary on Signs and Reasonings, vol. 1, p. 10.*)

relationship of either provenance or sameness of nature; no other relationship can exist between the sign and the predicate. In the first case, the sign is the effect of the predicate (and thus a separate entity), and in the second, the sign is the same nature (or entity) as the predicate.

In the system of Sautrāntika Following Reasoning, an effect is related with its cause by the relationship of provenance, but the reverse is not true: a cause is not said to be related with an effect. A cause can be inferred from its effect, because the effect must have arisen from a cause; but effects cannot in general be inferred from causes, because a cause may be blocked and prevented from producing its effect.

As for sameness of nature, a phenomenon such as an oak is related with tree in that relationship, but tree is not said to be related with oak. If tree is eliminated, then oak is necessarily also eliminated; but eliminating oak does not necessarily eliminate tree, for there are many trees other than oak trees.

If the pervasions are established in a particular proof, the sign and predicate must be in one of these two relationships. If signs were divided just on the basis of the type of relationship between the predicate and the sign, there would be only two types. But this is not the only criterion for the main division of correct signs; the other consideration is whether the predicate of the probandum is a positive or a negative phenomenon.[a]

EFFECT, NATURE, AND NONOBSERVATION SIGNS

The main division of correct signs combines these two criteria (the type of sign-predicate relationship and whether the predicate is a positive or negative phenomenon) to provide correct signs of three types: effect signs, nature signs, and nonobservation signs.[184] Correct effect and nature signs are correct signs in syllogisms in which the predicate of the probandum is a positive phenomenon. Lati Rin-po-che says,

> The first two types, correct effect signs and correct nature signs, are called "correct signs of a positive phenomenon (*sgrub rtags yang dag*)" because the predicate of the probandum is a positive phenomenon, in the sense that the explicit predicate of the probandum is a positive phenomenon.[b]

---

[a]   The predicate of the probandum is necessarily an existent, because only an existent can be known by valid cognition; and existents may be divided into positive and negative phenomena.

[b]   Commentary on *Signs and Reasonings*, vol. 1, p. 49. There is a disagreement among Geluk-pa scholars concerning whether the predicate of the probandum must be a positive

Nonobservation signs are correct signs in syllogisms in which the predicate of the probandum is a negative phenomenon. He continues,

> Correct nonobservation signs are called "correct signs of a negative phenomenon" because that which is held as the explicit predicate of the probandum is a negative phenomenon.[185]

The threefold division of correct signs does not originate with the Ge-luk-pa. This division of correct signs is also made by the eleventh-century Indian Buddhist logician Mokṣākaragupta.[a] Like the Ge-luk-pa scholars, he attributes the threefold division to Dharmakīrti, who wrote,

> Among [the three kinds of logical marks] the two [the identical and causal marks] are for establishing the existence of real entities, the other one [the mark of noncognition] is the probans for negation.[b]

There is apparent agreement among Ge-luk-pa scholars that correct effect and correct nature signs are signs of a positive phenomenon, and correct nonobservation signs are signs of a negative phenomenon. However, there is a disagreement: in the case of a proof involving a correct sign of a positive phenomenon, does the predicate of the probandum need to be a positive phenomenon? They agree that in such a proof, a positive phenomenon is being proved, but does it follow that the predicate must itself be a positive phenomenon? As Ge-shay Pel-den-drak-pa puts it,

> As to whether the predicate of the probandum itself has to be a positive phenomenon, there are two opinions [among the Ge-luk-pa]. One is that [whatever is] a correct effect sign or a correct nature sign must have a positive phenomenon as predicate of the probandum and the other is that it need not.[186]

According to Jam-yang-shay-pa, the textbook author of Go-mang

---

phenomenon; this is discussed below. The topic of signs of positive phenomena is discussed in chapter eight.

[a] Mokṣākaragupta writes, "Those [logical marks] which have three characteristics...are of three kinds. (1) The mark as the effect (*kārya*) [of *s*—the predicate] has the threefold character; (2) the mark identical in essence (*svabhāva*) [with *s*] has the threefold character; (3) the mark as the non-cognition (*anupalabdhi*) [of *s*] has the threefold character." Kajiyama, *Introduction to Buddhist Philosophy,* page 72.

[b] Ibid., p. 80. "Logical mark" is Kajiyama's translation for *rtags,* "sign," and "identical and causal marks" are the nature and effect signs. The Sanskrit for this passage is: *atra dvau vastusādhanau, ekaḥ pratiṣedhahetuḥ.*

College of Dre-pung Monastic University, a syllogism proving a positive phenomenon (whether it involves a correct effect sign or correct nature sign) need not have as its predicate a positive phenomenon. Ge-shay Pel-den-drak-pa goes on,

> In Jam-yang-shay-pa's opinion, the predicate of the probandum need not be a positive phenomenon; it is sufficient that the sign be proving [or establishing] a positive phenomenon.[187]

According to Jam-yang-shay-pa, the predicate of the probandum may be either a positive phenomenon or an affirming negative phenomenon.[a] This view is not shared by other Ge-luk-pa scholars, however. As Ge-shay Pel-den-drak-pa says, "most scholars hold that if [a proof involves] a correct sign of a positive phenomenon, the predicate of the probandum must itself be a positive phenomenon."[188]

In short, there is apparent agreement, among Ge-luk-pa scholars, that a correct sign must be proving either a positive or a negative phenomenon. If it is proving a positive phenomenon, the relationship between sign and predicate is that of either provenance or sameness of nature. If it is a relationship of provenance, the sign is a correct effect sign; if it is a relationship of sameness of nature, the sign is a correct nature sign. If, on the other hand, the correct sign is proving a negative phenomenon, it is a correct nonobservation sign, whatever the relationship (provenance or sameness) between sign and predicate.

Pur-bu-jok points out that the three main types of signs (effect, nature, and nonobservation signs) are contradictory in relation to a specific proof but are not contradictory in general. This means that whatever is, for example, a correct effect sign in a specific proof is necessarily not a nature sign or a nonobservation sign in that proof. However, something that is a correct effect sign in one proof may be a nature sign or a nonobservation sign in *other* proofs. Pur-bu-jok writes,

> In terms of one basis the three signs are contradictory, but in terms of different established bases they are not contradictory. This is because, for instance, created phenomenon is a correct

---

[a] An affirming negative phenomenon (*ma yin dgag, paryudāsapratiṣedha*) is a negative phenomenon that, through the terms expressing it, implies a positive phenomenon in the place of what is being eliminated. A frequently cited example is "mountainless plain" (*shing med pa'i thang*). According to Ge-shay Pel-den-drak-pa, one advantage to the Go-mang system (that is, that of Jam-yang-shay-pa) is that "it enables inclusion as a correct sign of a positive phenomenon the sign in the proof of opposite from nonfire (*me ma yin pa las log pa*), because it proves fire (a positive phenomenon)." Ge-shay Pel-den-drak-pa, commentary on *Signs and Reasonings*, vol. 2, p. 20.

effect sign in the proof of sprout as arisen from causes and conditions, but is a correct nature sign in the proof of sprout as impermanent and is a correct nature sign in the proof of sprout as without a self of person.[189]

In other words, "created phenomenon" is:

(1) a correct effect sign in the syllogism, "The subject, a sprout, is arisen from causes and conditions because of being a created phenomenon,"
(2) a correct nature sign in the syllogism, "The subject, a sprout, is impermanent because of being a created phenomenon," and
(3) a correct nonobservation sign in the syllogism, "The subject, a sprout, is without a self of person because of being a created phenomenon."

THE REASON FOR STUDYING THESE SIGNS

Correct effect, nature, and nonobservation signs have been set forth, according to the Ge-luk-pa tradition, as a guide toward understanding the four noble truths: the truth of suffering, the truth of the origin of suffering, the truth of the cessation of suffering, and the truth of the paths leading to the cessation of suffering. The tradition further explains how each type of sign contributes to this understanding. From this point of view, it is said that correct effect signs were set forth as a means of understanding the relationship (1) between the suffering of cyclic existence and the cause of suffering (ignorance), and (2) between the cessation of suffering and the causes of that cessation (true paths). In Lati Rin-po-che's words,

> The correct effect signs are set forth as a means of understanding the cause-and-effect relationship between the origin of suffering and true suffering. And, just as there is a cause-and-effect process with respect to entering into cyclic existence, so there is with respect to getting out of cyclic existence—that is, with respect to the latter two truths, those of path and cessation.[190]

To understand the four noble truths it is essential, according to Ge-luk-pa scholars, to understand the nature of cause and effect. Suffering arises as a result of its cause (ignorance) and is eliminated through elimination of that cause. As Lati Rin-po-che explains,

> We want happiness and don't want suffering; the cause of suffering is the afflictions, and thus we must give up the afflictions; the root of the afflictions is ignorance. If we can't destroy ignorance, we can't destroy the afflictions; if we can't destroy those, we can't sever the continuum of suffering. Therefore we have to destroy ignorance.[191]

Ignorance is eliminated through the cultivation of true paths. True paths are paths that cultivate wisdom and compassion; through wisdom and compassion, the causes of suffering—ignorance and its predispositions—are eliminated and suffering is ended.

EFFECT SIGNS

The Ge-luk-pa school emphasizes the understanding of cause and effect (and thus knowing that effects arise from causes and that whatever is produced has its own cause) because it helps one understand how to behave by helping one understand the principles of ethics and of spiritual practice in general. Put another way, understanding the cause-and-effect nature of action helps one understand the necessity of engaging in certain practices and avoiding others, for the sake of spiritual development.

In syllogisms that involve correct effect signs, an effect is stated as the sign, and the cause of that effect is stated as the predicate of the probandum. An example is: "With respect to the subject, on a smoky pass, fire exists because smoke exists." Roughly speaking, the forward pervasion (wherever smoke exists, fire necessarily exists) and the counterpervasion (wherever fire does not exist, smoke necessarily does not exist) are established because of the causal relationship between the predicate of the probandum (fire) and the sign (smoke).[a] The pervasions

---

[a] This is "roughly speaking" because these are not, strictly speaking, the pervasions. Strictly speaking, the forward pervasion is just "smoke" and the counterpervasion is just "smoke." The pervasions as phrases ("wherever smoke exists, fire necessarily exists" and "wherever fire does not exist, smoke necessarily does not exist") are the pervasions contained in the proof statements that facilitate understanding of the forward pervasion and counterpervasion. As explained in chapters two and three, there are two types of proof statements, positive (using a qualitative similarity between the subject and the example) and negative (using a qualitative dissimilarity).

A positive proof statement corresponding to the syllogism, "With respect to the subject, on a smoky pass, fire exists because smoke exists," is: "Wherever smoke exists, fire necessarily exists, as is the case with a kitchen; smoke also exists on a smoky pass."

A negative proof statement is: "Wherever fire does not exist, smoke necessarily does not exist, as is the case with a river; smoke, however, exists on a smoky pass." "Smoky

cannot be realized until one has realized the cause-and-effect relationship between fire and smoke.

NATURE SIGNS

As for correct nature signs, they were set forth as a means of understanding that all things are impermanent by nature: "Correct nature signs are set forth for the sake of realizing that true sufferings are impermanent and miserable."[192] Coarse impermanence, as illustrated by the shattering of a pot, is obvious and confirmed by direct perception. Subtle impermanence—the disintegration of things moment by moment—is a slightly hidden phenomenon (*cung zad lkog gyur; *kimcidparokṣa*) and does not immediately appear to direct perception. However, through reasoning one can generate an inferential consciousness capable of explicit realization of even this subtle impermanence.

In syllogisms involving correct nature signs, the predicate of the probandum must be of the same nature as the sign. An example is: "The subject, sound, is impermanent because of being a product." Roughly speaking, one can realize the forward pervasion (whatever is a product is necessarily impermanent) and the counterpervasion (whatever is permanent is necessarily not a product) only after having ascertained that the predicate of the probandum (impermanent) and the sign (product) share the same nature.[a]

NONOBSERVATION SIGNS

As for correct nonobservation signs, they were set forth for the sake of realizing that all things are selfless (*bdag med*). This means, according to the Consequence School (Prāsaṅgika-Madhyamaka), that they are empty of inherent existence (*rang bzhin kyis stong pa*). As Lati Rin-po-che says, "The correct nonobservation signs are set forth for the sake of

---

pass" and "river" are qualitatively dissimilar in relation to the existence of fire because fire exists on a smoky pass but not in a river.

Pur-bu-jok posits these proof statements in *Signs and Reasonings*, pp. 22b.3-4.

[a] A positive proof statement corresponding to this syllogism (that is, "The subject, sound, is impermanent because of being a product") is: "Whatever is a product is necessarily impermanent, as is the case with pot; sound also is a product." A negative proof statement is: "Whatever is permanent is necessarily not a product, as is the case with uncompounded space; sound, however, is a product." Sound and uncompounded space are qualitatively dissimilar in relation to impermanence because sound is impermanent but uncompounded space is not. Pur-bu-jok posits these proof statements in *Signs and Reasonings*, p. 22b.5-6.

realizing that true sufferings are empty and selfless."[193] In all proofs involving nonobservation signs, the predicate of the probandum must be a negative phenomenon. An example is, "The subject, the self of persons, is empty of inherent existence because of being a dependent-arising."[a]

CORRECT EFFECT SIGNS

On the topic of correct effect signs, Pur-bu-jok writes that the explanation has four parts: (1) definitions, (2) divisions, (3) explanation of the valid cognition that ascertains the definition in terms of an illustration, and (4) identification of the sign, the predicate of the probandum, and the basis of debate.[b]

DEFINITIONS

Pur-bu-jok provides four definitions of correct effect sign. The first is the most complete. The second, for use in debate, is extremely short, more an abbreviation or code phrase than a definition; the third is a slight expansion of the second. The fourth has some differences from the first that make it less correct technically but, in Pur-bu-jok's view, easier to understand. He begins:

1. The definition of something's being a correct effect sign in the proof of that[c] is:

    (1) It is a correct sign of a positive phenomenon and (2) there exists a common locus of (a) being that which is held as the explicit predicate of the probandum in the proof of that by the sign of it and (b) being its [the sign's] cause.[194]

---

[a] Another example is: "With respect to the subject, on a craggy cliff where trees are not observed, a juniper does not exist because trees do not exist." The corresponding positive proof statement is: "Wherever trees do not exist a juniper necessarily does not exist, as is the case with a treeless plain; on a craggy cliff where trees are not observed, trees also do not exist." The negative proof statement is: "Wherever a juniper exists, tree necessarily exists, as is the case with a forest; on a craggy cliff where trees are not observed, however, tree does not exist." Pur-bu-jok posits these proof statements in *Signs and Reasonings*, pp. 22b.6-23a.1.

[b] Ibid., p. 7a.6. It should be noted that in his treatment of this fourth topic, Pur-bu-jok touches on only the sign and the predicate of the probandum, not on the basis of debate.

[c] "In the proof of that" (*de sgrub*) means in any given proof.

According to Pur-bu-jok, in any given proof, there may be more than one explicit predicate of the probandum.[a] Since the definition requires a common locus of being the explicit predicate and being the sign's cause, at least one of the explicit predicates must be a cause of that which is set as the sign. For instance, in the syllogism, "With respect to the subject, on a smoky pass, fire exists because smoke exists," both "fire" (*me*) and "fire exists" (*me yod*) are explicit predicates. Fire is both the explicit predicate in that proof and a cause of the sign, smoke. Therefore, "fire" (not "fire exists") is sometimes called the "main object held as the predicate of the probandum (*bsgrub bya' chos su bzung bya'i gtso bo*)."[b] Of the other three definitions, Pur-bu-jok writes:

2. When debating, the definition of correct effect sign is:

    That which is the three effect modes.

Correct effect sign and compounded phenomenon (*'dus byas*) are equivalent (*don gcig*).

3. The definition of correct effect sign in the proof of something is:

    That which is the three effect modes in the proof of that.

4. From the point of view of understanding, the definition of its being a correct effect sign in the proof of something is:

    (1) It is a correct sign in the proof of that and (2) there exists a common locus of (a) being the main object held as the explicit predicate of the probandum in the proof of that by the sign of it and (b) being its cause.[195]

Pur-bu-jok's chief criteria for a correct effect sign are (1) that it must be a sign of a positive phenomenon and (2) that it must be in a relation of provenance with the predicate. This means the predicate must be the cause of the sign; or, to be more precise, that which is held as the predicate of the probandum must be a cause of that which is set as the sign. The "main object held as the predicate of the probandum" is "fire," which, of course, is the cause of "smoke," the sign. The fourth

---

[a] Pur-bu-jok's presentation of explicit and implicit predicates is explained in chapter one, in the section on the predicate of the probandum.

[b] Pur-bu-jok also posits "observation by valid cognition of fire" as an explicit predicate, but not all Ge-luk-pas agree.

definition is considered easier to understand because it is more specific, substituting "the *main* object held (*bzung bya'i gtso bo*)" for the phrase "that which is held (*bzung bya*)" in the first definition. Ge-shay Pel-den-drak-pa comments,

> For the sake of understanding, this definition is given, specifying that the cause is the main object held as the explicit predicate of the probandum. For example, "fire" (instead of "the existence of fire") is considered the *main* predicate of the probandum.[196]

Another way to express the second criterion is to say that the predicate of the probandum pervades the sign, while also being of a different substantial entity from that sign. The First Dalai Lama gives this definition of something's being a correct effect sign in the proof of that (that is, in a particular proof):

> (1) It is a correct sign of a positive phenomenon in the proof of that and (2) whatever is the explicit predicate of the probandum in the proof of that is necessarily the pervader that is of a different substantial entity from it.[197]

A sign is considered to be a correct sign only if there is irrefutable entailment between the sign and the predicate of the probandum. One way of expressing this requirement is to say that the predicate of the probandum must pervade the sign. Furthermore, as has been noted, the sign and the predicate must be in a relationship either of provenance or of sameness of nature.

Another way Ge-luk-pa scholars express the requirement of entailment is to say that the predicate of the probandum and the sign are either the same substantial entity or different substantial entities. A correct sign necessarily entails the predicate; therefore, the predicate pervades the sign. The sign is necessarily related with the predicate; therefore, it is either the effect of the predicate or of the same nature as the predicate. If it is the effect of the predicate, then the predicate and the sign are necessarily of different substantial entities because they are not simultaneous. If the sign is of the same nature as the predicate, then the predicate and the sign are said to be of the same substantial entity.

DIVISIONS: THE FIVE TYPES OF EFFECT SIGNS

After the definitions, Pur-bu-jok discusses the division of correct effect signs into five types,[a] correct effect signs that:

(1) prove an actual cause (*dngos rgyu; sākṣat-kāraṇa*),
(2) prove a preceding cause (*rgyu sngon song; *samanantara-hetu*),
(3) prove a general cause (*rgyu spyi; *sāmānya-hetu*),[b]
(4) prove a particular cause (*rgyu khyad par; asādhāraṇa-kāraṇa*), and
(5) provide a means of inferring causal attributes (*rgyu chos rjes dpog*).[198]

This fivefold division shows the variety of phenomena that may be inferred through the presence of an effect.

One of the subjects in the elementary *Collected Topics* is an introduction to the nature of cause and effect. At that time, students learn that any created thing is necessarily a cause and is necessarily an effect: thing, impermanent, cause, and effect are equivalent (*don gcig*) and mutually inclusive (*yin khyab mnyam*) in this context. These concepts they later apply to the study of logic. The division of correct effect signs indicates the inferences that can be drawn from the presence of an effect (the sign). From the effect one can infer:

that it necessarily has a cause (the third type),
that it necessarily has its own actual cause (the first type),
that it necessarily has its own preceding cause (the second type), and
that it necessarily has its full, complete cause; that is, that all the causes
     must be present (the fourth type);
finally, one can infer causal attributes (the fifth type).

1. Correct Effect Sign Proving an Actual Cause

As an illustration of this first type of correct effect sign, Pur-bu-jok posits "smoke" in the syllogism, "With respect to the subject, on a smoky pass, fire exists because smoke exists." He writes,

> One can state, "With respect to the subject, on a smoky pass, fire exists because smoke exists." In that, "smoke" is a correct effect sign proving an actual (or direct) cause in the proof of fire as existing on a smoky pass.[199]

Ge-luk-pa scholars value this syllogism as introducing beginners to the need for precise thinking. From the presence of a phenomenon (smoke), one can infer the existence of its actual cause (fire). Fire is the

---

[a] Mokṣākaragupta in the eleventh century posited only three types of correct effect sign. The difference in approach is discussed below.
[b] This type is also called an effect sign proving the colt isolate (*rang ldog*) of the cause

direct or actual cause of smoke; smoke must arise from fire. Having established in debate that smoke is a correct sign in this syllogism, teachers will move on to the following argument: then it follows that smoke
is a correct sign in the proof that fire exists in the mouth of a smoker.
The students know that is not true, and can set to work on the problem:
will they try to argue that the pervasion is not established—that wherever there is smoke there is not necessarily fire? Or will they decide
that there is pervasion, but the pervasion does not mean the direct
cause must occur in exactly the same place as its effect? As Ge-shay Pel-
den-drak-pa presents the question,

> Wherever smoke exists, fire must exist; wherever smoke exists,
> the direct cause of smoke must exist; these are the things being
> proved by this first type [of correct effect sign]. Then, it follows
> that in the mouth of a person who smokes, fire must exist be-
> cause smoke exists; because there is smoke in his [or her]
> mouth, there must be fire. Do you say there is no pervasion,
> that wherever there is smoke, there is not necessarily fire ? Or
> do you say there is pervasion, but it means that any instance of
> smoke must have arisen from a direct cause, which is fire, and
> does not mean that the direct cause must have occurred in ex-
> actly the same place as the resultant smoke? This is one exam-
> ple; another example is smoke that has drifted a long way and
> can be seen in the sky far from the fire that caused it; does one
> have to accept that fire exists there in the sky because smoke
> exists there?[200]

From such discussions it can be seen that this first type of sign (proving
an actual cause) cannot be used to prove that fire exists in the mouth of
a smoker; it is not used to pinpoint the fire in any proof. It is used to
indicate generally that given the presence of smoke (on a mountain
pass, in the sky, etc.), one can infer the existence of the fire that is the
direct or actual cause of that smoke. One does not go beyond that to
infer also the presence of fire in exactly the same place as smoke. In
Lati Rin-po-che's words,

> This syllogism is proving that fire exists in general. What is
> mainly being shown is the relationship between smoke and fire;
> if smoke exists, fire exists. But if smoke exists in a specific
> place, it is not necessarily the case that fire exists in that same
> place.[201]

The treatment of the topic of correct effect signs has apparently undergone considerable change since the time of Mokṣākaragupta. The Ge-luk-pas' division of effect signs differs chiefly in that they analyze the subject from a different point of view. Mokṣākaragupta was apparently interested in showing three ways in which the causal relationship between predicate and sign is ascertained. The Ge-luk-pas agree that the causal relationship must be ascertained in order to ascertain the pervasion, but do not use the ways of ascertaining it as the criteria for their division. The Ge-luk-pa analysis focuses on differences among types or aspects of causes that can be inferred from the presence of an effect.

Mokṣākaragupta lists only three types of effect signs, positing as the first:

> When fire and the like are the object to be proved, smoke and the like are to be determined [as the effect] by means of the three kinds of cognition consisting of perception and nonperception.[202]

He does not state explicitly the syllogism under consideration, but it can be understood that fire is the predicate and that smoke is the effect and is set as the sign in the proof of fire. His statement that smoke is ascertained (as the effect of fire) "by means of the three kinds of cognition consisting of perception and nonperception (*trividhapratyakṣānupalambha*)" is explained by Kajiyama,

> Perception here means the observation of the concomitance [association] in agreement, as well as in difference, of a cause and an effect.[203]

According to Kajiyama, this means that the causal relationship of fire and smoke "can be ascertained if we observe that smoke, which has not been there, occurs when fire has appeared and that when the fire has gone, the smoke disappears as well."[204] That is, we observe that smoke occurs with fire and observe its absence in the absence of fire.

The Ge-luk-pa presentation of effect signs in the topics of *Signs And Reasonings* does not address directly *how* the causal relationship is ascertained; this is studied later in the more detailed studies of the topics of "Valid Cognition." In these later studies, more emphasis is placed on the technical requirements of relationship than is explicitly expressed here in Mokṣākaragupta's *Tarkabhāṣā*. Ge-luk-pa scholars emphasize that, in any correct proof, the pervasions must be ascertained—which one can only do by ascertaining the relationship between the sign and the predicate. However, a concomitance or association in the occurrence of two things does not necessarily relate them in a such a way as to permit pervasion. Ge-luk-pa commentary on the nature of relationship specifies that it must be *by the force* of the elimination of the one that the other is eliminated.

In summary, Mokṣākaragupta's differentiation of types of effect signs is based on the way the causal relationship is established, and the Ge-luk-pas' on the type of cause being inferred. In all five Ge-luk-pa types there must be a causal relationship between predicate and sign—this relationship must be ascertained, as the most important part of establishing the pervasion—but the way in which it is ascertained is not the basis of the divisions.

2. Correct Effect Sign Proving a Preceding Cause

As an example of a correct effect sign proving a preceding cause, Pur-bu-jok posits "smoke" in the syllogism, "The subject, the bluish rising smoke in the intermediate space, is preceded by its own former cause, fire, because of being smoke." He writes,

> One can state, "The subject, the bluish rising smoke in the in-termediate space, is preceded by its own former cause, fire, be-cause of being smoke." In that, "smoke" is a correct effect sign proving the preceding cause in the proof of the bluish rising smoke in the intermediate space as having its own former cause, fire.[205]

The first type (actual cause) of correct effect sign was presented to prove that from the existence of smoke in general, one can infer the existence of fire in general. This second type (preceding cause) is pre-sented to indicate that every instance of an impermanent phenomenon (such as smoke) must have its own specific cause (such as fire). Pur-bu-jok's example can be a model for proving that any given phenomenon must be preceded by its own specific cause. As Lati Rin-po-che puts it,

> You can apply it to other instances; you could say, "The subject, the debater, is preceded by his own causes, former actions, be-cause of being a human." Or "The subject, the crop in the east, is preceded by its own causes, seeds, because of being a crop"; you could apply it to any impermanent thing.[206]

Thus, from the existence of an effect one can infer not only the exis-tence of the cause in general but also the existence of the specific cause of that particular effect.

3. Correct Effect Sign Proving a General Cause

As an example of a correct effect sign proving a general cause, Pur-bu-jok posits "occasionally produced thing" in the syllogism, "The subject, the appropriated aggregates (*nyer len kyi phung po*), have their own causes because of being occasionally produced things." His presentation is,

> One can state, "The subject, the appropriated aggregates, have their own causes because of being occasionally produced things." In that, "occasionally produced things" is a correct effect sign proving the general cause in the proof of the appropriated aggregates as having their own causes.[207]

Something's being produced occasionally means that its arising is dependent on specific causes and cannot occur without them. As Lati Rin-po-che says,

> That something is occasionally produced means that it is produced when all of its causes and conditions aggregate and is not produced when its causes and conditions have not aggregated; and thus [its] occasional production can be set as a sign that a thing is caused.[208]

According to Ge-luk-pa scholars, the purpose of this type of effect sign is to prove that every produced thing necessarily has its own cause. Specific causes are not being indicated, but rather the general condition of possessing a cause. Ge-shay Pel-den-drak-pa notes, "This is the proof of the existence of the cause, which means the existence of the cause *in general*."[209] Thus, the emphasis is on "cause" in general rather than a specific cause. As Lati Rin-po-che explains it,

> This is not a case of proving an actual cause, a former cause, or a particular cause; it is a case of proving the self-isolate of the cause, or the isolate-generality (*spyi ldog*) of the cause, and thus is called a correct effect sign proving the self-isolate of the cause.[210]

The first type of effect sign established the relationship between an effect and its "actual" or direct cause; the second established the relationship between an effect and its own "preceding" cause; and this third type establishes the relationship between being an occasionally produced thing and having a cause, in general.

Occasionally produced There is an important distinction between "occasionally produced thing" (*res 'ga' skye ba'i dngos po*) and occasional occurrence (*res 'ga'*). Whatever is an occasionally produced thing necessarily has a cause and thus is necessarily impermanent. However, whatever occurs occasionally is not necessarily impermanent; many permanent phenomena occur only occasionally, such as the suchness (*chos nyid*) of a pot, or the isolate of pot; however, although occurring occasionally, the suchness of a pot and the isolate of pot are not themselves impermanent and thus do not possess causes. Therefore, "occasional occurrence" could not be a correct sign in the proof that the appropriated aggregates have their own causes. Ge-shay Lob-sang-gya-tso explains,

> "Occasionally produced" (*res 'ga' skye ba*) refers to occasionally produced *thing* and is thus necessarily impermanent. Whatever is occasional (*res 'ga'*) [that is, occurs occasionally] is not necessarily impermanent; but whatever is produced occasionally (*res 'ga' skye ba*) is necessarily impermanent. Pot's isolate is occasional, in that it *occurs* occasionally [that is, whenever pot itself occurs]; but it is not *produced* occasionally [and thus is not an occasionally produced thing]. Whatever is produced occasionally necessarily has its own cause.[a]

When a pot comes into existence, so does its suchness; but the suchness of the pot is not impermanent; it is not an effect, does not arise from a cause. "Permanent" thus does not mean permanent in time; being permanent has nothing to do with duration over time. Whether a phenomenon is permanent or not is determined by the way it is apprehended by valid cognition. Those phenomena that are permanent are apprehended only by conceptual thought; what appears only to conceptual thought is always a permanent phenomenon.

Comment on the first three types. The first three types of effect signs, very closely related, reflect a subtle distinction not made in such earlier

---

[a] Commentary on *Signs and Reasonings*, vol. 3, p. 7. In the Lo-sel-ling logic manual, the syllogism under consideration is the same, except for the sign, which is "because of being occasionally produced (*res 'ga' skye ba*)," instead of "because of being an occasionally produced thing (*res 'ga' skye ba'i dngos po*)." The meanings of these two signs are considered to be the same by Ge-luk-pa scholars. There is no difference between *occasionally produced* and *occasionally produced thing*. Whatever is occasionally *produced* is necessarily a product and is necessarily a thing. However, whatever is occasional (that is, occurs occasionally) is not necessarily a product. For example, the emptiness or suchness of a pot.

works as the *Tarkabhāṣā*.[a] What is being inferred is slightly different in each of these cases.

- Proving an actual cause: smoke must have an actual, direct cause; therefore from the presence or existence of smoke one can infer the existence of its direct cause, fire.
- Proving a preceding cause: any impermanent phenomenon must have its own specific cause; thus from the presence of an impermanent phenomenon one can infer the existence of its preceding cause.
- Proving a general cause: whatever is impermanent, and therefore a created phenomenon, must possess a cause; it must be caused. This type of sign is proving the self-isolate of the cause. The self-isolate of cause is cause itself; not the actual cause or the specific cause, but rather just *cause*; that is, the quality of being caused. In other words, this type of sign proves the existence of causality—proves that any effect whatsoever necessarily possesses a cause.

4. Correct Effect Sign Proving a Particular Cause

As an example of a correct effect sign proving a particular cause, Purbu-jok posits "thing which is not produced without the existence of its observed object condition" in the syllogism, "The subject, a sense consciousness perceiving blue, has its own observed object condition because of being a thing that is not produced without the existence of its observed object condition." He writes,

> One can state, "The subject, a sense consciousness perceiving blue, has its own observed object condition because of being a thing that is not produced without the existence of its observed object condition." In that, "thing that is not produced without the existence of its observed object condition" is a correct effect sign proving a particular cause in the proof of a sense-consciousness perceiving blue as having its own observed object condition.[211]

The Ge-luk-pa tradition explains that an effect depends on its full cause; *all* of the separate particular causes that are required for its production. A sense consciousness, for example, is said to require the presence of three separate causes:

---

[a] Mokṣākaragupta's first type is replaced by the Ge-luk-pa types one, two, and three, as they are analyzed from a different point of view.

- an observed object condition (*dmigs rkyen, ālambanapratyaya*),[a]
- an immediately preceding condition (*de ma thag rkyen, samanan-tarapratyaya*), and
- a dominant or empowering condition (*bdag rkyen, adhipatipratyaya*).

Knowing this, one can conclude validly from the presence of the effect (an eye consciousness apprehending the color blue) that all three particular causes were necessarily present.

According to most Ge-luk-pa scholars, the purpose of effect signs proving a particular cause is to prove the existence of any one of the necessary causes, given the occurrence of a phenomenon that depends on multiple causes. As Lati Rin-po-che says, "In this type of proof, one is proving, from among many causes, the existence of one particular causal factor."[212] If there exists a phenomenon that requires for its occurrence a collection of causal factors, then from that phenomenon's existence one can infer the existence of any particular one of those factors—because if any one of them were missing, the phenomenon would not exist.

Ge-shay Pel-den-drak-pa comments that Pur-bu-jok's example syllogism presents problems:

> It follows that "a thing that is not produced without the existence of its observed object condition" is not a correct sign, because when the property of the subject is established, the probandum is also established. Having understood that it [that is, a sense consciousness perceiving blue] is a thing that is not produced without the existence of its observed object condition, one necessarily understands [the probandum, that is,] that it possesses its observed object condition.[213]

If establishing the property of the subject of a proof also automatically establishes the probandum, the proof cannot be valid. After making this point about the example syllogism, Ge-shay Pel-den-drak-pa goes on to say that the main purpose of this third type of correct effect sign is to indicate that all three conditions must be present for a sense consciousness to arise. This purpose is more clearly reflected in the example provided by Ge-shay Tsül-trim-nam-gyel, in the textbook used by Lo-sel-ling College. The example syllogism there is:

---

[a] This is sometimes phrased "object of observation condition"—its condition of being an object of observation.

With respect to the subject, a sense direct perception apprehending form, there exists its condition, which is other than its
dominant condition and its immediately preceding condition
because of (1) being produced occasionally and because of (2)
not being produced by merely the completion of its dominant
condition and its immediately preceding condition.[214]

According to Lati Rin-po-che, although the illustrations set forth by
Pur-bu-jok and Tsül-trim-nam-gyel are different, the mode of proof or
purpose is the same:

The way this [illustration] is stated [by Pur-bu-jok] is slightly
different from the way it is stated in the other logic manual
[that is, the one by Tsül-trim-nam-gyel] but the mode of proof
is the same. Both [Pur-bu-jok and the Lo-sel-ling author] are
proving, from among many causes, the existence of one particular causal factor.[215]

Commenting on the difference between this Lo-sel-ling example and
Pur-bu-jok's syllogism, Ge-shay Pel-den-drak-pa notes that Pur-bu-jok's
is faulty—and that he may have presented it to prompt debate. Indeed,
Lati Rin-po-che says of Pur-bu-jok on another occasion, "It is as if he
wanted to cause problems, to give rise to qualms"[216]—to make students
think. Ge-luk-pa scholars hold (or make the apologetic) that an author
sometimes includes problematical passages in order to provoke
thought—to increase debate among students. As Lati Rin-po-che says,
"If everyone [that is, all scholars] said the same thing, people would not
raise qualms."[217]

It is interesting to compare this Ge-luk-pa fourth type of correct
effect sign (proving a particular cause) with Mokṣākaragupta's second
type, which he posits as,

When [the function of] the visual organ, etc., is the object to be
proved, knowledge [visual and other] is to be determined [as
the effect] through the fact that the effect occurs occasionally
[that is, only when the organ functions].[218]

In Mokṣākaragupta's example, the function of the visual organ is the
predicate, and knowledge is the sign. Through the experience of visual
knowledge (that is, through its occurring occasionally) one infers the
function of the visual organ (that is, the eye sense power).
Mokṣākaragupta specifies that the causal relationship is established
through the occasional occurrence of the visual knowledge. Because
visual sense-consciousness does occur from time to time, one can know

that the sense power is functioning.

Although the Ge-luk-pa scholars use a similar example, the emphasis has changed in the Ge-luk-pa presentation, which stresses that a created thing must have all its causes; all the individual necessary causes must be present. The production of a complex phenomenon that requires several causal factors serves as proof of the existence of each of those causal factors.

In Ge-luk-pa logic manuals, the types of correct effect signs were not set forth to distinguish different ways in which the sign is determined to be the effect of that which is being proved. Rather, the emphasis is on understanding the types (or aspects) of causes that can be inferred. In the Ge-luk-pa system what is being proved by this syllogism is that a sense consciousness only arises through the existence of its complete cause, which means the coming together of all of its necessary causes; the point is that all three necessary factors must be present.

5. Correct Effect Signs That Are a Means of Inferring Causal Attributes

As an example of this type of correct effect sign, Pur-bu-jok posits "the present taste of molasses" in the syllogism, "With respect to the subject, with the lump of molasses in the mouth, there exists the capacity of the former taste of molasses to generate the later form of molasses because the present taste of molasses exists."[a] He writes,

> One can state, "With respect to the subject, with the lump of molasses in the mouth, there exists the capacity of the former taste of molasses to generate the later form of molasses because the present taste of molasses exists." In that, "the present taste of molasses" is a correct effect sign that is a means of inferring causal attributes in the proof that the capacity for generating the later form of molasses by the former taste of molasses exists with [the subject] the lump of molasses in the mouth.[b]

---

[a]   To follow the discussion of this type of sign, it will help to remember that in the Ge-luk-pa point of view, the category of form (*gzugs*) is made up of color (*kha dog*) and shape (*dbyibs*). "Color" will sometimes be used interchangeably with "form."

[b]   *Signs and Reasonings*, p. 8a.2-4. There is a small difference between Pur-bu-jok's syllogism and that posited by Tsül-trim-nam-gyel in the Lo-sel-ling text. In the latter the predicate is "there exists the capacity of the former taste of molasses to generate the present form of molasses" instead of Pur-bu-jok's "there exists the capacity of the former taste of molasses to generate the later form of molasses." Lati Rin-po-che says, "It

In the example of the fourth type of correct effect sign (one proving a particular cause), the effect arises from several different causes and depends equally on each; thus the production of the effect is proof of the presence of each. In this fifth type, however, the effect arises from one cause, which is a collection of distinct attributes (the form and the taste are understood to be two attributes of the molasses). The presence of the effect is not in itself direct proof of the presence of each of those attributes, but it is said to be a "means of inferring" (and thus serves as proof of) their presence.

Thus, this type of sign gives rise to inference realizing the attributes of the cause. As Ge-shay Pel-den-drak-pa says, "This type of sign has its name because the attributes of the cause are inferred from the sign of the effect; then, in dependence on that inference, the cause is understood."[219] In the syllogism under consideration, the attributes of the cause include the former moment of the taste and form of the molasses. The former moment of molasses has its taste and form as attributes; that is, if we consider the moment of taste, it is accompanied by another attribute, the moment of form.

The attributes of the former cause are its taste and form at that time. The former taste is a dominant or substantial cause (*nyer len*) leading to the later taste as its dominant or substantial effect (*nyer 'bras*); the former form is a substantial cause, leading to the later form as its substantial effect. Ge-shay Pel-den-drak-pa explains,

> This example deals with substantial causes and supporting or cooperative conditions (*lhan cig byed rkyen, sahakāripratyaya*). The former *form* and the present *form* are substantial cause and substantial effect. The former *form* and the present *taste* are related, not directly, but because the former form is a cooperative condition for the present taste.[220]

Taste leads to taste, form to form; the former taste is a "cause" of the later form of molasses only in its capacity as cooperative condition, and not as an actual cause or as a substantial condition. The former form is an attribute of the cause of the present taste, but it is not itself a direct cause of the present taste; the former form is a cooperative condition in the production of the present taste. Similarly, the former taste is an attribute of the cause of the present form, but is not a direct cause of

---

would be preferable to say 'the present form' rather than 'the later form'" (because the latter is ambiguous). He goes on to say that Pur-bu-jok probably phrased it this way to make the students think; to raise qualms. (Commentary on *Signs and Reasonings*, vol. 2, Apr. 15, 1977, p. 4.)

the present form; the former taste is a cooperative condition in the production of the present form. It is the Ge-luk-pa point of view that one can infer directly the attributes of the cause of the form from the presence of the taste of molasses; however, it is not possible to infer the form from the taste. This will become more clear when we look at the background of the discussion of this syllogism and at the syllogism itself in more detail.

The Ge-luk-pa discussion arises from a passage in the *Pramāṇavārttika* in which Dharmakīrti discusses the Sāṃkhya assertion that it is valid to prove the existence of the present form of molasses from the existence of the present taste.[a] The Buddhists do not consider this valid, because there is not a strictly defined logical relationship between taste and form. Before discussing the Sāṃkhya and Buddhist points of view, it may be helpful to make clear the basis of the debate under consideration.

In some Buddhist texts, the subject of the debate under consideration is "with the lump of molasses in the mouth." Of this, Ge-shay Pel-den-drak-pa notes,

> Some books use that as a subject, but I have qualms about it. It is strange; these [that is, the Buddhists and the Sāṃkhyas] are skilled opponents, and it doesn't make sense.[221]

In his opinion, the basis of debate, "a lump of molasses" is not very helpful. If a lump is present in the mouth, it will be directly perceived, and who then would have doubt concerning the existence of the form; why would a sign ever be needed? Ge-shay Pel-den-drak-pa suggests as an alternative basis of debate, "At the time when there is a sweet taste but the lump of molasses has dissolved and only a slight residue, visible as a yellow stain, remains."[222] There must be a time when doubt is possible concerning the existence of the form [of molasses]. He adds,

> The time when a doubt can exist is when there is a sweet taste but the lump of molasses has melted and only a brownish or

---

[a] In consequence of this assertion, the Sāṃkhyas add that evidently there are more than three kinds of correct signs (effect, nature, and nonobservation), because this sign (that is, the existence of the present taste) is clearly not one of those three. According to Ge-shay Pel-den-drak-pa, "Dharmakīrti answers that the Sāṃkhya argument depends on one's being able to realize the present form of molasses from the present taste of molasses. If that were true, there would be a fourth kind of sign; but there is no way to understand the present form from the present taste." This brief account of the background of the discussion of this syllogism is based on commentary from Ge-shay Pel-den-drak-pa, vol. 3, p. 4.

yellowish stain is left. At that time, there is a difference in the way the two opponents view the situation.[a]

At that time, there is no discernable form and thus there may be doubt regarding whether or not the form of molasses exists. Sāṃkhyas and Buddhists agree that the existence of the form of molasses can be inferred, but the reasons they employ are different. According to the Sāṃkhyas, one can infer the form directly from the taste; according to the Buddhists, one cannot do so because form and taste are not related. As Ge-shay Pel-den-drak-pa says,

> According to the Sāṃkhyas, one infers the present form from the present taste. However, for the Buddhists, the existence of the present taste is not a correct sign [in the proof of the existence of the present form] because there is no relationship between the sign [taste] and the predicate of the probandum [form].[223]

Thus, according to the Buddhists, the Sāṃkhyas would consider the following to be a correct syllogism: "With respect to the subject, on the tongue where there is the taste of molasses but no lump, form exists because taste exists." But from the Buddhist point of view this is not valid reasoning. The taste cannot prove the form because it is not related with the form. Taste and form occur together as parts of one collection; and they are simultaneous—if one is eliminated, the other is also necessarily eliminated because their production, abiding, and disintegration are simultaneous. But in the technical sense of relationship they are *not* related, because it is not *by the power* of the elimination of the one that the other is eliminated.

According to Ge-luk-pa scholars, this type of effect sign is set forth to explain that one can, in fact, *infer* the existence of the present form from the existence of the present taste; but one cannot use the existence of the present taste as a correct sign in the proof of the existence of the present form. It is only by inferring causal attributes (the fifth type of correct effect sign) that one is able to infer the present form. Lati Rin-po-che comments,

> There does exist in general an inferential consciousness that

---

[a] Ibid., vol. 3, p. 6. Ge-shay Pel-den-drak-pa also says here, "It is easier to understand this debate if one thinks of the form as being, in this case, not the shape of the molasses, but the color. If it is the color, then it is not correct to posit as the subject, 'with the lump of molasses,' because if there is a 'lump' there is shape; and if there is shape, there is no doubt concerning the existence of form."

realizes the existence of the present form of molasses in dependence on the existence of the present taste of molasses. However, it is not in dependence on the sign as stated in this syllogism, "The subject, with the lump of molasses in the mouth, there exists the present form of molasses because of the existence of the present taste of molasses."[224]

Thus, according to these scholars, the existence of the present taste cannot serve as a correct sign proving the existence of the present form because taste and form are not related. Having shown that it is not a correct sign, however, they go on to explain that from the presence of the present taste, the presence of the present form is, indeed, ascertained but only in combination with another ascertainment: ascertainment of the capacity of the prior taste to generate the present form.

There is apparent agreement among Ge-luk-pa scholars that two inferences are generated in dependence on the syllogism under consideration, "With respect to the subject, with the lump of molasses in the mouth, there exists the capacity of the former taste of molasses to generate the later form of molasses because the present taste of molasses exists." One is the inference realizing that the former taste has the capacity to produce the present form, and the other is the inference realizing the existence of the present form. As Lati Rin-po-che says,

> Thus in dependence on a correct effect sign that is a means of inferring causal attributes two different types of inferential consciousness are produced, one that realizes the existence of the capacity of the former taste of the molasses to produce the present form and one that realizes the existence of the present form of the molasses.[225]

Knowing that the cause of the present taste of molasses has as attributes both form and taste, one can conclude that the former taste of molasses serves as cause of the later form in its capacity as supporting condition. Then, from the present taste one can infer the capacity of the former taste to produce not only the later (that is to say, the present) taste, but also the present form (the attributes of form and taste go together). Ge-shay Pel-den-drak-pa puts it clearly,

> Here [in this illustration] we are dealing with cooperative conditions. One understands that the former taste of molasses has the capacity to produce the present form of molasses. If [one understands that] there exists the capacity of the former taste

of molasses to produce the next [moment of the] form of the molasses, then one has to understand also [the existence] of the present form of molasses.[226]

There are important similarities between Pur-bu-jok's fifth type of effect sign and Mokṣākaragupta's third:

When the colour, etc., [of a citron, etc.] is the object to be proved, the taste, etc., is to be determined [as the logical mark as effect] through both being dependent [for their production] on one and the same set of causes, as [we infer] the color of a citron from its taste.[227]

In this proof, the predicate is "color" and the sign is "taste"; according to Mokṣākaragupta, from taste one infers color because they depend on the same set of causes. He posits this type of effect sign to demonstrate how the causal relationship between phenomena such as color and taste is to be ascertained: through their depending on the same set of causes.

In Mokṣākaragupta's explanation and that of the Ge-luk-pas, a similar illustration is used, one that addresses the same problem of how form (or color) can be inferred from taste. Ge-luk-pa scholars would agree with Mokṣākaragupta that the color and taste of molasses (or of a "citron") depend on the same set of causes; as Lati Rin-po-che says, "The taste and form of the molasses are produced from one collection of causes."[228] Mokṣākaragupta explains his illustration this way:

In this...case, the preceding colour is the material cause in relation to the colour to be produced, and the [preceding] taste [which is the material cause of the subsequent taste, necessarily cooperates with the preceding colour] as the auxiliary cause (sahakārikāraṇa) [for the production of the subsequent colour]. This is the logical [relation] involved in the production of the lump [of citron] at the subsequent moment from that at the preceding moment.[229]

This is very similar to the Ge-luk-pa commentary on the example posited by Pur-bu-jok. The shared cause of the color and taste of molasses includes a former moment of color and of taste. The former taste is the dominant condition for the production of the present taste and is a supporting condition for the production of the present color. Ge-luk-pa scholars go on to emphasize the complexity of the inference involved: from the taste of molasses one does in fact infer its form, but the presence of the taste cannot serve alone as a correct sign of the presence of the form.[a]

Ge-luk-pa scholars explain that, in a correct proof, there must be a precise technical relationship between sign and predicate, but between taste and form there is not such a relationship (as there is between fire and smoke). It is acceptable to conclude from the presence of smoke that there is also fire, but to conclude from the presence of taste that there is form is a much more complex inference. This takes one into the background of the functioning of reasoning: It is only because one knows that fire is the cause of smoke that smoke can serve as a sign proving the presence of fire; and it is only because one knows that certain qualities of an object occur together (the color, shape, taste, etc., of molasses, for example) that one can infer from the presence of one the presence of the other. However, Ge-luk-pa scholars consider it important not to view this latter inference as arising simply—in the same way as the inference understanding the presence of fire arises.

There is no relationship between taste and form, and thus ascertaining form from taste is a more complex operation of inference than ascertaining fire from smoke. A person must know that form and taste occur together and that former and later moments of form and taste are in a relationship of cooperative cause and cooperative condition—understanding the relationship between the whole collection of causes and the collection of effects. In its capacity as cooperative condition, the former taste produces the present moment of form. By the presence of the present moment of taste one infers this complex relationship, giving rise to two inferences, one of which is of the present moment of form. Thus one does in fact ascertain the presence of the present moment of form, but not simply—not through ascertaining a simple cause-and-effect relationship.

Pur-bu-jok briefly presents another way of dividing correct effect signs. He writes,

> In another way, when correct effect signs are divided, there are two. This is because smoke is a correct effect sign that relates to the similar class as a pervader in the proof of the existence of the direct cause of smoke on a smoky pass, and smoke is an effect sign that relates to the similar class in two ways in the proof of the existence of fire on a smoky pass.[230]

The two types are (1) correct effect signs that relate to the similar class

---

[a] See, for example, the comments above by Ge-shay Pel-den-drak-pa and Lati Rin-po-che.

as a pervader and (2) those that relate to the similar class in two ways. As explained earlier, in a correct proof, the sign entails the predicate of the probandum, and this means that the predicate of the probandum pervades the sign. Within that being the case, there are two possibilities: either the sign pervades the predicate of the probandum in return (and thus relates to it "as a pervader") or it does not (and thus relates to the predicate "in two ways").

Pur-bu-jok's example of the first type is the sign in the syllogism, "With respect to the subject, on a smoky pass, the direct cause of smoke exists because smoke exists." His example of the second is the sign in the syllogism, "With respect to the subject, on a smoky pass, fire exists because smoke exists." He goes on to explain,

> The fact that [smoke] relates to the similar class as a pervader in the proof of [the existence of the direct cause of smoke on a smoky pass] means that wherever the direct cause of smoke exists, smoke necessarily exists.
>
> The fact that [smoke] relates to the similar class in two ways in the proof of the existence of fire on a smoky pass means that wherever fire exists, smoke does not necessarily exist [and also does not necessarily not exist].[231]

In the point of view of the system of Sautrāntika Following Reasoning, a cause can be inferred from an effect, but an effect cannot, in general, be inferred from a cause. This is because a cause does not necessarily produce an effect. Lati Rin-po-che explains,

> Wherever smoke exists, there fire necessarily exists, but wherever fire exists, smoke does not necessarily exist and does not necessarily not exist. Wherever fire exists smoke does not necessarily exist, because it is possible to have the cause but not have the effect; a cause may be obstructed [prevented from producing an effect]. It is not inevitable that an effect will be produced, unless the direct cause is present.[232]

If a direct cause is present, the arising of its effect is considered to be inevitable (e.g., wherever there is the direct cause of smoke, there is necessarily smoke). Thus the sign, smoke, is said to relate to the similar class (the existence of the direct cause of smoke) as pervader in Pur-bu-jok's first example, the proof of the existence of the direct cause of smoke on a smoky pass. However, if a cause is present (not specified as a "direct" cause), it is not inevitable that an effect will be produced; it may or may not be produced (e.g., wherever there is fire, there is not necessarily smoke and there is not necessarily not smoke). Thus smoke is said to relate to the similar class in two ways in Pur-bu-jok's second example, the proof of the existence of fire on a smoky pass.

Pur-bu-jok's discussion of correct effect signs has followed the outline he began with. Having discussed definitions and divisions, he now comes to the explanation of illustrations—an extremely brief comment:

> Proofs: With respect to the subject, smoke, it is an effect sign in the proof of fire as existing on a smoky pass because (1) it [smoke] is a correct sign in the proof of that and (2) it [smoke] is an effect of fire. This is just [one] illustration.[233]

Here Pur-bu-jok is referring to the illustration he gave of the first of the five main types of correct effect sign: effect sign proving an actual cause. He leaves it at that, but the same reasoning can be applied to his illustrations of the other four types. For example, smoke is a correct effect sign in the proof of the bluish rising smoke in the intermediate space as having its own former cause, fire, because it (smoke) is a correct sign in the proof of that and it is an effect of its own former cause, fire. And so on.

IDENTIFICATION OF THE SIGN AND PREDICATE

THE SIGN

In his concluding section on correct effect signs, Pur-bu-jok makes a distinction between "smoke" and "the existence of smoke." He writes:

> "Smoke" is a correct sign in the proof of fire as existing on a smoky pass; is both the stated sign (*bkod tshod kyi rtags*) and the sign that appears to the mind (*song tshod kyi rtags*) in the proof of that; and is also a correct sign [in the proof of fire as existing on a smoky pass] by the sign, smoke.
>
> "The existence of smoke" [on the other hand] is a correct sign and the stated sign in the proof of fire as existing on a smoky pass; but it is not the sign that appears to the mind in the proof of that; and it is not a correct sign [in the proof of that] by the sign, smoke.[234]

Fire is the direct or actual cause of smoke; smoke must arise from fire. The statement of the reason in that proof is "because smoke exists" (*du ba yod pa'i phyir*—which can also be translated as "because of the presence of smoke"). It is important to note that although the reason includes the word "exists," it is not "the existence of smoke" or "smoke exists" that is functioning as the correct effect sign in the syllogism. The sign in that proof is said to be simply "smoke." As Ge-shay Pel-den-drak-pa says,

> One says "because smoke exists," but the sign is just "smoke"; when "because smoke exists" is stated, what appears to the mind is "smoke," not "the existence of smoke."[235]

THE PREDICATE

Pur-bu-jok continues,

> "Fire" is the predicate of the probandum and the stated predicate of the probandum as well as the predicate of the probandum that appears to the mind in the proof of [fire as existing on a smoky pass] by the sign, smoke.
>
> "The existence of fire" is the predicate of the probandum and the stated predicate of the probandum in the proof of [fire as existing on a smoky pass] as well as the predicate of the probandum in the proof of that by the sign, smoke. It is not, however, the predicate of the probandum that appears to the mind in the proof of that.[236]

It is said that the sign is "smoke" and that the predicate of the probandum is both "fire" and "fire exists" (or "the existence of fire"). Problems arise, however, because if one takes "fire" to be the predicate, then the pervasion is not established; and if one takes "the existence of fire" to be the predicate, then "smoke" is not a correct effect sign. Two debates can arise concerning the identification of the predicate of the probandum in a syllogism involving a correct effect sign; the first is:

> Challenger (C): It follows that "With respect to the subject, on a smoky pass, fire exists because smoke exists" is a correct proof.
> Defender (D): I accept.
> C: Posit the predicate of the probandum in that proof.
> D: Fire exists (*me yod pa*).
> C: It follows that "fire exists" is the predicate of the probandum.
> D: I accept.
> C: It follows that the existence of fire is not permanent.
> D: Why?
> C: Because of being a cause of smoke.
> D: The reason is not established.

C: Then it follows that smoke is not a correct effect sign in that proof.

If one posits "fire exists" as the predicate of the probandum, then the sign "smoke" cannot be a correct effect sign. A correct effect sign must be the effect of that which is set as the predicate of the probandum. "Fire exists" is considered to be a permanent phenomenon and thus cannot be the cause of smoke. Another debate might run:

C: It follows that "With respect to the subject, on a smoky pass, fire exists because smoke exists" is a correct proof.

D: I accept.

C: Posit the predicate of the probandum in that proof.

D: Fire (*me*).

C: What is the predicate of the negandum in that proof?

D: Not being fire (*me ma yin pa*).

C: It follows that smoke exists in the dissimilar class in that proof because smoke exists in "not being fire."

One could argue in this way that smoke is not a correct sign in that proof because smoke exists in the dissimilar class; smoke exists in "not being fire" because smoke is not fire. Ge-shay Lob-sang-gya-tso says, "Any smoke you could posit is 'not fire'; and since smoke itself is something that is not fire, you cannot say that smoke does not exist in 'not being fire.'"[237]

If fire is the predicate, then the negandum is "not being fire"; if not being fire is the predicate of the negandum, then the pervasion is not established—because for the pervasion to be established, the sign must be just nonexistent in the dissimilar class.

Ge-shay Lob-sang-gya-tso adds that one has to posit each individually (fire and the existence of fire) as the predicate of the probandum. Then, when explaining why this is a correct effect sign, one takes the predicate as "fire" because the definition of effect sign specifies that there must be a common locus of being the predicate and being a cause. But when explaining why the pervasion is established, to satisfy the criteria of the pervasion, one needs to take the "existence of fire" as the predicate. The criteria of the pervasion are that the sign must exist in only the similar class and must be just nonexistent in the dissimilar class.[238]

The reason smoke can serve as a correct effect sign is that there is a causal relationship between fire and smoke. But when analyzing the pervasion between sign and predicate one must specify that the reverse of the predicate is the nonexistence of fire. According to Ge-shay

Lob-sang-gya-tso,

> The sign must not exist in the reverse of the predicate of the
> probandum; in the context of establishing the pervasion, the
> predicate of the probandum has to be "fire exists"; then the re-
> verse is "fire does not exist"; then the sign must not exist in
> "fire does not exist," which is the case, because where there is
> no fire, there can be no smoke.[239]

Pur-bu-jok's definition of a correct effect sign specifies that there must
occur a common locus of (1) being the predicate of the probandum and
(2) being a cause of the sign. In the proof of fire as existent on a smoky
pass by the sign, smoke, that common locus is fire.

Fire is said to be the explicit predicate of the probandum, the predicate of the probandum, the stated predicate of the probandum (*bkod
tshod kyi bsgrub bya'i chos*), and the predicate of the probandum that appears to the mind (*song tshod kyi bsgrub bya'i chos*). Pur-bu-jok explains
that the *existence of fire* is the predicate of the probandum and the
stated predicate of the probandum in that proof, but it is not the predicate of the probandum that appears to the mind in that proof.

As if anticipating the complications that arise in this topic, Pur-bu-
jok writes,

> From the point of view of understanding, the definition of
> something's being a correct effect sign in a given proof is:
>
>> (1) it is a correct sign in the proof of that and (2) there
>> exists a common locus of (a) being the main object held
>> as the explicit predicate of the probandum in the proof
>> of that by the sign of it and (b) being its cause.[240]

In his definition of correct effect sign "from the point of view of understanding,"[a] Pur-bu-jok specifies that there must exist a common locus
of being the *main object* held as the predicate and being a cause of the
sign. The main object held as the predicate is fire, which is the cause of
smoke. That is also the predicate of the probandum that appears to the
mind. This phrase "main object" indicates there is more than one object held as predicate. The other predicate ("the existence of fire") is
not the cause of smoke. But in specifying that the main object held is
the cause, he bypasses the objection that this cannot be a correct effect
sign because "existence of fire" is the predicate and is *not* a cause of
smoke.

---

[a] This is the fourth of his variant definitions of correct effect signs.

In summary, according to Pur-bu-jok, both "fire" and "fire exists" are explicit predicates in the proof of fire as existing on a smoky pass. However, if one posits "fire exists" as the predicate in that proof, certain problems arise, including that "smoke" cannot be a correct effect sign. Then if one posits "fire" as the predicate, other problems arise, including that the pervasions are not established. Pur-bu-jok's way around these problems is to specify that the "*main* object held as the predicate of the probandum" is the cause of the sign, smoke.

Pur-bu-jok ends his explanation of correct effect signs with a brief discussion of other phenomena that may be taken as the explicit predicates in the proof of fire as existing on a smoky pass by the sign, smoke. He writes,

> "Fire as observed by valid cognition" [the definition of the existence of fire] and "the hot and burning" [the definition of fire] are not, individually, that which is held as the explicit predicate of the probandum in the proof of fire as existing on a smoky pass because of being correct signs in the proof of that. However, those two are, individually, that which is held as the explicit predicate of the probandum in the proof of that by the sign, smoke. This is because there exists a common locus of (1) being that which is held as the explicit predicate of the probandum in the proof of that and (2) being a definition.[241]

There is a difference of opinion, among Ge-luk-pa scholars, concerning whether "fire as observed by valid cognition" and "the hot and burning" are explicit predicates of the probandum in the proof of fire as existent on a smoky pass by the sign, smoke. Concerning Pur-bu-jok's own meaning in this context, there appears to be at least a small amount of room for debate. Lati Rin-po-che says that in Pur-bu-jok's explanation, the words "in the proof of that" (in "However, those two are individually that which is held as the explicit predicate of the probandum *in the proof of that* by the sign, smoke") refer to (1) the proof of fire as observed by valid cognition on a smoky pass and (2) the proof of the hot and burning as existing on a smoky pass. According to Lati Rin-po-che, "fire as observed by valid cognition" is the explicit predicate of the probandum only in the proof of fire as observed by valid cognition and, similarly, "hot and burning" is the explicit predicate of the probandum only in the proof of hot and burning as existent on a smoky pass.[242]

According to Ge-shay Ge-dün-lo-drö, however, "fire as observed by valid cognition" and "hot and burning" are explicit predicates of the probandum in the proof of fire as existent on a smoky pass by the sign, smoke. Pur-bu-jok's own words are somewhat ambiguous in this context, but elsewhere in his text he asserts that there may be more than one explicit predicate in a proof. For example, he writes,

> The two, the impermanent and [its definition] the momentary are each the explicit predicate of the probandum in the proof of sound as impermanent by the sign, product.[243]

It is Pur-bu-jok's view that when a definiendum is ascertained its meaning (that is, its definition) must also be explicitly ascertained at that time.[a]

---

[a] This topic is discussed in more detail in the chapter eight section on "the division of correct signs by way of the modes of proof."

5. Correct Nature Signs

The important features of a correct nature sign in a particular proof are: (1) it is necessarily proving a positive phenomenon; and (2) it is necessarily related to the predicate of the probandum in a strictly defined relationship of sameness of nature.

POSITIVE PHENOMENON

The first important feature of a correct nature sign is that it must be proving a positive phenomenon; this means, according to most Ge-luk-pa scholars, that the explicit predicate of the probandum in the syllogism being proved must be a positive phenomenon. Pur-bu-jok's definition of a correct nature sign does not mention the predicate's being a positive phenomenon. He posits:

> (1) It (x) is a correct sign in the proof of something and (2) it is posited from the point of view that whatever is held as the explicit predicate of the probandum in the proof of that by the sign x must be of one nature with x.[a]

This leaves room for debate about the matter. Some Ge-luk-pa scholars think Pur-bu-jok's definition implies that the predicate of the probandum must be a positive phenomenon, others that the definition should be modified to make the specification explicit.

Ge-shay Pel-den-drak-pa, for example, is of the opinion that rephrasing would make this definition more useful; he says,

> Given the definition as phrased, one can posit many counterexamples [that satisfy the definition but are not actually correct nature signs]. You could posit, for example, "The subject, sound, is opposite from not being impermanent (*mi rtag pa ma yin pa las log pa*) because of being a product."[244]

The sign in that syllogism satisfies the requirements of the definition in that the predicate of the probandum, "opposite from not being

---

[a] *Signs and Reasonings*, p. 8b.6-7. This is the complete definition. Pur-bu-jok also posits two shorter ones: "The definition of a correct nature sign is: that which is the three nature modes. In another way, the definition of a correct nature sign in the proof of that (that is, in any proof) is: that which is the three nature modes in the proof of that." (Ibid., p. 8b.5-6.) These are not considered to be complete definitions; they are used as a kind of shorthand in debate.

impermanent," is of one nature with the sign, product; however, the ge-shay continues,

> "Product" is not a correct nature sign in that proof because the predicate of the probandum is a negative phenomenon; in order to be a correct nature sign, it must be proving a positive phenomenon.[245]

In Ge-shay Pel-den-drak-pa's opinion the definition of correct nature sign should be modified to reflect the requirement that the predicate of the probandum be a positive phenomenon; he writes,

> One should add to the definition the requirement that whatever is held as the explicit predicate of the probandum in that proof is necessarily a positive phenomenon or the requirement that the sign must be a sign of a positive phenomenon.[a]

On the other hand, another Ge-luk-pa scholar, Ge-shay Lob-sang-gya-tso, asserts that there is no flaw in Pur-bu-jok's definition. True, that definition may appear to be faulty because one can posit something that seems to satisfy the definition but is not actually a correct nature sign (for example, the sign, product, in the proof of sound as opposite from not being impermanent); someone might say that since one can posit such a counterexample, it follows that whatever is (that is, satisfies) that definition is not necessarily a correct nature sign. To such a statement, the ge-shay responds simply, "The three spheres ('khor gsum)!"—meaning that all aspects of its reasoning are incorrect.[b]

Ge-shay Lob-sang-gya-tso argues that one can interpret Pur-bu-jok's definition to mean that the predicate of the probandum must be a positive phenomenon, citing material from elsewhere in the text—for example:

• Pur-bu-jok writes, "Whatever is either a correct effect sign or a correct nature sign is necessarily a correct sign of a positive phenomenon,"[246] and

---

[a] Commentary on *Signs and Reasonings*, vol. 3, p. 15. The requirement that the sign be proving a positive phenomenon indicates, for most Ge-luk-pa scholars, that the predicate of the probandum is a positive phenomenon; but, as has been explained earlier, the scholars of Go-mang College of Dre-pung Monastic University, following the teaching of Jam-yang-shay-pa, say that a sign of a positive phenomenon (that is, one that is proving a positive phenomenon) may have, as predicate, a negative phenomenon.
[b] Commentary on *Signs and Reasonings*, vol. 3, p.15. The three spheres are explained in chapter eight, in the debate on whether product is a correct sign on the occasion of one's own purpose.

- in his definition of a correct sign of a positive phenomenon, he specifies that the explicit predicate of the probandum must be a positive phenomenon.[247]

Thus, if someone says that "product" is a correct nature sign in the proof of sound as opposite from not being impermanent because it satisfies Pur-bu-jok's requirements for a correct nature sign, Ge-shay Lobsang-gya-tso counters with the argument that "product is not a correct nature sign in the proof of sound as opposite from not being impermanent, because it is a sign of a negative phenomenon in that proof; and whatever is a sign of a negative phenomenon cannot be a sign of a positive phenomenon."[248]

Yet another point of view has been advanced by another Ge-luk-pa scholar, Lati Rin-po-che. He focuses on the phrase "posited from the point of view" in Pur-bu-jok's definition (the correct sign is "posited from the point of view that whatever is held as the explicit predicate of the probandum in the proof of that by the sign x must be of one nature with x"), saying that it indicates a qualification. Lati Rin-po-che explains,

> These words indicate that there is no pervasion; whatever is of one nature with that which is held as the explicit predicate of the probandum in a proof is not necessarily a correct nature sign in that proof. For example, "The subject, sound, is empty of being permanent because of being a product," or "The subject, sound, is opposite from not being impermanent because of being a product." In those two cases, the explicit predicate of the probandum is of one nature with the sign, but the sign is not a correct nature sign; it is a nonobservation sign.[249]

Thus, it is Lati Rin-po-che's opinion that the definition already allows for exceptions to the requirements as stated and therefore does not need to be altered.

If the definitions a text contains are occasionally ambiguous or incomplete, this is not generally considered to be a flaw. For the texts to be valuable training tools, it is not necessary that their meaning be entirely unambiguous. Texts are indeed used as a basis for study and debate, but the teachers are expected to and do provide instruction that fills out the idea and roots the simplified presentation into a broader context.

It is clear that there is widespread agreement among Ge-luk-pa scholars that a nature sign must be a "sign of a positive phenomenon" (sgrub rtags yang dag)—a sign proving a positive phenomenon. Only those of Go-mang College of Dre-pung Monastic University hold that a syllogism involving a sign of a positive phenomenon need not have as its predicate a positive phenomenon; although a positive phenomenon is being proved, the explicit predicate of the probandum itself need not be a positive phenomenon. According to the Go-mang scholars, a syllogism involving a correct nature sign may have as its predicate either a positive phenomenon or an affirming negative phenomenon. Scholars of the other Ge-luk-pa colleges, however, hold that, if the predicate of the probandum is a negative phenomenon, the sign cannot be an effect or nature sign; it must be a nonobservation sign. Pur-bu-jok's own view was made clear in the two examples cited above.

The First Dalai Lama makes this requirement—that the explicit predicate of the probandum must be a positive phenomenon—explicit in his definition of a correct nature sign in the proof of something:

> (1) It is a correct sign of a positive phenomenon in the proof of that and (2) whatever is the explicit predicate of the probandum in the proof of that is necessarily a pervader that is the same nature (*bdag gcig pa'i khyab byed*) as it.[250]

For a sign to be valid, there must be irrefutable entailment between the sign and the predicate of the probandum. One way of expressing this requirement is to say that the predicate of the probandum must pervade the sign. In the case of a correct effect sign, the predicate of the probandum is the pervader of the sign and is of a different entity from the sign (because the predicate of the probandum and the sign are cause and effect). In the case of a correct nature sign, the predicate of the probandum is the pervader of the sign and is of the same entity or the same nature as the sign.

SAMENESS OF NATURE

The second important feature of a correct nature sign in a given proof is that it must be in a strictly defined relationship with the predicate of the probandum—a relationship of sameness of nature. In their definitions of correct nature signs, Pur-bu-jok and the First Dalai Lama both specify that the predicate of the probandum is "the same nature" as the sign.

It was explained in the topic of the pervasions (chapters two and three) that in any correct proof the sign must be related with the predicate of the probandum in a relationship either of provenance or of sameness of nature. If the relationship is one of provenance, then the sign must be the effect of the predicate—and thus the predicate and the sign are necessarily different entities. If the relationship is one of sameness of nature, then the predicate and the sign are necessarily one entity. As Lati Rin-po-che says,

> In any proof involving a correct nature sign, that which is held as the explicit predicate of the probandum and that which is set as the sign must be of one nature.[251]

Being "of one nature (or the same nature)" (*bdag nyid gcig*) does not mean being "related in the relationship of sameness of nature" (*bdag gcig tu 'brel*). As explained earlier, in Tibetan logic, "relationship" (*'brel ba*) has a special technical meaning. It is said, for example, that oak and tree are of the same entity or of the same nature and that oak is of one entity or nature with tree; this is reciprocal. But, while it is accurate to say that oak is *related* with tree, it is not accurate to say that tree is *related* with oak. Oak is related with tree, because if tree is eliminated, oak is also automatically eliminated; but tree is *not* related with oak because if oak is eliminated tree is not necessarily eliminated—there are many trees that are not oaks.

In the same way, the predicate of the probandum in any proof involving a correct nature sign is necessarily the same nature (*bdag nyid gcig*) as the sign but is not necessarily *related* in the relationship of sameness of nature (*bdag gcig tu 'brel*). For example, in the syllogism, "The subject, the sound of a horn, is impermanent because of being arisen from exertion," "arisen from exertion" (the sign) is related with "the impermanent" (the predicate) in a relationship of sameness of nature, but the impermanent is not related with the arisen from exertion, because if the arisen from exertion is eliminated, the impermanent is not necessarily eliminated. This is because the impermanent is a broader category than the arisen from exertion; many impermanent phenomena—such as lightning and rain—are not arisen from exertion.

DIVISIONS OF CORRECT NATURE SIGNS

The main division of correct nature signs is made according to whether or not the signs themselves are expressed by terms that indicate an agent. From this point of view, Pur-bu-jok posits two types of correct nature signs: those that involve a qualification and those that are free of qualification.[a] He defines them as follows:

---

[a] *Signs and Reasonings*, pp. 8b.7-9a.1. As this discussion will explain, "involving qualification (or specification)" means that a cause is indicated by the terms used to express

The definition of a correct nature sign involving a qualification in the proof of something is: "A correct nature sign in the proof of that, which is posited from the point of view that the term expressing it indicates its own agent."

The definition of a correct nature sign that is free of qualification in the proof of something is: "A correct nature sign in the proof of that, which is posited from the point of view that the term expressing it does not indicate its own agent."[252]

This approach to the analysis of correct nature signs (whether they are expressed by terms that indicate their own agent) reflects their main use—as an aid in understanding impermanence. Although nature signs can be used in proving phenomena that are not impermanent, their presentation is geared toward helping students understand the meaning of "the impermanent." As was noted in chapter four, the reason for studying nature signs is for the sake of realizing that true sufferings are impermanent and miserable.[253]

All impermanent phenomena are necessarily produced phenomena; and being products, they necessarily have causal agents. Although all impermanent phenomena have causal agents, they are not necessarily expressed in terms that indicate those agents. Two terms that are said to express their agents are "product" and "arisen from exertion"; a term that is said to not express an agent is "thing."[a]

Nature signs are divided, then, according to whether or not the terms expressing them express (or indicate or specify) an agent. If an agent is specified, then it is a sign involving a qualification (or specification) of a cause; if an agent is not specified, it is a sign free of qualification of a cause.

NATURE SIGNS INVOLVING A QUALIFICATION

As the definition of a correct nature sign involving a qualification in the proof of something, Pur-bu-jok posited above, "A correct nature sign in the proof of that, which is posited from the point of view that the term expressing it indicates its own agent." The agent may be expressed explicitly or implicitly. He continues,

Correct nature signs involving a qualification are of two types:

---

the sign.

[a] For a discussion of "thing," see the section below on nature signs that are free of qualification.

those that explicitly indicate their agent and those that implicitly indicate their agent.

"Arisen from exertion" (*rtsol byung*) and "created phenomenon" (*skyes pa*) are [correct nature signs that explicitly indicate their own agent] in the proof of the sound of a conch as impermanent.[254]

The term "arisen from exertion" is said to explicitly indicate an agent, a particular or specific cause (*rgyu khyad par*)—the activity of the person who performed the exertion. The exertion of a person is that which is depended on (the cause or agent); that which is arisen from exertion is that which depends on that agent. Lati Rin-po-che explains,

> When one states, "the subject, the sound of a conch, is impermanent because of being arisen from exertion," "arisen from exertion" is a correct sign involving a qualification that is expressed by a term that explicitly indicates its agent. The agent is the exertion of a person; the words "arisen from exertion" explicitly indicate the exertion of a person—in this case, the person who made the sound of the conch. The word *khyad par* ("qualification" or "particular") refers to an agent or instrument. The agent is the particular cause (*rgyu khyad par*) of that which is arisen from exertion; the exertion of the person is that which is depended on, the agent. Thus, this is a correct nature sign which depends on a specific cause, which is the agent.[255]

Besides "arisen from exertion," Pur-bu-jok posits "created phenomenon" as an example of a term that explicitly indicates its agent. Ge-shay Pel-den-drak-pa disagrees; in his opinion, "created phenomenon" (like "product") indicates an agent only indirectly.[a]

As an example of a correct nature sign that implicitly indicates its agent, Pur-bu-jok posits "product" in the syllogism, "The subject, sound, is impermanent because of being a product."[256] The implied agents are the causes and conditions that generate a product. According to Ge-shay Lob-sang-gya-tso,

> In the case of the sign, product, the agents indicated are the causes and conditions through which there is production.

---

[a] Ge-shay Pel-den-drak-pa says, "The term 'created phenomenon' only indirectly indicates its agent." (Commentary on *Signs and Reasonings*, vol. 3, p. 15.) Lati Rin-po-che—though not actually disagreeing with Pur-bu-jok's statement—does say that the terms "product" and "created phenomenon" have no apparent difference in the way they indicate their agent. (Commentary on *Signs and Reasonings*, vol. 3, Apr. 18, 1977, p. 1.)

"Product" expresses implicitly "produced from causes and conditions."[257]

To summarize: "Arisen from exertion" *explicitly* indicates a causal agent, the exertion of a being. "Product" *implicitly* indicates causal agents, the causes and conditions from which the product arose. Because a specific agent is indicated by these signs, they are called signs involving qualification (or specification or specificity).

NATURE SIGNS THAT ARE FREE OF QUALIFICATION

The definition Pur-bu-jok gave above for a correct nature sign that is free of qualification in the proof of something is "a correct nature sign in the proof of that which is posited from the point of view that the term expressing it does not indicate its own agent." A correct nature sign that is free of qualification is one that does not indicate an agent. As an example, he posits "thing" in the syllogism, "The subject, sound, is impermanent because of being a 'thing' (*dngos po, bhava*)."[258] There is some debate about whether or not the word thing indicates its own agent (or cause). Ge-luk-pa scholars discuss this topic at some length; they apparently agree that the definition of thing[a] refers to its ability to produce its own effect (its own next moment) but does not explicitly or implicitly point to its own cause (or agent). As Ge-shay Pel-den-drak-pa puts it,

> In having "thing" as the sign, there is some debate about whether it indicates an agent; when one says "because of being a thing" one understands "being able to perform a function." At that time, one understands that it is the agent of something else, but one does not understand its own cause, its own agent.[259]

There is apparent agreement among Ge-luk-pa scholars that in order to ascertain a phenomenon like "thing" one must first ascertain its definition. Someone might then argue that when thing appears to the mind, its definition, that which is able to perform a function, also appears to the mind; and furthermore, since this definition expresses an agent, it follows that thing itself indicates an agent indirectly. Ge-shay Pel-den-drak-pa counters this argument by saying that—although when one understands thing one also understands being able to

---

[a] The definition of "thing" is "that which is able to perform a function" (*don byed nus pa*).

perform a function, and thus one understands that it (thing) is the agent of something else—one does *not* understand thereby the agent of "thing" itself, and thus "thing" is not a term that indicates its *own* agent.[260] Another teacher, Ge-shay Lob-sang-gya-tso, says that although "that which is able to perform a function" indicates an agent, "thing" itself does not, either explicitly or implicitly.[261]

As a general rule, if a term is composed of a verb or a verbal noun, it almost always indicates some agent or instrument, but if it is an adjective or a plain noun (not verb-derived), then it does not indicate an agent at all. This is made clear by Lati Rin-po-che when he says,

> If you have a verb [or verbal], some agent or instrument is always indicated, either explicitly or implicitly. If you have a [non-verb-derived] noun or adjective, then an agent is not indicated either explicitly or implicitly.[262]

An exception to this rule is "particularity of product" (*byas pa'i bye brag*) which is said to *not* indicate an agent, even though it includes the verbal noun "product." "Particularity of product" is a correct nature sign in the proof of sound as impermanent and is thus related with the impermanent in the relationship of sameness of nature. Most phenomena related with the impermanent are themselves also impermanent and therefore have causal agents. Particularity of product is an exception, because although whatever is a particularity of product is necessarily impermanent, "particularity of product" itself—that is to say, the phenomenon expressed by the term "particularity of product"—is a permanent phenomenon. Ge-shay Pel-den-drak-pa says,

> Correct nature signs that are permanent, such as "particularity of product" in "the subject, sound, is impermanent because of being a particularity of product," are cases of not expressing an agent.[263]

Thus, "thing" and "particularity of product" are examples of signs that do not indicate an agent. Thing, however, does in fact have an agent, and "particularity of product" in fact does not. Being a permanent phenomenon, particularity of product does not have a cause. The definition of "correct nature sign" specifies that the terms expressing them do not indicate "their own agent"; it might be argued that this phrase "their own agent" implies that they do in fact possess an agent, which is not, however, expressed. If that were the case, particularity of product could not be included as a nature sign. However, there is apparent agreement among Ge-luk-pa scholars that permanent phenomena

(such as particularity of product) are to be included, along with impermanent phenomena (such as thing) in the category of nature signs that
are free of qualification.

In the syllogism, "The subject, smoke, is impermanent because of
being an effect," the sign "effect" is said to be a correct nature sign that
does indicate its agent, but not explicitly. From the term "effect" one is
said to understand implicitly the existence of a cause. Ge-shay Pel-den-
drak-pa explains,

> If the sign is "because of being an effect," it is a case of implicit-
> ly understanding the cause; the cause is not explicitly stated. If
> the sign were "effect of fire," as in "The subject, smoke, is im-
> permanent because of being the effect of fire," in that case, the
> cause is explicitly expressed.[264]

Thus, in the proof of impermanence, the sign used may be expressed by
a term that indicates its agent or by a term that does not. The sign
proving impermanence may itself be permanent, as in the case of "particularity of product"; but if it is, it cannot indicate its agent, because it
has no agent.

Nature signs may also be used in the proof of phenomena other
than the impermanent. For example, in the syllogism, "The subject, the
isolate of thing, is permanent because of being a common locus of (1)
being a phenomenon and (2) not being momentary," the sign, "a common locus of being a phenomenon and not being momentary" (*chos
dang skad cig ma ma yin pa'i gzhi mthun pa*), is a correct nature sign in
that proof. Although "isolate of thing" refers only to "thing" itself (because nothing other than "thing" can be the isolate of thing), it is not
itself a thing. "Isolate of thing" is a permanent phenomenon. The definition of a permanent phenomenon specifies that it must be a phenomenon and that it must not be momentary; something that satisfies
these criteria is necessarily permanent.

Even though it is possible to posit nature signs other than those
proving impermanence, their primary use is for understanding impermanence. It is this use that determines both the way nature signs are
divided and the way those divisions are explained.

Pur-bu-jok briefly presents another way of dividing correct nature
signs. He writes,

> In another way, correct nature signs in the proof of sound as
> impermanent are of two types:

1. A correct nature sign in the proof of [sound as imperma-
   nent] that relates to the similar class as a pervader in the
   proof of that; an illustration of this is "product."
2. A correct nature sign in the proof of [sound as imperma-
   nent] that relates to the similar class in two ways in the
   proof of that. An illustration is "particularity of product."[265]

As explained earlier, in any correct proof, the sign must be related to
the predicate. Put another way, the sign must be existent in only the
similar class and only nonexistent in the dissimilar class. This means
that, in a correct proof, the similar class necessarily pervades the sign.
That being the case, there are then two possibilities: either the sign also
pervades the predicate or it does not. Pur-bu-jok continues,

Proof of the illustrations:

1. "Product" is [a correct nature sign in the proof of sound as
   impermanent that relates to the similar class as a pervader
   of it in the proof of that] because it [product] is a correct
   nature sign in the proof of that and whatever is impermanent is necessarily that [product].
2. "Particularity of product" is [a correct nature sign in the
   proof of sound as impermanent that relates to the similar
   class in two ways in the proof of that] because that [parti-
   cularity of product] is a correct nature sign in the proof of
   that and whatever is impermanent is not necessarily that
   [particularity of product].[266]

In the syllogism, "The subject, sound, is impermanent because of being
a product," the similar class is the impermanent; whatever is impermanent is necessarily a product and thus the sign is said to pervade the
similar class. In the syllogism, "The subject, sound, is impermanent because of being a particularity of product," the sign does not pervade the
similar class because whatever is impermanent is not necessarily a particularity of product. The sign, particularity of product, is said to be
related to the similar class (the impermanent) in two ways because, as
Lati Rin-po-che tells us,

(1) whatever is impermanent is not necessarily a particularity
    of product; for example, product is impermanent but is not
    a particularity of product because whatever is a particulari-
    ty of product must be different from product; and
(2) whatever is impermanent is not necessarily *not* a particu-
    larity of product; for example, a pot is both impermanent

and a particularity of product.[267]

Mokṣākaragupta's *Tarkabhāṣā* contains a short explanation of nature signs, including the following definition and example:

[The logical mark representing] essential identity is [defined] as follows: The nature [of *s*] itself is said [by Dharmakīrti to be] the *h* of the quality to be proved (*s*) when the latter depends for its existence on the existence of that (*h*) alone; the probans thus defined is to be understood as the essential nature of the quality to be proved.

For example, in the inference "This can be called a tree, because it can be called a *śiṃśapā*," "this" stands for *p*, that is, a thing being seen in front [of the inferring person]; "because it can be called a *śiṃśapā*" refers to *h*. What is the meaning of "because it can be called a *śiṃśapā*"? It means the applicability of the designation [*śiṃśapā* which connotes] particular branches, leaves, colour and form. The applicability of the designation "tree" is *s*.[a]

Mokṣākaragupta's example involves the relationship of sameness of nature between tree and *śiṃśapā* (a kind of tree). Any specific tree, an oak for example, is said to be pervaded by tree—that is, whatever is an oak is necessarily a tree.

Pur-bu-jok's main examples of a correct sign (e.g., the sign in the syllogism, "The subject, sound, is impermanent because of being a product") differ from Mokṣākaragupta's; but they are similar in that, in each, the sign entails the predicate of the probandum because of the relationship of sameness of nature between the sign and the predicate of the probandum.

Mokṣākaragupta completes his discussion of nature signs by bringing up a possible qualm and responding to it:

[The opponent:] If two things are identical, they cannot be [related to each other by] the relation of probans and probandum, because [in this case both of them] would be [one and the same] part of the thesis.

[The author:] The objection is untenable. It is true that both are not different in reality. But there may be a person

---

[a] Kajiyama, *Introduction to Buddhist Philosophy*, p. 76. Kajiyama's term for "nature sign" is "logical mark of essential identity." In his translation system, *s* refers to the *sādhya* (probandum) and *h* refers to the *hetu* (the sign).

who, seeing a certain thing, applies the name *śiṁśapā* which he learnt once, but does not identify it with the name "tree," since he imagines [through the name *śiṁśapā* not the essential qualities of the tree, but] something else [say, tallness] owing to confusion. Such a person may be now persuaded by means of this inference based on identity. Therefore, even if they are one in reality, they appear distinct when they occur in conceptual knowledge that depends on distinction from others (*vyāvṛtti*). This is the reason why [this kind of inference] is not incompatible with the relation of probans and probandum.[268]

Although tree and *śiṁśapā* are of the same nature, they appear separately to conceptual thought, and thus it is possible for someone to be familiar with the name *śiṁśapā* but not with the name "tree."

Ge-luk-pa discussion of this issue is similar; Ge-shay Pel-den-drak-pa explains that someone's ascertaining a specific type of tree, "oak," for example, does not necessarily entail that person's ascertaining "tree."[a]

Although there does not appear to be any conflict between Mokṣākaragupta's view of nature signs and that of Pur-bu-jok, there is one interesting difference. In Pur-bu-jok's presentation, nature signs are discussed in a way that emphasizes the importance of the concept of impermanence. This emphasis is discernable especially in the fact that all five example syllogisms posited by Pur-bu-jok involve proofs in which the predicate of the probandum is "the impermanent." This emphasis is also reflected in commentary on Pur-bu-jok's text by Ge-luk-pa scholars. Lati Rin-po-che indicates that the purpose for positing correct nature signs is to help students understand impermanence.[b]

---

[a] Commentary on *Signs and Reasonings*, vol. 5, p. 2. This discussion arises in explaining how the absence of trees can serve as a correct nonobservation sign proving the absence of an oak, discussed in chapter seven.

[b] Commentary on *Signs and Reasonings*, vol. 1, p. 58. (See the section "the reason for studying these signs" in chapter four.)

6. Correct Nonobservation Signs of the Nonappearing

NONOBSERVATION SIGNS

Nonobservation signs (*ma dmigs pa'i rtags*) are used in the proof of negative phenomena. That is, in a syllogism being proved by a nonobservation sign, the explicit predicate of the probandum is necessarily a negative phenomenon. Pur-bu-jok makes this requirement clear in his definition of a correct nonobservation sign in the proof of something:

> (1) It (x) is a correct sign in the proof of that and (2) there occurs a common locus of (a) being what is held as the explicit predicate of the probandum in the proof of that by the sign x and (b) being a negative phenomenon.[a]

For example, "product" is a correct nonobservation sign in the syllogism, "The subject, sound, is empty of being permanent because of being a product." The predicate of the probandum is a negative phenomenon: "empty of being permanent" (*rtag pas stong pa*). Lati Rin-po-che summarizes the terminology involved:

> In the case of a syllogism involving a correct nonobservation sign, there is a basis of debate, a predicate of the probandum, and a sign; the basis of debate is the basis of negation. There is also a predicate of the negandum, a negandum, and an object designated as the predicate of the negandum (*dgag bya'i chos su brtags pa'i don*). For example, when one states, "The subject, sound, is empty of being permanent because of being a product," sound is the basis of negation (*dkag gzhi*); that sound is permanent (*sgra rtag pa*) is the negandum; permanent is both the predicate of the negandum and the object designated as the predicate of the negandum.[269]

The object designated as the predicate of the negandum is not always identical to the predicate of the negandum. "The predicate of the

---

[a] *Signs and Reasonings*, pp. 9a.7-9b.1. Ge-luk-pa scholars agree that the predicate of the probandum must be a negative phenomenon, and most of them agree that it may be either an affirming negative phenomenon or a nonaffirming negative phenomenon. According to Jam-yang-shay-pa, however, and the scholars of Go-mang who adhere to his view, the predicate of the probandum must be a nonaffirming negative phenomenon. (Ge-shay Kön-chok-tse-ring, commentary on *Signs and Reasonings*, p. 0.)

negandum" refers to the opposite of the full predicate of the probandum as stated in the given syllogism, whereas "the object designated as
the predicate of the negandum" generally refers to the main object of
consideration within the predicate of the negandum.[a] This distinction
becomes especially important in the case of the nonobservation signs
of the nonappearing, as will be explained below.[b]

Pur-bu-jok posits two kinds of nonobservation signs: nonobservation signs of the nonappearing (*mi snang ba ma dmigs pa'i rtags*) and
nonobservation signs of the suitable to appear (*snang rung ma dmigs pa'i
rtags*).[c] This division depends on whether the object *designated* as the
predicate of the negandum (the main object of consideration within the
full predicate of the negandum) is a phenomenon that is "suitable to
appear" (*snang rung ba*)—that is, accessible to the valid cognition of the
opponent, in relation to the subject. Ge-shay Pel-den-drak-pa explains
the meaning of "suitable to appear" in this context:

> Suitable to appear means suitable to be realized by valid cogni-
> tion. In general, appearance (*snang ba*) and realization (*rtogs pa*)
> are different in meaning. In general, something's appearing
> does not [necessarily] mean it is realized. Here, however, the
> meaning [of "suitable or unsuitable to appear"—*snang rung mi
> rung*] is "suitable or unsuitable to be realized by valid cogni-
> tion" (*tshad mas rtogs rung mi rung*).[270]

In a syllogism involving a *nonobservation sign of the nonappearing*, the
object designated as the predicate of the negandum is a phenomenon
that is *not* accessible to the valid cognition of the opponent. As Ge-shay
Pel-den-drak-pa says,

> If the object designated as the predicate of the negandum exists
> in relation to the subject, but cannot be seen [by the opponent]
> through direct perception or inference, then the sign is a non-
> observation sign of the nonappearing.[271]

A phenomenon that is not accessible to a person's valid cognition—
whether direct or inferential—is a supersensory object (*skal don*) for

---

[a]   Ge-shay Pel-den-drak-pa explains that the object designated as the predicate of the
negandum is the main focus of thought within the predicate of the negandum. (Commentary on *Signs and Reasonings*, vol. 4, p. 1.)

[b]   See the subsection "consideration of the phrase 'object designated as the predicate of
the negandum,'" in this chapter.

[c]   *Signs and Reasonings*, p. 9b.1-2. Nonobservation signs of the suitable to appear are
discussed in chapter seven.

that person. In a proof involving any nonobservation sign, the predicate of the negandum is by definition a negative phenomenon; in a proof involving a nonobservation sign of the nonappearing, the *main* object under consideration within that predicate—the object designated as the predicate of the negandum—is a supersensory object for the opponent. Lati Rin-po-che comments,

> In the case of a correct sign of the nonappearing, the object designated as the predicate of the negandum in that proof is not suitable to appear to the opponent, whether it exists with the basis of negation [that is, the subject] or not. A supersensory object does not appear to an ordinary being, whether it is present or not. Thus, "nonappearing" means that the object designated as the predicate of the negandum [being a supersensory object for the opponent] is unsuitable to be perceived by the opponent—whether it exists with the basis of negation or not.[272]

On the other hand, in a syllogism involving a *nonobservation sign of the suitable to appear*, the object designated as the predicate of the negandum is a phenomenon that is "suitable to appear"—that is, accessible to the valid cognition of the opponent. A phenomenon that is suitable to appear—such as smoke—would be apprehendable, in general, if it were present. But even such an object, generally apprehendable by an ordinary person, may in certain circumstances be nonapprehendable; smoke may be invisible at night. According to Lati Rin-po-che,

> In the case of a correct nonobservation sign of the suitable to appear, the object designated as the predicate of the negandum exists with the basis of negation and is suitable to appear to the valid cognition of the correct opponent; however, due to certain circumstances, it is not perceived by the opponent.[273]

Phenomena that are not initially accessible to the valid cognition of ordinary beings fall into two categories: (1) hidden phenomena, which—although inaccessible to direct valid cognition—are accessible to inferential valid cognition, and (2) supersensory objects, which are not accessible—except in a general way—to either direct or inferential valid cognition.

In any valid proof, that which is being proved to a correct opponent must be a hidden phenomenon for that opponent; otherwise there would be no need for proof. Hidden phenomena may be established by valid cognition through correct signs. Objects that are supersensory for the correct opponent differ from hidden phenomena in that they are not accessible (except in a general way) to that opponent's valid cognition, whether direct or inferential.

Supersensory objects are not supersensory by their very nature—that is, they are not supersensory for all beings. What is inaccessible to the valid cognition of one person may be accessible to that of another. Categorizing phenomena as supersensory or not is always relative to the mind of the individual being. Here, as in other areas of Tibetan logic, the emphasis is on the specific person. This emphasis is reflected in the words of Ge-shay Pel-den-drak-pa:

> So-called supersensory objects are not such in general; they are supersensory in relation to specific persons' minds. For example, atoms are supersensory objects for us because their entity is subtle.[274]

Pur-bu-jok explains that there are three types of supersensory objects: those that are supersensory by way of place, by way of time, and by way of entity. He writes,

> Objects that are supersensory by way of place are, for example, the specifics of environments and beings that are very far away from oneself. Objects that are supersensory by way of time are, for example, the specifics of past and future eons. Although these are not supersensory in general, they are supersensory in terms of one's mind. Objects that are supersensory by way of entity are objects that are beyond one's ken even when nearby, because of their subtle entities; for example, a flesh-eater or an intermediate being of a god that is right in front [of oneself], or the aggregates (*phung po*) of those beings.[a]

Certain categories of sentient beings are thus considered to be supersensory objects in relation to the minds of ordinary beings; these include gods, demigods, hell-beings, hungry ghosts, flesh-eaters, and other beings whose nature is too subtle to be perceived by ordinary beings. Objects that are supersensory by way of entity also include the spiritual attainments and good qualities of beings: enlightenment, omniscience, liberation, *bodhicitta*, and other good qualities. As Ge-shay Pel-den-drak-pa says,

> The main point here [in this topic of nonobservation signs of

---

[a] *Signs and Reasonings*, p. 10b.5-7. Flesh-eaters (*piśāca*) are a class of demons that are said to be cannibals and to prey on human beings.

the nonappearing] is that we [as ordinary beings] cannot know, for example, if any given person is enlightened; that is something we cannot decide with any certainty. Whether or not someone is enlightened is not apparent to us through valid cognition. It is not suitable to talk about things that one cannot know with any certainty; we can't come to valid conclusions about such things. For example, the good qualities of another are things we cannot be certain about; so to talk about or come to conclusions about the qualities of another is unsuitable.[275]

One can know of certain qualities in another—such as honesty or dishonesty—which one might label as good or bad depending on one's point of view, but the deepest spiritual attainments of others are said to be inaccessible to the perception of ordinary beings.

It is said that the existence in general of each of these supersensory objects can be ascertained by valid cognition. Scriptural sources may serve as proof of the existence of phenomena such as omniscience and flesh-eaters.[a] One can gain valid inferential knowledge of the existence of the quality of omniscience, for example, by means of reasoning, through relying on correct signs of belief. One can know of the existence of omniscience, in general, as a spiritual attainment; but one cannot ascertain this quality in relation to specific persons—one cannot know its specific occurrences. Similarly, one can know of the existence of flesh-eaters, in general, by means of reasoning; but one cannot know if one is present in a particular place. As Ge-shay Pel-den-drak-pa puts it,

> If there were a flesh-eater present here, there would be no way to prove it [to an opponent for whom it is a supersensory object] with a reason; there is no reason by which one can prove that a flesh-eater is present to someone for whom it is a supersensory object.[276]

This, then, is the difference between hidden phenomena, such as subtle impermanence, and supersensory objects: when one develops valid cognition of subtle impermanence, it is necessarily in relation to a

---

[a] Lati Rin-po-che explains that ordinary beings are capable of ascertaining, in dependence on scriptural sources, the existence of flesh-eaters; he says, "Even though a flesh-eater is a supersensory object, we can posit that it exists. But with regard to this particular place in front of us, it would be an object of doubt for people like us. In dependence on scripture we *can* ascertain that flesh-eaters exist." (Commentary on *Signs and Reasonings* vol. 1, p. 67.)

particular subject—one ascertains a specific occurrence of subtle impermanence. Having understood by valid cognition the subtle impermanence of one thing—a pot, for example—one can apply the same reasoning to develop understanding of the subtle impermanence of other things—sounds, tables, mountains, etc.—and thereby ascertain the specific impermanence of each of these things. However, when one develops valid cognition of the existence of a supersensory object—a flesh-eater or omniscience, for example—such understanding is *not* in relation to specific occurrences; one for whom these are supersensory objects cannot know their specific occurrences.

To summarize, nonobservation signs are divided according to whether the phenomenon under consideration is supersensory (and thus "nonappearing" to the valid cognition of the opponent) or "suitable to appear" to the valid cognition of the opponent in relation to the subject. The terms "nonappearing" and "suitable to appear" refer to the object designated as the predicate of the negandum. Ge-shay Pel-den-drak-pa summarizes the basis of the division of nonobservation signs with these words,

> If, in relation to a basis of debate, the object designated as the predicate of the negandum is suitable to be seen by the valid cognition of the correct opponent, then it is a correct nonobservation sign of the suitable to appear. If it is not suitable to appear to the opponent, then it is a correct nonobservation sign of the nonappearing.[277]

NONOBSERVATION SIGNS OF THE NONAPPEARING

Pur-bu-jok's definition of a correct nonobservation sign of the nonappearing in the proof of something is:

> (1) It (x) is a correct nonobservation sign in the proof of that and (2) although, in general, the object designated as the predicate of the negandum in the proof of that by the sign x does exist, it does not appear to the valid cognition of the person for whom it has become the property of the subject in the proof of that.[278]

The object designated as the predicate of the negandum exists, in general, but it is a supersensory object for the opponent. Because it is supersensory, even if it were present in a particular place, the opponent could not ascertain it there. Someone who has had no experience of flesh-eaters has no way of knowing if one is present in a particular place. Such persons could not know of its presence by direct valid cognition, because even if it were present it would be invisible to them; and they could not know of its presence by inferential valid cognition, because even if it were present, its presence could not be proved by reasoning. According to Ge-shay Pel-den-drak-pa,

> For someone who has no experience of a sentient being such as a flesh-eater, there is no way to know either by direct perception or by inference if there is a flesh-eater here in this place or in any given place; there is no way for that person to say one way or the other.[279]

Similarly, ordinary beings have no way of knowing if another person has spiritual qualities, such as omniscience, because these are supersensory objects for them. Pur-bu-jok writes,

> Sutra says: "A person cannot estimate the measure of [another] person. [If one does so,] one will degenerate." By the mere fact of their not appearing to oneself, it is not reasonable to say that another does not have such-and-such good qualities.[a]
>
> To indicate this meaning, [we find in Dharmakīrti's *Commentary on (Dignāga's) "Compilation of Prime Cognition"*: "When a valid cognition is nonoperating and nonexistent, then it has as effect the nonoperation of a subsequent cognition."[280]

A valid cognition is a cause, having as its effect a factually concordant

---

[a] "By the mere fact of their not appearing *to* oneself" is a translation of *rang la mi snang ba tsam gyis.* This translation accords with the commentary of Lati Rin-po-che. Ge-shay Ge-dün-lo-drö's understanding of this line is somewhat different. In accordance with his commentary, it would be rendered "by the mere fact that they do not appear *in* oneself," or, more freely, "by the mere fact that one does not have [those qualities] oneself." The ge-shay explains, "Just because one does not have them [that is, certain good qualities] oneself, it is not reasonable to say that another does not have them. The words *rang la mi snang ba* ("not appearing to/in oneself") do not mean that one is not seeing [the qualities] in others, but rather that one does not have them oneself. The fault is to say: 'They don't have these good qualities because I don't have these good qualities.'" (Ge-shay Ge-dün-lo-drö, commentary on *Signs and Reasonings*, section 6, pp. 2-3.)

On the other hand, according to Lati Rin-po-che, this passage indicates that it is unreasonable to hold that what one does not see does not exist. He explains that this statement is directed, in part, at the Nihilists, who assert that liberation, omniscience, and the relationship of cause and effect of actions do not exist because they do not perceive them. He says, "The presentation of correct nonobservation signs of the nonappearing is set forth mainly to refute such views." (Lati Rin-po-che, commentary on *Signs and Reasonings*, vol. 2, April 18, pp. 2-3.)

subsequent cognition. When valid cognition does not operate, there is also no operation of subsequent cognition. It is said that one cannot estimate the measure of another person because that is a supersensory object. There is no way to prove or disprove the presence of a supersensory object in a particular place or in relation to a particular person. Valid cognition is thus "nonoperating and nonexistent" in relation to supersensory objects.

Pur-bu-jok goes on to divide nonobservation signs of the nonappearing into two types: (1) a correct sign that is a *nonobservation* of a "related object" (*'brel zla* or *'brel yul*) of the nonappearing and (2) a correct sign that is an *observation* of a "contradictory object" (*'gal zla*) of the nonappearing.[281]

It is important to keep in mind that the correct sign in a proof is always related to the predicate of the probandum in that proof. That being the case, there are two further possibilities among nonobservation signs: (1) the sign may involve the nonobservation of a "related object" (x) of the predicate of the negandum, in that the predicate of the negandum and x are related[a]; or (2) the sign may involve the observation of a "contradictory object" (y) of the predicate of the negandum, in that y is contradictory with the predicate of the negandum.

CORRECT SIGN THAT IS A NONOBSERVATION OF A RELATED OBJECT

This type of sign is used in this way: First let us posit an object a that is related with another object b, either by being the effect of b or by being of the same nature as b; b is thus the "related object" of a. It has been shown that because a and b are related in one of these two ways, the presence of a in a particular place establishes the presence of b in that place. It is also the case that, given that relationship, the absence of b in a particular place may establish the absence of a in that place.

In the context of nonobservation signs, this explains that—given that relationship between a and b, and given the right circumstances (that is, a correct or a prepared opponent)—the absence of b establishes the absence of a in a particular place; that is, the nonobservation of b

---

[a] If the sign involves the nonobservation of something that is a "related object" of the predicate of the negandum, then the opposite of the sign is the related object of the predicate of the negandum. Is this related object (*'brel zla*) of the predicate of the negandum itself related (*'brel ba*) with the predicate of the negandum? Is the predicate of the negandum related with its related object? The discussion of these questions is more relevant to the next chapter and appears there. In brief, some Ge-luk-ba scholars say that the related object of x *is* necessarily related with x and some say that it is not.

proves the nonexistence of *a* in that place. For example, oak is related with tree, and tree is the "related object" of oak. The absence of tree establishes the absence of oak in a particular place; that is, the nonobservation of trees in a particular place is conclusive proof of the nonexistence of oaks in that place.[a]

Pur-bu-jok posits the following as the definition of a correct sign of the nonappearing that is a nonobservation of a related object in the proof of something:

> That which is a common locus of (1) being a correct nonobservation sign of the nonappearing in the proof of that and (2) being a nonaffirming negative phenomenon.[282]

In this type of correct sign of the nonappearing, that which is set as the sign is the nonobservation of an object to which the predicate of the negandum is related. Being a nonobservation, the sign is of course a negative phenomenon; Pur-bu-jok's definition further specifies that it must be a nonaffirming negative phenomenon.[b]

It has already been shown that there are two types of relationships: of provenance and of sameness of nature. When Ge-luk-pa scholars, including Pur-bu-jok, analyze correct signs that are a nonobservation of a related object of the nonappearing, they distinguish three types: correct signs of the nonappearing that are a nonobservation of a cause, a pervader, and a nature.[283] "Pervader" and "nature" are two distinctions within the "sameness of nature" category. If *a* is related to *b* in a

---

[a]   The absence of oak cannot establish the absence of tree because there are trees other than oaks. As a complication, it is interesting to note that the situation is different in the case of phenomena related *causally*. For example, smoke is related with fire; the absence of fire may in certain circumstances establish the absence of smoke (for example, on a lake at night: smoke would be invisible, and fire, if present, would be visible; thus the absence of fire proves the absence of smoke). And the absence of smoke may in certain circumstances establish the absence of fire (in a situation in which smoke, if present, would be visible, for example from the chimney of a house; the fire would not be visible, but the smoke would; the absence of smoke thus proves the absence of fire). Does this mean that fire is related with smoke? This is a complicated issue. Some Ge-luk-pa scholars hold that the direct cause of something is related with it and some that it is not. Although a thorough analysis of this topic is beyond the scope of this book, the next chapter touches on it.

[b]   Ge-luk-pa scholars explain that any "nonobservation" (*ma dmigs pa*) of something must be a nonaffirming negative phenomenon; for example, the nonobservation of pot (*bum pa'i ma dmigs pa*) is a nonaffirming negative phenomenon. On the other hand, any "observation" of something must be either an affirming negative phenomenon (such as a mountainless plain) or a positive phenomenon (such as a pot).

relationship of provenance, then *b* is the cause of *a*; if *a* is related to *b* in a relationship of sameness of nature, then *b* is either the pervader of *a* or of the same nature as *a*.

Thus, the sign involves the nonobservation of something that is either a cause, a pervader, or a nature of the predicate of the negandum. Each of these three is a related object of the predicate of the negandum. In this context, as will be explained below, the nonobservation of the cause of x in a particular place serves as proof of the nonexistence of x in that place; and the same is true for the pervader and nature of x—wherever they do not exist, x cannot exist.

The distinction between the "pervader of *a*" and the "nature of *a*" identifies the two main ways in which phenomena may be related in the strictly defined way required for the relationship of sameness of nature. If *a* is the same nature as *b* in this relationship, then *b* is either (1) a category that is mutually pervasive with *a* or (2) a category that is broader than *a* and completely encompasses *a*; that is, it pervades *a*, but is not pervaded by *a*.

(1) Examples of phenomena that are mutually pervasive are "the impermanent" and "product." "The impermanent" is of the same nature as "product" and is mutually pervasive with "product"—whatever is a product is necessarily impermanent and whatever is impermanent is necessarily a product. Product is related with the impermanent; therefore, the nonobservation—in a certain place—of the impermanent (the related object of product) proves the nonexistence of product there. This is called the nonobservation of a nature.

(2) Examples of phenomena that have the same nature but are not mutually pervasive are "tree" and "oak." Oak is said to be of the same nature as tree, but tree is a broader category than oak and completely encompasses oak. Tree and oak are not mutually pervasive: whatever is an oak is necessarily a tree, but whatever is a tree is not necessarily an oak. Tree is "the related object" (*'brel zla*) of oak (because oak is related with tree) but is *not* "related" (*'brel ba*) with oak; if oak is eliminated, tree is not necessarily eliminated—there are many trees that are not oaks. Tree is not related with oak, but oak is related with tree; therefore, the nonobservation—in a particular place—of tree, the related object of oak, proves the nonexistence of oak there. This is called the nonobservation of a pervader.

Nonobservation of a Cause

To illustrate a correct sign that is a nonobservation of a cause, Pur-bu-jok posits,

> [One can state, "With respect to the subject, here in this place in front, there does not exist a factually concordant subsequent cognition—ascertaining a flesh-eater—in the continuum of a person for whom a flesh-eater is a supersensory object, because of the nonexistence of a prime cognition—observing a flesh-eater—in the continuum of a person for whom a flesh-eater is a supersensory object."] In that, "the nonexistence of a prime cognition—observing a flesh-eater—in the continuum of a person for whom a flesh-eater is a supersensory object" is a correct sign of the nonappearing that is a nonobservation of a cause in the proof that, here in this place in front, there does not exist a factually concordant subsequent cognition—ascertaining a flesh-eater—in the continuum of a person for whom a flesh-eater is a supersensory object.[284]

In this syllogism, the predicate of the probandum is the nonexistence of a factually concordant subsequent cognition ascertaining a flesh-eater in the continuum of a person for whom a flesh-eater is a supersensory object. The predicate of the negandum is the existence of such a subsequent cognition. The sign is the nonexistence of a prime cognition ascertaining a flesh-eater in the continuum of such a person.

The prime cognition is the cause of the subsequent cognition. Thus, this sign involves the nonobservation of a cause of the predicate of the negandum. Just as the presence of the effect (the subsequent cognition) may serve as proof of the presence of the cause (the prime cognition), so the absence of the cause (the prime cognition) may serve as proof of the absence of the effect (the subsequent cognition). As Ge-shay Ge-dün-lo-drö explains,

> In this syllogism, the predicate of the negandum is "a factually concordant subsequent cognition ascertaining a flesh-eater in the continuum of a person for whom a flesh-eater is a supersensory object." If that subsequent cognition existed, its cause would be "a prime cognition that observes a flesh-eater in the continuum of a person for whom a flesh-eater is a supersensory object." When the nonexistence of that cause is stated as the sign, it is a correct sign of the nonappearing that is a nonobservation of a cause.[285]

Pur-bu-jok explains, in four stages, why the nonexistence of that cause is "a correct sign of the nonappearing that is a nonobservation of a related cause." The reason in that syllogism is shown to be:

(1) a correct nonobservation sign;
(2) a correct nonobservation sign of the nonappearing;
(3) a correct sign of the nonappearing that is a nonobservation of a related object; and, finally,
(4) a correct sign of the nonappearing that is a nonobservation of a related cause.[286]

To repeat, the syllogism in question is: "With respect to the subject, here in this place in front, there does not exist a factually concordant subsequent cognition—ascertaining a flesh-eater—in the continuum of a person for whom a flesh-eater is a supersensory object, because of the nonexistence of a prime cognition—observing a flesh-eater—in the continuum of a person for whom a flesh-eater is a supersensory object." The stages of Pur-bu-jok 's reasoning are as follows.

(1) Concerning the sign's being a correct nonobservation sign, Pur-bu-jok writes,

> The subject, the nonexistence of a prime cognition—observing a flesh-eater—in the continuum of a person for whom a flesh-eater is a supersensory object, is a *correct nonobservation sign* in the proof that there does not exist a factually concordant subsequent cognition—that ascertains a flesh-eater in the place in front—in the continuum of a person for whom a flesh-eater is a supersensory object because (a) it is a correct sign in the proof of that and (b) the nonexistence of a factually concordant subsequent cognition that ascertains a flesh-eater in the place in front—in the continuum of a person for whom a flesh-eater is a supersensory object—is a negative phenomenon.[287]

As Pur-bu-jok points out, to be a correct nonobservation sign, the sign must first be a correct sign. He does not discuss or prove this further, because his main purpose in this section is to explain the distinguishing features of the nonobservation signs of the nonappearing and not of nonobservation signs in general. In addition to being a correct sign (and therefore being the three modes in that proof), the main criterion of a correct nonobservation sign is that the predicate of the probandum be a negative phenomenon. This is because the sign is proving the absence or nonexistence of something; that nonexistence (*med pa*) is necessarily a negative phenomenon.

(2) Pur-bu-jok then indicates the main criterion of something's being a nonobservation sign of the nonappearing:

> The subject, the nonexistence of a prime cognition—observing a flesh-eater—in the continuum of a person for whom a flesh-eater is a supersensory object, is *a correct nonobservation sign of the nonappearing* in the proof of that because (a) it is a correct nonobservation sign in the proof of that and (b) a flesh-eater is a supersensory object for a person for whom it [the sign] has become the property of the subject in the proof of that.
>
> If someone says that the latter part of the reason [that is, that a flesh-eater is a supersensory object for such a person] is not established, then [the response is] it follows with respect to the subject, a person for whom a flesh-eater is a supersensory object with respect to the place in front, that a flesh-eater is a supersensory object for him because it is that subject.[288]

There is apparent agreement among Ge-luk-pa scholars that the sign in this syllogism is a nonobservation sign of the nonappearing because the main object designated as the predicate of the negandum—flesh-eater—is, in relation to the basis of debate, a supersensory object for the opponent. There is a difference of opinion concerning the precise referent of the term "object designated as the predicate of the negandum." Pur-bu-jok does not specify that the object designated as the predicate of the negandum is a supersensory object; he merely asserts that "flesh-eater" itself is one. Some scholars limit the use of the term "object designated as the predicate of the negandum" to the supersensory object; but Pur-bu-jok does not. This will be discussed below.

Despite this difference concerning the use of the term, there is apparent complete agreement concerning the essential point: flesh-eaters are supersensory objects for the opponent in question, and therefore they are not "suitable to appear" to him or her; the sign in the proof in question is thus a nonobservation sign of the nonappearing.

Concerning the reason why "flesh-eater" is a supersensory object, Pur-bu-jok says only that it is one because it is specified as one in the subject of the syllogism. In Ge-shay Pel-den-drak-pa's view, this is not a useful explanation because it does not provide any information. He says,

> Here, the reason is "because of being that subject." A sign should be helpful; this one is not. It is like saying, "The subject, sound, is impermanent because of being a sound." You cannot posit the basis of debate as the sign.[289]

Ge-shay Pel-den-drak-pa explains that a flesh-eater is a supersensory object because it is not ascertainable (by the opponent) either by direct valid cognition or by inferential valid cognition.[290]

(3) Concerning the sign's being a correct sign of the nonappearing that is a nonobservation of a related object, Pur-bu-jok writes,

> The subject, the nonexistence of a prime cognition—observing a flesh-eater—in the continuum of a person for whom a flesh-eater is a supersensory object, is a correct sign of the nonappearing that is a nonobservation of a related object in the proof of that because of (a) being a correct nonobservation sign of the nonappearing in the proof of that and (b) being a nonaffirming negative phenomenon.[291]

As explained earlier, this type of sign necessarily involves a "nonobservation" (*ma dmigs pa*) of something; and whatever is a nonobservation of something is necessarily a nonaffirming negative phenomenon.

(4) Concerning the sign's being a correct sign that is a nonobservation of a related cause of the nonappearing, Pur-bu-jok writes,

> It follows with respect to the subject, object of knowledge, that the nonexistence of a prime cognition—observing a flesh-eater—in the continuum of a person for whom a flesh-eater is a supersensory object is a correct sign of the nonappearing that is a nonobservation of a related cause in the proof of that because (a) it is a correct sign of the nonappearing that is a non-observation of a related object in the proof of that and (b) a prime cognition that observes a flesh-eater is the cause of a factually concordant subsequent cognition that ascertains a flesh-eater.[292]

This reasoning is uncomplicated. A prime cognition that observes a flesh-eater is the cause of a factually concordant subsequent cognition that ascertains a flesh-eater. Thus, a subsequent cognition ascertaining a flesh-eater must be preceded by a prime cognition ascertaining flesh-eater. Because the nonobservation of a cause of the predicate of the negandum is set as the sign, it is a sign of the nonappearing that is the nonobservation of a cause.

The sign involves the nonobservation of a cause of the predicate of the negandum. The cause is thus the related object of the predicate of the negandum. Lati Rin-po-che explains more fully,

> The flesh-eater does not appear to the valid cognition in the

continuum of a person for whom flesh-eater is a supersensory object. The *effect* is the predicate of the negandum—a factually concordant subsequent cognition that ascertains the existence of flesh-eater in the place in front. That which is necessarily related with the predicate of the negandum is a preceding prime cognition; because the nonobservation of that prime cognition is being stated as the reason, this is a correct sign of the nonappearing that is the nonobservation of a related object."[293]

Lati Rin-po-che says of the sign (a preceding prime cognition) that it is "necessarily related with the predicate of the negandum." This seems to indicate that the preceding prime cognition is actually related (*'brel ba*) with the predicate of the negandum; however, generally speaking, a cause is said to be unrelated with its effect. It appears that Lati Rin-po-che here is using the term "related" loosely to mean "the related object" (*'brel zla*)—indicating that the prime cognition is the related object of the predicate of the negandum. Elsewhere he says that the related object of something (x) is not necessarily related with x; for example, the direct cause of fire is the related object of fire but is not related with fire.[a]

Consideration of the Phrase "Object Designated as the Predicate of the Negandum"

In the study of nonobservation signs of the nonappearing, a distinction is made between (1) "the predicate of the negandum" in a particular proof and (2) "the object designated as the predicate of the negandum" in that proof. There is some discussion among Ge-luk-pa scholars concerning the use of the second term; the disagreement is relatively superficial, being primarily terminological rather than conceptual, but it is a potential source of confusion and should be noted.

Some scholars, including Ge-shay Pel-den-drak-pa and Lati Rin-po-che, limit the application of "object designated as the predicate of the negandum" specifically to that part of the predicate (flesh-eater) that is a supersensory object for the opponent and therefore is not suitable to appear to him or her. Ge-shay Pel-den-drak-pa then identifies this as the main object under consideration within that predicate.

Pur-bu-jok applies the term more broadly. In the syllogism under

---

[a] Commentary on *Signs and Reasonings*, p. 65. There is disagreement in this regard; this topic is discussed more in the chapter on nonobservation signs of the suitable to appear.

discussion, the predicate of the negandum is "*the existence* of a factually concordant subsequent cognition ascertaining a flesh-eater in the continuum of a person for whom a flesh-eater is a supersensory object." This is the full expression of the "predicate of the negandum," and according to Pur-bu-jok it may also be posited as an object designated as the predicate of the negandum in that proof. He adds that two shorter phrases are also objects designated as the predicate of the negandum in this syllogism: (1) dropping "the existence of" from the complete predicate gives "a factually concordant subsequent cognition ascertaining a flesh-eater in the continuum of a person for whom a flesh-eater is a supersensory object"; and (2) a radical abbreviation gives the *main* object of consideration: "flesh-eater."

Pur-bu-jok's view regarding the difference between these two terms ("predicate of the negandum" and "object designated as the predicate of the negandum") is expressed in the following passage:

> Whatever is an "object designated as the predicate of the negandum" in the proof of something is not necessarily "the predicate of the negandum" in the proof of that.[a] This is because: (1) "The existence of a factually concordant subsequent cognition that ascertains the existence of a flesh-eater—in the continuum of a person for whom a flesh-eater is a supersensory object with respect to the place in front" is both an object designated as the predicate of the negandum in the proof of the nonexistence of such a factually concordant subsequent cognition and the predicate of the negandum in the proof of that. (2) However, a flesh-eater and a factually concordant subsequent cognition that ascertains it are, individually, objects designated as the predicate of the negandum in the proof of that but are not the predicate of the negandum in the proof of that.[294]

---

[a] In Pur-bu-jok's view, there are three possibilities (*mu*) between these two phenomena; he does not state this explicitly, but it can be inferred from his words. Ge-luk-pa scholars commenting on his text explain his view by summarizing the three possibilities. Ge-shay Pel-den-drak-pa says, "According to Pur-bu-jok, there are three possibilities between the predicate of the negandum and the object designated as the predicate of the negandum: (1) both; for example, *the existence* of a factually concordant subsequent cognition ascertaining a flesh-eater in the continuum of a person for whom a flesh-eater is a supersensory object; (2) whatever is the predicate of the negandum is necessarily an object designated as the predicate of the negandum; but whatever is an object designated as the predicate of the negandum is not necessarily the predicate of the negandum; for example, flesh-eater; and (3) neither; for example, the horn of a rabbit." (Ge-shay Pel-den-drak-pa, commentary on *Signs and Reasonings,* vol. 4, p. 13.)

Two points are raised here. The first is (1) that the full expression of the predicate of the negandum is both the predicate of the negandum and an object designated as the predicate of the negandum. The second is (2) that the two, "flesh-eater" and "factually concordant subsequent cognition that ascertains the existence of flesh-eater, in the continuum of a person for whom flesh-eater is a supersensory object," are objects designated as the predicate of the negandum, but are not the predicate of the negandum.

(1) Pur-bu-jok considers the first point to be obvious. He writes, "The first part of the reason is easy [to prove]"[295]—whatever *is* the predicate of the negandum is obviously an object designated as the predicate of the negandum. However, not all Ge-luk-pa scholars agree that the full expression of the predicate of the negandum is an object designated as the predicate of the negandum. Some limit the application of the term "object designated as the predicate of the negandum" to "flesh-eater."

The definition of a correct nonobservation sign of the nonappearing specifies that although, in general, the object designated as the predicate of the negandum exists, it does not appear to the valid cognition of the correct opponent. Furthermore, Ge-luk-ba scholars explain that "not appearing" means it is not suitable to be realized by valid cognition because it is a supersensory object. On the basis of this definition, one could argue that, according to Pur-bu-jok, the object designated as the predicate of the negandum is a supersensory object; and if that is the case, then the full expression of the predicate of the negandum must be a supersensory object, because it is the object designated as the predicate of the negandum.

Ge-shay Pel-den-drak-pa and Lati Rin-po-che apply the term "object designated as the predicate of the negandum" only to the part of the predicate of the negandum that is "not suitable to appear" to the opponent—that is, to the supersensory object, flesh-eater. Lati Rin-po-che explains that, in the syllogism under consideration, the object designated as the predicate of the negandum is "flesh-eater" because it is the object toward which the subsequent cognition would be directed *if* such a subsequent cognition existed. He says,

> Why is flesh-eater the object designated as the predicate of the negandum? The hypothetical predicate of the negandum would be the operation of a subsequent cognition; that with respect to which such a subsequent cognition would operate would be a flesh-eater; the flesh-eater, therefore, is the object designated

as the predicate of the negandum.[296]

Ge-shay Pel-den-drak-pa clarifies this by explaining that the flesh-eater is the *main* object of consideration in the predicate of the negandum. He says,

> In considering whether, in relation to flesh-eater, there does or does not exist a factually concordant subsequent cognition, the main object of thought is flesh-eater. That is the object appearing to one's mind, the object under consideration. Flesh-eater is the main focus of the mind, and is thus the [main] object designated as the predicate of the negandum.[297]

According to Ge-shay Pel-den-drak-pa, flesh-eater is the object designated as the predicate of the negandum not only because it is the main object under consideration but also because it is the main object of doubt in the mind of the opponent.[298]

In summary, there is apparent agreement among Ge-luk-pa scholars that the full expression of the opposite of the predicate of the probandum is the predicate of the negandum. There is disagreement concerning the scope of the phrase, "object designated as the predicate of the negandum." Pur-bu-jok applies it broadly, to the full expression of the predicate of the negandum and to its two abbreviations. Lati Rinpo-che and Ge-shay Pel-den-drak-pa limit its application to the main object under consideration within the predicate of the negandum—the supersensory object.

(2) The second point Pur-bu-jok makes is that, in the syllogism under consideration, a flesh-eater and a subsequent cognition that ascertains it are both, individually, objects designated as the predicate of the negandum but are not the predicate of the negandum. He writes,

> If someone says that the second part of the reason is not established [that is, it is not established that a flesh-eater and a factually concordant subsequent cognition that ascertains it are, individually, the object designated as the predicate of the negandum], then the response is that [a flesh-eater and a subsequent cognition that ascertains it are both, individually, objects designated as the predicate of the negandum in the proof of that] because an opponent in the proof of that doubts whether or not a flesh-eater exists in this place in front and because such [a correct opponent] doubts whether or not a factually concordant subsequent cognition exists.

The two—a flesh-eater and a factually concordant subsequent cognition that ascertains it—are not, individually, the predicate of the negandum in the proof of that. This is because, in general, flesh-eaters exist and also because, for example, smoke is not the predicate of the negandum in the proof of the nonexistence of smoke on a lake at night.[299]

Here again two points are made: The first is (a) that both flesh-eater and factually concordant subsequent cognition are, individually, the object designated as the predicate of the negandum; the second is (b) that these two are not, individually, the predicate of the negandum in that proof.

(a) Pur-bu-jok asserts that both flesh-eater and factually concordant subsequent cognition are, individually, the object designated as the predicate of the negandum because the opponent has doubt concerning both. As explained before, there is some disagreement among Ge-luk-pa scholars. Ge-shay Pel-den-drak-pa limits the use of the phrase "object designated as the predicate of the negandum" to flesh-eater because in his view this is the object in relation to which there is doubt in the mind of the opponent. He says,

> For a person for whom a flesh-eater is a supersensory object, there is no way to see whether a flesh-eater is there or not; so this is someone who has doubt about whether there is or is not a flesh-eater there.[300]

The sign in the syllogism in question is considered to be a correct sign; therefore there must be some doubt concerning the existence of the factually concordant subsequent cognition in the mind of the opponent. Otherwise there would be no need for proof. Ge-shay Pel-den-drak-pa, however, specifies that the main focus of the doubt is the flesh-eater, not the subsequent cognition.[a]

In summary, whereas Pur-bu-jok posits both flesh-eater and the factually concordant subsequent cognition ascertaining flesh-eater as objects designated as the predicate of the negandum, some later commentators posit only flesh-eater as such. Ge-shay Pel-den-drak-pa

---

[a] Ge-shay Pel-den-drak-pa says, "Through his own experience, [the opponent] will know if a subsequent cognition ascertaining a flesh-eater exists or not." (Commentary on *Signs and Reasonings*, vol. 4, p. 14.) Elsewhere, the ge-shay likens this knowledge to direct knowledge of one's own pain, saying, "Someone who has a toothache knows from his own experience that he has a toothache; the presence or absence of toothache he knows by his own experience." (Ibid., vol. 4, p. 11.)

notes that one reason for this is that the doubt is directed toward flesh-eater, not toward the subsequent cognition.

Ge-shay Pel-den-drak-pa has another comment to make on Pur-bu-jok's statement that both flesh-eater and factually concordant subsequent cognition are objects designated as the predicate of the negandum. He points out,

> If the subsequent cognition is taken as an object designated as the predicate of the negandum, then it follows that the sign in that proof is not a sign of the nonappearing. It is a sign of the suitable to appear, because the object designated as the predicate of the negandum is suitable to appear—if the subsequent cognition exists, it is suitable to appear. Through his [or her] own experience, the opponent will know if there is a subsequent cognition in his [or her] own mental continuum.[301]

This argument centers on the fact that the factually concordant subsequent cognition is not a supersensory object. If it existed there, it would be ascertainable by valid cognition by the opponent. If one interprets the definition of nonobservation sign of the nonappearing to mean that the object designated as the predicate of the negandum is a supersensory object, then one could argue that if the subsequent cognition is posited as the object designated as the predicate of the negandum, then subsequent cognition must be a supersensory object. Or one could argue, with Ge-shay Pel-den-drak-pa, that if subsequent cognition is posited as the object designated as the predicate of the negandum, then the sign is not a sign of the nonappearing but rather of the suitable to appear, because subsequent cognition is the object designated as the predicate of the negandum and it *is* suitable to appear.

Thus, it may be argued that the object designated as the predicate of the negandum cannot be, in this proof, the subsequent cognition or the existence of the subsequent cognition, because that object must be a supersensory object for the opponent. Within the predicate of the negandum, only flesh-eater is not suitable to appear to the opponent; a flesh-eater does not appear to the valid cognition of the person for whom it is a supersensory object. Thus it may be said that the main object designated as the predicate of the negandum is "flesh-eater."

(b) There is agreement, among Ge-luk-pa scholars, concerning Pur-bu-jok's second point (that flesh-eater and the factually concordant subsequent cognition that ascertains it are not, individually, the predicate of the negandum); only the full expression of the opposite of the predicate of the probandum is called "the predicate of the negandum."

Pur-bu-jok asserts in support of this view that flesh-eater exists in general and that, "for example, smoke is not the predicate of the negandum in the proof of the nonexistence of smoke on a lake at night." On this, Lati Rin-po-che comments:

> In this example, the predicate of the negandum is not smoke, but rather the existence of smoke. This is because the opponent does not have doubt about smoke in general but rather about the existence of smoke where it cannot be seen, such as on a lake at night.[302]

Similarly, the opponent in the proof involving flesh-eater does not have doubt about the existence of flesh-eater in general, but rather about the specific presence of flesh-eater in front of him or her. Where is the doubt focused? Not toward the existence of flesh-eater in general, but toward the specific presence of flesh-eater.

In summary, the most important point regarding a nonobservation sign of nonappearing is that it is used in a proof that involves a supersensory object regarding which the opponent can have no specific valid knowledge; that is, he or she cannot know either by inference or by direct perception of its specific occurrence.

Nonobservation of a Pervader

As an illustration of a correct nonobservation sign of the nonappearing that is a nonobservation of a pervader, Pur-bu-jok posits,

> [One can state, "With respect to the subject, here in this place in front, it is unsuitable for a person for whom a flesh-eater is a supersensory object to posit the existence of a flesh-eater because of the nonobservation by valid cognition of the existence of a flesh-eater by a person for whom the existence of a flesh-eater is a supersensory object."] In that, "the nonobservation by valid cognition of the existence of a flesh-eater by a person for whom the existence of a flesh-eater is a supersensory object" is a correct sign of the nonappearing that is a nonobservation of a pervader in the proof that it is unsuitable for a person for whom a flesh-eater is a supersensory object to posit the existence of a flesh-eater with respect to this place in front.[303]

The predicate of the probandum is the unsuitability—and the predicate of the negandum is the suitability—of a person for whom a flesh-eater is a supersensory object to posit the existence of a flesh-eater. The sign is such a person's nonobservation by valid cognition of the existence of a flesh-eater. The suitability of positing the existence of a flesh-eater is said to be pervaded by the observation by valid cognition of the existence of a flesh-eater. Whoever has observed a flesh-eater by valid cognition can appropriately posit its existence; the observation is a necessary condition for the suitability of a person to posit the existence of a flesh-eater. Ge-shay Ge-dün-lo-drö explains,

> In this proof, the predicate of the negandum—"the suitability of a person for whom a flesh-eater is a supersensory object to posit the existence of a flesh-eater"—is the object pervaded. The pervader is "the observation by valid cognition of the existence of a flesh-eater by a person for whom the existence of a flesh-eater is a supersensory object." In other words, the observation by valid cognition of the existence of a flesh-eater is a necessary condition for the suitability of a person to posit the existence of a flesh-eater.[304]

Lati Rin-po-che explains that although ordinary beings can ascertain the existence of flesh-eater, they cannot ascertain its presence in a particular place. He says,

> It is not suitable for a person for whom a flesh-eater is a supersensory object to posit the thesis that a flesh-eater exists, because for that person there is no observation by valid cognition of flesh-eater. Even though a flesh-eater is a supersensory object, we can posit that it exists; but with regard to this particular place in front of us, it would be an object of doubt for people like us. In dependence on scripture, we can ascertain that flesh-eater exists.[305]

For a person for whom flesh-eater is a supersensory object, there is no observation by valid cognition of flesh-eater. It is said that whether or not valid cognition of flesh-eater exists in relation to a particular place is ascertained by direct valid cognition. The opponent has direct knowledge of the lack of such valid cognition in his or her own mental continuum.[a]

Ge-shay Lob-sang-gya-tso notes that a debater might ask, "If the opponent realizes the nonobservation by valid cognition of flesh-eater, doesn't he realize the nonexistence of flesh-eater?" The answer is no.

---

[a] Thus, it is said that the property of the subject in this proof is established by direct perception.

The context must be kept in mind or misunderstanding will result. He explains,

> The property of the subject is established; therefore, the non-observation by valid cognition of the existence of a flesh-eater has to be realized in relation to the place in front. It has to be specified, however, in relation to a particular person for whom the flesh-eater is a supersensory object. Otherwise, if it is not specified, then the nonobservation by valid cognition of flesh-eater would have to establish the nonexistence of flesh-eater—and that is not what is being proved here.[306]

It is important to specify the context of the reasoning—that it is posited in relation to a person for whom flesh-eater is a supersensory object. There cannot be nonobservation of valid cognition ascertaining flesh-eaters, in general, because in general flesh-eaters exist; if *in general* there were no observation of valid cognition ascertaining flesh-eaters, then they could not exist.[307]

Clearly, the nonobservation by valid cognition of flesh-eaters by an ordinary person does *not* prove the nonexistence of flesh-eaters. An important purpose of the presentation of nonobservation signs of the nonappearing is to indicate that the nonobservation by valid cognition of a supersensory object does not prove its nonexistence.[a]

If the sign "nonobservation by valid cognition of a flesh-eater" does not prove the nonexistence of a flesh-eater, then what does it prove? It can prove only the nonexistence of phenomena related with the valid cognition of a flesh-eater; and flesh-eater itself is *not* related with the valid cognition of flesh-eater. That which is related with the valid cognition of flesh-eater is either (a) the effect of or (b) of the same nature as such a valid cognition:

(a) The effect of the valid cognition ascertaining flesh-eater is the subsequent cognition of flesh-eater. Thus the nonobservation by valid cognition of flesh-eater does prove the nonexistence of a subsequent cognition of flesh-eater.

(b) The suitability of positing the existence of flesh-eater is said to be the same nature as the valid cognition of flesh-eater, in that the suitability of positing the existence of flesh-eater is pervaded by the valid cognition of flesh-eater; it is not suitable to assert the

---

[a]   According to Lati Rin-po-che, one purpose of this type of sign is to counter the view, "What I don't see doesn't exist." (Commentary on *Signs and Reasonings*, vol. 2, Apr. 18, 1977, p. 3.)

existence of a flesh-eater in a particular place unless one has ascertained a flesh-eater there by valid cognition. Thus the nonobservation by prime cognition of flesh-eater does prove the unsuitability of positing the existence of flesh-eater.

To summarize, in the case of an ordinary being for whom flesh-eaters are supersensory objects, the nonobservation by valid cognition of a flesh-eater in a particular place does not prove the nonexistence of flesh-eaters in that place. It does, however, prove (1) the nonexistence of a subsequent cognition ascertaining a flesh-eater in that place and (2) the unsuitability of positing the existence of a flesh-eater (in that place by that person).

In more general terms, it can be said that the nonobservation by valid cognition of a supersensory object, x, does not prove the nonexistence of x. It proves only:

(1) the nonexistence of the effect of the valid cognition of x,
(2) the nonexistence of that which is the same nature as the valid cognition of x, and
(3) the nonexistence of that which is pervaded by the valid cognition of x.

The absence of the cause proves the absence of the effect, and the absence of the pervader proves the absence of the pervaded. Thus, from the nonexistence of x one can infer the nonexistence of whatever is x's effect, the nonexistence of whatever is pervaded by x, and the nonexistence of whatever is the same nature as x.

Nonobservation of a Nature

As an illustration of a correct sign of the nonappearing that is the nonobservation of a nature, Pur-bu-jok posits,

> [One can state, "With respect to the subject, here in this place in front, there does not exist a factually concordant subsequent cognition, ascertaining a flesh-eater, in the continuum of a person for whom a flesh-eater is a supersensory object because of the nonobservation by valid cognition of a factually concordant subsequent cognition, ascertaining a flesh-eater, in the continuum of a person for whom a flesh-eater is a supersensory object."] In that, "the nonobservation by valid cognition of a factually concordant subsequent cognition, ascertaining a flesh-eater, in the continuum of a person for whom a flesh-eater is a

supersensory object" is a correct sign of the nonappearing that is a nonobservation of a nature in the proof of the nonexistence of a factually concordant subsequent cognition—ascertaining a flesh-eater in this place in front—in the continuum of such a person.[308]

In this syllogism, the predicate of the negandum and the reverse of the sign, if existent, would be of one nature. Ge-shay Ge-dün-lo-drö explains,

> The predicate of the negandum is "the existence of a factually concordant subsequent cognition, ascertaining a flesh-eater, in the continuum of a person for whom a flesh-eater is a supersensory object." This is of one nature with the reverse of the sign, "the observation by prime cognition of a factually concordant subsequent cognition, ascertaining a flesh-eater, in the continuum" of such a person. This is because "that which is observed by prime cognition" is the definition of "existent." In this proof, the nonobservation of such a factually concordant subsequent cognition is stated as the sign; thus, it is a correct sign of the nonappearing that is a nonobservation of a nature.[309]

From the nonobservation by prime cognition of a factually concordant subsequent cognition ascertaining a flesh-eater, one cannot infer anything about a flesh-eater, but one *can* infer the nonexistence of a cognition ascertaining one. In this proof, the property of the subject (the first mode) is established because the opponent knows by his or her own direct experience whether or not there is such a cognition in his or her own mental continuum.

The pervasions are also established. If there is nonobservation by valid cognition of a factually concordant subsequent cognition in the continuum of such a person, then such a cognition is necessarily nonexistent in that person's continuum. If there exists such a cognition in the opponent's continuum, then it is necessarily observed by valid cognition.

CORRECT SIGN THAT IS AN OBSERVATION OF A CONTRADICTORY OBJECT

As the definition of a correct sign of the nonappearing that is an observation of a contradictory object in the proof of something, Pur-bu-jok posits:

That which is a common locus of (1) being a correct nonobservation sign of the nonappearing in the proof of that and (2) being either an affirming negative or a positive phenomenon.[310]

He offers the following illustration:

[One can state, "With respect to the subject, here in this place in front, there does not exist a factually concordant subsequent cognition, ascertaining a flesh-eater, in the continuum of a person for whom a flesh-eater is a supersensory object because of existing (*yod pa'i phyir*)."] In that, "existing" is a correct sign of the nonappearing that is an observation of a contradictory object in the proof that there does not exist a factually concordant subsequent cognition—which ascertains a flesh-eater in this place in front—in the continuum of a person for whom a flesh-eater is a supersensory object.[311]

Here, the predicate of the negandum is "the existence of a factually concordant subsequent cognition ascertaining a flesh-eater in the continuum of a person for whom a flesh-eater is a supersensory object." There can be no existence of such a cognition in the continuum of a person for whom a flesh-eater is supersensory; therefore, such a subsequent cognition cannot exist for that person. Being nonexistent, it is contradictory with existence. According to Ge-shay Ge-dün-lo-drö,

The existence of that factually concordant subsequent cognition does not in fact exist and, thus, is contradictory with existence. Because the sign—"existing"—is contradictory with the predicate of the negandum, it is a correct sign of the nonappearing that is an observation of a contradictory object.[a]

One Ge-luk-pa scholar, Lati Rin-po-che, asserts that the sign "existing" (or "existence") refers to the existence of the "place in front" (the subject); thus he understands the sign to be "because the place in front exists." In his view,

The name "correct sign of the nonappearing that is an observation of a contradictory object" means that the sign is contradictory with the predicate of the negandum. The sign is "because [the place in front] exists." Once the place in front exists, a

---

[a] Commentary on *Signs and Reasonings*, section 6, p. 6. It should be noted that a nonexistent is usually not considered to be contradictory with something else, because that which is "contradictory" (*'gal ba*) must be an existent. It is usually held to be more accurate to say that the nonexistent is contradicted by the existent.

subsequent cognition by a person for whom a flesh-eater is a supersensory object would not operate. The existence of the place in front is contradictory with the existence of such a factually concordant subsequent cognition.[a]

In explaining why "existent" is a correct sign that is an observation of a contradictory object, Pur-bu-jok himself writes,

> The subject, existent, (or existing, or exists—*yod pa*) is a correct sign that is an observation of a contradictory object in the proof that there does not exist a factually concordant subsequent cognition—that ascertains a flesh-eater in the place in front—in the continuum of a person for whom a flesh-eater is a supersensory object because it [existent] is a correct nonobservation sign in the proof of that and is either an affirming negative phenomenon or a positive phenomenon. [The latter reason is established] because [existent] is a positive phenomenon.[312]

As explained earlier, such a sign necessarily involves the observation of something, and an observation (*dmigs pa*) of an object is necessarily either a positive phenomenon or an affirming negative phenomenon. According to Ge-shay Kön-chok-tse-ring, the main point of this illustration is to indicate that a nonobservation sign need not be a negative phenomenon. He explains that the sign in this proof could be virtually any positive phenomenon: "because of being an established base," "because of being an object of knowledge," and so on.[313]

PURPOSE OF NONOBSERVATION SIGNS OF THE NONAPPEARING

The value of this category of correct signs is to show that one cannot know by valid cognition the full extent of the good qualities of another person. Pur-bu-jok summarizes the importance of this topic by writing:

> If there is a person for whom the two—an intermediate being who will be a god in the next life and a flesh-eater—are supersensory objects from the viewpoint of his doubting whether or

---

[a] Commentary on *Signs and Reasonings*, vol. 1, p. 68. Several other Ge-luk-pa scholars emphasize that "existence" itself is contradictory with the operation of the subsequent cognition. Ge-shay Pel-den-drak-pa says, "The sign is just 'existent'; it is existence in general." (Commentary on *Signs and Reasonings*, vol. 4, p. 7.) And Ge-shay Ge-dün-lo-drö says, "The predicate of the negandum, the existence of a factually concordant subsequent cognition ascertaining a flesh-eater in the continuum of a person for whom flesh-eater is a supersensory object, and existence are contradictory." (Commentary on *Signs and Reasonings, section 6, p. 6.)

not they exist in front of him, it is unsuitable for the person to decide whether or not those two exist in that place. Taking this as an example, the purpose of positing nonobservation signs of the nonappearing is to understand the unsuitability of reifying or deprecating any person's faults or good qualities when one has not ascertained the presence or absence of faults and virtues by valid cognition.[314]

If something is a supersensory object for a person, then that person cannot know it by valid cognition. The good qualities of another are supersensory objects for ordinary beings and therefore are not ascertained by valid cognition. This nonobservation by valid cognition is itself said to be established by direct perception, which makes it sound like something very obvious—but if it were obvious, there would be no need for such proofs. It is because people do, in fact, falsely attribute good and bad qualities to others and because people do attribute nonexistence to qualities such as omniscience, that such signs were set forth.

This topic of nonobservation signs of the nonappearing can be used to help break down students' resistance to new ideas concerning things they cannot see and to help them learn to verify for themselves the truth concerning such phenomena as omniscience, liberation, *bodhicitta*, flesh-eaters, and so forth. It can induce people to look closely at the basis for their judgments and conclusions. Ge-shay Pel-den-drak-pa tells us,

> The purpose of this discussion of nonobservation signs of the nonappearing is to make the point that concerning things of which we (ordinary beings) have no valid knowledge, we cannot make definite conclusions. This is especially true regarding the spiritual attainments of another person; we have no valid knowledge of them and thus cannot know them with certainty.[315]

The full extent of another's good qualities is necessarily a supersensory object for most of us; therefore judgments and conclusions concerning the merits and faults of another are necessarily faulty. As Lati Rin-po-che says,

> One has not in fact ascertained with valid cognition another person's faults or virtues. So, if one proceeds to state, "This is the person's fault; this is the person's virtue," one is either reifying something, positing existence to something that doesn't

exist, or deprecating, denying, that is, considering to be non-existent, something that actually does exist.[316]

After spending enough time in the debate courtyard to know these syllogisms thoroughly and to become at ease in playing with the ideas behind them; and after enough time among the teachers to appreciate the qualities of character many of them have, the student can begin to see that one's ordinary way of relating to people is faulty—is not based on valid knowledge. The correct way to relate to others is said to be one that is based on valid knowledge.

No claim is made that merely understanding nonobservation signs of the nonappearing will bring a valid relationship with others; however, this understanding is thought to support the cultivation of such a relationship because it (1) makes one less likely to jump to invalid conclusions concerning another's faults and good qualities and (2) gradually undercuts the mistaken idea that what one does not perceive (e.g., omniscience) does not exist. It is not surprising that the knowledge of the possibility of excellent qualities and attainments in human beings—together with the knowledge that one's perception may be mistaken—should support the cultivation of a "valid" relationship with others. Eventually such knowledge will serve as the basis for the cultivation of *bodhicitta*, which might be described, from a Buddhist point of view, as the most valid and true relationship with others because it is founded on a true appraisal of the nature and value of other beings.

7. Correct Nonobservation Signs of the Suitable to Appear

Nonobservation signs are divided into two types, depending on whether the object designated as the predicate of the negandum is or is not a supersensory object for the opponent. If the predicate is a supersensory object for that person, it is not suitable to appear to him or her, and the sign employed in proving the negandum is called a nonobservation sign of the nonappearing.[a] If the predicate is *not* a supersensory object, it is suitable to appear to him or her, and the sign used in the syllogism is called a nonobservation sign of the suitable to appear. "Suitable to appear" has the very precise meaning that the predicate of the negandum is suitable to be realized by valid cognition. If the object is present in a particular place, therefore, the opponent is able to realize its presence there by valid cognition—either direct or inferential.

Pur-bu-jok's definition of a correct nonobservation sign of the suitable to appear in the proof of something is:

> A common locus of (1) being a correct nonobservation sign in the proof of that and (2) its being true that the object designated as the predicate of the negandum in the proof of that is not a supersensory object for the person for whom [the sign] has become the property of the subject in the proof of that.[317]

As an illustration, we may take the syllogism: "With respect to the subject, on a lake at night, smoke does not exist because fire does not exist."[b]

The subject specifies the place or circumstance or context under consideration; in this syllogism, the subject is "on a lake at night." The predicate of the probandum is "smoke does not exist." The predicate of the negandum is "smoke exists." The object designated as the predicate of the negandum is "smoke."[c] Smoke is not a supersensory object—it is

---

[a] These signs are discussed in chapter six.

[b] A syllogism is introduced here to illustrate the general nature of nonobservation signs of the suitable to appear. Pur-bu-jok's discussion of this particular syllogism appears in its proper place, in the section on "nonobservation of a cause." Another nonobservation sign of the suitable to appear is in the syllogism, "The subject, sound, is impermanent because of being a product." For the correct opponent for whom impermanent is not a supersensory object, product is such a sign.

[c] On pages 14b.7-15a.1 of *Signs and Reasonings,* Pur-bu-jok posits two objects designated

suitable to appear; thus, the nonappearance of fire is a correct nonobservation sign of the suitable to appear.

Here, the object designated as the predicate of the negandum (smoke) is something that is accessible to the opponent's valid cognition but is not accessible—in the context specified by the subject—to his or her direct perception. That is, although the predicate of the negandum is *suitable to appear* in general, it is *not* suitable to appear in this particular situation. In some circumstances one may be unable to see an object that is usually visible, and thus one may be uncertain whether it is present or not. In that case, the absence of the object can be logically established by (1) the absence (nonobservation) of something else to which it is related that *is* suitable to appear in that place or (2) by the presence of something contradictory with it. As Pur-bu-jok puts it:

> When correct signs that are a nonobservation of the suitable to appear are divided, there are two types: (1) correct signs that are a nonobservation of a related object suitable to appear (*snang rung gi 'brel zla*) and (2) correct signs that are an observation of a contradictory object suitable to appear (*snang rung gi 'gal zla*).[a]

When something that is normally visible cannot be seen, doubt can arise concerning whether it is present or not. A correct opponent is necessarily a person wondering about it, and this is the occasion for the

---

as the predicate of the negandum: "smoke" and "the existence of smoke." However, in his main treatment of this category of signs, the first of these two is the more important.

[a]   *Signs and Reasonings*, p. 11a.2. These phrases deserve some comment:

- In this book, this main division of nonobservation signs is into "nonobservation signs of the nonappearing" and "nonobservation signs of the suitable to appear." This emphasizes the fact that the difference between them is whether or not the object designated as the predicate of the negandum is suitable to appear (the sign is a sign *of* something that is suitable to appear). A subcategory is here called "signs that are a nonobservation of a related object suitable to appear"; this is an effort to indicate that what is suitable to appear is *the related object* (the sign). Lati Rin-po-che makes this point when he says that, in this type of proof, that which is set as the sign is something which, if present, would be suitable to appear (commentary on *Signs and Reasonings*, vol. 1, p. 70).
- A case could be made for inserting "of the": "signs that are a nonobservation of a related object *of the* suitable to appear." The object that is not observed (the sign) is a related object of something that is suitable to appear (the object designated as the predicate of the negandum), which thus is not a supersensory object for the opponent.

debater to use a nonobservation sign of the suitable to appear. The reasoning is as follows:

(1) By the sign of the nonobservation (absence) of phenomenon *x*, whatever is related with *x* is also eliminated. For example, since smoke is related with fire, the presence of smoke may serve as valid proof of the presence of fire, and the absence of fire may serve as valid proof of the absence of smoke.[a]

(2) By the sign of the observation of phenomenon y, whatever is contradictory with y is eliminated. For example, fire is said to be contradictory with cold; this is because hot and cold are explicitly contradictory (*dngos 'gal*), and hot is said to be the nature of fire.[b] Because fire is contradictory with cold, the presence of fire eliminates the presence of cold.

Of these two categories of signs—nonobservation of a related object and observation of a contradictory object—Pur-bu-jok now takes up the first.

NONOBSERVATION OF A RELATED OBJECT SUITABLE TO APPEAR

As the definition of a correct sign that is a nonobservation of a related object suitable to appear, Pur-bu-jok posits:

> That which is a common locus of (1) being a correct nonobservation sign of the suitable to appear and (2) being a nonaffirming negative phenomenon.[c]

This type of sign involves the nonobservation of something (x) to which the object designated as the predicate of the negandum is related. The sign is the nonobservation of an object that, if present, would be "suitable to appear" to the opponent. When the absence of this object is observed, that absence proves the absence of whatever is related to it.

---

[a] See the section below on "nonobservation of a direct effect" for discussion of the cause-and-effect relationship.

[b] The definition of fire is "the hot and burning."

[c] *Signs and Reasonings*, p. 11a.3. In chapter four it was noted that "an affirming negative phenomenon, through the terms expressing it, implies a positive phenomenon in the place of what is being eliminated. A nonaffirming negative phenomenon does not." Positive phenomenon and negative phenomenon are also discussed briefly in chapter eight. In chapter six (in the discussion of "correct sign that is a nonobservation of a related object") it was noted that the "nonobservation" (*ma dmigs pa*) of something is a nonaffirming negative phenomenon

A general statement of reasoning using this type of sign is:

"With respect to the subject x (a specific context or situation), a does not exist because b does not exist (is not observed)."

Here, a is the object designated as the predicate of the negandum; it is a phenomenon suitable to appear in general, but not suitable to appear in the context specified by the subject. And the nonobservation of b is the sign—b itself is the opposite (or reverse) of the sign (*rtags log*). In addition, b is the related object (*'brel zla*) of a. B would be suitable to appear in the context specified by the subject, if it were present. Its absence serves as proof of the absence of a, because they are related. For example, smoke is not suitable to appear in the dark ("on a lake at night"), but fire is. Fire is the cause of smoke, and thus smoke is "related" (*'brel ba*) with fire, and fire is "the related object" (*'brel zla* or *'brel yul*) of smoke.

Correct signs that are a nonobservation of a related object suitable to appear are divided on the basis of the way in which the object designated as the predicate of the negandum (a) is related to the opposite of the sign (b). Two relationships are possible: if the predicate of the negandum a is related with the opposite of the sign b, it must be either the *effect* of b or of the *same nature* as b. Pur-bu-jok writes,

> There are four types [of correct signs that are a nonobservation of a related object suitable to appear]: correct signs that are a nonobservation of (1) a cause suitable to appear, (2) a pervader suitable to appear, (3) a nature suitable to appear, and (4) a direct effect suitable to appear.[a]

The first and fourth of these types involve the relationship of provenance, the second and third the relationship of sameness of nature. In each case, the sign is the nonobservation of something related to the predicate of the negandum, and that related object is suitable to appear. As Lati Rin-po-che puts it:

> If the pervader of the predicate of the negandum in the proof of that exists [that is, is present], it is suitable to appear. Similarly,

---

[a] *Signs and Reasonings*, p. 11a.4. Pur-bu-jok posits a brief definition of a correct sign which is a nonobservation of a cause suitable to appear: "That which is the three modes of the nonobservation of a cause suitable to appear." He adds that the form of this definition applies to the other three as well; thus, the definition of a correct sign which is a nonobservation of a pervader suitable to appear is "that which is the three modes of the nonobservation of a pervader suitable to appear," and so forth. (*Signs and Reasonings*, p. 11a.5.)

if the cause, the nature, or the direct effect of the predicate of the negandum exist, they are suitable to appear.[318]

In the nonobservation of a cause and of a direct effect suitable to appear, the object designated as the predicate of the negandum *a* is related to the opposite of the sign *b* (that is, the object that is not observed) in the relationship of provenance. That is, the nonobservation of *b* proves the absence of *a*, because *a* is the effect of *b*. In this connection, Ge-shay Lob-sang-gya-tso mentions the distinction between "cause" and "*direct* cause":

> There are the relationships of [direct cause and] direct effect (*dngos 'bras kyi 'brel ba*) and the relationships of cause and effect (*rgyu 'bras kyi 'brel ba*). In the case of a reason involving direct cause and direct effect, because the direct effect does not exist, the direct cause is eliminated. And in the case involving cause and effect, because the cause does not exist, the effect is eliminated.[319]

In the nonobservation of a pervader and of a nature, the predicate of the negandum (*a*) is related to the opposite of the sign (*b*) in the relationship of sameness of nature; that is, *a* is the same nature as *b*. In the case of a syllogism using a correct sign that is a nonobservation of a *pervader*, *a* is the same nature as *b* and *a* is pervaded by *b* (but *b* is not pervaded by *a*). In the case of a syllogism using a correct sign that is a nonobservation of a *nature*, *a* is the same nature as *b* and *a* and *b* are mutually inclusive (the pervasion goes both ways). Ge-shay Lob-sang-gya-tso says:

> ...there are the relationship of sameness of nature (*rang bzhin gyi 'brel ba*) and the relationship of pervader and pervaded (*khyab bya khyab byed kyi 'brel ba*)...Then by the nonexistence of the pervader the existence of the pervaded is eliminated.[320]

NONOBSERVATION OF A CAUSE

To illustrate his first type of correct nonobservation sign of a related object suitable to appear, Pur-bu-jok posits the sign in the following syllogism: "With respect to the subject, on a lake at night, smoke does not exist because fire does not exist." He writes:

> "The nonexistence of fire" (or "fire does not exist"—*me med pa*) is a correct sign that is a nonobservation of a cause suitable to appear in the proof of smoke as nonexistent on a lake at

night.[321]

Here, the object designated as the predicate of the negandum is smoke; its cause (and its related object) is fire—the opposite of the sign (*rtags log*).[322] Although smoke is normally visible, it would not be seen on a lake at night. Smoke is *not* suitable to appear to the opponent in that context; but fire—the cause of smoke—*is* suitable to appear. As Lati Rin-po-che says,

> Night is a time when you would see even a tiny fire; but even if there were a lot of smoke, you could not see it. The sign, then, of there not being any smoke is that there isn't any fire.[323]

Smoke is related with fire, being its effect. Because smoke is related with fire, the elimination of fire eliminates smoke also. In this syllogism, therefore, the nonexistence of fire (the cause of smoke) is a correct sign that is a nonobservation of a cause suitable to appear.

It should be noted that since this is a subcategory of correct nonobservation signs of the suitable to appear, the object designated as the predicate of the negandum (smoke) is not a supersensory object for the opponent and therefore is in general "suitable to appear." Ge-shay Ge-dün-lo-drö says:

> Because the object designated as the predicate of the negandum is not a supersensory object [for the opponent], if it exists it is suitable to appear to him [or her].[324]

If smoke is there, it must be apprehendable by valid cognition. But we are told that the context makes it invisible, since the night is too dark for direct perception by the sense of sight. Since smoke is suitable to appear, it must be ascertainable in some other way. According to Ge-shay Pel-den-drak-pa:

> How does this type of sign work? That which is designated as the predicate of the negandum is smoke, and the cause of smoke is fire. In the context of the syllogism, if smoke is there it is not perceivable by direct perception—but it *is* understandable by valid cognition. It must be known by valid cognition. But how?
>
> This being in the category of nonobservation signs of the suitable to appear, if smoke were there it would have to be ascertainable by valid cognition...there would have to be a way for the opponent to know of its presence. This might involve going out on the lake in a boat and smelling smoke. If it is

there, it must be ascertainable in one way or another. If it is impossible for the opponent to know if smoke exists there, this would become a nonobservation sign of the nonappearing rather than of the suitable to appear.[325]

To sum up: In the syllogism, "With respect to the subject, on a lake at night, smoke does not exist because fire does not exist," the sign "fire does not exist" is a nonobservation sign of the suitable to appear. Thus, the object designated as the predicate of the negandum (smoke) is not a supersensory object for the opponent. But in this context it is not visible. Its absence is proved by the nonobservation of a related object (the cause—fire) of the object designated as the predicate of the negandum (smoke).

NONOBSERVATION OF A PERVADER

As an illustration of his second type of sign that is a nonobservation of a related object, Pur-bu-jok posits the sign in the syllogism, "With respect to the subject, on a craggy cliff where trees are not observed by valid cognition, an oak does not exist because of the nonexistence of trees." He writes:

> [In that,] "The nonexistence of trees" is a correct sign that is a nonobservation of a pervader suitable to appear in the proof of the nonexistence of an oak on a craggy cliff where trees are not observed by valid cognition.[a]

The object designated as the predicate of the negandum is oak, which is pervaded by tree—the opposite of the sign.[b] An oak is not a supersensory object and thus must be ascertainable, if present. Ge-shay Pel-den-drak-pa comments:

> In relation to that [basis of debate], if the object designated as the predicate of the negandum [oak] exists, then it must be suitable to be perceived by the valid cognition of the opponent.[326]

Since this is a nonobservation sign of the suitable to appear, the predicate of the negandum is not a supersensory object for the opponent.

---

[a] *Signs and Reasonings*, p. 11a.5-6. Pur-bu-jok refers to a *sha pa* (Sanskrit, *aśoka*), a medium-sized tree with magnificent red leaves; I have used "oak" for simplicity.

[b] Ge-shay Ge-dün-lo-drö, commentary on *Signs and Reasonings*, section 7, p. 2b. The sign, of course, is "the nonexistence of tree," so "the existence of trees" (here abbreviated by the ge-shay to "trees") is the *rtags log*, the opposite of the sign.

Therefore, if it is present in relation to the subject, it is ascertainable by the opponent—somehow. If the hill is very far away, such ascertainment would probably have to be inferential. Ge-shay Pel-den-drak-pa suggests:

> One way would be to watch someone go there and bring back a branch of the tree; from the branch one could tell that those trees over there must be oaks. Such reasons can be posited to prove that there is an oak over there; but it can only be proved by a reason, because it is too far away to tell by direct perception.[327]

In Pur-bu-jok's illustration, the craggy cliff under consideration is understood to be close enough for the observer to ascertain the presence or absence of trees by direct perception, but too far away to identify a specific type of tree. Although the distance is too great to identify the genus, from the absence of *all* trees one can conclude with certainty that there are no oaks on that cliff. As Ge-shay Lob-sang-gya-tso says:

> If the object designated as the predicate of the negandum, oak, existed in that place, it would not be perceivable by direct perception. In this context [in relation to this basis of debate], the correct opponent would not be able to know the oak by direct perception if it were there. But the pervader, trees, if it existed there, would be suitable to appear to his or her direct perception. By the nonexistence of the pervader, the existence of the pervaded is eliminated.[328]

Whatever is an oak is necessarily a tree, but whatever is a tree is not necessarily an oak; thus tree pervades oak, but oak does not pervade tree. In the terminology of the Ge-luk-pa system, therefore, oak is related with tree, but tree is not related with oak. This is because if tree is eliminated, oak is also necessarily eliminated, but if oak is eliminated, tree is not necessarily eliminated. From the fact that oak is related with tree, one can conclude that the presence of oak proves the presence of tree, and the absence or nonobservation of tree proves the absence of oak.[329] Lati Rin-po-che comments:

> For example, there are two mountains: on the first you can see that there are trees, but you can't tell what kind; on the second you can see that there are no trees at all. If someone has doubt about whether there are oaks on the second mountain, you could state this reason ("the nonexistence of trees") to prove that there can't be any oaks. Because the nonobservation of the

pervader of the predicate of the negandum is stated as the sign, it is called a correct sign that is a nonobservation of a pervader.[330]

It is important to note the wording in Pur-bu-jok's example syllogism. The predicate of the probandum in this proof is "an oak does not exist" (not "an oak *tree* does not exist"). If the predicate of the probandum were to include the word "tree," then "the nonexistence of trees" would serve no purpose as a sign, and it would therefore not be a correct sign. As Ge-shay Pel-den-drak-pa says,

> If one understands that "trees" are not present, one does not necessarily understand that "oaks" are not present. If one has understood the presence of "oak *tree*," then one has necessarily understood the presence of *tree*, and if one has understood the absence of tree, then one has necessarily understood the absence of "oak tree." It would not be a correct sign if the predicate were "oak tree does not exist."[331]

The nonobservation of trees by valid cognition is useless as proof of the nonexistence of oak trees, because when one ascertains the absence of all trees in a particular place, one cannot wonder whether a specific tree is present, and therefore there is no use for a sign. However, one may still wonder whether an oak is present. As Ge-shay Pel-den-drak-pa says,

> There is the possibility of someone having doubt about whether or not there is an oak there in the distance. [The opponent] sees that there are no trees there and yet still has doubt about whether there is an oak. Having understood that there are no trees there, there is then no doubt about an oak tree or about any tree.... But if just "oak" is stated [as it is in the predicate here], then there can be doubt. There will not necessarily be doubt—but if there *is* doubt, then this is the type of sign used.[332]

Clearly, if one has eliminated the presence of trees in a place, one cannot have doubt about the presence of oak trees. But, one may have doubt about the presence of oak. This is because, as Ge-shay Pel-den-drak-pa says, "understanding that something is an oak does not necessarily mean that one has understood it to be a tree."[333]

NONOBSERVATION OF A NATURE

As an illustration of his third type of sign that is a nonobservation of a

related object, Pur-bu-jok posits the sign in the syllogism, "With respect to the subject, on a place where pot is not observed by valid cognition, pot does not exist because of the nonobservation of pot by valid
cognition." He says:

> [In that,] "the nonobservation of pot by valid cognition" is a
> correct sign that is a nonobservation of a nature suitable to ap-
> pear in the proof of the nonexistence of pot on a place where
> pot is not observed by valid cognition.[334]

Here, the object designated as the predicate of the negandum is "pot
exists" (*bum pa yod pa*). This is of one nature with "the observation by
valid cognition of pot" (*bum pa tshad mas dmigs pa*). Because the nonobservation of that is set as the sign, it is a sign that is the nonobservation
of a nature.[a]

A pot is not a supersensory object. Thus, according to Buddhists, if
a pot is present in a particular place it must be perceivable by valid
cognition, and if a pot is not perceived by valid cognition in that place,
then a pot does not exist there. For most students it would be obvious
whether or not a pot is present right in front of oneself. This proof is
said to be directed toward the Sāṃkhyas, who hold the view that an
effect exists in its cause. If a cause of pot (such as the clay from which it
is to be produced) exists, then the pot can also be said to exist, because—for the Sāṃkhya—the effect exists *in potential* at the time of its
cause.[b] Ge-shay Pel-den-drak-pa says,

> The object designated as the predicate of the negandum is
> "pot"; if it existed with the basis of debate [that is, in the place

---

[a] Ge-shay Ge-dün-lo-drö, commentary on *Signs and Reasonings*, section 7, p. 6. It should
be noted that the ge-shay identified the object designated as the predicate of the negandum as "pot exists." Ge-shay Pel-den-drak-pa (quoted in the paragraph that follows)
identifies the predicate of the negandum more briefly as "pot." It would be consistent
with Pur-bu-jok's view to say that both statements are correct. Later in the text, he
comments that both "smoke" and "the existence of smoke" are the object designated as
the predicate of the negandum in the proof that smoke does not exist on a lake at night.
(*Signs and Reasonings*, pp. 14b.7-15a.1. This is cited below in "identification of the sign,
predicate of the probandum, and basis of debate.")

[b] Two important principles in Sāṃkhya philosophy are *satkāryavāda* (the effect preex-
ists in the material cause) and *pariṇāmavāda* (the effect is a transformation of the
cause). Causation is the manifestation (*āvirbhāva*) of what is already potentially existent. *Prakṛti* (primordial matter) manifests what it already contains; this manifestation
is called the transformation (*pariṇāma*) of *prakṛti* into the world. *Prakṛti* is inert eternal
substance; all that exists (besides *puruṣa*, pure consciousness) is mere *pariṇāma* and
must already exist in *prakṛti* in latent form.

specified by the subject], it would be apprehendable by direct perception. For the proponents of the Sāṃkhya system, the cause of pot is there in the clay.... For them, if the cause of pot is there, the pot can be said to be there, because the effect exists at the time of the cause.

For someone with that tenet system...there would be need for this sign [nonobservation of a nature] to prove the nonexistence of the pot in that place. For people without such a strong mistaken idea, there would be no need for proof; it would be obvious to direct perception whether a pot is there or not.[a]

In this syllogism and illustration, the Buddhists are demonstrating to the Sāṃkhyas that a pot cannot exist at the time of its cause if the pot has not yet come into existence. It is not observed by valid cognition at the time of its cause and thus cannot be said to be existent at the time of its cause. As Ge-shay Lob-sang-gya-tso says, "The pot that the Sāṃkhyas say exists with pot's cause is a nonmanifest pot."[b]

NONOBSERVATION OF A DIRECT EFFECT

To illustrate his fourth type of sign that is a nonobservation of a related object, Pur-bu-jok posits the sign in the syllogism, "With respect to the subject, in a walled circle devoid of smoke, the direct cause of smoke does not exist because of the nonexistence of the direct effect, smoke." He writes:

[In that, the sign] "the nonexistence of the direct effect, smoke," is a correct sign that is a nonobservation of a direct

---

[a] Commentary on *Signs and Reasonings*, vol. 5, pp. 5-6. A somewhat different point of view is expressed by Ge-shay Kön-chok-tse-ring:

The property of the subject [in this proof—that is, that a pot does not exist in the place where pot is not observed by valid cognition] is established by direct perception. The pervasion is: "Whatever is not observed by valid cognition is necessarily nonexistent." The Sāṃkhyas say there is no pervasion; the fact that a pot is not observed by valid cognition does not mean it is not there. In their view, it is possible for something to exist without observation by valid cognition. They hold that the effect exists when the cause exists—otherwise there is no way to generate the effect. (Commentary on *Signs and Reasonings*, vol. 1, pp. 11-12.)

This view implies that the Sāṃkhyas will not be persuaded by that reasoning; they will just say "There is no pervasion."

[b] Literally, "a pot that does not occur as an object of the senses." (Commentary on *Signs and Reasonings*, vol. 4, p. 18.)

effect suitable to appear in the proof of the nonexistence of the direct cause of smoke in a walled circle devoid of smoke.[335]

Here the object designated as the predicate of the negandum is "the direct cause of smoke"—that is, fire. Its direct effect is "smoke"—the opposite of the sign. Since the nonobservation of smoke is set as the sign, it is a sign that is a nonobservation of a direct effect.[336] Lati Rin-po-che comments:

> The direct cause of smoke is fire. This sign is stated for some-one who is wondering whether or not there is fire there. Since the place is walled in, one would not see a fire; however, since there is no roof, one would see smoke if it were present.[337]

This is a situation in which smoke would be visible if it were present, but fire would be hidden by walls. In this case the absence of a direct cause is being inferred from the absence of its effect; does this mean that the direct cause is related with the effect? Pur-bu-jok lists this as the fourth of the correct signs that are nonobservations of a *related object* suitable to appear—but it is not universally agreed that the direct cause of smoke is related with smoke. Ge-shay Lob-sang-gya-tso says:

> There is debate about whether the unobstructed cause [that is, the direct cause] of smoke is related with smoke. There are two opinions; some say the unobstructed cause of smoke is related with smoke; some say that it is not. It is the case that smoke is related with the unobstructed cause of smoke because if the unobstructed cause of smoke is eliminated, then by the power of that, smoke is eliminated. But is the unobstructed cause of smoke related with smoke? If smoke is eliminated, is the unob-structed cause of smoke eliminated?[a]

There is apparent agreement among Ge-luk-pa scholars that—according to the tenet system of the Sautrāntika Following Reasoning—an effect is related with its cause and that, in general, a cause is not re-lated with its effect. But what about "direct cause" and "direct effect"—how are these related? Lati Rin-po-che comments:

> It is usually said that the effect is related with the cause, not that the cause is related with the effect; once a *direct* cause is present, however, its effect must follow. There is no certainty

---

[a] Commentary on *Signs and Reasonings*, vol. 4, p. 21. The meaning of unobstructed cause and direct cause of smoke is the same, according to Ge-shay Pel-den-drak-pa (commen-tary on *Signs and Reasonings*, vol. 5, p. 11).

that a cause will be followed by an effect, but a *direct* cause *must* be followed by its effect. Usually, it is not the causes of smoke that are related with smoke, but rather smoke that is related with the cause of smoke. It is only in the Prāsaṅgika-Madhyamaka system that cause is established in dependence on effect. In all other systems, from Svātantrika-Madhyamaka on down, this is not accepted.[338]

In general, in the tenet system of the Sautrāntika Following Reasoning, it is said that fire is not related with smoke. The presence of fire thus cannot prove the presence of smoke; and the absence of smoke cannot prove the absence of fire. A correct *effect* sign is posited, because the presence of an effect proves the presence of a cause.[339] However, the presence of a cause does not *necessarily* prove the presence of an effect, because the cause may be prevented from producing an effect. For the Sautrāntika Following Reason, the fact that the production of an effect can be obstructed means that (1) a cause cannot be used as proof of an effect; and (2) furthermore, the absence (nonobservation) of an effect cannot serve as proof of the absence of a cause.

Nevertheless, there is one case in which Pur-bu-jok apparently considers the cause to be related to the effect: when the cause under consideration is precisely and explicitly described as the "direct cause" of the effect. According to Pur-bu-jok, a direct and unobstructed cause will necessarily produce its own direct effect. This can be inferred from his positing "the nonexistence of a direct effect" as a fourth type of correct sign that is a nonobservation of a related object suitable to appear. Thus, just as the presence of a direct effect can be inferred from the presence of its direct cause, so also the absence of a direct unobstructed cause can be inferred from the absence of its direct effect. As Ge-shay Pel-den-drak-pa says,

> If the unobstructed cause [that is, the direct cause] of smoke exists, there will be smoke, so the reason [proving the existence of the unobstructed cause of smoke] would be the existence of smoke. By the sign of the existence of smoke there, one could infer that there also exists there the cause of smoke—fire. If the unobstructed cause of smoke is there, then smoke must arise in the very next moment.[340]

Smoke is related with the direct (unobstructed) cause of smoke (the effect is related with the cause—here there is no disagreement). Smoke is related with the direct cause of smoke because if the direct cause of smoke is eliminated, then by the power (or force) of that, smoke is eliminated. But is the direct cause of smoke related with smoke? If smoke is eliminated, is the direct cause of smoke eliminated?

There is apparent agreement that smoke is a related object of the direct cause of smoke; but opinion differs on whether the direct cause of smoke is related with smoke. Ge-shay Pel-den-drak-pa says, "If smoke is a related object of the direct cause of smoke, then the direct cause of smoke must be related with smoke."[341] On the other hand, Lati Rin-po-che says, "Smoke and the direct cause of smoke are *related objects*, but they are not *related*."[342]

To conclude his section on correct signs that are a nonobservation of a related object suitable to appear, Pur-bu-jok mentions a debate that could arise—one that essentially involves a play on words. He writes:

> Someone says, "fireless" is [an illustration of] the first [a correct sign that is a nonobservation of a cause suitable to appear] and that "treeless" is [an illustration of] the second [a correct sign that is a nonobservation of a pervader suitable to appear].
>
> The response to this is: "It [absurdly] follows with respect to the subject, horn of a rabbit, that smoke does not exist because of being fireless; and it follows with respect to the subject, horn of a rabbit, that an oak does not exist because of being treeless. You have accepted the pervasions."
>
> Both signs are established because the subject [horn of a rabbit] is not an established base. Since smoke is the direct effect of fire, one cannot assert that smoke does not exist; and since oak is an object of pervasion by tree, one cannot assert that oak does not exist.[343]

This debate centers on the signs in the following syllogisms:

- With respect to the subject, on a lake at night, smoke does not exist because "fire does not exist" (*me med pa*), and
- With respect to the subject, on a craggy cliff where trees are not observed by valid cognition, oak does not exist because "tree does not exist" (*shing med pa*).

Pur-bu-jok's hypothetical opponent is suggesting that the signs in these two syllogisms are "fireless" (*me med*) instead of "fire does not exist" (*me med pa*) and "treeless" (*shing med*) instead of "tree does not exist" (*shing med pa*). The syllogisms would then state: "...smoke does not exist because of being fireless" and "...oak does not exist because of being treeless."

The substitutions may at first appear to be acceptable, because the reasons (signs) are established; as Ge-shay Ge-dün-lo-drö points out, "There is no fault in saying that a fireless lake at night is fireless."[344] By extension, there is apparently no fault in saying that a place where trees are not observed by valid cognition is "treeless."

Pur-bu-jok is noting that a challenger might try to confuse an opponent by this substitution. A defender who accepts these proofs may forget that he or she is thereby accepting not only the reasons (the signs) but also the *pervasions*—that is, that the sign [fireless] is pervaded by (entails) the predicate of the probandum [smoke does not exist]. Accepting the pervasions means accepting that "with regard to whatever is fireless, smoke does not exist" and "with regard to whatever is treeless, oak does not exist."

Once the defender has done that, the challenger can say, "It follows that with respect to the subject, horn of a rabbit, smoke does not exist because of being fireless." The defender has already accepted the pervasion; and, as Pur-bu-jok points out, the reason is established because horn of a rabbit is not an established base (that is, it is nonexistent). This means that horn of a rabbit, being nonexistent, is fireless and treeless; and (Ge-shay Pel-den-drak-pa adds) it may be said to be "causeless, effectless, and so forth."[345] The defender must either contradict himself or herself by saying that the pervasions are not established or accept the absurd theses that smoke and oak do not exist.

Pur-bu-jok points out, however, that these theses are not acceptable: "Since smoke is the direct effect of fire, one cannot assert that smoke does not exist; and since oak is an object of pervasion by tree, one cannot assert that oak does not exist." (He has dropped the subject, horn of a rabbit, altogether and taken the predicate of the probandum alone to be the complete thesis.) Ge-shay Pel-den-drak-pa explains,

> The play here is on the difference in meaning between "fireless" and "fire does not exist." The horn of a rabbit is fireless because it is not an established base—horn of a rabbit is causeless, effectless, and so forth.
>
> But it is not correct to say, "With respect to the subject, horn of a rabbit, smoke does not exist," because smoke does in fact exist. In these cases, the predicate becomes a unit in itself. So it is a play on words. It is possible to be ambiguous and to confuse people. Here is an example of how one might play with the wording in debate.[346]

This debate sketched by Pur-bu-jok depends primarily on a slight shift in meaning: changing *me med pa* to *me med* changes the meaning from "fire does not exist" to "fireless." One can say, "horn of a rabbit is fireless," but one cannot say that "in relation to horn of a rabbit, fire does not exist." The debate also depends on the fact that the predicate of the probandum (in this case, fire does not exist) may be understood as complete in itself; when this happens, the subject becomes meaningless and can be disregarded.

Referring to these four types of signs that are a nonobservation of a related object that is suitable to appear, Lati Rin-po-che emphasizes their importance,

> In all four systems of tenets, the reasonings that prove emptiness are mostly cases of nonobservation of related objects that are suitable to appear. Therefore, if you don't understand this presentation [of this type of nonobservation sign], then you can't understand the reasoning proving emptiness.
>
> For example, [reasoning establishing] the lack of being one or many[a] would be a case of a nonobservation of a nature suitable to appear. This reasoning of the lack of being one and many is interpreted in two ways: as the nonobservation of a *nature* suitable to appear and as a *pervader* suitable to appear.[b]

These illustrations are reasonings that advanced students will use much later in the study of emptiness. The beginning student is made aware that this is the direction toward which his or her studies are leading.

OBSERVATION OF A CONTRADICTORY OBJECT SUITABLE TO APPEAR

The second type of correct nonobservation sign of the suitable to appear is those involving the observation of a contradictory object suitable to appear. Pur-bu-jok's definition is:

> That which is a common locus of (1) being a correct nonobservation sign of the suitable to appear in the proof of that and of (2) being either an affirming negative phenomenon or a positive phenomenon.[347]

---

[a] For a discussion of this type of reasoning, see Jeffrey Hopkins, *Meditation on Emptiness* (London: Wisdom), 1983, pp. 64-65.

[b] Commentary on *Signs and Reasonings*, vol. 2, Apr. 22, 1977, pp. 5-6. Lati Rin-po-che adds, "If you are proving the existence of emptiness for a person who does not understand emptiness, then there might be some purpose for stating a sign of nonobservation of that which is *not* suitable to appear." (Ibid., p. 6.)

When divided, correct signs that are observations of contradictory objects are of two types:

(1) correct signs that are an observation of an object suitable to appear that is contradictory in the sense of not abiding together (with the object designated as the predicate of the negandum) and
(2) correct signs that are an observation of an object suitable to appear that is contradictory in the sense of mutual exclusion.[348]

CONTRADICTORY IN THE SENSE OF NOT ABIDING TOGETHER

Pur-bu-jok gives the following definition of a correct sign that is an observation of an object suitable to appear that is contradictory in the sense of not abiding together in the proof that the continuous tangible object, cold, does not exist on a place in the east covered by a large powerful fire:

> That which is a common locus of (1) being a correct sign that is an observation of a contradictory object in the proof that the continuous tangible object, cold, does not exist on a place in the east covered by a large powerful fire and of (2) being contradictory with the continuous tangible object, cold, in the sense of not abiding together with it.[349]

In the case of the signs that are an observation of contradictories in the sense of not abiding together, the sign and the predicate of the negandum must be different substantial entities. Because only impermanent things can be different substantial entities, this category is limited to impermanent things.[a]

In the study of the *Collected Topics,* the student learns that the category "thing" is divided into three types:

(1) material phenomena (*bem po, kanthā*),
(2) consciousnesses (*shes pa, jñāna*), and

---

[a] Ge-shay Pel-den-drak-pa, commentary on *Signs and Reasonings,* vol. 5, p. 10. The requirement that the sign and the predicate of the negandum must be different substantial entities is made explicit in the definition (of a correct sign which is an observation of an object contradictory in the sense of not abiding together) posited by Ge-shay Tsül-trim-nam-gyel in the logic manual used at Lo-sel-ling:

> that which is a common locus of (1) being a correct sign which is an observation of a contradictory [object] in the proof of that and of (2) being a different substantial entity from the thing (*dngos po*) that is designated as the predicate of the negandum. (*Signs and Reasonings,* p. 10b.3-4.)

(3) nonassociated compositional factors (*ldan min 'du byed, viprayukta-saṃskāra*).[a]

Therefore, whatever is a thing is necessarily either a material phenomenon (for example, a color), a consciousness (for example, a consciousness apprehending a color), or a nonassociated compositional factor. Some nonassociated compositional factors are persons (*gang zag;* for example, an animal) and some are not persons (for example, qualities of things—such as impermanence, productness, and so forth).

Mirroring the division of things into three types, Pur-bu-jok posits: correct signs that are an observation of an object that is contradictory (with the object designated as the predicate of the negandum):

(1) in the sense of material phenomena not abiding together,
(2) in the sense of consciousnesses not abiding together, and
(3) in the sense of nonassociated compositional factors not abiding together.[350]

Material Phenomena Not Abiding Together

Pur-bu-jok's five illustrations of this type of correct sign all involve the relationship between hot and cold. A strong, blazing fire is necessarily very hot and therefore is contradictory with cold, in the sense that hot and cold cannot abide together: in the presence of strong heat, cold is eliminated; and in the presence of strong cold, heat is eliminated.

Fire is thus said to be contradictory with cold: if fire is present, cold is eliminated. Furthermore, when cold is eliminated, all that is related with cold is necessarily also eliminated. Being contradictory with cold, fire is also contradictory with whatever is related with cold.

The observation of fire in a particular place eliminates from that place everything that is contradictory with fire; and thus it eliminates cold and whatever is related with cold. Something is related with cold if it is (1) the same nature as cold, (2) the direct unobstructed cause of cold, (3) pervaded by cold, or (4) the effect of cold. Thus the presence of fire eliminates the nature of cold, the direct unobstructed cause of cold, the pervader of cold, and the effect of cold.

Correct signs in the category "observation of objects contradictory in the sense of material phenomena not abiding together" are divided by Pur-bu-jok into five formal types. First he posits three correct signs that are an observation of a *nature* that is contradictory with (a) the

---

[a] This division of "thing" into three is discussed in Daniel Perdue's *Debate in Tibetan Buddhism*, pp. 354-376.

nature, (b) a cause, or (c) a pervader of the object designated as the predicate of the negandum. Then he posits two correct signs that are an observation of an *effect* that is contradictory with (d) the nature or (e) a cause of the object designated as the predicate of the negandum.[351]

A Nature Contradictory with a Nature

As an illustration of a correct sign that is an observation of a nature contradictory with the nature of the object designated as the predicate of the negandum, Pur-bu-jok posits the sign in the syllogism, "With respect to the subject, on a place in the east covered by a large power-ful fire, the continuous tangible object,[a] cold, does not exist because of being a place covered by a large powerful fire." He writes:

> [In that,] "a place covered by a large powerful fire" is a correct sign that is an observation of a nature contradictory with the nature [of the object designated as the predicate of the negan-dum] in the proof that the continuous tangible object, cold, does not exist on a place in the east covered by a large powerful fire.[352]

The object designated as the predicate of the negandum is the "conti-nuous tangible object, cold," which is of one nature with "cold"; fire is contradictory with cold, and a place covered by a large powerful fire is of one nature with fire. The presence of fire establishes the absence of the tangible object, cold; thus here the absence of cold is proved by a sign (a place covered with a large powerful fire) which is an observa-tion of a nature (fire) contradictory with a nature (cold).[b]

---

[a]   Tangible object (*reg bya*) means object of touch, as distinguished from object of sight, object of smell, etc.

[b]   Ge-shay Ge-dün-lo-drö, commentary on *Signs and Reasonings,* section 7, p. 7. Ge-shay Lob-sang-gya-tso points out that in this context "fire" refers not to the color and shape of a fire seen at a distance, but to the heat of a fire; that is, to the tangible object, fire. (The literal "object of touch" might be a more useful translation.) Objects of sight (per-ceptions of shape and color) are different from objects of touch, which include cold, heat, roughness, smoothness, etc. It would be more accurate to say that the object of touch, "heat" (instead of "fire") is contradictory with the object of touch, cold. Ge-shay Lob-sang-gya-tso makes this point because problems can arise in debate if "fire" is con-sidered to be an object of sight rather than an object of touch. (Commentary on *Signs and Reasonings,* vol. 5, pp. 1-2.)

A Nature Contradictory with a Cause

To illustrate a correct sign that is an observation of a nature that is contradictory with a cause of the designated predicate of the negandum, Pur-bu-jok posits the sign in the syllogism, "With respect to the subject, on a place in the east covered by a large powerful fire, continuous goose bumps that are an effect of the cold do not exist because of being a place covered by a large powerful fire." He writes:

> [In that,] "a place covered by a large powerful fire" is a correct sign that is an observation of a nature that is contradictory with a cause in the proof that continuous goose bumps that are an effect of cold do not exist on a place in the east covered by a large powerful fire.[353]

Here the object designated as the predicate of the negandum is "continuous goose bumps." Fire is contradictory with cold and contradictory with the effect of cold—goose bumps. It is understood that "a place covered by a large powerful fire" is of one nature with "fire." The presence of fire establishes the absence of that effect of cold, and the sign that proves this is one that is an observation of a nature contradictory with a cause. Thus, in Pur-bu-jok's proof, "a place covered by a large powerful fire" is a correct sign that is an observation of a nature (fire) contradictory with a cause (cold) of the designated predicate of the negandum (goose bumps).[354]

A Nature Contradictory with a Pervader

Pur-bu-jok's illustration of a correct sign that is an observation of a nature contradictory with a pervader of the designated predicate of the negandum is the sign in the syllogism, "With respect to the subject, on a place in the east covered by a large powerful fire, the continuous tangible object, snow, does not exist because of being a place covered by a large powerful fire." He writes:

> [In that,] "a place covered by a large powerful fire" is a correct sign that is an observation of a nature contradictory with the pervader [of the designated predicate of the negandum] in the proof that the continuous tangible object, snow, does not exist on a place covered by a large powerful fire.[355]

The object designated as the predicate of the negandum is "the continuous tangible object, snow," which is pervaded by the tangible object, cold. Fire is contradictory with that tangible object, and a place covered by a large powerful fire is of one nature with fire. The presence of fire establishes the absence of that which is pervaded by cold, and the sign proving this is one that is an observation of a nature contradictory with a pervader. Thus, in Pur-bu-jok's proof, "a place covered by a large powerful fire" is a correct sign that is an observation of a nature (fire) contradictory with a pervader (the tangible object, cold) of the designated predicate of the negandum (the tangible object, snow).[356]

The Missing "Contradictory with an Effect" Category

Pur-bu-jok has now listed correct signs that are observations of a *nature* that is contradictory with (a) the nature, (b) the cause, and (c) the pervader of the designated predicate of the probandum. He does not mention another possible category: a nature that is contradictory with the effect of the designated predicate of the negandum.

It is notable that the Lo-sel-ling logic manual does include such a sign. The manual's illustration is the sign in the syllogism, "The subject, the fire in the east, does not abide together harmlessly with the unobstructed capacity that is the cause of cold, because of being fire."[357]

Some Ge-luk-pa scholars say that the direct cause of cold is related with cold; if that is accepted, the presence of fire contradicts the presence of the direct cause of cold. This is proved by a sign that is an observation of something (fire) that is contradictory with the effect (cold) of the object (the unobstructed capacity that is the cause of cold) to be negated in that proof.

Pur-bu-jok does not entirely exclude "effect of the predicate of the negandum" from the discussion in this chapter. In his discussion of signs that are a nonobservation of a related object suitable to appear, he includes a correct sign that is a nonobservation of a direct effect suitable to appear. This functions as a correct sign because the absence of smoke (the effect) is seen as proof of the absence of the direct cause of smoke, fire. Thus, nonobservation of something that is the direct effect of fire (smoke) eliminates the presence of fire (the direct cause) in that place.

By including "effect" in that earlier category, the author indicated willingness to consider that the direct unobstructed cause of something is related with that thing. Why does he not include "effect" in the category under consideration now? One might answer that Pur-bu-jok is probably not trying to include every possible type of proof, but to provide models of appropriate reasoning upon which the student can build. One could posit Pur-bu-jok's five categories or the six in the

Lo-sel-ling text—or even more. However, this use of "effect" tangles with the definition of relationship and becomes highly debatable. The questions it raises are interesting but beyond the scope of an introductory manual.

In the above discussion of observations of a contradictory nature, Pur-bu-jok has illustrated that since fire is contradictory with cold, the presence of fire can serve as proof of the absence not only of cold but also of whatever is related with cold. The next point is that, since fire is contradictory with cold, whatever is related with fire is also contradictory with cold; from which it follows that the presence of something related with fire may serve as proof of the absence of cold and as proof of the absence of something related with cold.

Fire is contradictory with cold. Smoke is related with fire; thus, smoke is contradictory with cold; furthermore, the presence of smoke may also serve as proof of the absence of those things that are related with cold—e.g., that which is of one nature with cold (the tangible object, cold), that which is pervaded by cold (snow), and that which is the effect of cold (goosebumps). To illustrate this, Pur-bu-jok posits two signs that are observations of *effects* contradictory with (1) the nature and (2) a cause of the designated predicate of the negandum.

An Effect Contradictory with a Nature

To illustrate a correct sign that is an observation of an effect contradictory with the nature of the designated predicate of the negandum, Pur-bu-jok posits the sign in the syllogism, "With respect to the subject, on a place in the east covered by strongly billowing smoke, the continuous tangible object, cold, does not exist because of being a place covered by strongly billowing smoke." He writes:

> [In that,] "a place covered by strongly billowing smoke" is a correct sign that is an observation of an effect contradictory with the nature of the designated predicate of the negandum in the proof that the continuous tangible object, cold, does not exist on a place in the east covered by strongly billowing smoke.[358]

Ge-shay Ge-dün-lo-drö explains this succinctly:

> The object designated as the predicate of the negandum is "the continuous tangible object, cold"; the nature of that is cold. Fire, the cause of smoke, is contradictory with the tangible object, cold; and "a place covered by strongly billowing smoke" is of one nature with fire. Since "a place covered by strongly

billowing smoke" is set as the sign here, this is a correct sign
that is an observation of an effect (smoke) contradictory with
the nature (cold) of the designated predicate of the negandum
(the continuous tangible object, cold).[359]

Smoke is the effect of (and so related with) fire; and fire is contradictory with the tangible object, cold. Thus the presence of smoke proves
the absence of cold and also of that which is of one nature with cold:
the continuous tangible object, cold.

An Effect Contradictory with a Cause

Pur-bu-jok's illustration of a correct sign that is an observation of an
effect contradictory with a cause of the designated predicate of the negandum is the sign in the syllogism, "With respect to the subject, on a
place in the east covered by strongly billowing smoke, continuous
goose bumps that are an effect of cold do not exist because of being a
place covered by strongly billowing smoke." He writes:

> [In that,] "a place covered by strongly billowing smoke" is a
> correct sign that is an observation of an effect contradictory
> with a cause of the designated predicate of the negandum in
> the proof that continuous goose bumps that are an effect of
> cold do not exist on a place covered by strongly billowing
> smoke.[360]

Here the presence of smoke is being used as proof of the absence of
goose bumps. Smoke is the effect of fire; fire is contradictory with cold;
and goose bumps are the effect of cold. Thus in this proof, "a place covered by strongly billowing smoke" is a correct sign that is an observation of an effect (smoke, the effect of fire) contradictory with a cause
(cold) of the designated predicate of the negandum (goose bumps).[361]

Pur-bu-jok does not spell out every conceivable possibility. He posits only two illustrations involving the use of the presence of smoke as
a correct sign of the absence of cold and what is related with cold. The
first uses the presence of smoke as a sign proving the absence of that
which is the same *nature* as cold, and the second uses it as a sign proving the absence of that which is related to cold in a relationship of *provenance*. With that, he drops the topic, although one could posit examples of the presence of smoke proving the absence of that which is pervaded by cold (snow) or the absence of the unobstructed cause of cold.
The teacher or debate opponent could lead the student to work out
these points independently.

Summary: Material Phenomena Not Abiding Together

The point of this section is to show that in the case of material pheno-mena, if *a* is contradictory with *b*, then whatever is related with *a* is also contradictory with *b*. Not only that, but *a* is contradictory with whatever is related with *b*, and whatever is related with *a* is contradic-tory with whatever is related with *b*. Therefore, from knowing that fire is contradictory with cold, one can conclude that:

(1) the presence of fire serves as proof of the absence of cold;
(2) the presence of fire also serves as proof of the absence of whatever is related with cold (that is, the effect of cold, that which is the same nature as cold, and that which is pervaded by cold); and
(3) whatever is related with fire (smoke) serves as proof of the absence of cold and of whatever is related with cold.

Consciousnesses Not Abiding Together

To illustrate a correct sign that is an observation of an object contradic-tory in the sense of consciousnesses not abiding together, Pur-bu-jok writes,

> One can state, "The subject, a noninterrupted path of a Hearer path of meditation that is an actual antidote to the conception of a self of persons, does not abide harmlessly together with the conception of a self of persons because of being an actual anti-dote to the conception of a self of persons." In that, ["an actual antidote to the conception of a self of persons" is a correct sign that is an observation of a contradictory object in the sense of consciousnesses not abiding together].[a]

Two consciousnesses cannot "abide together" if one is contradictory with the other. In the Ge-luk-pa philosophy, this is a very precise use of the term "contradictory." It is not unusual for people to accommodate ideas that are fundamentally incompatible, that contradict each other in some way. It is normal, for example, to expect things to stay as they are and to be astonished if important things change in fundamental ways—if a house tumbles down or a shopping mall disappears in an earthquake or fire. Although one knows that things are temporary, one is shocked when they change. These are incompatible states of mind,

---

[a] *Signs and Reasonings*, p. 12a.5-6. Here Pur-bu-jok is relying on the Prāsaṅgika-Madhyamaka presentation of selflessness.

but they can and do abide together. Thus, a general awareness that things are subject to change is not, for most people, an *antidote* to conceiving of something as permanent.

If a consciousness is to serve as an antidote to a mistaken thought, then it must be contradictory with that mistaken thought. And that means not just incompatible but absolutely canceling one another out. Contradictory ideas cannot abide together; if one is present, there is no possibility of the other being present. One eliminates the other—or, as the Tibetans say, harms or destroys the other. Contradiction in this Geluk-pa sense always involves a "harmer" and a "harmed."[362]

In order to understand the quality of impermanence in relation to a particular object, for example, one must first eliminate permanence in relation to that object (one must understand that it is not permanent). Permanent and impermanent are contradictories; the presence of one eliminates the other.

Someone who has, through reasoning, generated inferential understanding of the impermanence of sound can no longer conceive of sound as permanent. Similarly, a person who through reasoned analysis has understood the emptiness of inherent existence of the self can no longer conceive of an inherently existent self. The person who has attained the uninterrupted path of a Hearer path of meditation is someone who has attained an actual antidote to the conception of a self of persons. If that antidote is present, there is no possibility of the presence of the conception of a self of persons. The consciousnesses are contradictory and cannot abide together. Lati Rin-po-che makes this clear when he says,

> The two never exist together. The seeds of the conception of a self of persons have to cease in order for the noninterrupted path to be generated in a person's continuum.[363]

This has practical application in a student's attempt to eradicate mistaken conceptions; ignorance is overcome through the eradication of mistaken ideas. One eradicates a mistaken idea by developing a consciousness that is an antidote to it; one develops a new understanding that makes it impossible to maintain the former mistaken idea, because the new is contradictory with the old in the sense of consciousnesses not abiding together. By means of reasoning, the student cultivates a correct consciousness (path of consciousness) that harms the mistaken consciousness. These new consciousnesses eliminate the mistaken ones as irrefutably as the presence of fire eliminates the presence of cold.

Nonassociated Compositional Factors Not Abiding Together

To illustrate a correct sign that is an observation of an object contradictory in the sense of nonassociated compositional factors not abiding together, Pur-bu-jok writes:

> One can state, "The subject, a crow in the east, does not abide harmlessly together with an owl because of being a crow."[364]

In that, "crow" is a correct sign of this type. Crows and owls, being persons (*gang zag*), are "nonassociated compositional factors." Ge-shay Ge-dün-lo-drö comments on Pur-bu-jok's illustration:

> The object designated as the predicate of the negandum is "owl," which is contradictory—in the sense of not abiding together—with a crow. Thus, crow is a correct sign that is an observation of a contradictory object in the sense of nonassociated compositional factors not abiding together.[365]

In the preceding type (consciousnesses) of contradictory objects not abiding together, the two—the mistaken consciousness and its direct antidote—are never together. In this third type (nonassociated compositional factors), the two—the crow and the owl—can be together for a short time, but then they inevitably fight; they will not stay together without one harming the other. The same is true of Pur-bu-jok's first type (material phenomena) of contradictory objects not abiding together—a strong fire and the touch of cold; they can be together for a short time, but then the very strong fire overwhelms the cold and eliminates it.[366]

Pur-bu-jok has concluded his outline of the topic of contradictories in the sense of not abiding together. It should be noted, however, as Lati Rin-po-che points out, that within each of the three classes (material phenomena, consciousnesses, and nonassociated compositional factors not abiding together) there are two varieties: direct and indirect contradictories. Lati Rin-po-che explains:

> An example of a direct contradictory is the syllogism, "The subject, the fire in the east, does not abide together harmlessly with the touch of cold because of being fire." In this, the two, fire and the touch of cold, are *direct* contradictories in the sense of not abiding together.
>
> However, in the syllogism, "The subject, the strongly billowing smoke in the east, does not abide together harmlessly

with the touch of cold because of being strongly billowing smoke," smoke and the touch of cold are *indirect* contradictories in the sense of not abiding together.

The conception of a self of persons and the uninterrupted path of a Hearer path of meditation that is an actual antidote to the conception of a self of persons are *direct* contradictories.[367]

CONTRADICTORY IN THE SENSE OF MUTUAL EXCLUSION

Definitions

In defining correct signs that are an observation of an object suitable to appear that is contradictory in the sense of mutual exclusion, Pur-bu-jok refers to two proofs, that sound is not permanent and that a horned mass is not a horse.

The proof that sound is not permanent. Pur-bu-jok's definition of a correct sign that is an observation of an object suitable to appear that is contradictory in the sense of mutual exclusion in the proof of sound as not permanent is:

> That which is a common locus of (1) being a correct sign that is an observation of a contradictory object in the proof that sound is not permanent and of (2) not being contradictory with permanent in the sense of not abiding together.[a]
>
> An illustration of such a sign is "product," [as in "The subject, sound, is not permanent because of being a product."][b]

Ge-shay Ge-dün-lo-drö comments:

> The object designated as the predicate of the negandum is

---

[a] To track this double negative, remember that Pur-bu-jok divides signs which are an observation of contradictory objects into two types: those involving (1) observation of an object contradictory in the sense of not abiding together [with the object designated as the predicate of the negandum] and (2) observation of an object contradictory in the sense of mutual exclusion. Here he takes up the second type, which is *not* "...not abiding together."

[b] *Signs and Reasonings,* p. 12a.7- b.1. In the case of a correct sign which is an observation of contradictories in the sense of not abiding together, the two—the object designated as the predicate of the negandum and the sign—must be different substantial entities. But in the case of a correct sign which is a nonobservation of contradictories in the sense of mutual exclusion, those two must not be different substantial entities. This requirement is made explicit in the definition posited by Ge-shay Tsül-trim-nam-gyel in his *Signs and Reasonings,* p. 12a.2-3.

"permanent," which is mutually contradictory with product. Thus, in the proof that sound is not permanent, product is a correct sign "that is an observation of a contradictory object in the sense of mutual exclusion."[368]

Product and permanent are mutually contradictory; as Ge-shay Pel-den-drak-pa notes, this means that when one appears to the mind the other is necessarily eliminated.[369] Product and permanent are not contradictory in the sense of not abiding together, because this category is limited to phenomena that are of different substantial entities, which is not the case with product and permanent. Ge-shay Pel-den-drak-pa explains,

> Only impermanent phenomena are said to be of one substantial entity or of different substantial entities; and here the predicate of the negandum is "permanent," which is itself a permanent phenomenon.[370]

Thus, it may be argued that permanent and product are not contradictory in the sense of not abiding together because they are not different substantial entities; whatever phenomena are contradictory in the sense of not abiding together must be different substantial entities, such as hot and cold.

The proof that a horned mass is not a horse. It is possible, however, for phenomena to be contradictory and also be different substantial entities—and yet not necessarily be contradictory in the sense of not abiding together. To make this point, Pur-bu-jok posits the definition of a correct sign that is an observation of objects contradictory in the sense of mutual exclusion in the proof that a horned mass in front [of oneself] is not a horse:

> That which is a common locus of (1) being a correct sign that is an observation of a contradictory object in the proof that a horned mass in front [of oneself] is not a horse and of (2) not being contradictory with horse in the sense of not abiding together [with it—that is, it *is* contradictory in the *other* sense: of mutual exclusion. When one states, "The subject, the horned mass in front of oneself is not a horse because of being horned,"] "horned" is such a sign.[a]

---

[a]   *Signs and Reasonings*, p. 12b.3. As usual, toward the end of a set of similar presentations, Pur-bu-jok elides the words that are to be understood; they are supplied here in brackets.

Ge-shay Ge-dün-lo-drö comments that horse and the horned mass (which is probably an ox or a yak) are mutually contradictory:

> The object designated as the predicate of the negandum, horse, is mutually contradictory with being horned. Thus, in the proof that the horned mass in front of oneself is not a horse, "being horned" is a correct sign that is an observation of an object suitable to appear that is contradictory in the sense of mutual exclusion.[371]

Pur-bu-jok specifies that the horned mass and a horse are not contradictory in the sense of not abiding together; but this time the reason is not because of not being different substantial entities (as it was in the case of permanent and product). Horned mass and horse *are* different substantial entities. Although they are different substantial entities, they are not contradictory in the sense of not abiding together. They are not considered to be contradictory in this sense, because these animals do not generally fight each other. Ge-shay Pel-den-drak-pa explains that "contradiction in the sense of not abiding together must involve a harmer and an object harmed."[372]

In short, Pur-bu-jok specifies that permanent and product, though contradictory, are not contradictory in the sense of not abiding together. This is because they are not different substantial entitles. He also specifies that a horned mass and a horse, though contradictory, are not contradictory in the sense of not abiding together, because they do not generally harm each other. Hot and cold, crow and owl, are considered to harm each other in the sense that they cannot remain together for any length of time, but that is not true of a horse and an ox, which are able to coexist peacefully.

Divisions and Illustrations

Pur-bu-jok continues: "This section [contradictories in the sense of mutual exclusion] is divided into two parts: (1) correct signs that, through dependence, refute definiteness and (2) correct signs that, through definiteness, refute dependence."[373] To illustrate the first of these types, he writes:

> One can state, "The subject, white cloth, is not definite in possessing a dyed color from its mere establishment, because its becoming that which has a dyed color must depend on causes arising later than itself." In that, "its becoming that which has dyed color must depend on causes arising later than itself" is a

correct sign in the proof of that, which, through dependence, refutes definiteness.[374]

For a white cloth to become colored, it must be subjected to certain conditions, dyeing. Lati Rin-po-che comments:

> At first the cloth has no color. To get that, it must be dyed. Its becoming something with color thus depends on a cause [being dyed].[375]

Of the second type, correct signs that, through definiteness, refute dependence, Pur-bu-jok writes:

> One can state, "With respect to the subject, product, its disintegration does not depend on other causes and conditions arising later than itself because of being definite to disintegrate from its mere establishment." In that, [the reason given] is a correct sign in the proof of that, which, through definiteness, refutes dependence.[376]

According to Ge-shay Ge-dün-lo-drö, the phrase "because of being definite to disintegrate" has the same meaning (*don dag gcig*) as "because of being impermanent."[377] Being impermanent, product is necessarily momentary and definite to disintegrate, right from its own production; no other cause is necessary.

Next, Pur-bu-jok suggests a debate that could arise on this subject:

> The statement, "It follows that impermanent is not a correct sign in the proof of sound as a product because product is a correct sign in the proof of sound as impermanent," is refuted in dependence on this reasoning [because, if the pervasion were true, one could state]:
>
> "It [absurdly] follows with respect to the subject, object of knowledge, that [being] definite to disintegrate from its mere establishment is not a correct sign in the proof that product does not depend for its own disintegration on other causes arising later than itself, because a thing that does not depend for its own disintegration on other causes arising later than itself is a correct sign in the proof of product as definite to disintegrate from its mere establishment."[378]

Lati Rin-po-che comments briefly:

> Product is a correct sign in the proof of sound as impermanent, and impermanent is a correct sign in the proof of sound as a

product.[379]

Clearly, the fact that product is a correct sign in the proof of sound as impermanent does not eliminate the possibility that impermanent can be a correct sign in the proof of sound as a product. Similarly, the fact that "being a thing that does not depend for its disintegration on other causes arising later than itself" is a correct sign in the proof of product as definite to disintegrate from its mere establishment does not eliminate the possibility that "being definite to disintegrate from its mere establishment" can be a correct sign in the proof that product does not depend for its own disintegration on other causes arising later than itself.

Pur-bu-jok continues:

> With regard to this, someone [an opponent] says, "It follows that the subject, that which possesses horns, is a correct sign that is an observation of a contradictory object in the sense of not abiding together in the proof that the horned mass in front [of oneself] is not a horse (1) because of being a correct sign that is an observation of a contradictory object in the proof of that and (2) because of being a different substantial entity from horse."
>
> [In response to that, one would state that] there is no pervasion.[380]

To say that there is no pervasion means that the predicate does not necessarily follow from the reason. The predicate is: "that which possesses horns is a correct sign that is an observation of a contradictory object in the sense of not abiding together in the proof that the horned mass in front [of oneself] is not a horse." The reason is: "because of being a correct sign that is an observation of a contradictory object in the proof of that and because of being a different substantial entity from horse."[a] Lati Rin-po-che comments:

---

[a] By holding that the pervasion is established, the opponent (above) is essentially asserting that if something (x) is a correct sign which is an observation of a contradictory object in a given proof and is a different substantial entity (from the object designated as the predicate of the negandum), then x is a correct sign which is an observation of an object contradictory in the sense of not abiding together.

It is interesting to note at this juncture that the definition posited by Ge-shay Tsül-trim-nam-gyel (in the Lo-sel-ling logic manual) of a correct sign which is an observation of a contradictory in the sense of not abiding together is:

> That which is a common locus (1) of being a correct sign which is an observation of a contradictory [object] in the proof of that and (2) of being a different

"That which possesses horns" is a correct sign that is an observation of a contradictory object in the proof that the horned
mass in front of oneself is not a horse and is also a different
substantial entity from horse. Thus, the opponent's reason is
established in the proof of that. This does not entail, however,
that "that which possesses horns" is a correct sign that is an
observation of a contradictory object in the sense of not abiding together in the proof of that. For that which possesses
horns and a horse can abide together peacefully; they do not
fight each other as do a crow and an owl, and thus are contradictories, not in the sense of not abiding together but rather in
the sense of mutual exclusion.[381]

Thus, in Pur-bu-jok's view, something (x) can be (1) a correct sign
that is an observation of a contradictory object in a given proof and (2)
a different substantial entity from the predicate of the negandum—but
this does *not* prove (as was stated by the opponent, above) that x is a
correct sign that is a contradictory in the sense of not abiding together.
He makes this clear by pointing out the consequence of that view:

"It [absurdly] follows with respect to the subject, object of
knowledge, that whatever are different substantial entities
must be contradictories in the sense of not abiding together
because of your assertion."
    If the opponent accepts this, [then one can state the conse-
quence,] "It follows that the subject, the two, fire and smoke,
are contradictories in the sense of not abiding together because
of your assertion."
    If this is accepted, [one can say,] "It [absurdly] follows that
the subject, the two, fire and smoke, are harmer and object
harmed because of your assertion." This cannot be accepted,
because they are assister and object assisted. This, in turn, is
because [fire and smoke] are cause and effect.[382]

Fire and smoke are different substantial entities that are also contradictory; according to the position the opponent has stated above, they
must therefore be contradictory in the sense of not abiding together—

---

substantial entity from the thing which is designated as the predicate of the
negandum in the proof of that. (*Signs and Reasonings*, p. 12a.2-3.)

Clearly, Pur-bu-jok would find fault with this definition; someone who posits it would
be likely to make the assertion of the opponent cited above, the assertion that Pur-bu-
jok argues against.

but that is not the case. Fire and smoke are different substantial entities and they are contradictory, but not in the sense of not abiding together. This is because phenomena that are contradictory in the sense of not abiding together must be harmer and harmed. As Pur-bu-jok points out, fire and smoke are cause and effect; these do not harm each other, rather they are related, the effect depending on the cause; thus they cannot be considered harmer and harmed.

Pur-bu-jok is pointing out that there is more to being contradictory in the sense of not abiding together than merely being contradictories that are different substantial entities. The objects involved must also be harmer and harmed, that is, not able to stay together for any length of time without one harming the other.

CONCLUDING TOPICS

In his *Signs and Reasonings,* Pur-bu-jok ends his presentation of nonobservation signs (covered here in chapters six and seven) with two sections. The first is an "explanation of the ascertainment of definitions in terms of illustrations," a brief discussion of the criteria for several types of nonobservations signs. The second, called "identification of the sign, predicate of the probandum, and basis of debate," is a brief discussion of the predicate and sign of several syllogisms—but *not* the subject (basis of debate), despite his heading.

EXPLANATION OF THE ASCERTAINMENT OF DEFINITIONS IN TERMS OF ILLUSTRATIONS

This section begins with a discussion of several illustrations of nonobservation signs of the nonappearing; this was presented in chapter six and will not be repeated here. The text then takes up nonobservation signs of the suitable to appear, discussing briefly the criteria of the six following signs:

(1) correct nonobservation sign of the suitable to appear,
(2) correct sign that is a nonobservation of a related object suitable to appear,
(3) correct sign that is a nonobservation of a cause suitable to appear,
(4) correct sign that is an observation of a contradictory object suitable to appear,
(5) correct sign that is an observation of an object suitable to appear that is contradictory in the sense of not abiding together, and
(6) correct sign that is an observation of an object suitable to appear

that is contradictory in the sense of mutual exclusion.

Nonobservation Sign of the Suitable to Appear

In his discussion of the correct nonobservation sign of the suitable to appear, Pur-bu-jok writes:

> The subject, product, is a correct nonobservation sign of the suitable to appear in the proof that sound is not permanent (1) because of being a correct nonobservation sign in the proof of that and (2) because permanent is not a supersensory object for a person for whom it has become the property of the subject in the proof of that. The first reason is easy.[383]

Pur-bu-jok indicates that the first reason (that is, that product is a correct nonobservation sign in the proof of that) is easy (to prove); Ge-shay Ge-dün-lo-drö elaborates,

> The subject, product, is a correct nonobservation sign in the proof of that because (1) it is a correct sign in the proof of that and (2) there occurs a common locus of (a) being what is held as the explicit predicate of the probandum in the proof of that by such-and-such a sign and (b) being a negative phenomenon.[384]

Here the ge-shay is repeating the criteria that Pur-bu-jok himself posited (in chapter six) for a correct nonobservation sign. Pur-bu-jok continues,

> The latter reason [that permanent is not a supersensory object...] is established because it follows with respect to the subject, a person for whom product has become the property of the subject in the proof that sound is not permanent, that permanent is not a supersensory object for that person because it [the person] is that subject.[385]

On this extremely brief explanation, Ge-shay Pel-den-drak-pa comments:

> When a reason like this one ["because it is that subject"] is used, it is hard to say whether the pervasion is established or not [that is, whether the sign entails the predicate of the probandum]. This is not a useful reason.[386]

It is clear that, according to Pur-bu-jok, "permanent" is not a supersensory object for a person for whom product has become the property of the subject in the proof of sound as not permanent. While not necessarily considering Pur-bu-jok's reasoning to be helpful, Ge-luk-pa scholars apparently agree that "permanent" is not generally a supersensory object. Lati Rin-bo-chay says,

> It can be decided [by ordinary beings] whether sound is permanent or not, whereas it is impossible to decide whether a flesh-eater is present or not.[387]

A flesh-eater is a supersensory object, and thus its presence cannot be ascertained by an ordinary being. Permanent, on the other hand, is generally considered by Ge-luk-pa scholars to be apprehendable by the valid cognition of ordinary beings and thus to be a nonsupersensory object.

Nonobservation of a Related Object Suitable to Appear

In discussing this type of correct sign, Pur-bu-jok writes,

> The subject, the nonexistence of fire, is a correct sign that is a nonobservation of a related object suitable to appear in the proof of smoke as nonexistent on a lake at night because of (1) being a correct sign that is a nonobservation of the suitable to appear in the proof of that and (2) being a nonaffirming negative phenomenon.[388]

A correct sign that is a nonobservation of a related object suitable to appear must first of all be a nonobservation sign of the suitable to appear. This means that it must be a correct nonobservation sign (that is, the predicate of the probandum must be a negative phenomenon), and the object designated as the predicate of the negandum must not be a supersensory object for the correct opponent in that proof.

Pur-bu-jok adds that the sign must be a nonaffirming negative phenomenon. As mentioned earlier, there is apparent agreement among Ge-luk-pa scholars that the nonobservation of something must be a nonaffirming negative phenomenon, while the observation of something must be either an affirming negative or a positive phenomenon. Some Ge-luk-pa scholars consider that this reasoning is not the most effective way of explaining the criteria of this type of sign. Ge-shay Ge-dün-lo-drö suggests an alternative explanation: in addition to being a nonobservation sign of the suitable to appear, the sign must involve the nonobservation of something (in this case, fire) that is a related object of the object designated as the predicate of the negandum (smoke). He says,

The object designated as the predicate of the negandum in the proof of that is "smoke," which is an object related to fire. "The nonexistence of fire" is set as the sign in the proof of that and, thus, is a correct sign that is a nonobservation of a related object suitable to appear.[389]

Nonobservation of a Cause Suitable to Appear

On this topic, Pur-bu-jok writes,

> With respect to the subject, object of knowledge, the nonexistence of fire is a correct sign that is a nonobservation of a cause suitable to appear in the proof of smoke as nonexistent on a lake at night because (1) it [the nonexistence of fire] is a correct nonobservation sign of the suitable to appear in the proof of that and (2) fire is the cause of smoke. Extend this reasoning to the [three] other [correct signs that are nonobservations of a pervader, of a nature, and of a direct effect suitable to appear].[390]

The nonexistence of fire is a correct sign that is a nonobservation of a cause suitable to appear in the proof of smoke as nonexistent on a lake at night because, first, it is a nonobservation sign of the suitable to appear in that proof. It is therefore a correct sign, and the object designated as the predicate of the negandum is not a supersensory object for the correct opponent in that proof. Secondly, the sign involves the nonobservation on something (fire) that is the cause of the object designated as the predicate of the negandum (smoke).

If we extend this reasoning as Pur-bu-jok suggests, we see that the nonexistence of trees is a correct sign that is a nonobservation of a pervader suitable to appear in the proof of oak as nonexistent on a craggy cliff where trees are not observed by valid cognition because:

(1) it is a correct nonobservation sign of the suitable to appear in the proof of that (thus, it is a correct nonobservation sign and the object designated as the predicate of the negandum, oak, is not a supersensory object for the correct opponent in that proof), and

(2) the sign involves the nonobservation of something (tree) that is the pervader of the object designated as the predicate of the negandum (oak).

The same reasoning can be applied to the nature and the direct effect sub-categories of correct signs that are a nonobservation of a related object suitable to appear.

Observation of a Contradictory Object Suitable to Appear

In discussing correct signs that are an observation of a contradictory object suitable to appear, Pur-bu-jok writes,

> The subject, product, is a correct sign that is an observation of a contradictory object suitable to appear, in the proof that sound is not permanent because of (1) being a correct nonobservation sign of the suitable to appear in the proof of that and (2) being either an affirming negative or a positive phenomenon.[391]

Because the sign involves the *observation* of something, it must be either an affirming negative or a positive phenomenon.

Ge-shay Ge-dün-lo-drö suggests another way of explaining the criteria for this type of sign. He says,

> Pur-bu-jok's reasoning does not convey the full meaning. Another way of carrying out this proof is: With respect to the subject, product, it is a correct sign that is an observation of a contradictory object suitable to appear in the proof that sound is not permanent because:
>
> (1) it is a correct nonobservation sign of the suitable to appear in the proof of that, and
> (2) the object designated as the predicate of the negandum in the proof of that by the sign of it is "permanent," with which product is contradictory.
>
> Since the observation of it [product] is set as the sign, it is a correct sign that is an observation of a contradictory object suitable to appear.[392]

This is clear: a correct sign that is an observation of a contradictory object suitable to appear must first of all be a correct nonobservation sign of the suitable to appear; and furthermore the opposite of the sign (*rtags log*)—in this case, product—must be contradictory with the object designated as the predicate of the negandum.

Observation of an Object Suitable to Appear That Is Contradictory in the Sense of Not Abiding Together

Pur-bu-jok continues,

With respect to the subject, object of knowledge, a place covered by a large powerful fire is a correct sign that is an observation of a contradictory object in the sense of not abiding together in the proof that the continuous tangible object, cold, does not exist on a place in the east covered by a large powerful fire because (1) of being a correct sign that is an observation of a contradictory object in the proof of that and (2) that place covered by a large powerful fire is a contradictory object that does not abide together with the continuous tangible object, cold.[393]

Ge-shay Ge-dün-lo-drö elaborates:

In another way: With respect to the subject, object of knowledge, a place covered by a large powerful fire is a correct sign that is an observation of a contradictory object in the sense of not abiding together in the proof of that because:

(1) it is a correct sign that is a nonobservation of a contradictory object in the proof of that, and
(2) the object designated as the predicate of the negandum in the proof of that by the sign of it is the continuous tangible object, cold, together with which a place covered by a large powerful fire does not abide.

Since it (a place covered by a large powerful fire) is set as the sign, it is a correct sign that is an observation of a contradictory object in the sense of not abiding together.[394]

To summarize: A place covered by a large powerful fire is this type of sign because, first, it is a nonobservation sign of the suitable to appear—the object designated as the predicate of the negandum (the continuous tangible object, cold) is not a supersensory object—and, second, "a place covered by a large powerful fire" is contradictory with the "cold" in the sense of not abiding together.

Observation of an Object Suitable to Appear That Is Contradictory in the Sense of Mutual Exclusion

Pur-bu-jok writes,

With respect to the subject, product, it [product] is a correct sign that is an observation of a contradictory object in the sense of mutual exclusion in the proof that sound is not permanent because (1) it [product] is a correct sign that is an observation of a contradictory object in the proof of that and (2) it [product] is not contradictory with permanent in the sense of not abiding together. This is because it [product] is not of a substantial entity different from permanent.[395]

To elaborate on these two criteria:

(1) Product is a correct sign that is an observation of a contradictory object in the proof of that. Thus, product is a correct nonobservation sign of the nonappearing, and product is contradictory with the object designated as the predicate of the negandum (permanent).

(2) Product is not contradictory with permanent in the sense of not abiding together.

Pur-bu-jok explains this by saying that product is not of a substantial entity different from permanent. It should be remembered that even if contradictory phenomena *are* different substantial entities, they are not necessarily contradictory in the sense of not abiding together. In order for phenomena to be contradictory in *that* sense, they must not only be different substantial entities but also be unable to remain together without one eventually harming the other.

Identification of the Sign, Predicate of the Probandum, and Basis of Debate

Pur-bu-jok ends his explanation of nonobservation signs with a short discussion of the sign (reason) and predicate of the probandum (and predicate of the negandum) in various syllogisms. (He does not actually discuss the basis of debate at all here.) He tells us,

> "The nonexistence of fire" is the reason in the proof of smoke as nonexistent on a lake at night by the sign, nonexistence of fire. "Fireless" is *not* the reason in the proof of smoke as nonexistent on a lake at night by the sign, nonexistence of fire.
>
> The nonexistence of smoke is both (1) the predicate of the probandum in the proof of smoke as nonexistent on a lake at night by the sign, nonexistence of fire, and (2) that held as the explicit predicate of the probandum in the proof of that. Smokeless is not either of those. The same reasoning [applies] to treeless, and so forth.[396]

The syllogism under consideration is: "With respect to the subject, on a lake at night, smoke does not exist because fire does not exist." As explained earlier, the meaning of the sign is changed if the language is altered from the nonexistence of fire (or fire does not exist—*me med pa*) to fireless (*me med*). There is a similar difference in meaning between the nonexistence of smoke (*du ba med pa*) and smokeless (*du ba med*), and between the nonexistence of tree (*shing med pa*) and treeless (*shing med*).

Pur-bu-jok continues,

> The nonobservation of pot by valid cognition is the reason in the proof that pot does not exist on a place where pot is not observed by valid cognition. The nonexistence of pot is both (1) the explicit predicate of the probandum in the proof that pot does not exist on a place where pot is not observed by valid cognition, and (2) that held as the explicit predicate of the probandum in the proof of that. Extend this to others of similar type.[397]

The syllogism is: "With respect to the subject, on a place where pot is not observed by valid cognition, pot does not exist because of the nonobservation of pot by valid cognition." Elsewhere in the text (chapter one), Pur-bu-jok discusses the explicit and implicit predicate of the probandum; there he defines the explicit predicate of the probandum in a given proof as "that held as the explicit predicate of the probandum" in that proof.

We can extend Pur-bu-jok's reasoning to another of this type (correct signs that are a nonobservation of a related object suitable to appear). In relation to the syllogism, "With respect to the subject, in a walled circle devoid of smoke, the direct cause of smoke does not exist because of the nonexistence of the direct effect, smoke," the nonexistence of the direct effect, smoke, is the reason in that proof, and the nonexistence of the direct cause of smoke is both (1) the explicit predicate of the probandum in that proof, and (2) that held as the explicit predicate of the probandum in that proof.

Pur-bu-jok then turns to consideration of the predicate of the negandum:

> "Smoke" is *an object designated* as the predicate of the negandum in the proof of smoke as nonexistent on a lake at night but is *not* the predicate of the negandum in the proof of that. "The existence of smoke" there is *both* an object designated as the predicate of the negandum in the proof of smoke as nonexistent on a lake at night *and* the predicate of the negandum in the

proof of that.[398]

In Pur-bu-jok's view, the phrase "object designated as the predicate of the negandum" refers not only to the full predicate of the negandum but also to abbreviations of that predicate. The phrase generally refers to the main object of consideration within the predicate of the negandum (in this case, "smoke"). However, the phrase, "predicate of the negandum" refers *only* to the reverse of the *full* predicate of the probandum.

Thus, it is "smoke exists" (or "the existence of smoke"), and not "smoke," that is the predicate of the negandum. Lati Rin-po-che comments:

> In this example, the predicate of the negandum is not smoke, but rather the existence of smoke. This is because the opponent does not have doubt about smoke in general but rather about the existence of smoke where it cannot be seen, such as on a lake at night.[399]

Ge-shay Ge-dün-lo-drö points out a parallel:

> Consider the syllogism, "With respect to the subject, on a smoky pass, fire exists because smoke exists." In that, one can posit *fire* (*me*) as the predicate of the probandum, and one can also posit *fire exists* (*me yod*) as the predicate of the probandum.
>
> Now, [if we apply what Pur-bu-jok has written about the negandum to this] one could say that *fire exists* is the predicate of the probandum but *fire* is not. Why? Because although "smoke" is an object designated as the predicate of the negandum in the proof that smoke does not exist on a lake at night, "smoke" is not the predicate of the negandum.[400]

Assume that, as Pur-bu-jok says, smoke is the *object designated* as the predicate of the *negandum* (in the proof that smoke does not exist on a lake at night) but is *not* the predicate of the negandum. Would it not follow that *fire* is the *object designated* as the predicate of the *probandum* (in the proof of fire as existent on a smoky pass) but is *not* the predicate of the probandum? Suggesting this parallel, Ge-shay Ge-dün-lo-drö asks, "If one were to say that smoke is indeed the predicate of the negandum, what fault would there be?"[401]

Pur-bu-jok continues,

> Permanent is an object designated as the predicate of the negandum in the proof that sound is not permanent but is not the

predicate of the negandum in the proof of that."[402]

These words imply that the predicate of the negandum in the proof of sound as not permanent is "being permanent" instead of "permanent" alone. Ge-shay Pel-den-drak-pa comments,

> This must mean that the predicate of the negandum is "being permanent" (*rtag pa yin pa*) instead of "permanent" (*rtag pa*). But if that is the case, then (in the proof of sound as impermanent) the predicate of the probandum would be not "impermanent" (*yin pa*) but rather "being impermanent" (*mi rtag pa yin pa*).[403]

Elsewhere (chapter one), Pur-bu-jok himself says that, in the proof of sound as impermanent, the predicate of the negandum is "permanent" (he does not say it is "being permanent"). Thus, according to Ge-shay Pel-den-drak-pa, it would be appropriate to assert "permanent" as the predicate of the negandum here, in the proof that sound is not permanent. If one posits (as Pur-bu-jok appears to do here) that, in the proof that sound is not permanent, "permanent" is not the predicate of the *negandum* but "being permanent" is, then shouldn't one also hold that, in the proof of sound as impermanent, "impermanent" is not the predicate of the *probandum* but "being impermanent" is? Are the situations parallel? This is the issue raised by Ge-shay Pel-den-drak-pa.

Ge-shay Ge-dün-lo-drö presents a possible solution. He comments, on Pur-bu-jok's passage,

> In the syllogism, "The subject, sound, is not permanent because of being a product," the predicate of the probandum is not "permanent," it is "being permanent." That is what [the text] indicates, but [in this context] there is no difference between "permanent" and "being permanent" [that is, each is the predicate of the negandum].[404]

He then suggests that there may be a mistake in the text, that words may have been omitted, perhaps by a copyist. Given the possibility that we are trying to analyze a "typo," what might Pur-bu-jok have originally written? Ge-shay Ge-dün-lo-drö suggests that the text might have contained words like those here italicized:

> "Permanent" is *both* an object designated as the predicate of the negandum *and the predicate of the negandum* in the proof that sound is not permanent. *"Not being impermanent" is an object designated as the predicate of the negandum in the proof that sound is*

not permanent but is not the predicate of the negandum in the proof of that.[405]

COMPARISON WITH MOKṢĀKARAGUPTA'S PRESENTATION

The Ge-luk-pa distinction between nonobservation signs of the nonappearing and of the suitable to appear is not made by Mokṣākaragupta. All the nonobservation signs that he described would fit into what in the Ge-luk-pa system is the category of nonobservation signs of the suitable to appear.

It may be useful to review the Ge-luk-pa approach to this topic. It divides nonobservation signs on the basis of the main focal point within the predicate of the negandum (the object designated as the predicate of the negandum)—whether it is supersensory or not for the opponent.

Nonobservation signs of the nonappearing (discussed in chapter six) are used in proofs in which the predicate of the negandum is supersensory; an example is the sign in the syllogism:

> With respect to the subject, here in this place in front, there does not exist factually concordant subsequent cognition— ascertaining a flesh-eater—in the continuum of a person for whom a flesh-eater is a supersensory object, because there does not exist valid cognition—observing a flesh-eater—in the continuum of a person for whom a flesh-eater is a supersensory object.

The nonobservation by valid cognition of flesh-eater does not prove the nonexistence of flesh-eater, but it does prove the nonexistence of whatever is related with valid cognition of flesh-eater; for example, the effect of such a valid cognition. Thus, the existence of a subsequent cognition ascertaining flesh-eater (the effect of the valid cognition ascertaining flesh-eater) is refuted by this proof.

An example of a nonobservation sign of the suitable to appear is:

> With respect to the subject, on a lake at night, smoke does not exist because of the nonexistence of fire.

Smoke is suitable to appear in general, but not in this context, on a lake at night. However, fire *is* suitable to appear, and thus nonobservation of fire in that place proves the nonexistence there of smoke.

Mokṣākaragupta's discussion of nonobservation signs is limited to what in the Ge-luk-pa system is the category of nonobservation signs of the suitable to appear. Mokṣākaragupta begins his discussion of nonobservation signs:

> [The logical mark of] noncognition is illustrated: In this place there is no jar, because it is not cognized though it is by nature perceptible. "Perceptible by nature" means "to be seen." [*Question:*] How can a nonexistent thing be cognized? [*Answer:*] When a place and other things are being cognized by one and the same sense perception, if a jar were present, it would be necessarily perceived..."[406]

In explanation of this, he continues,

> The qualifier of noncognition "though it is by nature perceptible" means, [(1) that all conditions for perception must be present and (2)] that the mere nonoccurrence of cognition regarding objects that are inaccessible in space, time, and essence, does not establish *a convention of nonexistence* [of the object concerned]; such objects are illustrated by Mt. Sumeru [which is spatially inaccessible], the future emperor Sankha [who is inaccessible in time] and a ghost [which is inaccessible in essence].[a]

Although Mokṣākaragupta mentions these three types of supersensory objects, he does not posit a category corresponding to the Ge-luk-pas' nonobservation signs of the nonappearing.

Mokṣākaragupta goes on to posit sixteen nonobservation signs, all of which fall into the Ge-luk-pas' category of nonobservation signs of the suitable to appear. Within this category, there are minor differences between the signs posited by Mokṣākaragupta and those posited by Pur-bu-jok. Briefly stated, Mokṣākaragupta's nonobservation signs are:

(1)   Firstly, the noncognition of an entity itself is illustrated: "Here there is no smoke, because it, being by nature perceptible, is not perceived."

(2)   Noncognition of an effect: "The actually efficient (*apratibaddhasāmarthya*, lit., whose efficiency is not impeded) causes producing smoke do not occur here, because there is no smoke."

(3)   Noncognition of a cause: "There is no smoke here, because

---

[a] Kajiyama, *Introduction to Buddhist Philosophy*, p. 80; the italicized words represent Mokṣākaragupta's *abhāvavyavahāra*. Kajiyama's translation ("practical activities concerning absence") seems less helpful than "a convention of nonexistence."

there is no fire."

(4) Noncognition of a pervader: "There is no *aśoka* tree here, because there are no trees here."[407]

These correspond to Pur-bu-jok's four types of sign in the category of correct signs that are a nonobservation of a related object suitable to appear:

(1) correct signs that are a nonobservation of a cause suitable to appear (like Mokṣākaragupta's third),
(2) a pervader suitable to appear (like Mokṣākaragupta's second),
(3) a nature suitable to appear (like Mokṣākaragupta's first), and
(4) a direct effect suitable to appear (like Mokṣākaragupta's fourth).

The corresponding signs are not identical, but they are similar.

The next nonobservation signs posited by Mokṣākaragupta are:

(5) Perception of something incompatible with the presence [of what is to be negated]: "Here there is no sensation of cold, because there is fire here."

(6) Perception of what is incompatible with an effect: "Here there are no actually efficient causes of the sensation of cold, because there is fire here."

(7) Perception of something incompatible with a cause: "He betrays no symptoms such as the bristling of the hair of the body specially [caused by cold], because he is near fire of a particular kind [that is, efficient enough to dispel cold]."

(8) Perception of what is incompatible with a pervader: "Here there is no sensation of freezing, because there is fire here."

(9) Perception of the effect of something incompatible with the essence [of what is to be negated]: "Here there is no sensation of cold, because there is smoke here."

(10) Perception of the effect of something incompatible with the effect [of what is negated]: "Here there are no actually efficient causes of cold, because here there is smoke."

(11) Perception of an effect of something incompatible with the causes [of what is to be negated]: "In this place there is no one who betrays the sensation [of cold] connected with symptoms such as the bristling of the hair of the body specially [caused by cold], because here there is smoke."

(12) Perception of the effect of something incompatible with a

pervader [of what is to be negated]: "Here there is no sensation of freezing because here there is smoke."

(13) Perception of what is pervaded by something incompatible with the existence [of what is to be negated]: "Here there is no fire because of the sensation of freezing."

(14) Perception of what is pervaded by a thing incompatible with the effect [of the object of negation]: "Here there are no actually efficient causes of fire because of the sensation of freezing."

(15) Perception of what is pervaded by a thing incompatible with the cause [of the object of negation]: "Here there is no smoke because of the sensation of freezing."[408]

These eleven signs (five through fifteen) would all fit into Pur-bu-jok's category of correct signs that are an observation of objects contradictory in the sense of material phenomena not abiding together. Pur-bu-jok posits five:

(1) a nature contradictory with a nature—like Mokṣākaragupta's fifth,

(2) a nature that is contradictory with a cause—like Mokṣākaragupta's seventh,

(3) a nature that is contradictory with a pervader—like Mokṣākaragupta's eighth,

(4) an effect that is contradictory with the nature—like Mokṣākaragupta's ninth, and

(5) an effect that is contradictory with a cause—like Mokṣākaragupta's eleventh.

Mokṣākaragupta's other signs (6, 10, 12, 13, 14, and 15) do not have parallels in Pur-bu-jok's presentation, but this is not a serious difference. In both systems it is clear that the listing is not meant to be definitive. Mokṣākaragupta writes, "Further subordinate forms may be enumerated according to the various circumstances of application,"[409] and the discussion in this chapter has shown that Ge-luk-pa scholars do not consider Pur-bu-jok's list to be rigid; more could be posited.

The final type of sign posited by Mokṣākaragupta is:

(16) Perception of what is pervaded by a thing incompatible with the pervader [of the object of negation]: "This is not permanent because it produces the effect only occasionally."[410]

This type does not have an exact parallel in Pur-bu-jok's text. In the category of correct signs that are an observation of an object suitable to appear that is contradictory in the sense of mutual exclusion, however, Pur-bu-jok posits "product" as a correct sign in the proof that sound is not permanent. The examples are slightly different, their names are different, but clearly they are similar in that something is being shown to be not permanent by the observation of x, which is contradictory with permanence.

In short, the presentations are not incompatible. Mokṣākaragupta's presentation of nonobservation signs is very similar to the Ge-luk-pa presentation of nonobservation signs of the suitable to appear. Mokṣākaragupta presents more types that would fall in the category of material phenomena not abiding together, however, and Pur-bu-jok extends the application of the reasoning to proofs that involve impermanent things other than material phenomena—consciousnesses and nonassociated compositional factors.

The significant difference—the inclusion of a category of nonobservation signs of the nonappearing in Pur-bu-jok and other Ge-luk-pa logic manuals—reflects the Ge-luk-pa emphasis on the practical application of logic. Pur-bu-jok makes it clear that this type of sign is presented to convey to students the importance of understanding that there are phenomena about which one can know very little. These are objects inaccessible in space, time, and entity—which include the deepest spiritual qualities of others. Students learn that such qualities are beyond one's ken, and therefore it is wise not to jump to conclusions about others or to assume that what one does not perceive does not exist.

8. Other Divisions of Correct Signs

The main division of correct signs into three types—correct effect, correct nature, and correct nonobservation signs—is called, by Pur-bu-jok, and other Ge-luk-pa textbook authors, the division "by way of the entity" (*ngo bo'i sgo nas*). As explained earlier, there are two criteria for this division: one is whether the sign and the predicate of the probandum are the same entity or different entities; the other is whether the predicate of the probandum is a positive or a negative phenomenon. Besides this main division, five other ways of dividing correct signs are set forth in Ge-luk-pa logic manuals. These five are divisions by way of:

(1) the predicate of the probandum (*bsgrub bya'i chos*),
(2) the mode of proof (*sgrub tshul*),
(3) the probandum (*bsgrub bya*),
(4) the mode of relating to the similar class (*mthun phyogs la 'jug tshul*), and
(5) the opponent (*rgol ba*).[a]

All of these divisions can be included in the main division into three. The other ways of categorizing signs were set forth in order to emphasize several different important aspects of correct signs.

Whatever is being proved by a correct sign is necessarily an existent—a phenomenon, an object observed by valid cognition:

- The division of correct signs by way of the predicate of the probandum is made depending on whether the phenomenon being proved is a positive phenomenon or a negative phenomenon.
- The division by way of the mode of proof is made depending on whether the phenomenon being proved is a definition or a definiendum.
- The division by way of the probandum is made depending on whether the phenomenon being proved is a slightly hidden phenomenon (*cung zad lkog gyur*), a very hidden phenomenon (*shin tu lkog gyur*), or a terminological suitability (*sgra byung grags pa*).
- The division by way of the mode of relating to the similar class is made depending on whether the sign pervades the similar class or not.
- And, finally, the division by way of the opponent is made depending on whether the reasoning is being used by one person in

---

[a] Pur-bu-jok cites this division in *Signs and Reasonings*, p.7a.4-5.

solitary analysis or by two people in debate. If one person is using the reasoning for his or her own sake to understand something new, that use involves a correct sign for one's own sake. If one person is using the reasoning for the sake of another person, in order for the other person to generate new understanding, then that use involves a correct sign for the sake of another.

(1) Division by Way of the Predicate of the Probandum

The division of correct signs by way of the predicate of the probandum is made depending on whether the phenomenon being proved is a positive phenomenon (*sgrub pa*) or a negative phenomenon (*dgag pa*). Whatever is being proved in a correct proof is necessarily an existent; only existents can be known by valid cognition. The Ge-luk-pa student knows from his or her study of the *Collected Topics* that the definition of an existent is "that which is observed by valid cognition"; thus, whatever is not observed by valid cognition is not an existent. One way of dividing existents is into positive and negative phenomena. This division of existents or phenomena is made depending on how the phenomena are realized by conceptual thought. Phenomena that are realized through the explicit elimination of an object of negation are called negative phenomena; phenomena that are realized by conceptual thought without the *explicit* elimination of an object of negation are called positive phenomena.

Pur-bu-jok, in his own text book on the *Collected Topics*, defines a positive phenomenon as:

> A phenomenon that is not an object realized by the conceptual consciousness apprehending it in the manner of an explicit elimination of its object of negation.[411]

Fire, for example, is a positive phenomenon. A conceptual consciousness that realizes fire does not explicitly eliminate an object of negation. The nature of conceptual thought is such that there is necessarily, even in its apprehension of positive phenomena, elimination of an object of negation; the conceptual consciousness apprehending fire does so by *implicitly* eliminating nonfire (*me ma yin pa*). However, this implicit elimination of nonfire does not mean that fire is a negative phenomenon; fire is a positive phenomenon because the conceptual consciousness apprehending it does so without having to *explicitly* eliminate anything.

Pur-bu-jok defines a negative phenomenon as:

> An object realized by the conceptual consciousness apprehending it in the manner of an explicit elimination of its object of negation.[412]

A negative phenomenon, such as "nonfire" or "the absence of fire" (*me med pa*) is realized by conceptual thought through the explicit elimination of an object of negation; in this case through the explicit elimination of "fire" (*me*).

Thus, from the point of view of the type of existent being proved, there are two types of correct signs: correct signs of a positive phenomenon (*sgrub rtags yang dag*) and correct signs of a negative phenomenon (*dgag rtags yang dag*). This division into two is called the division by way of the predicate of the probandum.

CORRECT SIGNS OF A POSITIVE PHENOMENON

According to Pur-bu-jok, the definition of a correct sign of a positive phenomenon is:

> (1) It is a correct sign in the proof of that and (2) there exists a common locus of being that held as the explicit predicate of the probandum in the proof of that by the sign of it and of being a positive phenomenon.[413]

The phrasing of this definition is significant. Among the various Ge-luk-pa monastic colleges, there are differences of opinion concerning the definition of "correct sign of a positive phenomenon." The definition posited by the textbook author of Lo-sel-ling College of Dre-pung Monastic University, Ge-shay Tsül-trim-nam-gyel, is:

> That which is the three modes in the proof of that and with respect to which whatever is held as the explicit predicate of the probandum in the proof of that is necessarily a positive phenomenon.[414]

Ge-shay Tsül-trim-nam-gyel's presentation of this topic accords with that of Jay-tsün Chö-kyi-gyel-tsen, in whose system there is only one explicit predicate of the probandum in any given proof; this definition, therefore, specifies that the explicit predicate of the probandum must be a positive phenomenon. However, according to Pur-bu-jok and Paṇ-chen Sö-nam-drak-pa, there may be more than one explicit predicate of the probandum. This difference of opinion is discussed in detail in the next section on "divisions by way of the mode of proof."

In brief, according to Pur-bu-jok, in the proof of sound as

impermanent by the sign, product, there are two explicit predicates of the probandum: "impermanent" and "momentary." Momentary is the definition of impermanent, and therefore, in order to apprehend "impermanent" by valid cognition, one must first apprehend "momentary" by valid cognition. When "impermanent" appears to the mind, "momentary" must also appear to the mind; therefore momentary is considered to be an explicit predicate of the probandum in the proof of sound as impermanent. However, according to Ge-shay Tsül-trim-nam-gyel, there is only one explicit predicate in any given proof.

Pur-bu-jok's definition reflects his position on this issue, as Ge-shay Pel-den-drak-pa explains,

> The definition is phrased this way because for Pur-bu-jok there may be more than one explicit predicate of the probandum [in any given proof].[415]

Pur-bu-jok includes the words "there exists a common locus of being that held as the explicit predicate of the probandum and being a positive phenomenon" so as to allow for the possibility that there may exist an explicit predicate of the probandum that is *not* a positive phenomenon. If these words are not included, a problem will arise in regard to syllogisms in which the predicate of the probandum is, for example, "positive phenomenon." The definition of "positive phenomenon" is "a phenomenon that is not an object realized by the conceptual consciousness apprehending it in the manner of an explicit elimination of its object of negation," which is itself a *negative* phenomenon.

This poses an interesting problem. According to Pur-bu-jok, when a definiendum is proved, its definition necessarily appears simultaneously to the mind of the correct opponent and thus is considered to be an equally explicit predicate of the probandum in that proof. Thus, were "positive phenomenon" to be proved, would not the explicit predicate of the probandum include both a positive and a negative phenomenon? If that were the case, then would the sign be a sign of a positive phenomenon or a sign of a negative phenomenon? Can a sign in a given proof be *both* a sign of a positive phenomenon and a sign of a negative phenomenon? No. There is apparent agreement, among Ge-luk-pa scholars, that "a sign of a positive phenomenon" and "a sign of a negative phenomenon" must be mutually exclusive in relation to any one proof.

Pur-bu-jok is able to maintain this position by including the above-mentioned words ("there exists a common locus...") in the definition. In the case of the proof of sound as a positive phenomenon, that common locus would be "positive phenomenon" itself. The fact that there may be another explicit predicate of the probandum that is a negative phenomenon (that is, the definition of positive phenomenon) does not pose a problem; as long as one of the explicit predicates is a positive phenomenon, the requirements of his definition are satisfied.

Pur-bu-jok posits a division of correct signs of a positive phenomenon; he writes,

> When [correct signs of a positive phenomenon are] divided, there are two [types], correct effect signs and correct nature signs. Whatever is a correct effect sign or a correct nature sign is necessarily a correct sign of a positive phenomenon.[416]

Correct effect and correct nature signs are necessarily correct signs of a positive phenomenon. An example of the first is the sign, smoke, in the syllogism, "With respect to the subject, on a smoky pass, fire exists because smoke exists." The explicit predicate of the probandum, fire, is a positive phenomenon. An example of a correct nature sign is "product" in the syllogism, "The subject, sound, is impermanent because of being a product."

CORRECT SIGNS OF A NEGATIVE PHENOMENON

The definition posited by Pur-bu-jok of a correct sign of a negative phenomenon is:

> (1) It is a correct sign in the proof of that and (2) there exists a common locus of being that held as the explicit predicate of the probandum in the proof of that by the sign of it and of being a negative phenomenon.[417]

This definition is identical to Pur-bu-jok's definition of "a correct nonobservation sign";[418] and, in fact, the two categories are equivalent, according to Pur-bu-jok, who states,

> The two, correct sign of a negative phenomenon and correct nonobservation sign, are equivalent (*don gcig*).[419]

While effect and nature signs are necessarily signs of a positive phenomenon, nonobservation signs are necessarily signs of a negative phenomenon. Earlier, Pur-bu-jok specified that effect, nature, and nonobservation signs are mutually exclusive, meaning specifically that whatever is one *in a particular proof* cannot be the others in that same proof. The same restriction applies in relation to signs of a positive phenomenon and signs of a negative phenomenon; these are also mutually exclusive in relation to any given proof. This does not eliminate the possibility of one phenomenon being—in different contexts—a sign of a positive phenomenon *and* a sign of a negative phenomenon. Pur-bu-jok explains,

> Although correct sign of a negative phenomenon in the proof of that [that is, in any given proof] and correct sign of a positive phenomenon in the proof of that are contradictory, correct sign of a negative phenomenon and correct sign of a positive phenomenon are not contradictory. This is because product is both [a correct sign of a negative phenomenon and a correct sign of a positive phenomenon]. This [in turn] is because it [product] is both a correct sign of a negative phenomenon in the proof that sound is not permanent and a correct sign of a positive phenomenon in the proof that sound is impermanent.[420]

"Product" may be a correct sign of a positive phenomenon or of a negative phenomenon, depending on context. For example, "product" is a correct sign of a negative phenomenon in the syllogism, "The subject, sound, is not permanent because of being a product." The predicate of the probandum in that proof, "is not permanent" (*rtag pa ma yin pa*), is a negative phenomenon. The conceptual consciousness apprehending it does so through the explicit elimination of "permanent." "Product" can, of course, also function as a correct sign of a positive phenomenon; for example, in the syllogism, "The subject, sound, is impermanent because of being a product," "product" is a correct sign of a positive phenomenon; this is because the predicate of the probandum in that proof, "impermanent," is a positive phenomenon. The conceptual consciousness apprehending "impermanent" does so without the explicit elimination of an object of negation.

Although in general "product" may be either a sign of a positive phenomenon or a sign of a negative phenomenon, it must be one or the other in any given proof; it cannot be both. This is because what is being proved is either a positive phenomenon or a negative phenomenon, and cannot be both, as Ge-shay Lob-sang-gya-tso makes clear when he says,

> That which is held as the explicit predicate of the probandum is never both a positive phenomenon and a negative phenomenon.[421]

Positive phenomenon and negative phenomenon are contradictory;

thus no one phenomenon can be both; it follows then that whatever is held as the explicit predicate of the probandum in any given proof cannot be both.

A complication arises however when one considers complex predicates containing more than one part. Ge-shay Pel-den-drak-pa explains the problem:

> The two, a correct sign of a positive phenomenon and a correct sign of a negative phenomenon have to be contradictory. That being the case, what about the syllogism, "The subject, sound, is impermanent and opposite from being nonimpermanent (*mi rtag pa ma yin pa las log pa*) because of being a product"? This [that is, "product," in this proof] is considered to be a sign of a positive phenomenon. To assert in the definition [of sign of a positive phenomenon] that the predicate is necessarily a positive phenomenon poses a problem when this syllogism is considered.[422]

The explicit predicate of the probandum in this syllogism is made up of both a positive phenomenon and a negative one. That being the case, is "product" both a sign of a positive phenomenon and a sign of a negative phenomenon? No. According to Ge-luk-pa scholars, even in cases involving such complex predicates, the explicit predicate is always considered to be either positive or negative; never both. There is a difference of opinion concerning whether in the syllogism just cited, the predicate of the probandum is a positive phenomenon or a negative one. According to Ge-shay Lob-sang-gya-tso, it is a positive phenomenon. In his view, if a predicate contains more than one part, one negative and the other positive, then the first one stated is considered to be the "explicit" one. He comments,

> If the explicit predicate of the probandum is a positive phenomenon, the sign is a sign of a positive phenomenon; and if the explicit predicate of the probandum is a negative phenomenon, then it is a sign of a negative phenomenon. The explicit predicate of the probandum is never made up of both a positive and negative phenomenon. In the case of the syllogism, "The subject, sound, is impermanent and opposite from nonimpermanent because of being a product," the explicit predicate is just "impermanent." If the predicate is just "opposite from nonimpermanent," then it is a sign of a negative phenomenon. The sign in the syllogism, "With respect to the subject, on a smoky pass, fire exists because smoke exists," is a sign of a positive

phenomenon. "With respect to the subject, on a smoky pass, opposite of nonfire exists because smoke exists"—in that, smoke is a sign of a negative phenomenon. If you posit, as predicate, "fire and opposite of nonfire exist," then it is a sign of a positive phenomenon. If you posit "opposite of nonfire and fire exist," then [smoke] is a sign of a negative phenomenon. [The one you state first is the explicit one.][423]

Lati Rin-po-che, on the other hand, asserts that the predicate of the probandum in this syllogism, "The subject, sound, is impermanent and opposite from being nonimpermanent because of being a product," is a negative phenomenon. According to him, if the predicate of the probandum contains a negative phenomenon, then the whole predicate is considered to be a negative phenomenon. Lati Rin-po-che makes his view clear when he says,

> In the syllogism, "The subject, sound, is impermanent and opposite from being nonimpermanent because of being a product," the predicate of the probandum is a negative phenomenon because an aspect of a negative phenomenon appears to the mind; it is true that the aspect of a positive phenomenon also appears, but it does not follow from that that it [the predicate of the probandum] is a positive phenomenon. You cannot break the predicate of the probandum into two parts and say that each is an explicit predicate of the probandum; there is only one, the compound predicate, that is a negative phenomenon.[424]

According to Lati Rin-po-che, any compound that includes a negative phenomenon is itself then considered to be a negative phenomenon; he gives as example, "negative and positive phenomenon" (*dgag sgrub*); one part is positive, but the whole is considered to be negative.

(2) DIVISION BY WAY OF THE MODE OF PROOF

The division of correct signs by way of the mode of proof is made depending on whether the phenomenon being proved is a definition or a definiendum. This is not an all-inclusive division; not all correct signs can be included in this division because many objects are not categorized as either definitions or definienda; for example, "the suitability of being expressed by the term 'moon,'" is said to be neither a definition not a definiendum. Thus, in the following syllogism, the explicit predicate of the probandum is neither a definition nor a definiendum: "The subject, the rabbit-bearer, is suitable to be expressed by the term 'moon' because of existing among objects of conceptuality." In some parts of the world there is a tradition of seeing in the moon a face which is referred to as "the man in the moon"; in Indo-Tibetan culture, there is a tradition of seeing the image of a rabbit in the moon; from this comes the tradition of referring to the moon as "the rabbit-bearer."

Some scholars, including the author of the Lo-sel-ling College text-book, posit only two types of correct signs by way of the mode of proof—correct signs proving the meaning and correct signs proving the expression.[425] In this context, "meaning" (*don*) refers to a definition and "expression" (*tha snyad*) refers to a definiendum. A correct sign proving the meaning (*don sgrub kyi rtags yang dag*) is a correct sign in a proof in which the explicit predicate of the probandum is a definition; thus it is a correct sign proving a definition, or a "meaning." A correct sign proving the expression (*tha snyad sgrub kyi rtags yang dag*) is a correct sign in a proof in which the explicit predicate of the probandum is a definiendum; thus it is a correct sign proving a definiendum, or an "expression."

According to Pur-bu-jok, however, when correct signs are divided by way of the mode of proof, there are five types—correct signs proving the meaning, the expression, only the meaning, only the expression, and both the meaning and the expression.[426]

This difference in the number of signs posited in the division by way of the mode of proof arises because of a difference of opinion concerning the nature of the explicit predicate of the probandum in a valid proof. Both Pur-bu-jok and Ge-shay Tsül-trim-nam-gyel posit the same definition for "explicit predicate of the probandum": "that which is held as the explicit predicate of the probandum." However, they disagree in their identification of "that which is held as the explicit predicate of the probandum" in a given proof. For example, they disagree in their identification of the explicit predicate of the probandum in the following syllogism, "The subject, sound, is impermanent because of being a product." It is the opinion of Ge-shay Tsül-trim-nam-gyel that the explicit predicate of the probandum in that proof is "impermanent" and that no other explicit predicate of the probandum can be posited in that proof. Therefore, the sign in that proof is necessarily a sign proving a definiendum or "expression," because "impermanent" is a definiendum. However, according to Pur-bu-jok, there is more than one explicit predicate of the probandum in that proof. Pur-bu-jok writes,

The two, the impermanent and the momentary, are each the

explicit predicate of the probandum in the proof of sound as impermanent by the sign, product.[427]

According to Ge-shay Tsül-trim-nam-gyel, when one ascertains the impermanent, only the impermanent appears to one's mind; and therefore, impermanent is the sole object of ascertainment at that time. According to Pur-bu-jok, however, when one ascertains "the impermanent," its definition, "the momentary," also appears to the mind; thus the ascertainment of "the momentary" accompanies the ascertainment of "the impermanent" and for that reason "the momentary" is said also to be the explicit predicate of the probandum in the proof of sound as impermanent by the sign, product.

To summarize this difference of opinion, according to Ge-shay Tsül-trim-nam-gyel's Lo-sel-ling textbook, when a correct opponent gains realization of the impermanent in dependence on the sign in the syllogism, "The subject, sound, is impermanent because of being a product," only "impermanent" appears explicitly to his or her mind. According to Pur-bu-jok, however, both "impermanent" and "momentary" appear to his or her mind at that time. It is Pur-bu-jok's view that when an expression (definiendum) is being ascertained, its meaning (definition) must also be *explicitly* ascertained at that time; thus, in his view, one sign may establish both a meaning and an expression. Because in Pur-bu-jok's view it is possible to posit two explicit predicates of the probandum of the same proof, he does not limit his division of correct signs by way of the mode of proof to two types. When he divides correct signs from this point of view, he posits five types.

CORRECT SIGNS PROVING THE MEANING

The definition posited by Pur-bu-jok of something's being a correct sign proving the meaning in a particular proof is:

> It is a correct sign in the proof of that, and there exists a common locus of being that held as the explicit predicate of the probandum in the proof of that by the sign of it and of being a definition.[428]

An illustration of a correct sign proving the meaning is the sign in the following syllogism, "The subject, sound, is momentary, because of being a product." In that proof, product is a correct sign proving the meaning because product is a correct sign in the proof of that and there occurs a common locus of being that held as the explicit predicate of the probandum in that proof and of being a definition. "Momentary," the definition of "impermanent," is posited as that common locus.[a]

CORRECT SIGNS PROVING THE EXPRESSION

The definition posited by Pur-bu-jok of something's being a correct sign proving the expression in the proof of that is:

> It is a correct sign in the proof of that and there exists a common locus of being that held as the explicit predicate of the probandum in the proof of that by the sign of it and of being a definiendum.[429]

An illustration of a correct sign proving the expression is the sign in the syllogism, "The subject, sound, is impermanent because of being a product." In that proof, product is a correct sign proving the expression because of being a correct sign in that proof and because there exists a common locus of being that held as the explicit predicate of the probandum in that proof and of being a definiendum. "Impermanent," the definiendum of "momentary," is posited as that common locus.

CORRECT SIGNS PROVING ONLY THE MEANING

The definition posited by Pur-bu-jok of something's being a correct sign proving only the meaning in the proof of that is:

> It is a correct sign in the proof of that and there does not exist a common locus of being that held as the explicit predicate of the probandum in the proof of that by the sign of it and of being a definiendum, but there does exist a common locus of being that held as the explicit predicate of the probandum in the proof of that by the sign of it and of being a definition.[430]

An illustration of a correct sign proving only the meaning is the sign in the syllogism, "The subject, sound, is momentary because of being a product." There does not occur a common locus of being that held as the explicit predicate of the probandum in that proof and of being a definiendum. "Momentary" is the definition of "impermanent," and thus must be ascertained before "impermanent." When "momentary"

---

[a] Pur-bu-jok posits definitions of each of the five types, but provides no further explanation of any type other than "correct signs proving only the expression" and "correct signs proving both the meaning and the expression." The illustrations of the other types were provided by Ge-shay Ge-dün-lo-drö (commentary on *Signs and Reasonings*, vol. 1, April 30, pp. 4-5).

is newly ascertained by inferential valid cognition by means of a reason, "impermanent" has not yet been ascertained.

This view appears to be shared by all the Ge-luk-pa scholars. However, Ge-shay Tsül-trim-nam-gyel calls "product" a correct sign proving the meaning in the proof of sound as momentary,[431] while Pur-bu-jok would call "product" a correct sign proving *only* the meaning in that proof. This distinction arises because according to Ge-shay Tsül-trim-nam-gyel all signs proving the meaning are necessarily proving only the meaning but, for Pur-bu-jok, in some cases a correct sign proves only a meaning and in some cases a correct sign proves both a meaning and an expression.

CORRECT SIGNS PROVING ONLY THE EXPRESSION

The definition posited by Pur-bu-jok of something's being a correct sign proving only the expression in the proof of that is:

> It is a correct sign in the proof of that and there does not exist a common locus of being that held as the explicit predicate of the probandum in the proof of that by the sign of it and of being a definition, but there does exist a common locus of being that held as the explicit predicate of the probandum in the proof of that by the sign of it and of being a definiendum.[432]

Pur-bu-jok then provides an illustration:

> [When one states, "The subject, sound, is impermanent because of being momentary,"] momentary is a correct sign proving only the expression in the proof of sound as impermanent.[a]

There occurs a common locus of being that held as the explicit predicate of the probandum in that proof and of being a definiendum; "impermanent," the definition of "momentary," is that common locus. However, there does not exist a common locus of being that held as the explicit predicate of the probandum in that proof and of being a definition.

In this proof, the definition of "impermanent," "momentary," is being used as a sign in the proof of sound's impermanence. The correct opponent must be someone who, having ascertained sound as

---

[a] *Signs and Reasonings*, p. 15b.7. Pur-bu-jok adds: "However, [momentary] is not a correct sign proving sound as impermanent by the sign, product. This is because whatever is a correct sign in the proof of sound as impermanent by the sign, product, must be one with product." (Ibid., pp. 15b.7-16a.1.)

momentary, is wondering whether sound is impermanent. This opponent is therefore someone who has ascertained the meaning ("the momentary") but not the expression ("the impermanent"). Thus only the expression is being proved newly.

Another example posited of a correct sign proving only the expression is "product" in the syllogism, "The subject, sound, is impermanent because of being a product." It should be noted that only in certain circumstances is this the case. The correct opponent must be someone who has already ascertained "the momentary" but not "the impermanent." If the opponent has not already ascertained "the momentary," then product is a correct sign proving both the meaning and the expression in the proof of sound as impermanent. As Lati Rin-po-che puts it,

> Is "product" necessarily a correct sign proving only the expression in the proof of sound as impermanent? No. It is only for a specific type of opponent, one who has already realized that sound is momentary and for whom product has become the property of the subject in the proof of sound as impermanent.[433]

CORRECT SIGNS PROVING BOTH THE MEANING AND THE EXPRESSION

Pur-bu-jok posits as the definition of something's being a correct sign proving both the meaning and the expression in the proof of that:

> It is a correct sign in the proof of that and there exists a common locus of being that held as the explicit predicate of the probandum in the proof of that by the sign of it and of being a definition and there exists a common locus of being that held as the explicit predicate of the probandum in the proof of that by the sign of it and of being a definiendum.[434]

As an illustration of a correct sign proving both the meaning and the expression, Pur-bu-jok suggests the sign in the syllogism, "The subject, sound, is impermanent because of being a product." He explains,

> Product is a correct sign proving only the expression in the proof of sound as impermanent for a correct opponent who has already established by valid cognition that sound is momentary. However, in general, [product] is a correct sign proving both the meaning and the expression in the proof of sound as impermanent. This is because [product] is a correct sign proving both the meaning and the expression for a correct opponent

who has not ascertained by valid cognition that sound is momentary.[435]

In summary, according to Pur-bu-jok, in the syllogism, "The subject, sound, is impermanent because of being a product," product is necessarily a sign proving the expression; it is also either a sign proving only the expression or a sign proving both the meaning and the expression. If the opponent has already ascertained "momentary," then product is a correct sign proving only the expression. If the opponent has not already understood "momentary," then product is a correct sign proving both the meaning and the expression in that proof. This is because in order for the opponent to understand "impermanent" he or she must first understand "momentary"; thus, for such an opponent, product may be said to be establishing both "impermanent" and "momentary."

Other scholars disagree, saying that the person who has not already ascertained "momentary" must first ascertain "momentary" by means of a sign proving the meaning; only then can he or she ascertain impermanent, by means of a sign proving the expression. This is the point of view of Paṇ-chen Sö-nam-drak-pa, as Ge-shay Pel-den-drak-pa comments,

> For Paṇ-chen Sö-nam-drak-pa, there are only signs proving the meaning and signs proving the expression. Thus, [the syllogism,] "The subject, sound is impermanent because of being a product," will always be proving an expression and never both an expression and a meaning. The meaning will have to have been proved earlier; but it will not be proved by this proof. This is because there is always [for Paṇ-chen Sö-nam-drak-pa] only one explicit predicate of the probandum, only one thing being proved explicitly. However, for Pur-bu-jok, there can be two explicit predicates of the probandum, two separate things being proved explicitly by the same proof.[436]

The Application of Connection between Illustration, Definiendum, and Definition

The most important issue to consider in understanding the explanation of this division of correct signs (by way of the mode of proof) is the order of ascertainment of definitions and definienda. By the time students in a Ge-luk-pa monastic university begin the study of logic, they already know, from their study of the *Collected Topics*, that in order to ascertain an object, one must first ascertain the meaning of that object. It is specified in the *Collected Topics* that in order to ascertain an object, that object's definition must first be understood; otherwise what is known is only a word without any meaning attached to it. For example, it is clearly explained in the *Collected Topics* that the ascertainment of "thing" by valid cognition must be preceded by the ascertainment by valid cognition of the definition of thing: "that which is able to perform a function." Thus, the ascertainment of a definiendum must always be preceded by ascertainment of its definition.

Pur-bu-jok explains that before one can ascertain by valid cognition "pot," one must ascertain the definition of pot: "that which is bulbous, flat based, and able to perform the function of holding water." Having understood that meaning in relation to an illustration, the name "pot" can then be attached to that meaning; this process is called the "application of the connection" (*mtshon sbyor*) between illustration, definiendum, and definition.

In order for this "application of the connection" to be correct, the definition must be correct and complete, and the illustration must be a correct one. With regard to ascertaining "thing" (*dngos po*), for example, the formal expression of an application of connection between illustration, definiendum, and definition is:

> Pot is the illustration and is exemplified as being a thing through being able to perform a function.[437]

This is considered to be a correct application of the connection between illustration, definiendum, and definition, and therefore its use may bring new understanding to the appropriate person. The person for whom this functions as a correct application of connection is someone who has seen a thing without knowing that its name is "thing." Such a person will come to understand the relationship between the illustration, the definition, and the definiendum through hearing this correct application of connection; he or she will then understand the following: "That which is able to perform a function is a thing." This will be explained below (pp. 303ff.).

Incorrect applications of the connection between illustration, definiendum, and definition cannot serve to bring understanding. Applications of connection are incorrect due to the use of an incorrect illustration or an incorrect definition. For example, it is said that "golden pot" cannot be an illustration of "pot" and "cypress pillar" cannot be an illustration of "pillar." Applications of the connection between illustration, definition, and definiendum that use these as illustrations are thus necessarily mistaken. According to Pur-bu-jok,

> Someone says: "Cypress pillar is the illustration and is exempli-
> fied as being a pillar through being that which is able to per-
> form the function of supporting beams; this application of con-
> nection between an illustration (cypress pillar), a definiendum
> (pillar), and a definition (that which is able to perform the
> function of supporting beams) is a proper one."
>
> [The response is:] "It follows that that is not correct be-
> cause there does not exist a person who, having ascertained
> cypress pillar by valid cognition, does not ascertain pillar by va-
> lid cognition, and thus cypress pillar cannot be an illustration
> of pillar."[438]

"Cypress pillar" is not considered to be a correct illustration of "pillar"
because it cannot be ascertained separate from pillar. Just as there is no
way to ascertain "big man" without also ascertaining "man," so also,
there is no way to ascertain "cypress pillar" without ascertaining "pillar." A correct illustration must be both separate from and easier to
ascertain than the definiendum it illustrates.

Pur-bu-jok continues,

> If someone says that the reason is not established, [then, the
> response is,] "It follows that [such a person] does not exist be-
> cause any person who has ascertained cypress pillar by valid
> cognition must be a person who has ascertained cypress pillar
> as pillar by valid cognition."[439]

Someone says the reason is not established, meaning that it is not established that there does not exist a person who, having ascertained
cypress pillar by valid cognition, does not ascertain pillar by valid cognition and thus cypress pillar cannot be an illustration of pillar. This
person therefore holds that such a person *does* exist. To prove that the
reason *is* established and therefore that such a person does not exist,
Pur-bu-jok argues that any person who has ascertained cypress pillar
by valid cognition has necessarily ascertained cypress pillar as pillar by
valid cognition; and this, in turn, is because such a person must have
ascertained cypress pillar as cypress pillar by valid cognition. Pur-bu-
jok writes,

> If someone says that the reason is not established [that is, it is
> not established that any person who has ascertained cypress
> pillar by valid cognition must be a person who has ascertained
> cypress pillar as pillar by valid cognition, then the response is,

"Any person who has ascertained cypress pillar by valid cognition must be a person who has ascertained cypress pillar as pillar by valid cognition] because any person who has ascertained cypress pillar by valid cognition must be a person who has ascertained cypress pillar as cypress pillar by valid cognition."[440]

Having ascertained a cypress pillar by valid cognition, one has necessarily ascertained that a cypress pillar is, in fact, a cypress pillar. To use another example, if someone sees a pot and does not know its name, but only its qualities, that person ascertains the qualities of the pot, but not "pot." To ascertain "pot" one must recognize the pot *as* a pot. Similarly, one who sees a cypress pillar, but does not know the name "cypress pillar," knows the qualities of that pillar by direct perception but does not know "cypress pillar." To ascertain cypress pillar, one must ascertain cypress pillar as cypress pillar; and, as Pur-bu-jok points out, if one has ascertained cypress pillar as cypress pillar, one has necessarily also ascertained cypress pillar as pillar.

Similarly, "golden pot" cannot be a proper illustration of "pot" because there does not exist a person who, having ascertained "golden pot" by valid cognition, has not ascertained "pot" by valid cognition. Pur-bu-jok comments,

> Someone says: "Golden pot is the illustration [and] is exemplified as being a pot [through] being that which is bulbous, flat based, and able to perform the function of holding water." This application of connection [between an illustration (golden pot), a definiendum (pot), and a definition (that which is bulbous, flat based, and able to perform the function of holding water)] is a proper one."
>
> Response: "It follows that that is not correct because there does not exist a person who, having ascertained golden pot by valid cognition, has not ascertained pot by valid cognition." Extend the reasoning and mode of proof.[441]

Pur-bu-jok indicates that the reasoning proving this is the same as that used earlier to prove that there does not exist a person who, having ascertained cypress pillar, has not ascertained pillar. Thus, in order to prove that there does not exist a person who, having ascertained golden pot, has not ascertained pot, Pur-bu-jok would use this reasoning:

> There does not exist a person who, having ascertained "golden pot" by valid cognition, has not ascertained "pot" by valid cognition because any person who has ascertained "golden pot" by

valid cognition must be a person who has ascertained "golden pot" as "pot" by valid cognition. This is because any person who has ascertained golden pot by valid cognition must be a person who has ascertained "golden pot" as "golden pot" by valid cognition.[442]

In the two preceding examples of mistaken applications of the connection between illustration, definiendum, and definition, the mistake is with the illustration itself. Pur-bu-jok goes on to explain that even when a correct illustration is used, the application of connection will be incorrect if the definition is incorrect. He says:

> Someone says: "Golden pot is the illustration [and] is exemplified as being a pot [through] being bulbous. This application of connection [between an illustration (golden pot), a definiendum (pot), and a definition (bulbous)] is a proper one."
>
> The response is: "It follows that that is not correct because bulbous is not the definition of pot."
>
> If someone says that the reason is not established, [then the response is,] "It [absurdly] follows that whatever is bulbous must be a pot because [according to you] bulbous is the definition of pot. You have accepted the reason."[443]

The opponent has posited "bulbous" as the definition of "pot." Definition and definiendum are necessarily mutually inclusive (*yin khyab mnyam*); therefore, if being bulbous is posited as the definition of pot, it must follow that whatever is bulbous is necessarily a pot. Pur-bu-jok counters that view with the following arguments:

> If the consequence [that whatever is bulbous must be a pot] is accepted, then it [absurdly] follows that the subject, bottomless pot [that is, a broken pot, a pot without any bottom and thus incapable of holding water], is a pot because of being bulbous.
>
> If someone says that the reason is not established, [then the response is, "It absurdly follows that the subject, a bottomless pot,] is bulbous because of being directly (*mngon sum du*) established as bulbous.
>
> If the consequence [that a bottomless pot is a pot] is accepted, then it follows that the statement of "able to perform the function of holding water" is not necessary as part of the definition of pot because a bottomless pot is a pot. The consequence cannot be accepted.[444]

It is generally accepted among the Ge-luk-pa that being bulbous is not enough to distinguish a pot; it must also be able to perform the characteristic function of a pot, to hold water. From this point of view, then, a broken pot, one that cannot hold water, is not, in fact, a pot.

Pur-bu-jok illustrates a proper application of the connection between an illustration, definiendum, and definition as follows:

> Golden thing that is bulbous, flat based, and able to perform the function of holding water is the illustration [and] is exemplified as being a pot [through] being that which is bulbous, flat based, and able to perform the function of holding water. Such an application of connection [between an illustration, a definiendum, and a definition] is a proper one.[445]

Through the application of such a connection, it is possible to make known to another person what name to apply to the object that possesses the characteristics of being bulbous, flat based, and able to perform the function of holding water. A person who has seen such an object but does not know its name will understand this connection newly through hearing such a correct application of the connection between illustration, definiendum, and definition. Pur-bu-jok explains the process, using another example, "pillar," and its definition, "that which is able to perform the function of supporting beams":

> For someone to whom an object appears to mind but who does not know what verbal convention to designate to that [object], one must make a terminological connection and cause it to become known, [saying,] "The verbal convention for this type of object is such-and-such." For example, there is a person who, although having already ascertained that which is able to perform the function of supporting beams, does not know to apply the convention "pillar" to it. When that person is told, "That which is able to perform the function of supporting beams is the definition or meaning of pillar," he [or she] will be able to understand the relationship between the name and the meaning—thinking, "That which is able to perform the function of supporting beams is a pillar." Thus, between the two, definition and definiendum, the definition is easier to understand and the definiendum is more difficult to understand in relation to that.[446]

It is easier to apprehend the characteristics of the object than its verbal designation; the one can be observed directly; the other must be learned. The characteristics of the object can be seen by direct perception; the name must be learned from someone who knows it; the name must be affixed to the object, based on the object's possessing the required characteristics.

Pur-bu-jok posits other correct applications of connection:

> Furthermore, [the following] are also proper applications of connection [between illustration, definiendum, and definition]:
> (1) The application of the connection: sound is the illustration [and] is exemplified as being impermanent [through] being momentary.
> (2) The application of the connection: pot is the illustration [and] is exemplified as being a thing [through] being able to perform a function.
> (3) The application of the connection: the first moment of a sense direct perception apprehending blue is the illustration [and] is exemplified as being a valid cognition [through] being a new, incontrovertible knower.

Others are to be known through extension of this reasoning.[447]

A correct application of connection includes a valid illustration and a valid definition. It is interesting to note that if the elements of a correct application of the connection between illustration, definition, and definiendum are arranged into a syllogism, they produce a syllogism that is also valid.

The syllogisms that correspond to the three examples posited by Pur-bu-jok of correct applications of connection are as follows:

(1) "The subject, sound, is impermanent because of being momentary."
(2) "The subject, pot, is a thing because of being able to perform a function."
(3) "The subject, the first moment of a sense direct perception apprehending blue, is a valid cognition because of being a new, incontrovertible knower."

Ge-shay Ge-dün-lo-drö explains the similarity between a correct syllogism and a correct application of connection:

> A correct syllogism and a proper application of connection between illustration, definiendum, and definition can be very similar. For example, the syllogism, "The subject, sound, is impermanent because of being momentary," is similar to the application of connection: sound is the illustration and is exemplified as being impermanent through being momentary. They

differ, however, in that the syllogism directly expresses a reason whereas the application of connection merely expresses the relationship between an illustration, a definiendum, and a definition without directly expressing a reason.[448]

If the elements of a correct application of connection are arranged as a syllogism, they will produce a valid syllogism, but a valid syllogism will not necessarily produce a correct application of connection. The ge-shay goes on,

> There is not a great difference between an application of connection and a correct syllogism; however, they are not the same. If we state the syllogism, "The subject, sound, is impermanent because of being a product," this is not a correct application of connection [that is, the elements of this syllogism cannot form a correct application of connection] because product is not the definition of impermanent. However, if we state the syllogism, "The subject, sound, is impermanent because of being momentary," this syllogism is very similar to a correct application of connection.[449]

Just as the elements of a correct application of connection will form a valid syllogism, similarly, the elements of an invalid application of connection will produce invariably an invalid syllogism. As Ge-shay Ge-dün-lo-drö points out,

> If we say, "The subject, oak pillar, is a pillar because of being able to perform the function of supporting beams," this is not a correct syllogism and [the parts—oak pillar, pillar, and being able to perform the function of supporting beams] do not constitute a correct application of connection. It is not a correct syllogism because, having ascertained the basis of debate ("oak pillar"), one would also ascertain the probandum ("oak pillar is a pillar"); there would then be no subject of enquiry (or "subject sought to be known," *shes 'dod chos can*).[450]

This is not a correct syllogism because, having realized the basis of debate, one also realizes the probandum. Any person who has ascertained "oak pillar" by valid cognition also necessarily has ascertained "pillar" by valid cognition. Therefore, there is no subject of enquiry; there can be no one who wonders whether "oak pillar" is a "pillar"; such doubt does not arise.

Summary

There is apparent agreement among Ge-luk-pa scholars that a connection must be made between the meaning (the definition) and the expression (the definiendum) by means of an illustration; and there is apparent agreement concerning the order of such ascertainment: first the definition must be understood; then the proper connection must be made between the definition and the definiendum by means of an illustration. Someone who has not ascertained by valid cognition the definition, "that which is bulbous, flat based, and able to perform the function of holding water," cannot ascertain the definiendum, "pot," by valid cognition. Similarly, someone who has not ascertained "that which is able to perform a function" by valid cognition cannot ascertain "thing" by valid cognition because "that which is able to perform a function" is the definition of "thing"; and someone who has not ascertained "the momentary" by valid cognition cannot ascertain "the impermanent" by valid cognition because "the momentary" is the definition of "the impermanent."

Disagreement among Ge-luk-pa scholars arises due to a difference of opinion concerning the nature of the explicit predicate of the probandum in a given proof. According to Ge-shay Tsül-trim-nam-gyel, there is never more than one explicit predicate in any given proof, and thus, in a division of signs from the point of view of the mode of proof, there can be only two types: those proving only the meaning and those proving only the expression.

According to Pur-bu-jok, however, there may be two explicit predicates in any given proof because he posits the possibility of proving a meaning and an expression by means of the same proof. He posits five types of signs in the division by way of the mode of proof.

Some Ge-luk-pa scholars, including Ge-shay Pel-den-drak-pa, feel that it would be more appropriate for Pur-bu-jok to posit three types: those proving only the meaning, those proving only the expression, and those proving both the meaning and the expression. This is because there is no discernable difference between those proving the expression and those proving only the expression; nor is there any apparent difference between those proving the meaning and those proving only the meaning. Ge-shay Pel-den-drak-pa explains,

> Positing them this way [that is, making separate categories of (1) those proving the meaning and (2) those proving only the meaning and of (3) those proving the expression and (4) those proving only the expression] is like positing a division of

objects of knowledge into three: impermanent phenomena, permanent phenomena, and forms. Whatever is a form is necessarily impermanent, so there would not seem to be a reason for making separate categories.[451]

Any sign proving the meaning is necessarily either proving only the meaning or proving both the meaning and the expression; similarly, any sign proving the expression is necessarily either proving only the expression or proving both the meaning and the expression. It is apparent, therefore, that there are only three distinct categories: those proving only the meaning, those proving only the expression, and those proving both the meaning and the expression. It is not clear why Pur-bu-jok posits signs proving the meaning and signs proving only the meaning as two separate categories.

(3) Division by Way of the Probandum

The division of correct signs by way of the probandum is made depending on whether the phenomenon being proved is a slightly hidden phenomenon, a very hidden phenomenon, or a terminological suitability. These are said to be the three types of objects of comprehension (*gzhal bya, prameya*) of inferential valid cognition.[a]

An object of comprehension of inference is necessarily a hidden phenomenon. Phenomena that are apprehended by direct perception do not require proof; only hidden phenomena require proof. Hidden phenomena must be initially ascertained by reasoning in dependence on correct signs. As has been explained earlier, correct signs are those that are capable of inducing—in the mind of a correct opponent—new and valid inferential understanding of something formerly hidden to that person. In a correct proof, the predicate of the probandum is necessarily something that, for the opponent in question, cannot be initially ascertained by direct perception; it must be hidden *for that opponent.*

Then, a distinction is made between those hidden phenomena that are slightly hidden and those that are very hidden.[b] Although hidden

---

[a] Whatever exists is realized by valid cognition, which is said to be of two types, direct valid cognition and inferential valid cognition. Direct valid cognition is necessarily nonconceptual. Inferential valid cognition is conceptual, and, being valid, it is also necessarily incontrovertible (*mi bslu ba*) in regard to its own object of comprehension (*gzhal bya, prameya*).

[b] Slightly hidden phenomena are, for example, subtle impermanence and emptiness; very hidden phenomena include specific subtle features of the causes and effects of actions. This is discussed in the pages that follow.

phenomena are considered to be of two types, the objects of comprehension of inferential valid cognition are said to be of three types: slightly hidden phenomena, very hidden phenomena, and terminological suitabilities. Three types are posited rather than two because a distinction is made, among slightly hidden phenomena, between those that are terminological suitabilities and those that are not. Any terminological suitability requiring proof is necessarily a slightly hidden phenomenon; however, "terminological suitability" is treated as a category separate from "slightly hidden phenomenon" in order to make a clear distinction between objects apprehended by inference of renown and objects apprehended by inference by the power of the thing. Lati Rin-po-che explains,

> The reason for separating out "correct sign of renown" from other correct signs is for the sake of separating out the type of object [that is, terminological suitability], which is different from the object [ascertained by means] of a sign by the power of the fact.[452]

It should be noted that not all terminological suitabilities are necessarily hidden phenomena in relation to any given opponent; what is hidden to one may not be to another. However, if a person requires proof of a terminological suitability, then for that person the terminological suitability is a slightly hidden phenomenon. The difference between these two types of objects—(1) terminological suitabilities and (2) other slightly hidden phenomena—will be explained below.

An inferential valid cognition realizing a slightly hidden phenomenon is called an inference by the power of the fact (*dngos stobs rjes dpag*, **vastu-bala-anumāna*); one realizing a terminological suitability is called an inference of renown (*grags pa'i rjes dpag*, **prasiddha-anumāna*); and one realizing a very hidden phenomenon is called an inference of belief (*yid ches rjes dpag*, **āpta-anumāna*). Each of these inferential valid cognitions is generated in dependence on a correct sign and, thus, the division of signs by way of the probandum contains three types: (1) correct signs by the power of the fact (*dngos stobs kyi rtags yang dag*); (2) correct signs of renown (*grags pa'i rtags yang dag*); and (3) correct signs of belief (*yid ches kyi rtags yang dag*).[453]

CORRECT SIGNS BY THE POWER OF THE FACT

The definition posited by Pur-bu-jok of a correct sign by the power of the fact is,

That which is a correct sign in the proof of that and is a producer of an inferential valid cognition—by the power of the fact-—of the probandum in the proof of that.[454]

An illustration is, for example, product in the syllogism, "The subject, sound, is impermanent because of being a product." Impermanence is not something attributed to sound arbitrarily, the way a name might be. The name "sound" (*sgra*) is attributed to objects of hearing (*nyan bya*) by worldly convention; the name does not in any way inhere in the object and thus the name itself is said to be known through "renown" (*grags pa*). On the other hand, sound is by its very nature impermanent; impermanence is a quality of sound and not merely attributed to sound by worldly convention. This means that the nature of impermanence is not attributed to sound arbitrarily, but rather is found to be of the very nature of sound, to be there "by the power of the thing itself." Thus, impermanence is said to be known, not through renown, but rather by the "power of the fact" (*dngos stobs*).

Impermanence is just one of many slightly hidden phenomena, all of which are ascertained initially by means of reasoning. Others are posited by Lati Rin-po-che:

There are many examples of slightly hidden phenomena: liberation, omniscience, valid person, subtle impermanence, selflessness of persons, the pervasive suffering of composition, and so forth. These are all phenomena that must initially be realized by an ordinary being in dependence on a correct sign through the power of the fact.[455]

A problem arises, centering on the phrasing Pur-bu-jok uses in his definition of correct sign of renown. There, he specifies that the sign is "a producer of inferential valid cognition." Relying on this definition, one could argue that whatever is a correct sign of renown is necessarily impermanent because of being a producer (*skyed byed*), and therefore a cause (*rgyu*). Whatever is a producer and a cause is necessarily impermanent. Ge-shay Pel-den-drak-pa addresses this issue:

There is a problem with this definition; for example, consider the syllogism, "The subject, space, is empty of a self of persons because of being permanent." The sign [permanent] is a correct sign by the power of the fact, but the sign is not the producer of inferential valid cognition [because it is not a "producer" at all]; it cannot be phrased that way. The definition should include [the words] "in dependence on the positing of the correct sign" [that is, in dependence on the positing of the sign, inferential valid cognition is generated].[456]

Ge-shay Pel-den-drak-pa points out that, as phrased, the definition is a source of potential problems and debate. As phrased, it can be argued that whatever is set as a sign by the power of the fact must be a cause, which is not correct. By changing the wording, he eliminates the problem. Problems like this arise in the study of any topic. Ge-luk-pa students are taught to look for problems like this one; to look for contradictions, no matter how minor. These are used then as the basis for debate.

After defining correct signs through the power of the fact, Pur-bu-jok goes on to posit divisions and illustrations:

Divisions
Correct signs through the power of the fact are of three types: correct effect, nature, and nonobservation signs through the power of the fact.

Illustrations

(1) [One can state, "With respect to the subject, on a smoky pass, fire exists because smoke exists." In that,] smoke is a correct effect sign through the power of the fact in the proof of fire as existing on a smoky pass.
(2) [One can state, "The subject, sound, is impermanent because of being a product." In that,] product is a correct nature sign through the power of the fact in the proof of sound as impermanent.
(3) [One can state, "With respect to the subject, on a lake at night, smoke does not exist because fire does not exist." In that,] the nonexistence of fire is a correct nonobservation sign through the power of the fact in the proof of smoke as nonexistent on a lake at night.[457]

In each of these cases, the probandum is a slightly hidden phenomenon, which must be initially ascertained by a correct opponent through reasoning by the power of the fact.

(1) "With respect to the subject, on a smoky pass, fire exists because smoke exists." The presence or absence of fire on a smoky pass is being established, not by worldly convention, but by the power of the fact. Smoke is the effect of fire. Fire is by nature the cause of smoke. This is not merely attributed to fire by worldly convention.

(2) "The subject, sound, is impermanent because of being a product."
Impermanent is the nature of sound and is not attributed to sound
merely by renown.

(3) "With respect to the subject, on a lake at night, smoke does not exist because fire does not exist." "Smoke does not exist" is a negative
phenomenon. The presence or absence of smoke does not rely on
convention or renown. Fire is the cause of smoke; in certain contexts the absence of fire may serve as proof of the absence of
smoke.

It should be noted that phenomena that are not ordinarily hidden
may become hidden under certain circumstances; for example,
"smoke" is considered to be a correct sign in the syllogism, "With respect to the subject, on a smoky pass, fire exists because smoke exists";
the predicate of the probandum is fire; does this mean fire is a hidden
phenomenon? Ge-shay Pel-den-drak-pa discusses the question:

> With regard to whatever is a sign by the power of the fact, the
> predicate of the probandum must be a slightly hidden pheno-
> menon; therefore, it follows that the predicate of the proban-
> dum in the proof of fire as existing on a smoky pass by the sign,
> smoke, is a slightly hidden phenomenon. If you accept this,
> then it follows that fire is a hidden phenomenon; but fire is not
> a hidden phenomenon because of being a manifest phenome-
> non. Fire is a manifest phenomenon in general. In this particu-
> lar situation and for this person [the opponent] fire is a hidden
> phenomenon. However, the context has to be specified; other-
> wise, since fire is a manifest phenomenon in general, this could
> not be an example of a sign by the power of the fact.[458]

Fire is not a hidden phenomenon in general. In the context of a particular proof, such as that of fire as existing on a smoky pass, fire is said to
be a hidden phenomenon for the correct opponent. Lati Rin-po-che explains that the opponent is wondering whether fire is present on a
smoky pass; he or she is not wondering about fire in general. Thus it
would seem that the hidden phenomenon is "the presence of fire," not
"fire" itself; however, "smoke" is posited as a correct effect sign in this
proof and therefore fire—the cause of smoke—is considered to be the
predicate of the probandum. Thus, fire is itself a hidden phenomenon
in this context.

The meaning of "by the power of the fact" will become more clear
when compared to the meaning of "by renown," below.

CORRECT SIGNS OF RENOWN

The definition posited by Pur-bu-jok of a correct sign of renown is,

> That which is a correct sign in the proof of that and is a pro-
> ducer of an inferential valid cognition—of renown—of the pro-
> bandum in the proof of that.[459]

An illustration is the sign in the syllogism, "The subject, the rabbit-
bearer, is suitable to be expressed by the term 'moon' because of existing among objects of thought." As mentioned earlier, in Indo-Tibetan
culture there is a tradition of calling the moon "rabbit-bearer." Lati
Rin-po-che observes,

> Because there is a full image of a rabbit that can be seen in the
> moon, it is called a rabbit-bearer. What is being proved by this
> reasoning is that it is alright to call the rabbit-bearer by the
> term "moon" (*zla ba, candra*).[460]

It is not by the power of the thing that a terminological suitability is
ascertained. The suitability of calling the shining object in the sky at
night "moon" is entirely dependent upon convention and not on the
nature of the object. A name is attached to a thing by mere convention
or renown. "By renown" means by the power of the mind, and not by
the power of the thing itself. As Ge-shay Pel-den-drak-pa says,

> It is not by the power of the thing that it is suitable to call
> something this or that; it is by the power of one's own mind,
> not by the power of the thing [or of the fact]. The suitability
> does not inhere in the thing; it depends on the mind.[461]

The suitability of using a certain name for an object does not inhere in
or depend on the object, but rather depends on the mind; this means
that the suitability of designating a name to an object depends on one's
own wish or intention.[a]

To understand the difference between ascertainment "by power of
the fact" and "through renown," it may be helpful to consider the dif-

---

[a] Lati Rin-po-che explains that renown (*grags pa*) is considered in two aspects, the intention to call an object by a certain name and then actually doing so; he says, "The
actual renown is either thought (*nyams rtog*) or sound (*sgra*); these refer to the motivation for saying 'moon' and the sound itself [respectively]. Renown indicates that it is in
accordance with one's wish. Wish is the motivational thought (the intention); acting in
accordance with that wish means to make the sound." (Commentary on *Signs and Reasonings*, vol. 1, p. 97.)

ference between a name, such as "fire," and the meaning to which it is attached, "hot and burning." The name "fire" is attached by convention to the phenomenon that is hot and has the capacity to burn; the name itself does not exist with that phenomenon, but rather is attached to it by convention. However, the qualities of being hot and having the capacity to burn are said to exist right with the object and are not merely attributed to it through renown. Thus, the qualities of being hot and burning are said to be present in that object "by the power of the fact," whereas the name "fire" is said to exist in relation to that object only by renown.[462]

As explained earlier (p. 288), the Ge-luk-ba point of view is that in order to ascertain any object, its meaning must first be understood. The meaning is determined by the nature of the object; but the name affixed to an object is determined by convention. The *meaning* of an object, however, is not attributed to it by mere convention. For example, in order to understand thing, one must first understand the definition of thing: "that which is able to perform a function." This definition is not attributed to thing by mere convention; it reflects an essential quality of thing. The *name* thing, however, is attached to "that which is able to perform a function" by mere convention. Any name could be used. The name, thing, does not exist right with the object, as an essential characteristic. As Ge-shay Pel-den-drak-pa notes,

> We choose the name thing or [its Tibetan equivalent] *dngos po* depending on convention, on renown. The quality of being able to perform a function, however, *does* exist right with the object and is not posited there only by renown or by convention.[463]

Correct Nature Signs of Renown

Pur-bu-jok posits a division of correct signs of renown into two types, correct nature signs of renown and correct nonobservation signs of renown. His illustration of the first type is:

> [One can state, "The subject, rabbit-bearer, is suitable to be expressed by the term 'moon' because of existing among objects of thought." In that,] "existing among objects of thought" is a correct nature sign of renown in the proof of the rabbit-bearer as suitable to be expressed by the term "moon."[464]

The predicate of the probandum—that which is being proved—is the suitability of being expressed by the term, "moon." The sign is "existing among objects of thought." Because the rabbit-bearer is an object of thought, it may be expressed by the term "moon." Ge-shay Pel-den-drak-pa adds,

> Whatever exists is necessarily an object of thought and whatever is an object of thought may be expressed by whatever term one chooses.[465]

This is a correct nature sign because (1) the predicate of the probandum and the sign are considered to be of one nature and (2) the predicate of the probandum is a positive phenomenon. It is a sign of renown because it is proving a terminological suitability.

Correct Nonobservation Signs of Renown

For this type, Pur-bu-jok posits the illustration:

> [One can state, "The subject, rabbit-bearer, is not suitable to be expressed by the term 'moon' through the power of the fact because of existing among objects of thought." In that,] "existing among objects of thought" is a correct nonobservation sign of renown in the proof of the rabbit-bearer as not suitable to be expressed by the term "moon" through the power of the fact.[466]

This is a nonobservation sign because the predicate of the probandum is a negative phenomenon. The predicate of the probandum is the lack of the suitability of being expressed by the term "moon" through the power of the fact. The sign is "existing among objects of thought." Because rabbit-bearer is an object of thought, it may be expressed by the term "moon"; but it may not be expressed by the term "moon" through the power of the fact. Whatever is an object of thought may be called anything one wishes; this is not through the power of the fact, however, but rather by one's own choice; that is, by the force of worldly convention.

It should be noted that no effect sign of renown is posited. Ge-shay Pel-den-drak-pa explains why this is so:

> There is no effect sign of renown because a terminological suitability is necessarily permanent; being permanent, no effect [of it] can be posited. Whatever terminological suitability one can posit will always be permanent.[467]

Whatever is permanent is necessarily without cause or effect; if there were a correct effect sign of renown it would have to be possible to posit a proof of some x that is the cause of a terminological suitability, but such does not exist.

CORRECT SIGNS OF BELIEF

The definition that Pur-bu-jok posits for a correct sign of belief is:

> That which is a correct sign in the proof of that and is a producer of an inferential valid cognition—of belief—of the probandum in the proof of that.[468]

The predicate of the probandum in a syllogism involving a correct sign of belief is necessarily a very hidden phenomenon. Very hidden phenomena are those that are ascertainable only by an inference of belief; they are not accessible to inference by the power of the fact. Pur-bu-jok's illustration of a correct sign of belief is the sign in the syllogism,

> The subject, the scripture, "Through giving, resources; through ethics, happy transmigrations," is incontrovertible with respect to the meaning that is its object of indication (*bstan bya'i don*) because of being a scripture that is pure by way of the three analyses.[469]

That which is being proved is a very hidden phenomenon; this scripture deals with the cause and effect relationship of actions. In general, the cause and effect relationship of actions is *not* a very hidden phenomenon; for example, in order to understand that there is a cause and effect relationship between engaging in ethics and attaining happy transmigrations, one need not depend on a sign of belief; this is not a very hidden phenomenon. However, in order to understand the *specific* causes and effects of actions, one must rely on correct signs of belief. According to Lati Rin-po-che,

> Very hidden phenomena are such things as the subtle features of the cause and effect of actions, as taught in the scripture, "Through giving, resources," in which the object given, the recipient of the gift, the giver, the time of giving, and so forth (leading to a specific resource) are all very hidden phenomena.[470]

A scripture is found to be valid if it is not contradicted by the three types of valid cognition. The three analyses refer to analysis of a scripture by the three types of valid cognition: direct valid cognition, inferential valid cognition by the power of the fact, and inferential valid cognition of belief. Lati Rin-po-che goes on,

> What does it mean to be pure by way of the three analyses? It means that there is no damage from any of the three valid

cognitions.[471]

Ge-shay Pel-den-drak-pa expresses the same idea when he says,

> One has to check what one hears against what one knows. One has to check through direct perception, through inference of renown, and through inference of belief.[472]

If a scripture is to be pure by way of the three analyses, and thus "devoid of the three contradictions," the following three conditions must exist with regard to that scripture, Lati Rin-po-che tells us:

- If it contains teachings of manifest phenomena, then these must not be damaged or contradicted when analyzed by direct valid cognition.
- If it contains teachings of slightly hidden phenomena, then these must not be damaged when analyzed by inference by the power of the fact.
- If it contains teachings of very hidden phenomena, then these must be free of inner contradictions of assertion when analyzed by inference of belief.[473]

Inference of belief is generally explained in relation to topics of scripture that are inaccessible to direct perception and inference by the power of the fact. Belief in such a topic is said to depend largely on there being consistency within the scripture itself. Lati Rin-po-che says,

> Inference of belief, scriptural inference itself, is a matter of there being no contradiction between earlier and later parts of the scripture.[474]

However, inference of belief cannot be separated from the functioning of the other two types of inference. As explained by Ge-luk-pa scholars, first one must analyze the teachings contained in the scripture that pertain to phenomena that are *not* very hidden, and thus can be assessed for accuracy by means of inference by the power of the fact or by direct perception. Having found these to be correct, the test of consistency must be applied in relation to topics of a very hidden nature; if there is no contradiction between various parts of the scripture, then the scripture is deemed to be valid; because the author has already been found to be valid in regard to his or her teachings on topics of slightly hidden and manifest phenomena. Having found a teacher to be incontrovertible regarding the matters that can be checked, one concludes that he or she is also incontrovertible with regard to the rest, the very hidden, as long as the words are consistent, without inner contradiction.

Pur-bu-jok posits a division of correct signs of belief into three types, correct effect, nature, and nonobservation signs of belief.

Correct Effect Signs of Belief

As an illustration for this type of sign, Pur-bu-jok posits,

> [One can state, "The subject, the scripture, 'Through giving, resources; through ethics, happy transmigrations,' is preceded by a valid cognition that realizes the meaning indicated by it because of being a scripture that is devoid of the three contradictions." In that,] "scripture that is devoid of the three contradictions" is a correct effect sign of belief in the proof that the scripture, "Through giving, resources; through ethics, happy transmigrations," is incontrovertible with respect to the meaning that is its object of indication.[475]

In this syllogism, the predicate of the probandum is "preceded by a valid cognition that realizes the meaning indicated." To say that the scripture is preceded by a valid cognition means that whoever set forth the scripture must have ascertainment of its meaning. In this context this refers primarily to Nāgārjuna, according to Lati Rin-po-che, but it may refer to others as well. He tells us,

> If you say, "The subject, the scripture, 'Through giving, resources; through ethics, happy transmigrations,' is preceded by a valid cognition that realizes the meaning indicated," who [that is, what valid cognition] are you talking about? Nāgārjuna before he spoke the scripture. Or, if someone taught that scripture to you, then it refers to the valid cognition [ascertaining the meaning of the scripture] in that person's continuum.[476]

Lati Rin-po-che explains that what one ascertains by inference of belief is taught to one by someone else who already ascertains it by valid cognition. And, through analyzing thoroughly oneself to see that it is not contradicted by any one of the three types of valid cognitions, one develops an inferential valid cognition of belief in relation to it.

Correct Nature Signs of Belief

For this type of sign, Pur-bu-jok provides the following illustration:

[One can state, "The subject, the scripture, 'Through giving, resources; through ethics, happy transmigrations,' is incontrovertible (mi bslu pa) with respect to the meaning that is its object of indication because of being a scripture that is devoid of
the three contradictions." In that,] "scripture that is devoid of
the three contradictions" is a correct nature sign of belief in
the proof that the scripture, "Through giving, resources;
through ethics, happy transmigrations," is incontrovertible
with respect to the meaning that is its object of indication.[477]

Here, the predicate of the probandum is "incontrovertible with respect
to the meaning that is its object of indication," which is considered to
be a positive phenomenon. "Incontrovertible" is apparently considered
by most Ge-luk-pa scholars to be a positive phenomenon even though it
contains the negative particle "in-" (mi). According to Ge-shay Pel-den-
drak-pa,

If you consider incontrovertible to be a positive phenomenon,
then this is a nature sign; but if you consider it to be a negative
phenomenon, then this is a nonobservation sign.[478]

Just as "impermanent" is considered by many to be a positive phenomenon, so is "incontrovertible." Ge-shay Pel-den-drak-pa points out
that whatever is expressed in negative phrasing (that is, including negative words or particles) is not necessarily a negative phenomenon; he
says,

Whatever is phrased negatively is not necessarily a negative
phenomenon (dgag tshig yin na dgag pa yin pas ma khyab) and
whatever is phrased positively (sgrub tshig) is not necessarily a
positive phenomenon. For example, suchness (chos nyid) and
space are negative phenomena but are expressed with positive
words. "Incontrovertible" is expressed with negative words but
is not a negative phenomenon. When it [incontrovertible] appears to the mind, a positive phenomenon appears. What appears to the mind is that it [the scripture] is true, is absolutely
correct; a positive phenomenon appears to the mind.[479]

Correct Nonobservation Signs of Belief

Pur-bu-jok then posits, as an illustration of this third type,

[One can state, "The subject, the scripture, 'Through giving,
resources; through ethics, happy transmigrations,' is not

controvertible (*bslu ba ma yin pa*) with respect to the meaning that is its object of indication because of being a scripture that is devoid of the three contradictions." In that,] "scripture that is devoid of the three contradictions" is a correct nonobservation sign of belief in the proof that the scripture, "Through giving, resources; through ethics, happy transmigrations," is incontrovertible with respect to the meaning that is its object of indication.[480]

While "incontrovertible" is, according to some, a positive phenomenon, "not being controvertible" or "is not controvertible" (*bslu ba ma yin pa*) is said to be a negative phenomenon.

(4) Division by Way of the Mode of Relating to the Similar Class

The division of correct signs by way of the mode of relation to the similar class is made depending on whether the sign in a given proof pervades the similar class or not. As explained earlier, in order for a sign to be correct, it must be related with that which is held as the predicate of the probandum. This means that the sign is necessarily pervaded by the similar class in that proof.[a]

For example, product is a correct sign in the proof of sound as impermanent and thus is pervaded by the similar class: whatever is a product is necessarily impermanent. If circles are drawn to indicate the size of the two categories (the similar class and the sign), the circle representing the sign must be contained within the circle representing the similar class. Within that being the case, there are then two possibilities.

(1) The sign may be a category that is equal in size to the similar class; in this case, the circle representing the sign is the same size as that representing the similar class; they are mutually pervasive, and thus the sign is said to relate to the similar class as pervader.

(2) The sign may be a category that is smaller than, and completely

---

[a] As explained earlier, in Ge-luk-pa introductory logic manuals, the relationship (*'brel ba*) between the sign and the predicate in a syllogism is analyzed in terms of how the sign relates to the similar class. If the sign is correct in a given proof, then the sign must be existent in only the similar class and just nonexistent in the dissimilar class. This means, for example, that product must be existent in only the impermanent (that is, whatever is product is impermanent) and that the product must be only nonexistent in the dissimilar class (that is, whatever is permanent is necessarily not a product).

included in, the similar class. The circle representing the sign will be smaller than that representing the similar class; and the sign is said to relate to the similar class in two ways.

Thus the division of correct signs by way of the mode of relating to the similar class is into two types, correct sign that relates to the similar class as pervader and correct sign that relates to the similar class in two ways.

Pur-bu-jok's discussion of this topic is brief. He provides the following definitions and illustrations:

1) Correct sign that relates to the similar class as pervader

The definition of a correct sign that relates to the similar class as pervader [in the proof of sound as impermanent] is:

> That which is the three modes and relates to the similar class as pervader in the proof of sound as impermanent.

Product is an illustration [of a correct sign that relates to the similar class as pervader in the proof of sound as impermanent].

2) Correct sign that relates to the similar class in two ways

The definition of a correct sign that relates to the similar class in two ways [in the proof of sound as impermanent] is:

> That which is the three modes and relates to the similar class in two ways in the proof of sound as impermanent.

Particularity of product is an illustration [of a correct sign that relates to the similar class in two ways in the proof of sound as impermanent].[481]

Product is a correct sign that relates to the similar class as pervader in the proof of sound as impermanent. Ge-shay Lob-sang-gya-tso explains why:

> Product is a correct sign that relates to the similar class as a pervader in the proof of sound as impermanent; this is because whatever is impermanent is necessarily a product.[482]

The sign, product, relates to the similar class as pervader because product pervades impermanent; whatever is impermanent is necessarily a product. Product and impermanent are mutually inclusive phenomena.

Particularity of product is also considered to be a correct sign in the proof of sound as impermanent. Being a correct sign, it must be the case that it is pervaded by the similar class (impermanent); that is, whatever is a particularity of product is necessarily impermanent. But in this proof, the sign does not pervade the similar class; rather it relates to the similar class in two ways; this is because whatever is impermanent is not necessarily a particularity of product (for example, product) and is not necessarily not a particularity of product (for example, pot). Product itself is impermanent but is not a particularity of product. A particularity of product must be different from product.

Lati Rin-po-che provides another example of a sign that relates to the similar class in two ways:

> Another example is "arisen from exertion" in the syllogism, "The subject, the sound of a conch, is impermanent because of being arisen from exertion." Whatever is impermanent is not necessarily arisen from exertion and is not necessarily not arisen from exertion.[483]

The sign is necessarily pervaded by the similar class; thus, whatever is arisen from exertion is necessarily impermanent. However, the sign does not pervade the similar class, but rather relates to it in two ways. Whatever is impermanent is not necessarily arisen from exertion because, for example, the sound of the wind or a mountain, are impermanent but are not arisen from exertion. Whatever is impermanent is also not necessarily *not* arisen from exertion; for example the sound of a conch or a clay pot are both impermanent and also arisen from exertion. The sound of a conch arises from the exertion of the person who blows into it and the clay pot arises from the exertion of the potter who creates it.

A third example of a sign that relates to the similar class in two ways is "smoke" in the syllogism, "With respect to the subject, on a smoky pass, fire exists because smoke exists." This is because wherever fire exists smoke does not necessarily exist and does not necessarily not exist. Lati Rin-po-che comments,

> Where there is fire, there is not necessarily smoke and there is not necessarily not smoke. Wherever fire exists smoke does not necessarily exist because it is possible to have a cause but not an effect; a cause may be obstructed [that is, prevented from producing an effect]. It is not inevitable that the effect will be

produced unless the *direct* cause is present.[484]

Wherever smoke exists, fire exists, but wherever fire exists, smoke does not necessarily exist. A frequently used example is a red-hot coal. Fire is considered to be present in a red-hot coal, but no smoke is emitted. The example posited by Ge-shay Tsül-trim-nam-gyel of the existence of fire without the existence of smoke is: "a smokeless red burning coal in a blacksmith's shop."[a]

(5) DIVISION BY WAY OF THE OPPONENT

This division of correct signs is made depending on whether the reasoning is being used by one person in solitary analysis or by two people in debate. From this point of view, correct signs are of two types, correct signs on the occasion of one's own purpose (*rang don skabs kyi rtags yang dag*) and correct signs on the occasion of another's purpose (*gzhan don skabs kyi rtags yang dag*).[485] Pur-bu-jok posits a definition and illustration of each; he writes,

> Correct sign on the occasion of one's own purpose
>
> Definition:
>
>> It is a common locus of (1) being a correct sign in the proof of sound as impermanent and (2) there not existing a correct second party (*phyi rgol*) in the proof of that by the sign of it.
>
> Illustration: The first party (*snga rgol*) states to himself (or herself) that product is a sign in the proof of sound as impermanent. At the time of that proof, product is a correct sign on the occasion of one's own purpose in the proof of sound as impermanent.
>
> Correct sign on the occasion of another's purpose
>
> Definition:
>
>> It is a common locus of (1) being a correct sign in the proof of that and (2) there existing a correct second party in the proof of that by the sign of it.

---

[a] Ge-shay Tsül-trim-nam-gyel writes, "...wherever there is fire there is not necessarily smoke. This is because...it is indefinite in terms of a smokeless red burning coal in a blacksmith's shop." (*Signs and Reasonings*, p. 15b.3.)

Illustration: "Product" is a correct sign on the occasion of another's purpose in the proof of sound as impermanent.[a]

If one person is using reasoning for his or her own sake to understand something new, that use involves a correct sign on the occasion of one's own purpose. According to Ge-shay Pel-den-drak-pa,

> Thinking about [the proof] oneself, without stating it to another person—in that context, product is a correct sign on the occasion of one's own purpose in the proof of sound as impermanent.[486]

Pur-bu-jok specifies that there is no second party, no "latter opponent" (*phyir rgol*); only one person is involved. Lati Rin-po-che explains,

> A correct sign on the occasion of one's own purpose is a case of taking a reason as object of awareness in order to realize—for oneself—the meaning of the probandum. There is no need for another person, an opponent.[487]

THE TERMS "FORMER OPPONENT" AND "LATTER OPPONENT"

Pur-bu-jok uses the term "first (or former) party (or opponent)" (*snga rgol*) to refer to this person engaged in solitary analysis. This use of the term differs from the usual use. The usual use of the terms "former opponent" and "latter opponent" (or "second party") is in the context of distinguishing between two parties in a debate. That is, the usual use of these terms is in the context of the use of a correct sign "on the occasion of another's purpose." If one person is using the reasoning for the sake of another person, in order for the other person to generate new understanding, then that use involves "a correct sign on the occasion of another's purpose."

In the context of a correct sign on the occasion of one's own purpose, it may be said that there is neither a former party nor a latter party. There is only one person, using reasoning to develop understanding of something formerly hidden. Lati Rin-po-che says,

---

[a] Ibid., pp. 16b.6-17a.2. Concerning the term "party" or "opponent" (*rgol pa*), as will be explained, its usual use is in the context of debate, when *snga rgol* means former party or opponent and *phyi rgol* means latter party or opponent. Elsewhere, I have translated *phyi rgol yang dag* as "correct opponent"; this term usually refers to the person who is developing new understanding of a thesis. When only one person is involved, this term (*phyi rgol yang dag*) is not used to refer to the person who, in solitary analysis, is developing new understanding of a thesis; that person is called a *snga rgol yang dag*, literally, a correct former opponent."

In the case of a correct sign on the occasion of one's own purpose, there is no second party. In the case of a correct sign on
the occasion of another's purpose there *is* a second party. Since
on the occasion of one's own purpose there is no second party,
there is also no first party; the two depend on each other. That
being the case, one can say that, in the context of a correct sign
on the occasion of one's own purpose, there is neither a former
nor a latter party; one is merely positing the reason for oneself.[488]

In the context of meditation (on emptiness or impermanence, for example) one person is engaging in reasoning on a topic for his or her
own sake; that is, in order to generate new understanding in his or her
own mental continuum. There is no latter opponent in that there is no
external one; however, there may be said to be an internal opponent, in
that the meditator is trying to overcome his or her own mistaken
views.

As explained by Ge-luk-pa scholars, in the context of debate,

- The name "former party" (*snga rgol*) usually designates the challenger in the debate, the one who asks the questions. This is the
one who posits a sign for the sake of another person's understanding.
- The name "latter party" (*phyi rgol*) usually designates the defender,
answering the challenge; this is also translated "latter opponent"
or "second party." This is the person who is developing new understanding of the thesis. The second party is also called the correct
party or correct latter opponent (*phyi rgol yang dag*)—the one for
whom a reasoning is being employed, the person who is ready to
ascertain the probandum, the person who, having ascertained the
three modes, is wondering about the thesis.

Lati Rin-po-che continues,

A full-fledged correct former party must have realized the probandum, whereas the correct latter party (or second party)
must be someone who has realized the three modes of the application of the reason of the syllogism. The person doing the
proving is the former party, the person for whom it is being
proved is the latter party. For instance, when doctrine is being
explained to someone, the explainer should be someone who
has realized it [that is, the meaning of the doctrine] with valid
cognition, and the person who is listening should be someone

who has not. So from that point of view, the one who is doing the proving is "the former party," and the one for whom it is being proved is "the latter party."[489]

The former party should be someone who has already ascertained the probandum; and the latter party should be someone who is newly as-certaining the three modes of the reasoning, is wondering about the thesis. But indeed if the prover has not realized it, then he or she can-not be (in this strict use of the term) the former party. To be a correct former party, one has to have realized the probandum; to be a correct latter party one has to have realized the three modes of the sign. The person who is trying to prove the probandum to someone else has to be someone who has realized it. Lati Rin-po-che mentions another aspect of this:

> From the point of view of words, it would seem to be the same thing for the listener, whether the former party has realized the probandum or whether he or she is just repeating words without having realized them. From the point of view of the lis-tener, the words would be the same. From the point of view of the speaker, of course, it would be different. There probably is a difference in the force of what is said if you have realized it. For example, you could have two people say the word "pot," one who knows what it means and one who does not. For the listen-er, they are both saying "pot," but there is a difference in the power of it.[490]

Clearly this use of these terms is in the context of two people debating, one who already knows the probandum, and one who is newly develop-ing understanding of the probandum, with the help of the reasoning presented by the former party.

It should be noted that even in this standard usage, there are in-consistencies; it is not always possible to correlate the former opponent with the challenger and the latter opponent with the defender. Lati Rin-po-che explains this complication in the use of terms:

> There is no way to correlate challenger and defender definitely with former and latter party. In various treatises, the Buddhist is sometimes presented as the former party, with the non-Buddhist the latter party; sometimes it is the other way around. Traditionally, the defender first stated a position and then the challenger attacked that; so, in that case, the defender is the former party (that is, the one who speaks first). However, that

is not always the case. When the challenger speaks first, he is the former party. Thus, how former and latter relate to challenger and defender depends on the specific debate.[491]

If the name "former party" refers to the one who speaks first, then there is no certainty that it is indicating the challenger; depending on the context, it may refer to the challenger or the defender because either one may speak first. Nevertheless, it is usual for the term "former party" to mean the challenger and the "latter party" the defender.

When correct signs on the occasion of one's own purpose are considered, however, the terminology becomes confusing. There are not two people involved. One person is stating the reason to himself or herself in order to understand the probandum newly. In his definition of a correct sign on the occasion of one's own purpose, Pur-bu-jok specifies that there is no latter opponent because there is no external opponent, no other person. Pur-bu-jok calls the person thus engaged in solitary analysis the "former party." In order to be a "correct former party" (*snga rgol yang dag*), in Pur-bu-jok's terminology, this person should have ascertained the three modes. Ge-shay Pel-den-drak-pa points out,

> If one does not realize the three modes, then it is not a correct sign for one's own purpose. He [or she] is not a correct former opponent unless he or she has realized the three modes.[492]

In the context of correct signs on the occasion of one's own purpose, the "former opponent" is *not* someone who already understands the thesis, but rather is someone who is analyzing it newly. There is *no* party involved who has already ascertained the thesis. Although "latter party" normally refers to the one who is developing ascertainment of the thesis, the term has come to be associated with the second party in a debate; it is therefore not surprising that, when only one person is involved, this person is called a "former party." But it must be kept in mind that in the context of solitary analysis the former party is someone who does not understand the thesis yet, but is developing new understanding of it.

However confusing the terminology, there is apparent agreement among Ge-luk-pa scholars that reasoning may be used for one's own purpose, in which case one is developing new understanding of a thesis in one's own mind. Without an external opponent, one is attempting to overcome one's own mistaken views; thus one becomes a correct opponent, in the sense that one is about to generate understanding of the thesis. In short,

> The person who, having thought about it [the reasoning] and having established the three modes, is wondering whether or not sound is impermanent is one for whom product is a correct sign on the occasion of one's own purpose.[493]

When Pur-bu-jok posited an illustration of a correct sign on the occasion of one's own purpose, he specified the context very clearly: "The first party (*snga rgol*) states to himself or herself that product is a sign in the proof of sound as impermanent. At the time of that proof, product is a correct sign on the occasion of one's own purpose in the proof of sound as impermanent."[494] When positing an illustration of a correct sign on the occasion of another's purpose, however, he did not specify the context. He wrote, "'Product' is a correct sign on the occasion of another's purpose in the proof of sound as impermanent."[495]

Some scholars consider it necessary to specify the context; Ge-shay Ge-dün-lo-drö expresses the context clearly when he says,

> Product is a correct sign on the occasion of one's own purpose in the proof of sound as impermanent and it is also a correct sign on the occasion of another's purpose. When product becomes a correct sign on the occasion of one's own purpose [when it is used as such] in the proof of sound as impermanent, it is a correct sign on the occasion of one's own purpose. It is both: when it is used as a correct sign on the occasion of another's purpose, it is a correct sign on the occasion of another's purpose and when it is used as a correct sign on the occasion of one's own purpose, it is a correct sign on the occasion of one's own purpose.[496]

As the discussion below will show, Ge-shay Ge-dün-lo-drö and Ge-shay Pel-den-drak-pa hold that if the context is not specified, problems will follow. If, as Pur-bu-jok says, "Product is a correct sign on the occasion of another's purpose in the proof of sound as impermanent," then is product always a correct sign on the occasion of another's purpose in the proof of sound as impermanent? Is there such a thing as a correct sign on the occasion of one's own purpose in the proof of sound as impermanent by the sign, product?

Whether a correct sign on the occasion of one's own purpose exists

Pur-bu-jok himself presents several problems that arise, centering primarily on the issue of whether correct signs on the occasion of one's own purpose exist or not. He plays with various debate topics, without presenting in detail his own position on the issues involved. In the pages that follow, Pur-bu-jok argues *against* the following positions:

(1) product is both a correct sign on the occasion of one's own purpose and on the occasion of another's purpose in the proof of sound as impermanent;

(2) a correct sign on the occasion of one's own purpose does not exist;

(3) product is a correct sign on the occasion of one's own purpose in the proof of sound as impermanent; and

(4) when product has become a correct sign on the occasion of one's own purpose in the proof of sound as impermanent, product is a correct sign on the occasion of one's own purpose in the proof of sound as impermanent.

Stated in the opposite way, the positions Pur-bu-jok *holds* in the following debates are:

(1) product is not both a correct sign on the occasion of one's own purpose and a correct sign on the occasion of another's purpose in the proof of sound as impermanent;

(2) a correct sign on the occasion of one's own purpose exists;

(3) product is not a correct sign on the occasion of one's own purpose in the proof of sound as impermanent; and

(4) when product has become a correct sign on the occasion of one's own purpose in the proof of sound as impermanent, product is not a correct sign on the occasion of one's own purpose in the proof of sound as impermanent.

These do not appear to be consistent. Perhaps his purpose is to show how problematic the issues involved are.

It is interesting to note that Pur-bu-jok treats the topic of correct signs on the occasion of one's own purpose as he does quasi-signs: in his view, quasi-signs are nonexistent in general, and the fact that one can be posited in a given context does *not* indicate that quasi-signs exist in general.[497] Similarly, Pur-bu-jok argues that although instances can be posited of correct signs on the occasion of one's own purpose, one cannot assert their existence in general. In this regard, he differs from some other Ge-luk-pa scholars, notably Ge-shay Pel-den-drak-pa and Ge-shay Ge-dün-lo-drö, who hold that it is important to posit the existence of correct signs on the occasion of one's own purpose. Their views are cited in the appropriate contexts, below.

Is product a correct sign on the occasion of both one's own and another's purpose?

First Pur-bu-jok argues against the assertion that product can be both a sign for one's own sake and for another's. These two types of signs are considered to be mutually contradictory; thus a sign must be one or the other; it cannot be both. He writes,

> Someone says: "Product is both a correct sign on the occasion of one's own purpose in the proof of sound as impermanent and a correct sign on the occasion of another's purpose in the proof of sound as impermanent.
>
> [The response to that is:] "It [absurdly] follows that with respect to the subject, product, there does not exist a correct second party in the proof of sound as impermanent by the sign, product, because it [product] is a correct sign on the occasion of one's own purpose in the proof of sound as impermanent."[498]

There appears to be a difference of opinion concerning whether it is correct to say that product is both a sign on the occasion of one's own purpose and a sign on the occasion of another's purpose. Pur-bu-jok asserts that this is a mistaken view. His argument makes sense if one considers that the two types of sign are mutually contradictory; that being the case, if something is one, it cannot be the other. If product is a correct sign on the occasion of one's own purpose, then it cannot be a correct sign on the occasion of another's purpose; and thus a correct sign on the occasion of another's purpose in the proof of sound as impermanent by the sign, product, does not exist. A further consequence is that a correct second party would not exist in the proof of sound as impermanent because a correct sign on the occasion of another's purpose would not exist in the proof of sound as impermanent.

Others approach the issue differently. Ge-shay Ge-dün-lo-drö asserts that product is both a correct sign on the occasion of one's own purpose in the proof of sound as impermanent and a correct sign on the occasion of another's purpose in the proof of sound as impermanent, meaning that both exist—although in different contexts.[499] These two types of signs are mutually exclusive only in relation to a specific context, to a specific proof. Ge-shay Pel-den-drak-pa says,

> In a specific proof, then, they are contradictory, but not otherwise; product can be a correct sign on the occasion of one's own purpose in one context and a correct sign on the occasion of another's purpose in a different context.[500]

Pur-bu-jok continues his argument:

> If this is accepted [that is, if someone accepts that there does not exist a correct second party in the proof of sound as impermanent by the sign, product], then [the response is]: "With respect to the subject, [product], there does exist a correct second party in the proof of sound as impermanent by the sign, product, because it [product] is a correct sign on the occasion of another's purpose in the proof of sound as impermanent.[501]

Product is a correct sign on the occasion of another's purpose; therefore, a correct second party exists.

Earlier, Pur-bu-jok argued that if product is a correct sign on the occasion of one's own purpose, then a correct opponent does not exist. That is, if product is a correct sign on the occasion of one's own purpose in the proof of sound as impermanent, then it cannot be a correct sign on the occasion of another's purpose in that proof—and therefore a correct opponent does not exist (in the proof of sound as impermanent by the sign, product). Now he argues that product *is* a correct sign on the occasion of another's purpose. One might therefore conclude, on the basis of his former reasoning, that product cannot be a correct sign on the occasion of one's own purpose in the proof of sound as impermanent. If product cannot be a correct sign on the occasion of one's own purpose in the proof of sound as impermanent, then a correct sign on the occasion of one's own purpose does not exist in the proof of sound as impermanent.

Someone might conclude in this way that, in Pur-bu-jok's view, a correct sign on the occasion of one's own purpose does not exist. However, he goes on to refute that.

Does a correct sign on the occasion of one's own purpose exist?

Pur-bu-jok continues,

Furthermore, if someone says, "A correct sign on the occasion of one's own purpose does not exist," [the response is,] "That is not correct because when product becomes a correct sign on the occasion of one's own purpose in the proof of sound as impermanent, product is a correct sign on the occasion of one's own purpose in the proof of sound as impermanent.

Further, a correct sign on the occasion of one's own purpose exists because there exists a correct sign on the occasion of one's own purpose in the proof of sound as impermanent.

If someone says that the reason is not established [that is, it is not established that there exists a correct sign on the occasion of one's own purpose in the proof of sound as impermanent], [then the response is,] "It [absurdly] follows that with respect to the subject, object of knowledge, whatever is a correct sign in the proof of sound as impermanent is necessarily not a correct sign on the occasion of one's own purpose in the proof of that because [according to you] that reason is not established."[502]

Pur-bu-jok is arguing that a correct sign on the occasion of one's own purpose exists because a situation can be posited in which such as sign is used.

If someone questions this (saying that there does not exist a correct sign on the occasion of one's own purpose in the proof of sound as impermanent), Pur-bu-jok counters this by saying that it then follows that any correct sign in the proof of sound as impermanent is necessarily *not* a sign on the occasion of one's own purpose, because such a sign does not exist. He continues,

If this is accepted [that is, if it is accepted that with respect to the subject, object of knowledge, whatever is a correct sign in the proof of sound as impermanent is necessarily not a correct sign on the occasion of one's own purpose in the proof of that], then it [absurdly] follows that when product becomes a correct sign on the occasion of one's own purpose in the proof of sound as impermanent, the subject, product, is not a correct sign on the occasion of one's own purpose in the proof of that because of being a correct sign in the proof of that. [You have accepted] the three spheres.[503]

Ge-shay Pel-den-drak-pa explains the three spheres:

(1) The opposite of the consequence—that when product becomes a

correct sign on the occasion of one's own purpose in the proof of sound as impermanent, the subject, product, is a correct sign on the occasion of one's own purpose in the proof of that.

(2) The reason—that product is a correct sign in the proof of sound as impermanent.

(3) The pervasion—that whatever is a correct sign in the proof of sound as impermanent is necessarily not a correct sign on the occasion of one's own purpose in the proof of that.[504]

Pur-bu-jok's opponent has accepted that whatever is a correct sign in the proof of sound as impermanent is necessarily a correct sign on the occasion of another's purpose.

To summarize his arguments to this point, Pur-bu-jok has found fault with saying (1) that "product" is both a correct sign on the occasion of one's own purpose and a correct sign on the occasion of another's purpose; and also with saying (2) that a correct sign on the occasion of one's own purpose does not exist; and also with saying (3) that a correct sign on the occasion of one's own purpose in the proof of sound as impermanent does not exist. Now he seems to be asserting the *existence* of a correct sign on the occasion of one's own purpose in general and also on the occasion of one's own purpose in the proof of sound as impermanent.

Is product a correct sign on the occasion of one's own purpose in the proof of sound as impermanent?

Now Pur-bu-jok argues *against* the view that product is a correct sign on the occasion of one's own purpose in the proof of sound as impermanent. He writes,

> Further, it follows that product is not a correct sign on the occasion of one's own purpose in the proof of sound as impermanent because that [product] is a correct sign on the occasion of another's purpose in the proof of that. This is because the syllogism, "The subject, sound, is impermanent because of being a product," is a pure application of a correct sign on the occasion of another's purpose.[505]

A correct sign on the occasion of one's own purpose and a correct sign on the occasion of another's purpose are mutually contradictory. If something is one, it cannot be the other. If product is a correct sign on the occasion of another's purpose, it cannot be a correct sign on the occasion of one's own purpose. Pur-bu-jok continues,

[Someone] objects: It [absurdly] follows that when there does not exist a correct second party in the proof of sound as impermanent by the sign, product, there does exist a correct second party in the proof of sound as impermanent by the sign, product, because when product has become the correct sign on the occasion of one's own purpose in the proof of sound as impermanent, product is a correct sign on the occasion of another's purpose in the proof of sound as impermanent.[506]

Here, someone (Pur-bu-jok's opponent) is positing an absurd consequence of Pur-bu-jok's arguments. Pur-bu-jok argued that product cannot be a sign on the occasion of one's own purpose because it is a sign on the occasion of another's purpose. Being one it cannot be the other. It is reasonable to argue, then, that—if product is necessarily a sign on the occasion of another's purpose—no matter what the context, it is necessarily a sign on the occasion of another's purpose and, therefore, involves a second party. If product is necessarily a sign on the occasion of another's purpose in the proof of sound as impermanent, then product must always be posited by one person to another, a second party. If that is the case, then there is always a second party, even when none exists, as in the case of using the product for one's own sake.

This is a reasonable objection, because Pur-bu-jok did imply above that product is necessarily a correct sign on the occasion of another's purpose. However, he proceeds to reject this objection as well:

Answer to the objection: The reason is not established [that is, it is not established that when product has become the correct sign on the occasion of one's own purpose in the proof of sound as impermanent, product is a correct sign on the occasion of another's purpose in the proof of sound as impermanent].[507]

Pur-bu-jok asserted above that "product is not a correct sign on the occasion of one's own purpose in the proof of sound as impermanent because of being a correct sign on the occasion of another's purpose in the proof of that." The objector then attempted to show a consequence of that view. Pur-bu-jok implied that a correct sign on the occasion of one's own purpose does not exist, and a consequence of this is that any correct sign will necessarily be one on the occasion of another's purpose. But he denies that, saying that it does not follow that in *every* situation (even including the case of a sign for one's own purpose) a sign is for another's purpose.

Pur-bu-jok has denied the reason posited by the objector ("when product has become the correct sign on the occasion of one's own purpose in the proof of sound as impermanent, product is a correct sign on the occasion of another's purpose in the proof of sound as impermanent"). He has also indicated rejection of the consequence ("when there does not exist a correct second party in the proof of sound as impermanent by the sign, product, there does exist a correct second party in the proof of sound as impermanent by the sign, product"). Now he argues explicitly against the consequence:

> If it were accepted [that when there does not exist a correct second party in the proof of sound as impermanent by the sign, product, there does exist a correct second party in the proof of sound as impermanent by the sign, product,] then it would [absurdly] follow that when product is nonexistent, product exists because when a correct second party in the proof of sound as impermanent by the sign, product, does not exist, a correct second party in the proof of sound as impermanent by the sign, product, exists. You have accepted the reason.[508]

If someone accepts that even when there is no second party, there is a second party, that would be absurd. One would then have to accept that when there is no tree, there is a tree, and so on. It should be noted that on this point he and the objector are in complete agreement. The consequence was being presented by the objector as one that followed necessarily from Pur-bu-jok's own previous arguments.

When product has become a correct sign on the occasion of one's own purpose in a given proof, is it such a correct sign?

Pur-bu-jok now argues that a correct sign on the occasion of one's own purpose does not exist. He begins by presenting a view he considers to be mistaken:

> Someone says, "Although correct sign on the occasion of one's own purpose does not exist, when product has become a correct sign on the occasion of one's own purpose in the proof of sound as impermanent, product is a correct sign on the occasion of one's own purpose in the proof of sound as impermanent."[509]

Here, someone is asserting that a correct sign on the occasion of one's own purpose does not exist, in general, but, in a particular situation product is a correct sign on the occasion of one's own purpose. From this point of view, one cannot posit, in general, the existence of correct sign on the occasion of one's own purpose, just as one cannot posit the existence of quasi-signs in general; in general, whatever is an established base is necessarily a correct sign; similarly, in general, whatever is a correct sign is necessarily a correct sign for another's purpose. Pur-bu-jok continues,

> [The response is:] "That is not correct. It [absurdly] follows that a correct sign on the occasion of one's own purpose exists because a correct sign on the occasion of one's own purpose in the proof of sound as impermanent exists. This [in turn] is because (1) when product has become a correct sign on the occasion of one's own purpose in the proof of sound as impermanent, product exists and (2) when product has become a correct sign on the occasion of one's own purpose in the proof of sound as impermanent, product is a correct sign on the occasion of one's own purpose in the proof of sound as impermanent. The reason has been accepted."
>
> Further, it [absurdly] follows that a correct sign on the occasion of one's own purpose in the proof of sound as impermanent exists because there exists a product that has become a correct sign on the occasion of one's own purpose in the proof of sound as impermanent. [This is] because there exists a person for whom product has become a correct sign on the occasion of one's own purpose in the proof of that. This [in turn] is because there exists a person for whom smoke has become a correct sign on the occasion of one's own purpose in the proof of fire as existent on a smoky pass.[510]

Here, Pur-bu-jok argues against asserting the existence of a correct sign on the occasion of one's own purpose. He does not assert its existence in general, and, according to him, the existence of instances does not justify the general statement that it exists, just as the existence of instances of quasi-signs does not justify assertion of the existence of quasi-signs in general.

It seems inconsistent. Earlier, Pur-bu-jok argued against saying that a correct sign on the occasion of one's own purpose does not exist, and now he posits it as absurd that a correct sign on the occasion of one's own purpose exists. To be more precise, he asserts that (1) it is not accurate to say that "correct sign on the occasion of one's own purpose exists" and (2) it is not accurate to say that "correct sign on the occasion of one's own purpose in the proof of sound as impermanent exists." He then concludes that if someone says (point 2, above), "product is a correct sign on the occasion of one's own purpose in the proof of sound as impermanent," then you have to assert the *existence* of a correct sign on the occasion of one's own purpose in the proof of sound as impermanent. According to Pur-bu-jok, it is not suitable to assert this; but according to Ge-shay Pel-den-drak-pa and Ge-shay Ge-dün-lo-drö, it is important to assert the existence of such signs, and there can be no fault in doing so. Ge-shay Ge-dün-lo-drö asserts that a correct sign on the occasion of one's own purpose exists. It is his point of view that this is not a fault; in fact this has to be accepted; he says, "in our system, this type exists."[511]

Summary of the Debates

To summarize Pur-bu-jok's views, he does not accept that "product" is a correct sign on the occasion of one's own purpose and does not accept the existence of a correct sign on the occasion of one's own purpose. To do so would be like accepting the existence of quasi-signs. However, he also does not accept the *nonexistence* of signs on the occasion of one's own purpose. Other Ge-luk-pa scholars have different views on these issues.

It seems clear that Pur-bu-jok is pointing out topics of debate, rather than setting forth a clear and consistent position. By pointing out how various views can be argued against, he shows how problematic the issues are and how carefully they must be considered. Rather than settle every issue himself, Pur-bu-jok apparently prefers to encourage and even provoke debate. His aim may be to encourage the analysis of contradictions, no matter how small, because of the importance of such analysis in the development of a powerful path of reasoning.

9. Quasi-Reasons

Pur-bu-jok has shown on numerous occasions that a debater may posit a syllogism in which the sign is incorrect; the examples that were given and analyzed were chosen to illustrate the topic of the particular chapter. Here, Pur-bu-jok pulls together all the various incorrect uses of signs (some will be familiar) to consider in what way they are incorrect.

Reasons that are not correct are quasi-reasons (*gtan tshigs ltar snang*) (or quasi-signs—*rtags ltar snang*); they fail to satisfy one or another of the criteria necessary for correct signs. To be correct in a given proof, a sign must be the three modes in that proof. This means that the sign must satisfy the criteria established by the definitions of the property of the subject, the forward pervasion, and the counter-pervasion.

DEFINITION AND DIVISIONS

Pur-bu-jok begins this discussion of quasi-reasons:

> The explanation of the opposite of correct signs, quasi-reasons, has two parts: definition and divisions. The first of these also has two parts: (1) the refutation of another's view and (2) the presentation of our own system.

Definition:

> *Another's view*: In accordance with another's system, someone says, "The definition of a quasi-reason is: that which is not the three modes."
> *Refutation*: That is not correct because a quasi-reason does not exist. This is because whatever is an established base [that is, whatever exists] is necessarily a correct sign.
> *Our own system*: The definition of a quasi-reason is: that which is not the three modes in the proof of that.[512]

Pur-bu-jok implies that to posit "that which is not the three modes" as the definition would be to assert that, in general, a quasi-reason exists. To that he objects that whatever exists is potentially a correct sign. It is from this point of view that quasi-signs are said to be nonexistent *in general*. In chapter two we saw Pur-bu-jok's argument that:

- in general, dissimilar class does not exist, because whatever is an established base is necessarily a similar class, and that

- in general, dissimilar example does not exist, because whatever is an established base is necessarily a similar example.

By the same reasoning, he asserts here that, in general, quasi-reasons do not exist.

The reasoning appears likely to provoke debate. Lati Rin-po-che, for example, points out a qualm based on the fact that, for a sign to be correct in a given proof, there has to be a correct, prepared opponent in that proof. He says,

> One could then ask [the person who makes the assertion that whatever is an established base is necessarily a correct sign] if the extremely subtle arrangements of actions and their effects are correct signs. [These are very hidden phenomena and not generally accessible to usual inference.] Could a prepared opponent realize these?
>
> Or, to take an easy example, is "the two, permanent and thing" (*rtag dngos gnyis*) a correct sign? It is an established base; but how can you state "...because of being the two, permanent and thing"? There is nothing that is permanent and a thing.[513]

Suppose, as Pur-bu-jok asserts, that whatever is an established base—each and every phenomenon—is potentially a correct sign. In that case, whatever phenomenon one chooses, one should be able to posit a proof in which it could function as a correct sign. But how could such a phenomenon as "the two, permanent and thing" be used as a correct sign? "The two, permanent and thing" is *itself* considered to be an object of knowledge, an existent, an established base; but there is not anything that *is* both permanent and thing. This is an example of an object of knowledge whose being does not occur (*yin pa mi srid pa'i shes bya*).[a]

Pur-bu-jok continues,

Divisions

Although in general quasi-reasons do not exist, in application to specific instances, there are three types:

- contradictory reasons in the proof of that,
- indefinite reasons in the proof of that, and
- nonestablished reasons in the proof of that.[514]

Just as a dissimilar class and a dissimilar example may be said to exist in

---

[a]   Daniel Perdue discusses this category of phenomena in his *Debate in Tibetan Buddhism*, pp. 331-344.

relation to specific proofs, so also do quasi-reasons. It is from this point of view—that is, in application to specific proofs and not in general—that the three types of quasi-reasons can be identified.

CONTRADICTORY REASONS

Pur-bu-jok's presentation of contradictory reasons has four parts: (1) definition, (2) divisions, (3) illustrations, and (4) statements of proof.[515]

Definition

Pur-bu-jok posits a definition of a contradictory reason in a specific proof:

> The definition of a contradictory reason in the proof of sound as permanent is:
>
> > That which is a common locus of (1) being the property of the subject in the proof of sound as *permanent* and (2) being the forward pervasion in the proof of sound as *not permanent*.[516]

In a correct proof, the sign is the three modes; it is the property of the subject and the two pervasions in that proof. In the proof of sound as impermanent by the sign, product:

(1) For the sign, product, to be the property of the subject means that:
  - product exists with sound in accordance with the mode of statement (in other words, sound is a product), and
  - there exists a correct opponent who, having ascertained that sound is a product, is wondering whether sound is impermanent.
(2) For product to be the pervasions in that proof means that:
  - product exists in only the similar class (the impermanent)—that is, it exists in some but not necessarily all of the similar class; and
  - product is just nonexistent in the dissimilar class (the permanent)—that is, it does not exist at all in the dissimilar class.

On the other hand, a contradictory reason in a particular proof is the first mode (property of the subject), but not the second and third (the forward pervasion and counterpervasion) in that proof. Thus, a contradictory reason does not fulfill all the criteria above for a correct sign.

Looking at Pur-bu-jok's definition, and taking as an example product in the proof of sound as *permanent*, we see that the sign, product, is the contradictory reason in the proof of sound as permanent because it is:

(1) the property of the subject in the proof of sound as permanent (sound is a product) and
(2) the forward pervasion in the proof of sound as *not* permanent. In other words, product exists in only the similar class, the not permanent, and is just nonexistent (does not exist at all) in the dissimilar class, the permanent.

From this it can be seen that a contradictory reason in the proof of sound as permanent is necessarily the forward pervasion in the proof of the opposite—that is, in the proof of sound as *not* permanent.

Another way to express the same idea is to say that the contradictory reason in the proof of sound as permanent is necessarily the perverse forward pervasion in the proof of sound as permanent. This phrasing is found in the definition posited by Ge-shay Tsül-trim-nam-gyel in the Lo-sel-ling logic manual:

> The definition of something's being a contradictory sign in the proof of that is:
>
> > that which is ascertained as the perverse forward pervasion and the perverse counterpervasion in the proof of that by the sign of it by a person for whom it has become the property of the subject in the proof of that.[517]

To make the points briefly,

- in the case of a correct sign (for example, product in the proof of sound as impermanent), the sign is the property of the subject and the two pervasions (the forward pervasion and counterpervasion) in that proof;
- in the case of a contradictory reason (for example, product in the proof of sound as permanent), the property of the subject is established, but the forward pervasion and counterpervasion are not established in that proof.

This is because in the case of a contradictory reason the sign is actually proving the opposite of the probandum.

There are two ways to look at this situation, and two different ways to express the same point. One is to say that the sign is the forward pervasion in the proof of the opposite (that is, in the proof of sound as *not* permanent). The other way is to say that the sign is the perverse pervasions in that proof (that is, in the proof of sound as *permanent*). It is, as Ge-shay Ge-dün-lo-drö puts it, the perverse forward pervasion in that proof, because whatever is a product is necessarily not permanent.[518]

Divisions and Illustrations

Pur-bu-jok writes,

> Divisions
>
> Contradictory reasons are of two types: (1) a contradictory reason that relates to the dissimilar class as pervader and (2) a contradictory reason that relates to the dissimilar class in two ways.[519]

In a correct proof the sign is pervaded by the similar class, whereas in a contradictory proof the sign is pervaded by the dissimilar class. Just as a correct sign can relate to the *similar* class either as pervader or in two ways, so in the case of contradictory reasons the sign can relate to the *dissimilar* class either as pervader or in two ways. Pur-bu-jok continues,

> Illustrations
>
> (1) Product is a contradictory reason that relates to the dissimilar class as a pervader in the proof that sound is not impermanent.
> (2) Particularity of product is a contradictory reason that relates to the dissimilar class in two ways in the proof that sound is not impermanent.[520]

In his discussion of correct nature signs (chapter five), Pur-bu-jok pointed out that product is a correct sign that relates to the similar class as pervader in the proof of sound as impermanent and that particularity of product is a correct sign that relates to the similar class in two ways. Here he posits these two signs as illustrations of contradictory reasons in the proof of sound as not impermanent.

Statements of Proof

Concerning his first illustration, Pur-bu-jok writes,

It follows that the subject, product, is a contradictory reason that relates to the dissimilar class as a pervader in the proof that sound is not impermanent (1) because of being a contradictory reason in the proof of that and (2) [because] whatever is impermanent is necessarily it [product].[521]

Concerning his second illustration, he does not explain why particularity of product is a contradictory reason that relates to the similar class in two ways—perhaps because the explanation is easy. In the syllogism, "The subject, sound, is not impermanent because of being a particularity of product," particularity of product relates to the dissimilar class in two ways because whatever is impermanent is not necessarily a particularity of product and is not necessarily not a particularity of product. Ge-shay Ge-dün-lo-drö makes this point, adding:

Something that is impermanent and a particularity of product is "thing"; something that is impermanent and is not a particularity of product is "product" itself. Product itself is not a particularity of product.[522]

Pur-bu-jok continues, proving why particularity of product is a contradictory reason in the proof that sound is not impermanent:

It follows that the subject, particularity of product, is a contradictory reason in the proof that sound is not impermanent because of being a contradictory reason in the proof of sound as permanent. This is because of (1) being the property of the subject in the proof of that [that is, the proof of sound as permanent] and (2) being ascertained as a perverse forward pervasion in the proof of that by the sign of it [particularity of product].[523]

In this proof, Pur-bu-jok's first reason (that particularity of product is the property of the subject in the proof of sound as permanent) is easy to prove by applying the definition of "property of the subject." Roughly speaking, it is established because sound is a particularity of product. Concerning the second reason, Ge-shay Ge-dün-lo-drö comments:

If someone says that the second reason is not established, then the response is: "It follows that the subject, particularity of product, is ascertained as a perverse forward pervasion in the proof of sound as permanent by the sign, particularity of product, because whatever is a particularity of product is necessarily not permanent.[524]

Pur-bu-jok offers an alternative reason why particularity of product is a contradictory reason in the proof of sound as permanent:

> Further, it follows that the subject, particularity of product, is a contradictory reason in the proof of sound as permanent because of being a correct sign in the proof of sound as impermanent.[525]

These two are equivalent: being a correct sign in the proof of sound as impermanent and being a contradictory reason in the proof of sound as permanent.

Mistaken Views

Pur-bu-jok next addresses two mistaken views expressed by opponents:

> An opponent's view: "It follows that a contradictory reason in the proof of sound as impermanent exists because a contradictory reason in the proof of sound as permanent exists."
>
> Response: "That does not follow from the reason. To accept the statement [that a contradictory reason in the proof of sound as impermanent exists] is incorrect because whatever is a quasi-reason in the proof of sound as impermanent must be either an indefinite reason in the proof of that or a nonestablished reason in the proof of that."[526]

Ge-shay Ge-dün-lo-drö comments that a more effective response would be to say "posit one" (*zhog*)! That is, he would challenge the opponent: "Go ahead and posit a contradictory reason in the proof of sound as impermanent, since you say that one exists!"[527] The fact that there exists a contradictory reason in the proof of sound as permanent does not entail that there exists a contradictory reason in the proof of sound as impermanent.

In the proof of sound as permanent, the reason is contradictory with the predicate of the probandum.[528] It actually proves the opposite of the probandum. In the proof of sound as impermanent, however, there cannot be a contradictory reason: if there existed a contradictory reason in the proof of sound as impermanent, there would have to be a correct sign in the proof of sound as permanent. According to Pur-bu-jok's definition, something, x (for example, product), is a contradictory reason in the proof of sound as permanent because it is the forward pervasion in the proof of the opposite (that is, in the proof of sound as *not* permanent). It follows that if x is a contradictory reason in the proof of sound as impermanent, then x must be the forward pervasion in the proof of the opposite (that is, in the proof of sound as not impermanent). But that is not possible; there is nothing to posit that fulfills this requirement for x; there is no x that is the forward pervasion in the proof of sound as permanent, nothing to posit as x. This is why Ge-shay Ge-dün-lo-drö says it is better not to argue the point as Pur-bu-jok does, but just to say to the opponent: posit one!

We do learn, however, from Pur-bu-jok's response to the opponent, that a quasi-reason in the proof of sound as impermanent cannot be a contradictory reason. There is no correct sign in the proof of sound as not impermanent, so whatever is a quasi-reason in that proof must be one of the other two types: indefinite or nonestablished.

Pur-bu-jok goes on to present and then refute another mistaken view:

> An opponent's view: "If there exist three modes in the proof of that, there necessarily exists a correct sign in the proof of that."
>
> Response: "It [absurdly] follows that with respect to the subject, object of knowledge, there exists a correct sign in the proof of sound as permanent because there exist three modes in the proof of sound as permanent. You have accepted the pervasion."[529]

This issue was discussed briefly in the complication section of chapter one, in the context of explaining how the beginning student is shown that the wording of the definition of correct sign ("that which is the three modes") is significant. Someone might think, as does the opponent here, that if the three modes are present in a given proof then there is a correct sign in that proof. The problem here is that it is possible to posit the existence of the three modes in an absurd proof—the proof of sound as permanent—but only by using two different signs. Pur-bu-jok demonstrates:

> If someone says that the reason is not established, [the response is]: "It follows that there exist three modes in the proof of sound as permanent because
>
> (1) there exists a property of the subject in the proof of that,
> (2) there exists a forward pervasion in the proof of that, and
> (3) there exists a counterpervasion in the proof of that."

The first [root] reason is established because product is the property of the subject in the proof of sound as permanent.

> If someone says that the reason is not established, [the

response is]: "It follows that the subject, product, is the property of the subject in the proof of sound as permanent because of being a contradictory sign in the proof of that. This is because [product] is a correct sign in the proof of sound as impermanent."[530]

Here, Pur-bu-jok shows that there exists a property of the subject in the proof of sound as permanent by positing product as the sign. But he will show the existence of the pervasions in that proof by positing a different sign: "the common locus of being a phenomenon and not being momentary" (*chos dang skad cig ma ma yin pa*). He writes,

The second [root] reason ["there exists a forward pervasion in the proof of sound as permanent"] is established because a common locus of being a phenomenon and not being momentary is the forward pervasion in the proof of sound as permanent.

If someone says that the reason is not established, [the response is]: "It follows that the subject, a common locus of being a phenomenon and not being momentary, is the forward pervasion in the proof of sound as permanent because (a) there exists a correct similar example that possesses the two, the sign and the predicate, in the proof of that by the sign of it and (b) it [a common locus of being a phenomenon and not being momentary] is ascertained by valid cognition as just existing, in accordance with the mode of statement, in only the similar class in the proof of sound as permanent."[531]

Here Pur-bu-jok is applying the criteria of forward pervasion as specified in his definition of forward pervasion in chapter three. He goes on,

The first reason (a) is established because uncompounded space is a correct similar example that possesses the two, the sign and the predicate, in the proof of that by the sign of it.[532]

Ge-shay Ge-dün-lo-drö amplifies this reasoning:

One can state, "The subject, sound, is a permanent phenomenon because of not being a momentary phenomenon, as is the case with uncompounded space." In that, uncompounded space is a correct similar example that possesses the two, the sign and the predicate in the proof of that. This is because uncompounded space is permanent and is not momentary.[533]

Pur-bu-jok continues,

> The second reason (b) is established because it [a common locus
> of being a phenomenon and not being momentary] exists, in
> accordance with the mode of statement, in only the similar
> class in the proof of that. This is because it is the definition of
> permanent phenomenon.[534]

In the proof of sound as permanent, the similar class is the permanent.
The common locus of being a phenomenon and not being momentary
exists in only the similar class because it exists in only the permanent.
There is no instance of a common locus of being a phenomenon and not
being momentary that is not permanent.

Pur-bu-jok now takes up of the last part of his proof of a consequence of the opponent's mistaken view:

> The third [root] reason ["there exists a counterpervasion in the
> proof of sound as permanent"] is established because a com-
> mon locus of being a phenomenon and not being momentary is
> that.
>
>   If someone says that the reason is not established, [the re-
> sponse is]: "It follows that the subject, a common locus of being
> a phenomenon and not being momentary, is the counterperva-
> sion in the proof of sound as permanent because (a) there exists
> a dissimilar example that does not possess the two, the sign and
> the predicate, in the proof of that by the sign of it and (b) it is
> ascertained by valid cognition as only nonexistent in the dissi-
> milar class in the proof of that."[535]

Here Pur-bu-jok is applying the criteria specified in his definition of the
counterpervasion in chapter three.

Pur-bu-jok has shown how the opponent's view entails that there
would exist three modes in the proof of sound as permanent. If the opponent then agrees to this, Pur-bu-jok shows the opponent to be wrong
again; he writes,

> If the basic consequence [that there exists a correct sign in the
> proof of sound as permanent] is accepted, [then, the response
> is:] it follows with respect to the subject, sound, that there does
> not exist a correct sign in the proof of it as permanent because
> it is not permanent.[536]

There does not exist a correct sign in the proof of sound as permanent
because there is no *single* sign that is the three modes in that proof. The
three modes exist only if one posits two separate signs ("product" and
"the common locus of being permanent and not being momentary").

The original mistaken view being discussed here is the opponent's saying that if there exist three modes in a proof, there necessarily exists a correct sign in that proof. Pur-bu-jok refutes the view by positing two separate signs in the proof of sound as permanent. In a correct proof, however, the three modes refer to just one phenomenon. The point being made is that although three modes exist in the proof of sound as permanent, there is nothing that *is* the three modes in the proof of sound as permanent.

Pur-bu-jok goes on to imagine a determined opponent arguing that there *does* exist something that is the three modes:

> Someone objects: That which *is* the three modes in the proof of sound as permanent exists, because
>
> (1) that which is the property of the subject in the proof of that exists,
> (2) that which is the forward pervasion in the proof of that exists, and
> (3) that which is the counterpervasion in the proof of that exists.
>
> Answer to the objection: That does not follow from the reason.[537]

The opponent is arguing that if, in relation to each of these three, there exists something that is it, then there necessarily exists something that is all three. There is indeed something that is the first (product); there is something that is the second (common locus of being permanent and not being momentary); and there is something that is the third (that same common locus). But this reason does not entail that some *one* thing is all three. There is no such thing.

Ge-shay Ge-dün-lo-drö drives this point home:

> In response to the [opponent's] objection, one could state the absurd consequence: "It follows from your view that that which is a pillar and a pot exists because that which is a pillar exists and that which is a pot exists." This is mistaken because there does not exist a common locus of being both a pillar and a pot.[538]

In an indefinite reason, as in a contradictory reason, the property of the subject has to be established. The difference between these two types of quasi-signs is that in the case of the contradictory reason, the opponent is someone who has ascertained the perverse forward pervasion and the counterpervasion.

INDEFINITE REASONS

Pur-bu-jok defines an indefinite reason in the proof of sound as permanent in this way:

> That which is a common locus of (1) being the property of the subject in the proof of sound as permanent, (2) not being the forward pervasion in the proof of sound as permanent, and (3) not being the forward pervasion in the proof of sound as not permanent.[539]

Before the detailed discussion of indefinite reasons, it is interesting to consider the distinction between them and the previous category, contradictory reasons. A contradictory reason (for example, in the proof of sound as permanent) is the property of the subject in that proof and is the forward pervasion in the proof of the opposite of the probandum (that is, in the proof of sound as not permanent); this means that the sign is pervaded by the dissimilar class. So a contradictory reason in the proof of sound as permanent:

- is the property of the subject in the proof of sound as permanent,
- is not the forward pervasion in the proof of sound as permanent, but
- *is* the forward pervasion in the proof of sound as *not* permanent (this last is equivalent to saying that it is the perverse forward pervasion in the proof of sound as permanent).

An indefinite reason in the proof of sound as permanent:

- is the property of the subject in the proof of sound as permanent,
- is not the forward pervasion in the proof of sound as permanent, and
- is not the perverse forward pervasion in the proof of sound as permanent.

Another way of comparing these two quasi-signs is that (1) in both the contradictory and the indefinite reasons, the property of the subject has to be established; (2) in both, the forward pervasion and counterpervasion are not established; and (3) the perverse forward pervasion and perverse counterpervasion are established in the contradictory reasons but not in the indefinite reasons.

There are two types of indefinite reasons, uncommon and common.

Uncommon Indefinite Reasons

Pur-bu-jok's definition of something's being an uncommon indefinite reason in a given proof is:

> (1) it is an indefinite sign in the proof of that and (2) it is a common locus of (a) not being ascertained as existent in the similar class in the proof of that by a person for whom it has become the property of the subject in the proof of that, and (b) that person does not ascertain it as existing in the dissimilar class in the proof of that.[540]

That is, the sign is not ascertained as existing in either the similar or the dissimilar class. Pur-bu-jok provides the following illustrations:

> Object of hearing, opposite from nonsound, and sound-isolate— each of these is an uncommon indefinite reason in both the proof of sound as permanent and the proof of sound as impermanent.[541]

Sound is said to have a particularly close relationship with each of these—object of hearing, opposite from nonsound, and sound-isolate— which makes it impossible for a person to ascertain whether one of these is impermanent without simultaneously understanding that sound is impermanent. Ge-shay Ge-dün-lo-drö explains:

> None of these three can serve as a correct sign in the given proofs [that is, the proofs of sound as impermanent and of sound as permanent] because it is not possible for a person—for whom sound has become the property of the subject—to ascertain the relationship between any one of these three and the similar and dissimilar classes in those proofs without simultaneously understanding the thesis.
>
> In general it is possible, and in fact necessary, to ascertain the definition of a particular phenomenon before ascertaining that phenomenon itself. However, this is not the case with sound and its definition, object of hearing, because of their unusually close relationship.[542]

The ge-shay points out that it is not possible to ascertain object of hearing, etc. without also ascertaining sound. It is therefore impossible to posit a similar example in the proof of sound as impermanent by the sign, object of hearing; thus, the forward pervasion in that proof is not established. It has been explained that the forward pervasion in any

given proof must first be ascertained in relation to a similar example—
one realizes the pervasion in relation to a similar example before realizing it in relation to the subject. In this case, therefore, one would
have to be able to ascertain the pervasion, "whatever is an object of
hearing is necessarily impermanent," in relation to a similar example
before realizing it in relation to sound; but it is not possible to ascertain
object of hearing without simultaneously ascertaining sound. Ge-shay
Pel-den-drak-pa makes this point:

> When you understand that object of hearing is impermanent,
> you also understand that sound is impermanent; therefore
> there is no similar example in that proof [of sound as imper-
> manent by the sign, object of hearing]; and thus, the forward
> pervasion is not established.[543]

In the opposite syllogism, "The subject, sound, is permanent because of
being an object of hearing," the perverse pervasion happens to be true:
whatever is an object of hearing is necessarily not permanent. Is this a
contradictory reason, then? For some opponents it is, but for others it
is an indefinite reason. If object of hearing is to be a contradictory reason, the opponent (a person for whom the reason has become the
property of the subject) would have to ascertain the perverse pervasion
in that proof—that is, that whatever is an object of hearing is necessarily not permanent. In the case of its being an indefinite reason, the perverse pervasion is established, generally speaking (in that it is true), but
the opponent has not ascertained it.

Ge-shay Lob-sang-gya-tso comments:

> For someone who has ascertained the perverse forward perva-
> sion and counterpervasion, it is a contradictory sign, but for
> someone who has not ascertained them, it is not a contradicto-
> ry sign; it is an indefinite sign.
>
> The property of the subject is established, but the perverse
> forward pervasion is not ascertained and the perverse counter-
> pervasion is not ascertained—that is an indefinite sign.[544]

Whether a sign is contradictory or indefinite depends in large part on
the opponent, on the opponent's understanding. Therefore, one cannot
assert, in the proof of sound as impermanent because of being a product, that product is necessarily a correct sign; it depends on the understanding of the opponent. For someone who knows that sound is a
product but does not know whether product is impermanent or permanent, the sign is an uncommon indefinite reason. Product is also an

uncommon indefinite reason in the syllogism, "The subject, sound, is permanent because of being a product."

In short, for an opponent who knows nothing about the permanence or impermanence of product, product is an indefinite reason in both the proof of sound as impermanent and the proof of sound as permanent.

Common Indefinite Reasons

Pur-bu-jok defines a common indefinite reason in a given proof as:

> (1) It is an indefinite reason in the proof of that and (2) it is a common locus of either (a) its being ascertained as existent in the similar class in the proof of that by a person for whom it has become the property of the subject in the proof of that or (b) its being ascertained as existent in the dissimilar class in the proof of that by that person [or both].[545]

In brief, the opponent has ascertained (1) the property of the subject and has ascertained either (2) that the sign, product, exists in the similar class or (3) that product exists in the dissimilar class.

When someone says, "The subject, sound, is impermanent because of being a product," sound is the subject sought to be known. Because product is established as the property of the subject, product is ascertained as applying to sound (that is, sound is a product); for the opponent, product is ascertained as a feature of sound, it is ascertained as existent in or with respect to sound.

Here the similar class is impermanent. If the opponent ascertains product as existent among impermanent, then he or she has ascertained product as existent in both the subject and the similar class. That is, he or she has ascertained that product exists *in common* in the basis of relation of the pervasion (the similar class) and in the subject sought to be known.

Another possibility is that the opponent will ascertain product as existent among permanent. In this case, he or she ascertains that it exists *in common* in the subject sought to be known and in permanent (the dissimilar class in the proof of sound as impermanent).

Lati Rin-po-che explains that "common" and "uncommon" thus refer to the ascertainment of the opponent. He says,

> In order to have a common ascertainment, one must realize the existence of the sign in the subject and in at least one of the two, similar class or the dissimilar class. If someone ascertains

that the sign exists in the subject but does not ascertain it with regard to either the similar class or the dissimilar class, that is uncommon ascertainment.[546]

Common and uncommon refer to whether the sign is ascertained in both (in common in) the subject and one of the two bases of relation of the pervasions—similar and dissimilar class. If the sign is ascertained as existing in the subject and the similar class or as existing in the subject and the dissimilar class: it is a common ascertainment and thus a common indefinite reason.

If the sign is ascertained as existing in the subject but not in either the similar class or the dissimilar class: that is uncommon ascertainment, and thus the sign is an uncommon indefinite reason.

An example of a common indefinite reason is "object of hearing" in the proof of sound as impermanent, described above as an *uncommon* indefinite reason in that proof. Lati Rin-po-che comments that object of hearing can be either a common or an uncommon indefinite reason in that proof, depending on the understanding of the opponent. He says,

> A person for whom object of hearing has become the property of the subject in the proof of sound as impermanent ascertains object of hearing as a feature of sound, as existent with sound. If that person also ascertains object of hearing as existent among permanent (the similar class), that is "common" ascertainment. On the other hand, if that person ascertains object of hearing as existent among impermanent (the dissimilar class), that is also common ascertainment. If one does not ascertain either of those—that is, if one ascertains that object of hearing exists with sound but one does not ascertain that it exists in either the similar class or the dissimilar class—that is called "uncommon" [ascertainment].[547]

Pur-bu-jok divides common indefinite reasons into three types: (1) actual indefinite reason in the proof of that, (2) indefinite reason having remainder in the proof of that, and (3) indefinite reason that is not either of those in the proof of that.[548]

Actual Indefinite Reasons

The definition of something's being an actual indefinite reason in a given proof is:

(1) it is an indefinite reason in the proof of that and (2) it is

ascertained as existing in both the similar and the dissimilar class by a person for whom it has become the property of the subject in the proof of that.[549]

The sign is ascertained as existing in both the similar and the dissimilar classes. Lati Rin-po-che poses a question:

How can it be ascertained in both? For example, in the syllogism, "The subject, sound, is permanent, because of being an object of knowledge," object of knowledge is ascertained as existing in both the similar class and the dissimilar class. Object of knowledge exists in the similar class [permanent] because permanent is an object of knowledge and it exists in the dissimilar class [impermanent] because impermanent is an object of knowledge.[550]

Pur-bu-jok goes on to list four types of actual indefinite reasons and to give illustrations. He writes,

When actual indefinite reasons are divided, there are four types:

(1) actual indefinite reason that relates to the similar class as pervader and to the dissimilar class as pervader in the proof of that,
(2) actual indefinite reason that relates to the similar class as pervader and to the dissimilar class in two ways in the proof of that,
(3) actual indefinite reason that relates to the dissimilar class as pervader and to the similar class in two ways in the proof of that, and
(4) actual indefinite reason that relates to both the similar and dissimilar classes in two ways in the proof of that.[551]

For the first of these, he posits the illustration:

[One can state, "The subject, sound, is permanent because the horn of a rabbit does not exist." In that,] "the horn of a rabbit does not exist" is an actual indefinite reason that relates to the similar class as pervader in the proof of sound as permanent and to the dissimilar class as pervader in the proof of that.[552]

Ge-shay Ge-dün-lo-drö explains the proof of this:

It follows that the subject,[a] "the horn of a rabbit does not exist," relates to the similar class as a pervader in the proof of sound as permanent, because the similar class in the proof of that is "permanent," and with respect to whatever is permanent, the horns of a rabbit necessarily do not exist.

It follows that the subject, "the horn of a rabbit does not exist" relates to the dissimilar class as pervader in the proof of sound as permanent, because the dissimilar class in the proof of that is "impermanent," and with respect to whatever is impermanent the horns of a rabbit necessarily do not exist.[553]

In illustration of the second type, Pur-bu-jok posits,

[One can state, "The subject, the sound of a conch, is arisen from exertion because of being impermanent." In that,] impermanent is an actual indefinite reason that relates to the similar class as pervader and to the dissimilar class in two ways in the proof of the sound of a conch as arisen from exertion.[554]

Again, Ge-shay Ge-dün-lo-drö provides a proof:

It follows that the subject, impermanent, relates to the similar class as pervader in the proof of the sound of a conch as arisen from exertion because the similar class in the proof of that is "arisen from exertion," and whatever is arisen from exertion is necessarily impermanent.

It follows that the subject, impermanent, relates to the dissimilar class in two ways in the proof of the sound of a conch as arisen from exertion because the dissimilar class in the proof of that is "not arisen from exertion," and whatever is not arisen from exertion is not necessarily impermanent (for example, uncompounded space) and is not necessarily not impermanent (for example, a river).[555]

Pur-bu-jok's next illustration is an interesting variant:

[One can state, "The subject, the sound of a conch, is not arisen from exertion because of being impermanent." In that,] impermanent is an actual indefinite reason that relates to the dissimilar class as pervader and to the similar class in two ways in the proof of the sound of a conch as not arisen from exertion.[556]

---

[a] The ge-shay does not mean that "the horn of a rabbit does not exist" is the subject of Pur-bu-jok's syllogism; he means it is the subject he is discussing, the focus of his attention here.

Ge-shay Ge-dün-lo-drö's comment on this is,

> It follows that the subject, impermanent, relates to the dissimilar class as pervader in the proof of the sound of a conch as not arisen from exertion because the dissimilar class in the proof of that is "arisen from exertion" and whatever is arisen from exertion is necessarily impermanent.
>
> It follows that the subject, impermanent, relates to the similar class in two ways in the proof of the sound of conch as not arisen from exertion because the similar class in the proof of that is "not arisen from exertion" and whatever is not arisen from exertion is not necessarily impermanent and is not necessarily not impermanent.[557]

Pur-bu-jok concludes his list of actual indefinite reasons with this illustration:

> [One can state, "The subject, a sense consciousness apprehending two moons, is a direct perception because of being a sense consciousness." In that,] "sense consciousness" is an actual indefinite reason that relates to both the similar class and the dissimilar class in two ways in the proof that a sense consciousness apprehending two moons is a direct perception.[558]

Ge-shay Ge-dün-lo-drö explains that this is because the similar class in the proof of that is "direct perception," and whatever is a direct perception is not necessarily a sense consciousness (for example, a yogic direct perception) and is not necessarily not a sense consciousness (for example, a sense consciousness apprehending blue). Sense consciousness also relates to the *dissimilar* class in two ways here, because the dissimilar class in the proof of that is "*not* a direct perception," and whatever is not a direct perception is not necessarily a sense consciousness (for example, a pot) and is not necessarily not a sense consciousness (for example, a sense consciousness apprehending two moons).[559]

Indefinite Reasons Having Remainder

Pur-bu-jok's definition of this type of indefinite reason is:

> (1) It is a common indefinite reason in the proof of that and (2) a person for whom it has become the property of the subject in the proof of that
>
> • either, (a) having ascertained it as existing in the similar

class in the proof of that, doubts whether or not it exists in
the dissimilar class

- or, (b) having ascertained it as existing in the dissimilar
class in the proof of that, doubts whether or not it exists in
the similar class.[560]

He divides this section into two parts, indefinite reasons having correct
remainder and indefinite reasons having contradictory remainder.

Indefinite Reasons Having Correct Remainder

Pur-bu-jok's definition of something's being an indefinite reason having correct remainder in a given proof is:

(1) it is an indefinite reason having remainder in the proof of
that and (2) a person for whom it has become the property of
the subject in the proof of that, having ascertained it as existing
in the similar class, doubts whether or not it exists in the dissimilar class.[561]

Ge-shay Pel-den-drak-pa explains that reasons having correct remainder are so called because something remains to be done, for it to
be a correct sign.[562] A "correct remainder" has almost met the requirements of a correct sign, that is, has almost been ascertained as the forward pervasion and counterpervasion. In the case of the syllogism,
"Sound is impermanent because of being a product," for example,

- When someone has ascertained the property of the subject and the
pervasions (forward and counter-), product is a correct sign.
- When someone has ascertained that product exists in the similar
class but has not ascertained the relationship between product and
the dissimilar class, product is an indefinite sign having correct
remainder.

This is because something remains to be ascertained by the opponent
before product can be a correct sign.

In this case, the indefinite reason having correct remainder is in
fact a potentially correct sign; however, as Ge-shay Pel-den-drak-pa
says, "Some reasons having correct remainder are potentially correct
signs, but some are not."[563] One that is not is posited by Pur-bu-jok as
illustration:

[One can state, "The subject, Devadatta who speaks speech, is
not omniscient because of speaking speech." In that,] "speaking
speech" is an indefinite reason having correct remainder for a

person who has doubts with regard to omniscience in the proof that Devadatta, who speaks speech, is not omniscient.[564]

In this case, the opponent has ascertained that speaking speech exists in the similar class (speaking occurs among the nonomniscient) but has not ascertained whether speaking speech exists among the omniscient or not. According to Ge-shay Pel-den-drak-pa, "The sign is called a reason having correct remainder, even though it is not in fact potentially a correct sign."[565] It is not even potentially correct—the opponent will not be able to ascertain the relationship between sign and dissimilar class (the omniscient), because omniscience is a supersensory object. Ge-shay Pel-den-drak-pa continues,

> The opponent does not know whether speaking speech exists among the omniscient or not. The opponent has ascertained that speech exists in the similar class (the nonomniscient). So it is called a reason having correct remainder, even though it is not in fact even potentially a correct sign.[566]

Indefinite Reasons Having Contradictory Remainder

Pur-bu-jok's definition and illustration of something's being an indefinite reason having contradictory remainder in the proof of that are,

Definition:

(1) It is an indefinite reason having remainder in the proof of that and (2) a person for whom it has become the property of the subject in the proof of that, having ascertained it as existing in the dissimilar class, doubts whether or not it exists in the similar class.[567]

Illustration:

[One can state: "The subject, Devadatta who speaks speech, is omniscient because of speaking speech." In that,] "speaking speech" is an indefinite reason having contradictory remainder for a person who has doubts with regard to omniscience in the proof that Devadatta who speaks speech is omniscient.[568]

Here the similar class and dissimilar class are reversed from the illustration given for signs having correct remainder. In this case, contradictory remainder, the similar class is the omniscient and the dissimilar class is the nonomniscient. In this case the sign is ascertained as existing in the dissimilar class, but the person for whom it has become the property of the subject has not ascertained whether or not it exists in the similar class.

Here the opponent ascertains the relationship between sign and dissimilar class, but not that between sign and similar class. Thus, part of the requirements for a contradictory reason are fulfilled; and this is called an indefinite reason having contradictory remainder.

The reason for labeling this pair of signs either "having correct remainder" or "having contradictory remainder" is explained in the Lo-sel-ling logic manual as follows:

> The meaning of the two types of reasons having remainder exists. This is because:
>
> (1) it is ascertained as existing in the similar class in the proof of that by a person for whom it has become the property of the subject in the proof of that, and thus it is about to become a correct sign in the proof of that; but it has not been ascertained as not existing in the dissimilar class in the proof of that by that person. Thus it is posited as a reason having correct remainder, and
>
> (2) it is ascertained as existing in the dissimilar class in the proof of that by such a person and thus it is about to become a contradictory sign in the proof of that; but since it is not ascertained as not existing in the similar class in the proof of that by that person, it is posited as a reason having contradictory remainder.[569]

Even so, as Ge-shay Pel-den-drak-pa has said, the signs may or may not have correct or contradictory remainders in actuality.

Indefinite Reasons That Are Neither

The third type of common indefinite reasons is that which is neither of the first two types (actual indefinite reasons and indefinite reasons having remainder). Pur-bu-jok's definition and illustration are,

> Definition:
>
> (1) it is a common indefinite reason in the proof of that and (2) a person for whom it has become the property of the subject in the proof of that either ascertains that it exists in only the similar class in the proof of that or ascertains that it is nonexistent in only the dissimilar class in the proof of that.

> Illustration:

[One can state: "With respect to the subject, with the lump of molasses in the mouth, the present form of molasses exists because the present taste of molasses exists." In that,] the present taste of molasses is an illustration of a common indefinite reason that is not either of those two in the proof that the present form of molasses exists with the lump of molasses in the mouth.[a]

There is apparent agreement among Ge-luk-pa scholars that the sign in the syllogism is not correct. If it were a correct sign, it would have to be either a correct effect, correct nature, or correct nonobservation sign. Ge-shay Ge-dün-lo-drö eliminates all three as possibilities when he says,

Because the present form and the present taste of molasses are simultaneous, there cannot be a causal relationship between them. Thus, "the present taste of molasses" cannot be a correct effect sign in that proof...

If it were a correct nature sign in that proof, it would have to be of one nature with the present form of molasses, the predicate of the probandum in that proof. However, the present taste and form of molasses are not of one nature because of being separate substantial entities...

Further, "the present taste of molasses" is not a correct nonobservation sign in the given proof, because the predicate of the probandum is a positive phenomenon.[570]

Another way to approach this issue is to consider the relationship between the sign and the predicate of the probandum. For this to be a correct sign, these would have to be in a relationship either of provenance or of sameness of nature. At issue is the relationship between the present taste of molasses and the present form of molasses. In the Ge-luk-pa view, these are not related. Ken-sur Ye-shay-tup-ten comments,

If the present taste of molasses exists, the present form of molasses necessarily exists; nevertheless, the forward pervasion is not established. Why? Because these [the present form and present taste] are not related. They are separate substantial entities.[571]

Phenomena that are separate substantial entities may be related; but if

[a] *Signs and Reasonings*, p. 21a.4-6. This syllogism is also discussed in chapter four in the section on correct effect signs that are a means of inferring causal attributes.

so, they are necessarily related causally. This cannot be the case for the present taste and present form of molasses; these are simultaneous.

The present form and present taste of molasses, therefore, are not in a relationship of provenance. They are also not in a relationship of sameness of nature; phenomena related that way are not separate substantial entities. Ken-sur Ye-shay-tup-ten explains,

> These two [the present taste and the present form of molasses] are not in a relationship of sameness of nature because of being separate substantial entities. They appear separately to direct perception. Phenomena that are suitable to be perceived separately by direct perception are separate entities.[572]

To sum up, the present taste of molasses is not related to the present form of molasses—either in relationship of provenance or relationship of nature—and thus cannot function as a correct sign in this proof.

NONESTABLISHED REASONS

Pur-bu-jok begins his explanation of nonestablished reasons by positing a definition and divisions:

> The definition of a nonestablished reason in a given proof is:
>
> > (1) it is stated as a sign in the proof of that and (2) it is not the property of the subject in the proof of that.
>
> When divided, nonestablished reasons are of three types:
>
> - nonestablished reason in relation to the fact,
> - nonestablished reason in relation to a mind, and
> - nonestablished reason in relation to an opponent.[573]

In each of these three cases, the property of the subject is not established—one of the criteria set forth in the definition of property of the subject is not satisfied. Those criteria are that there must be a flawless subject and the sign must exist with the subject in accordance with the mode of statement.

Nonestablished Reasons in Relation to the Fact

In this division of nonestablished reasons, Pur-bu-jok identifies seven types:

> This section has seven parts: nonestablished reasons due to

(1) the nonexistence of the entity of the sign,
(2) the nonexistence of the entity of the subject,
(3) the nondifference of the sign and the predicate of the pro-
     bandum,
(4) the nondifference of the basis of debate and the sign,
(5) the nondifference of the basis of debate and the predicate
     of the probandum,
(6) the nonexistence of the sign, in accordance with the mode
     of statement, with the subject sought to be known, and
(7) the nonexistence in the subject sought to be known of a
     portion of the reason.[574]

He takes up each type in turn and provides an illustration. Of nonestablished reasons due to the nonexistence of the entity of the sign, he
writes:

(1) One can state, "The subject, a being, is miserable because of
     being pierced by the horn of a rabbit." In that, ["pierced by
     the horn of a rabbit" is a nonestablished reason due to the
     nonexistence of the entity of the sign in the proof of a be-
     ing as miserable].[575]

If either the subject or the sign is a nonexistent, then the property of
the subject cannot be established. The sign, "pierced by the horn of a
rabbit," does not exist—so it is a nonestablished reason. If a sign does
not exist at all, it cannot satisfy the requirement of existing with the
subject, in accordance with the mode of statement, as is specified by
the definition of the property of the subject.

  To illustrate the second type, Pur-bu-jok posits,

(2) One can state, "The subject, the horn of a rabbit, is imper-
     manent because of being a product." In that, ["product" is a
     nonestablished reason due to the nonexistence of the sub-
     ject].[a]

---

[a] Ibid., p. 21b.4-5. Later in *Signs and Reasonings,* Pur-bu-jok brings up a complication
which will not be pursued here because it is beyond the scope of this book. He writes,

> Someone asks, "Does there exist a correct sign in a syllogism in which some-
> thing nonestablished is held as the subject? If such exists, how would the pre-
> dicate of the probandum be established? If it does not exist, then how could
> [the statement,] 'The subject, the horn of a rabbit, is selfless because of being
> either an existent or a nonexistent' be a correct syllogism?"
>   Although there are differing assertions with regard to this, Gyel-tsap
> Rin-po-che explains that among signs of a positive phenomenon there does

The subject, horn of a rabbit, does not exist, and thus is not a flawless subject. To be flawless, there must be an opponent who, having ascertained by valid cognition that the horn of a rabbit is a product, is wondering if it is impermanent; there can be no such opponent. In addition, product does not exist with the horn of a rabbit, because product is not a quality of a nonexistent.

Types three, four, and five of nonestablished reasons hinge on nondifferences. If there is no difference (a) between the sign and the predicate of the probandum, or (b) between the subject and the sign, or (c) between the subject and the predicate of the probandum, then the property of the subject cannot be established. The first situation, (a), is illustrated by Pur-bu-jok's third type:

> (3) One can state, "The subject, sound, is impermanent because of being impermanent." In that, ["impermanent" is a nonestablished reason due to the nondifference of the sign and the predicate of the probandum].[576]

Sound is not a flawless subject here, because there cannot be an opponent who—having ascertained that sound is impermanent—is wondering if it is impermanent.

To illustrate the situation (b) in which there is no difference between the subject and the sign, Pur-bu-jok posits:

> (4) One can state, "The subject, sound, is impermanent because of being a sound." In that, ["sound" is a nonestablished reason due to the nondifference of the basis of debate and the sign].[577]

The property of the subject is not established. In discussing the criteria of something's being the property of the subject in the proof of sound as impermanent, Pur-bu-jok specifies that "it is *with* the subject, sound" (*sgra chos can gyi steng du khyod yin*).[578] Ge-shay Pel-den-drak-pa comments that something's being "with" sound means it is a quality or feature of sound.[579] Sound is not itself a quality of sound and therefore cannot be the property of the subject in that proof.

The third (c) of these nonestablished reasons is:

> (5) One can state: "The subject, sound, is sound because of

---

not exist a correct sign of that which is held to be a nonestablished basis of debate, but that among signs of a negative phenomenon, [such] does exist. Although there is much to be examined, let us leave it. (*Signs and Reasonings*, pp. 23a.6-23b.1.)

being a product." In that, ["product" is a nonestablished reason due to the nondifference of the basis of debate and the predicate of the probandum in the proof of sound as sound].[580]

Sound is not a flawless subject here, because there cannot be an opponent who, having ascertained by valid cognition that sound is a product, wonders if sound is a sound. To ascertain by valid cognition that sound is a product, one must ascertain both sound and product by valid cognition; to ascertain sound by valid cognition means that one knows sound to be sound.

For the next type of nonestablished reason, Pur-bu-jok provides the illustration,

(6) One can state: "The subject, sound, is impermanent because of being the object of apprehension by an eye consciousness." In that, ["object of apprehension by an eye consciousness" is a nonestablished reason due to the nonexistence of the sign, in accordance with the mode of statement, with the subject sought to be known in that proof].[581]

In this syllogism, "object of apprehension of an eye consciousness" is a nonestablished reason because the sign does not exist with the subject in accordance with the mode of statement. Lati Rin-po-che explains,

Object of apprehension by an eye consciousness does not exist, in accordance with the mode of statement, with sound because

(1) the mode of statement is an "is" statement, and
(2) sound is not an object of apprehension by an eye consciousness.

Sound is not an object of apprehension by an eye consciousness because it is an object of apprehension by an ear consciousness.[582]

The seventh type is called a nonestablished reason due to the nonexistence in the subject of a portion of the reason. For the sake of understanding, however, one might better think of it as a nonestablished reason due to the nonexistence in the reason of a portion of the subject. Pur-bu-jok's illustration is,

(7) One can state: "The subject, a tree, is sentient because of sleeping at night with curled leaves." In that, ["sleeping at night with curled leaves" is a nonestablished reason due to

the nonexistence in the reason of a portion of the subject sought to be known].[583]

The sign is a nonestablished reason due to the nonexistence in the reason, "sleeping at night with curled leaves," of a portion of the subject sought to be known (a tree). It is not a correct sign in that proof, because it does not apply to all instances of the subject. Ge-shay Ge-dün-lo-drö comments,

> Whatever is a tree (the subject sought to be known) does not necessarily sleep at night with curled leaves; for example, an oak tree.[584]

Among trees, some present an appearance of sleeping at night by the curling of their leaves and others do not.

These seven examples illustrate Pur-bu-jok's first division: nonestablished reasons in relation to the fact. In this type, the sign is nonestablished because of the nature of the entity of what is posited as the subject or the sign, and because of the nature of the relationship between the parts of the syllogism. The signs in his seven illustrations are nonestablished because of the very nature of the parts of the syllogism.

Nonestablished Reasons in Relation to a Mind

Pur-bu-jok's second division involves signs that are not established due to the understanding of the opponent involved:

> This section has four parts: nonestablished reasons due to
>
> (1) doubt with regard to the entity of the sign,
> (2) doubt with regard to the entity of the subject,
> (3) doubt with regard to the relationship of the basis of debate and the sign, and
> (4) the nonexistence of the subject sought to be known.[585]

If the opponent has doubt concerning the existence of that which is set as the sign, or concerning the existence of that which is set as the subject in a syllogism, then the sign in that syllogism cannot serve as a correct sign. Pur-bu-jok's illustration of a nonestablished reason due to doubt with regard to the entity of the sign is,

> (1) One can state: "The subject, sound, is impermanent because of being an object of comprehension of the valid cognition [in the continuum] of a flesh-eater." For a person for whom flesh-eater is a supersensory object, ["object of

comprehension of the valid cognition in the continuum of a flesh-eater" is a nonestablished reason due to doubt with regard to the entity of the sign in that proof].[586]

For someone for whom flesh-eater is a supersensory object, the sign, "an object of comprehension of the valid cognition of a flesh-eater," cannot be ascertained by valid cognition.

Pur-bu-jok continues,

(2) One can state: "The subject, the song of an odor-eater, is an impermanent phenomenon because of being a product." For a person for whom an odor-eater is a supersensory object [product is a nonestablished reason due to doubt with regard to the entity of the subject].[587]

A person for whom an odor-eater is a supersensory object cannot ascertain the subject by valid cognition.

The third type is the case of the opponent having doubt concerning the basis of debate and the sign. Pur-bu-jok cites the traditional illustration:

(3) One can state: "With respect to the subject, in the middle of three mountain ridges, a peacock exists because the call of a peacock exists." For a person who does not know where the peacock exists [the call of a peacock is a nonestablished reason due to doubt with regard to the relationship of the basis of debate and the sign in that proof].[588]

The call of the peacock will be clearly heard, echoing here and there from the mountain sides, but, as Den-ma Lo-chö Rin-po-che points out,

A person, having heard the call of a peacock, knows that a peacock exists somewhere on the three mountain ridges. However, hearing the peacock's call is not a sufficient reason for establishing the peacock as existing in the middle of the three mountain ridges.[589]

Pur-bu-jok's fourth type of reason that is nonestablished in relation to a mind is the case in which there does not exist a subject sought to be known. For someone who already knows that sound is impermanent, product in the proof of sound as impermanent is this type of nonestablished reason. Pur-bu-jok's illustration is,

(4) One can state: "The subject, sound, is impermanent because of being a product." For the glorious Dharmakīrti, [product

is a nonestablished reason due to the nonexistence of the subject].[590]

Lati Rin-po-che adds,

> The glorious Dharmakīrti has already ascertained by valid cognition that sound is impermanent. Thus, for him, sound does not exist as a subject sought to be known in the proof of sound as impermanent.[591]

The flawless subject sought to be known does not exist, because—in order for there to be a flawless subject—the opponent has to be actively wondering whether sound is impermanent. This is not a subject of wonder for an enlightened being.

Nonestablished Reasons in Relation to an Opponent

Pur-bu-jok tells us,

> There are three types of nonestablished reasons in relation to an opponent: nonestablished reason in relation to (1) the former opponent, (2) the latter opponent, and (3) both former and latter opponents.[a]

In this context it is clear that Pur-bu-jok's "former opponent" refers to the party who is stating the reason, and the "latter opponent" refers to the party to whom the reason is stated. It has been specified that in order for a sign to be correct, the former party must have ascertained the probandum and the latter party must be someone who has not yet done so. The latter is newly developing understanding and becoming a correct opponent (one who, having ascertained the three modes of the sign, is then ready to ascertain the probandum).

If the former party does not ascertain the probandum by valid cognition, then the sign is not a correct sign. To illustrate this first division of nonestablished reasons, Pur-bu-jok posits,

> (1) When a Sāṃkhya states to a Buddhist: "The subject, awareness (*buddhi*) is mindless because of having production and disintegration," [having production and disintegration is a nonestablished reason in relation to the former party].[592]

---

[a] *Signs and Reasonings*, p. 22a.5-6. For a discussion of the terms "former opponent" and "latter opponent," see the chapter eight section on the division of correct signs by way of the opponent.

Lati Rin-po-che comments,

> That awareness has production and disintegration is established for a Buddhist but not for a Sāṃkhya. Thus, "having production and disintegration" is a nonestablished reason in terms of the former party—a Sāṃkhya—in the proof of awareness as being mindless.[593]

Pur-bu-jok's second illustration is,

> (2) When a Nirgrantha states to a Buddhist: "The subject, a tree, has mind because of dying when the bark is peeled," [dying when the bark is peeled is a nonestablished reason in relation to the latter party].[594]

From the point of view of the Buddhist, according to Lati Rin-po-che, when the tree's bark is peeled the tree dries but does not die. Thus, dying when the bark is peeled is a nonestablished reason in terms of the latter party—the Buddhist—in the proof of a tree as having mind.[595]

And, finally, Pur-bu-jok says:

> (3) When a Sāṃkhya states to an Ayata [Nihilist]: "The subject, sound, is impermanent because of being an object of apprehension by an eye consciousness," [object of apprehension by an eye consciousness is a nonestablished reason in relation to both the former and latter parties].[596]

For neither the Sāṃkhya nor the Nihilist is sound established as an object of apprehension by an eye consciousness.[597]

In short, if the reason is nonestablished for one or the other of the opponents, or for both opponents, then it is a quasi-reason of the nonestablished type. To be established, the reason must be established for both opponents; the former opponent should be someone who has already ascertained the probandum, and the latter party should be someone who is newly developing understanding of the probandum.

10. The Text and Its Study

Pur-bu-jok's text on *Signs and Reasonings* is a manual for introducing Ge-luk-pa beginners to the principles, vocabulary, and concepts of the system of logic. The place of this topic in the Ge-luk-pa curriculum is shown by its title: *The Topic of Signs and Reasonings from the "Great Path of Reasoning" in the Magic Key to the Path of Reasoning, Explanation of the Collected Topics Revealing the Meaning of the Texts on Prime Cognition.* Valid cognition is one of the five main topics that make up the curriculum of the Ge-luk-pa monastic universities (the other four are perfection of wisdom, phenomenology, Madhyamaka philosophy, and monastic discipline).

A path of reasoning is a consciousness that has been trained in reasoned analysis until it can use analysis to realize, first, the meaning of religious texts and, eventually, the true nature of reality. The purpose of reasoning (logic) is to develop valid knowledge, and the study of this text is to lay a foundation for understanding how valid cognition is acquired. What is validity? How is valid knowledge acquired? What can be known? Further, and more specifically, what knowledge can be acquired through reasoning that will help lead one to self-transformation, to spiritual development, even to liberation, omniscience, and buddhahood?

The beginner is not dealing with these profound questions directly, but is laying a foundation of knowledge and experience that will serve as basis for their study. Pur-bu-jok's manual is "unlocking the door"—introducing fundamental vocabulary and concepts and laying the foundation for more difficult studies of valid cognition that will center on the works of Dignāga and Dharmakīrti and Tibetan commentaries on them. The text is a very brief presentation of basic principles of logic. Teachers amplify it with explanations and examples. The students strengthen their grasp of the issues by debating them daily in lively sessions with their classmates. And they begin to apply the principles of reasoning in individual analysis and reflection. The correct (or prepared) opponent is one who is able to benefit from the reasoning; this may be an external opponent (in debate) or oneself (in meditation). In either situation, reasoning is used to bring new understanding of a thesis to a prepared "opponent."

Pur-bu-jok's logic manual is about reasons (signs) and their use. Signs are used in syllogisms, the phrasing of which, though very precise, is simple and easily mastered by the Ge-luk-pa student. The syllogism is a statement of reasoning containing a subject, predicate, and sign. The thesis or probandum, that which is being proved, is made up of the subject and predicate. The negandum, that which is being eliminated, is the subject combined with the opposite of the predicate. For example, in the syllogism, "The subject, sound, is impermanent because of being a product," that which is being proved is that sound is impermanent and that which is being eliminated is that sound is permanent.

Students also learn the nature of the two modes of statement, the copular (the subject, sound, is impermanent because of being a product) and the ontological (the subject, on a smoky pass, fire exists because smoke exists). Then, having understood well the precise terminology and modes of statement in logic, they are ready for the two main lessons of this study: (1) What makes a sign valid—what are the requirements of a correct sign; what is an incorrect sign (a quasi-sign)? and (2) What are the varieties of correct signs?

VALIDITY: THE NATURE OF CORRECT SIGNS

A correct (valid) sign is used to prove something, x, that is hidden to the opponent, and for which he or she needs proof. It may be hidden by nature (something the ordinary person has no experience of) or by circumstance. Smoke is not usually a hidden phenomenon, it is usually ascertainable by direct perception; but in certain circumstances a reason may be needed to prove its presence or absence. On the other hand, impermanence and emptiness are said to be hidden phenomena (not ascertainable initially by direct valid cognition) that must initially be ascertained through reasoning. Tibetan Buddhism holds that direct (nonconceptual) valid cognition of these phenomena is possible and desirable; and the Ge-luk-pa school teaches that an important step on the way toward this direct valid cognition is inferential valid cognition, which arises from intellectual understanding—which must depend on a correct sign.

That is the purpose of Tibetan logic: to acquire understanding of something (a thesis) not previously understood. Something is hidden, and it may be ascertained in reliance on a reason. The manual sets forth very precise requirements for validity of reasons. A correct sign necessarily has three qualities—the three modes: the property of the subject, the forward pervasion, and the counterpervasion.

THE FIRST MODE: THE PROPERTY OF THE SUBJECT

The first mode, the property of the subject, requires that (1) the sign must relate to (be present in) the subject and (2) there must be a "flaw-less subject." In the syllogism, "The subject, sound, is impermanent be-cause of being a product," the sign must be present in the subject; that is, sound must in fact be a product. In the frequently occurring ontolog-ical example, "The subject, on a smoky pass, fire exists because smoke exists," the sign is present in the subject (is the property of the sub-ject). This means primarily that there must in fact be smoke on that pass. Thus, validity depends in part on the *content* of the syllogism (that is, on the phenomena referred to and their relationship). If there is a fault in the content, then the sign cannot be correct. In the syllogism, "The subject, sound, is impermanent because of being a nonproduct," the content is mistaken. Sound is not in fact a nonproduct; thus the reasoning is invalid.

In addition, the subject must be "flawless"—this means someone must be wondering about the thesis. Thus, validity does not depend on content alone; the sample syllogisms are considered to be only poten-tially correct. They become truly correct only when they contribute to *ascertainment* by a correct opponent. A fully prepared opponent is one who is able to benefit from the reasoning, able to achieve new under-standing based on it. In the Tibetan view, therefore, validity is relative. If someone has not already realized that sound is a product, he is not ready for this reasoning; and if he has already ascertained that sound is impermanent he is not a proper recipient of this reasoning, because no proof is needed—for him. In both cases, the property of the subject is not established, the proof is futile, the sign is ineffective and thus is not correct.

In summary, the first mode, the property of the subject, is not es-tablished if the content is invalid or if ascertainment is invalid.

THE SECOND AND THIRD MODES: THE PERVASIONS

The second and third modes (the forward pervasion and the counter-pervasion) require that there be irrefutable and inevitable entailment between the predicate of the probandum and the sign. For the reason-ing to generate understanding of the thesis, the sign must entail the predicate; for example, productness must entail impermanence. How is such entailment to be proved? One might try investigating products to see if any are permanent; but, finding none, could one conclude that none exists? Ge-luk-pa scholars say one could never be sure of having investigated all possible products. Their way to determine entailment without possibility of doubt is to establish the relationship between the predicate and the sign. By thoroughly understanding the relationship between (for example) impermanent and product, one can arrive at a knowledge of entailment so powerful and complete that it is established irrefutably.

The establishment of the pervasions depends on relationship. This relationship is such that if impermanent is eliminated, product is also necessarily eliminated. In the proof of sound as impermanent, that which is being eliminated (the predicate of the negandum) is permanent. Permanent and impermanent are directly contradictory; if one is present the other must be absent. The presence of impermanent is thus strictly eliminated from the permanent. Because product is related with impermanent, whenever impermanent is eliminated, so is product eliminated. Since impermanent cannot exist in the permanent (no instance of impermanent is permanent)—so also product cannot exist in the permanent (there is no instance of product that is permanent). There can be no instance of permanent (that is, no permanent phenomenon) that is a product and no instance of product (that is, no product) that is permanent (in other words, product is empty of permanent and permanent is empty of product).

Beginners do not go into the subtleties of relationship. Pur-bu-jok's text presents the relationship between the predicate and sign in an uncomplicated way: the sign must exist in only the similar class (this is the forward pervasion) and must be just nonexistent in the dissimilar class (this is the counterpervasion). In the proof of sound as impermanent, the similar class is the impermanent and the dissimilar class is the nonimpermanent.

The similar class is the impermanent, and product exists in only the impermanent; this means that whatever is a product is necessarily impermanent (that every instance of product is impermanent). The dissimilar class is the nonimpermanent, and product is just nonexistent in the nonimpermanent; this means that whatever is a product is necessarily not nonimpermanent (that there is no instance of product that is nonimpermanent). Thus "existing in *only* impermanent" means the phenomenon's existence is strictly limited to the impermanent; and "*just* nonexistent in nonimpermanent" means it is not existent at all in the nonimpermanent.

For the second and third modes (the pervasions) to be established, there must be (1) the proper relationship between the predicate and the sign and (2) ascertainment of that relationship by the opponent. Thus, once again, the validity of the reasoning depends both on the content and on ascertainment by the opponent.

An example of a syllogism in which the pervasions are not established is, "The subject, sound, is impermanent because of being a nonproduct." Nonproduct is not related with impermanent; nonproduct is *not* existent in just the impermanent (in fact it is not existent in the impermanent at all); and nonproduct is not just nonexistent in the nonimpermanent (in fact it is existent in the nonimpermanent). The pervasions are not established; and thus nonproduct is an incorrect sign—a quasi-sign—in that proof.

On the other hand, in the potentially correct syllogism, "The subject, sound, is impermanent because of being a product," if the opponent has not ascertained fully the relationship between product and impermanent, then the pervasions are not established. If the opponent still has doubt concerning whether product exists in only the similar class; or has not yet ascertained that permanent is utterly empty of product and that product is utterly empty of permanent; or does not see that there is no possibility of a common locus of permanent and product—then the pervasions are not established and the reasoning is invalid.

Another example of a syllogism in which the pervasions are not established is, "The subject, someone who speaks, is not omniscient because of speaking." An ordinary person has no experience of omniscience and so cannot be sure whether the omniscient speak or not; the relationship between speaking and omniscience cannot be fully ascertained. The reasoning cannot prove that thesis, because there is no way for the opponent to establish the relationship between the sign and the predicate. Thus the sign in that proof cannot bring ascertainment of the thesis and cannot be a correct sign.

In brief, the pervasions cannot be established (1) if the phenomena are not related appropriately or (2) if the opponent does not ascertain the relationship fully. Validity always depends on both *content* and *ascertainment*. Both must be valid; if either is invalid, the reasoning is invalid.

PROOF STATEMENTS

The main features of the three modes are: the presence of the sign in the subject, the relationship between sign and predicate, and the existence of a correct opponent. But how are the three modes and the thesis ascertained? The Ge-luk-pa schools use proof statements to bring understanding of the three modes to a correct opponent. The positive proof statement is said to express the forward pervasion explicitly and the counterpervasion to express it implicitly (while the negative proof statement expresses the counterpervasion explicitly and the forward pervasion implicitly). In "whatever is a product is necessarily impermanent, as is the case with pot; sound also is a product," the statement, "whatever is a product is necessarily impermanent," explicitly expresses the forward pervasion and implicitly expresses the counterpervasion. In "whatever is permanent is necessarily a nonproduct, as is the case with uncompounded space; sound, however, is a product," the statement, "whatever is permanent is necessarily a nonproduct," explicitly expresses the counterpervasion and implicitly expresses the forward pervasion. By means of the proof statements, the opponent ascertains that "whatever is a product is necessarily impermanent" (the forward pervasion) and that "whatever is a product is necessarily not nonimpermanent" (the counterpervasion)—in relation first to the similar example, pot, and next to the sign, product.

At this point it is said that the opponent understands the relationship between product and impermanent in relation to product (any product whatsoever is impermanent) but has not yet directed this ascertainment to sound, the subject of the syllogism; and thus he is still wondering about the thesis. "Sound also is a product" and "sound, however, is a product" explicitly express the property of the subject. A fully prepared opponent is one who, having ascertained the three modes, is ready to ascertain the thesis. All that remains is for him to turn his attention to the subject and ascertain the pervasions in relation to it. Having ascertained the pervasions (that whatever is a product is impermanent and whatever is a product is not non-impermanent) in relation to sound, he has ascertained the thesis: that sound is impermanent.

SUMMARY

The explanation of correct signs (that is, the explanation of the three modes of a correct sign) shows much about the Tibetan system of logic. The concept of validity includes both consciousness and content. In the Ge-luk-pa discussion of validity, there is little mention of formal considerations; the proper form of a syllogism, although important, can be quickly explained and then taken for granted; it does not feature in discussions. This is a point of contrast between Tibetan and Western logic systems. Western presentations of logic to beginners rely heavily on explanation of types of syllogistic statements; the emphasis is on form rather than on content or on what is in the mind of the person who is to make use of the reasoning. In the Tibetan system of logic, the emphasis is on both content and consciousness; that is, on specific phenomena and their nature, and on what the correct opponent ascertains about them. The least possible attention is given to the structure of propositional statements.

In short, the most important factors that must be present in order for the sign in a proof to be valid and thus capable of producing inferential valid cognition in the mind of a prepared opponent are:

- The first mode, property of the subject. This requires that the sign be present in the proper way in the subject. Product is present in sound, in that sound is in fact a product and every instance of sound is a product.
- The second and third modes, the forward pervasion and counterpervasion. These require that the sign be related to the similar class in the strictly defined way: when impermanent is eliminated, product is also necessarily eliminated. This relationship is explained to beginners in terms of the similar and dissimilar classes.

There are only two types of relationship that enable the establishment of the pervasions—only two possible relationships between sign and predicate. These are:

- The relationship of cause and effect. This may also be called the relationship of provenance; the sign is in the relationship of provenance with the predicate (must be the effect of the predicate).
- The relationship of sameness of nature or entity. In this case, the sign is of the same nature as the predicate.

Unless there is one of these relationships between the sign and the predicate, the pervasions will not be established and the sign will not be valid.

DIVISIONS OF CORRECT SIGNS

The academic tone of these lessons in reasoning notwithstanding, Ge-luk-pa scholars consider the study to be immensely practical for someone whose goal is spiritual development. Signs are considered correct because they provide valid knowledge to prepared opponents; it must of course be knowledge they did not have before. What new knowledge will be most helpful to an opponent? Analysis of the Ge-luk-pas' primary way of classifying correct signs will show their answers to that question. There are several ways of dividing or categorizing correct signs, but the one Pur-bu-jok discusses first and at greatest length is recognized as the "main division." (The rest are discussed under "other divisions.") The main division into correct effect, correct nature, and correct nonobservation signs draws attention to the importance of three fundamental concepts: cause and effect, impermanence, and emptiness.

THE MAIN DIVISION

Of the three types in the main division, Ge-luk-pa scholars say that effect signs were set forth to help students understand cause and effect; nature signs, to help them understand impermanence; and nonobservation signs, to help them understand emptiness. The criteria for this threefold division are (1) the type of relationship between the sign and the predicate of the probandum and (2) whether that predicate is a positive or a negative phenomenon.

When the predicate of the probandum is a positive phenomenon, the emphasis is on whether the relationship between sign and predicate is one of provenance or one of sameness of nature (the sign will be called an effect sign or a nature sign, respectively). If the predicate is a negative phenomenon, the sign is a nonobservation sign.

Effect Signs

In proofs using correct effect signs, the predicate is a positive phenomenon, and the sign is necessarily related with the predicate in a relationship of provenance. (The phenomenon used as the *sign* is the *effect* of the phenomenon used as the predicate.) An effect is a sign—of what? What can be inferred from the presence of an effect? This is the emphasis in the Ge-luk-pa presentation of effect signs. From the presence of an effect one can infer: (1) that it necessarily has a cause, (2) that it necessarily has its own actual cause (its direct cause), (3) that it necessarily has its own preceding cause, (4) that it necessarily has its full, complete cause (all the factors necessary for the arising of the effect); and (5) one can infer attributes of the cause.

An example Pur-bu-jok gives is, "The subject, on a smoky pass, fire exists because smoke exists"; smoke is a correct effect sign here. From the presence of an effect, smoke, one can infer (1) that it possesses a cause in general, (2) that it has a direct cause (fire), and (3) that it has an immediately preceding cause (the former moment of smoke). In the case of phenomena that depend on several causes, (4) one can infer the existence of each of the contributing causes; and, in the case of a phenomenon that depends on a complex cause (one possessing numerous attributes), (5) one can infer the attributes of the cause. Examination of these various aspects of the cause-effect relationship makes clear the essential point: that from an effect one can infer a cause.

The deeper purpose of this study is to strengthen one's understanding of the Buddha's Four Noble Truths concerning suffering and the cessation of suffering. The student is to understand that suffering arises from causes—as do spiritual goals. To attain the goals of elimination of suffering, attainment of good qualities, and liberation, one must cultivate the full complete causes of those attainments. Without a cause, the effect cannot occur.

Nature Signs

In proofs using correct nature signs, the predicate is a positive phenomenon, and the predicate and sign are in a relationship of sameness of nature. The text presents nature signs in a way that emphasizes the understanding of impermanence.

Nature signs are divided depending on whether the terms expressing them indicate a causal agent or not. For example, in the syllogism, "The subject, sound, is impermanent because of being arisen from exertion," arisen from exertion is said to express a causal agent (exertion). In "The subject, sound, is impermanent because of being a thing," thing does not express a causal agent. Thing is a correct nature sign in the proof of sound as impermanent (whatever is a thing is necessarily impermanent and is necessarily a caused phenomenon)—but the term "thing" itself does not express an agent.

There are a number of potentially correct signs in the proof that something is impermanent: because of being a thing, because of being a product, because of being an effect, because of being arisen from exertion, etc. All impermanent phenomena are necessarily produced phenomena; and, being produced, they necessarily have causal agents, whether their names explicitly express those agents or not. The criterion for the two categories of nature signs—whether or not they are expressed by terms that indicate their own agent—reflects their main use: to help a student understand the meaning of impermanence.

Nonobservation Signs

In the case of effect and nature signs, the predicate of the probandum is necessarily a positive phenomenon. When the predicate is a negative phenomenon, the sign is a nonobservation sign. The predicate of the *probandum* (that which is being proved) is the *absence* of x. This phrase can be reversed: the predicate of the *negandum* is "the *presence* of x"; and x (what one's mind is focused on) is "the object designated as the predicate of the negandum."

Pur-bu-jok covers these signs in much more detail than the others; he devotes three times as many pages to nonobservation signs alone as he does to effect and nature signs together. In general, nonobservation signs are said to have been set forth in order to prepare students for understanding emptiness. Emptiness is a hidden phenomenon and a negative phenomenon and thus must be ascertained initially through reliance on nonobservation signs.

Nonobservation signs (signs proving a negative phenomenon) are not divided according to the relationship between the predicate and the sign (as are signs proving a positive phenomenon—into effect and nature signs) but according to the nature of x, the object designated as the predicate of the negandum. The division depends on whether x is a supersensory object or not. If the object is supersensory, the sign is called a nonobservation sign of the nonappearing; if it is not supersensory, the sign is a nonobservation sign of the suitable to appear.

Nonobservation Signs of the Nonappearing

Certain phenomena are considered to be supersensory (which is defined as beyond the reach of one's senses, being either too subtle or too far away in space or time). Supersensory objects are beyond the reach of logic in one important respect: ordinary beings cannot ascertain their specific occurrence by either direct or inferential valid cognition. Many such objects are beings: gods, hell-beings, or (the example Pur-bu-jok uses) flesh-eaters, a type of demon. In addition, the deepest spiritual attainments of beings (omniscience, *bodhicitta*, etc.) are considered to be—in their specific occurrence—supersensory objects (although they are not so in general).

Working on nonobservation signs of the nonappearing shows the student how little can be known about supersensory objects. These are phenomena regarding which the opponent can have no specific knowledge, either by inference or by direct perception. The point made by this study is that nonobservation by valid cognition of a supersensory object (whether a being or a spiritual quality) does not prove its nonexistence. The nonexistence of valid cognition of x proves only the absence of whatever is related with that cognition—it proves nothing about x itself.

Pur-bu-jok's example is, "With respect to the subject, here in this place in front, there does not exist a factually concordant subsequent cognition—ascertaining a flesh-eater—in the continuum of a person for whom a flesh-eater is a supersensory object because of the nonexistence of a prime cognition—observing a flesh-eater—in the continuum of a person for whom a flesh-eater is a supersensory object." The nonobservation by prime (that is, valid) cognition of flesh-eater does not prove the nonexistence *of the flesh-eater*; what it *does* prove is the nonexistence of the *effect* of such a prime cognition. (The effect of a prime cognition is a factually concordant subsequent cognition.) The absence of the cause proves the absence of the effect: just as, for example, there does not exist a memory of the taste of mangos in someone who has never eaten a mango.

All Pur-bu-jok's examples of nonobservation of the nonappearing involve one supersensory object, a flesh-eater, but he makes it clear that the study of this type of sign has a deeper purpose. Just as nonobservation by valid cognition does not prove the nonexistence of a particular supersensory being, so the nonobservation by ordinary beings of liberation or omniscience or any other spiritual quality in another being does not prove that those qualities are not there.

The emphasis on this topic shows how important it is that students understand how little one can know about certain phenomena, including the deepest spiritual qualities of others. Pur-bu-jok quotes from a sūtra, "A person cannot estimate the measure of [another] person. [If one does so,] one will degenerate," and comments, "By the mere fact of their not appearing to oneself, it is not reasonable to say that another does not have such-and-such good qualities."[598]

Study of this topic is intended to help the student understand that we as ordinary beings are easily mistaken in our judgments of other beings; their deepest spiritual attainments are necessarily beyond one's ken, and therefore it is wiser to reserve judgments about their qualities. One gradually becomes less likely to jump to invalid conclusions about others and—more fundamentally—gradually abandons the mistaken idea that what one does not perceive does not exist.

Nonobservation Signs of the Suitable to Appear

A nonobservation sign is eliminating (proving the absence of) something. In this second type of nonobservation sign, the object (x) designated as the predicate of the negandum is not a supersensory object but one that would generally be apprehendable by the opponent. The Ge-luk-pa analysis of nonobservation of the suitable to appear presents the concepts of (1) relatedness and (2) contradiction in some detail. One of Pur-bu-jok's examples is, "The subject, on a lake at night, smoke does not exist because fire does not exist." Smoke, the object designated as the predicate of the negandum, is normally accessible to an opponent's valid cognition—but it is not accessible to direct perception in the specified context. Being unable to see an object that is usually visible, one may be uncertain whether it is present or not. In that case, its absence can be logically established by (1) the absence (nonobservation) of something else (fire—to which the object, smoke, is *related*) that *is* suitable to appear in that context.

The predicate (the absence of the object) can also be established by (2) the presence of something *contradictory* with the object. One of Pur-bu-jok's examples is, "With respect to the subject, in a place in the east covered by strongly billowing smoke, continuous goose bumps that are an effect of cold do not exist, because of being a place covered by strongly billowing smoke." Smoke is related with fire; fire is contradictory with cold and with whatever is related with cold; and whatever is related with fire is contradictory with cold as well as with whatever is related with cold. Therefore smoke (which is related with fire, being its effect) is contradictory with cold and also is contradictory with whatever is related with cold, such as goose bumps.

Pur-bu-jok's discussion of nonobservation signs of the suitable to appear is the longest section in the text, showing in detail what can be known about phenomena and how it can be known. He presents a number of syllogisms involving the three different kinds of impermanent phenomena: forms, consciousnesses, and nonassociated compositional factors. An example proving the absence of x by the presence of something contradictory to x is: "The subject, a noninterrupted path of a Hearer path of meditation that is an actual antidote to the conception of a self of persons, does not abide harmlessly together with the conception of a self of persons because of being an actual antidote to the conception of a self of persons." Here, two consciousnesses are directly contradictory: if one is present, the other must be absent. "The conception of a self of persons" refers to a conception of the inherent existence of a person.[a] The consciousness that is directly contradictory with that (and therefore a direct antidote) is a wisdom consciousness realizing the emptiness of inherent existence of a person. If such a wisdom is present, the conception of inherent existence is necessarily absent.

---

[a] This discussion of the conception of a self of persons reflects the Prāsaṅgika-Madhyamaka presentation of selflessness.

Nonobservation signs in general and nonobservation signs of the suitable to appear in particular are presented to help the student understand the reasons proving emptiness. The true nature of reality—its emptiness of inherent (or true) existence—is something that can be ascertained by valid cognition through the use of reasoning (and thus depending on correct signs). The text does not explicitly treat the difficult topic of emptiness, and Pur-bu-jok's examples are simple, not profound. However, he does point to the deeper purpose of nonobservation signs when he writes:

> In the Madhyamaka system, all correct signs proving nontrue existence are [signs that are an] observation of a contradictory object in the proof of that; they are mainly nonobservation signs of the suitable to appear....[For example,] one can state, "The subject, a sprout, is empty of true existence because of being a dependent-arising." The sign in that is a correct sign that is an observation of a contradictory object.[599]

Beyond this, his introductory manual makes little mention of emptiness and the reasonings proving emptiness. The beginner will hardly be ready to apply the principles of reasoning to this profound purpose—but that is the ultimate aim of this study.

OTHER DIVISIONS

Besides the main division into effect, nature, and nonobservation signs, Pur-bu-jok discusses five other divisions, which focus attention on other facets of correct signs. Of these, the first three depend on the type of phenomenon being proved:

- Is the predicate of the probandum a positive phenomenon or a negative phenomenon?
- Is the probandum a very hidden phenomenon, a slightly hidden phenomenon, or a terminological suitability?
- Is the explicit predicate of the probandum a definition or a definiendum?

The fourth division concerns the relationship between the sign and the predicate (whether the sign pervades the predicate or not), and the fifth concerns the opponent—whether the reasoning is being used by one person in solitary analysis or by two persons in debate.

It was noted in the discussion of what constitutes validity that Pur-bu-jok's manual focuses on two things: content (the phenomena involved and their relationship) and consciousness (the ascertainment by a correct opponent). The same twofold concern can be observed in the ways of dividing correct signs. The main division and four of the five others are concerned with the type of phenomenon being proved and the relationship between the sign and the predicate. The fifth, the division by way of the opponent, focuses on the use to which the reasoning is being put.

Division by Way of the Predicate of the Probandum

Is the predicate a positive or a negative phenomenon? This criterion is already present in the main division of correct signs; positing it as a separate criterion is a way of emphasizing the fact that in any correct proof, the predicate of the probandum is necessarily one or the other. For a sign to be valid, it must be capable of producing inferential valid cognition in the mind of an opponent concerning the thesis that is being proved. That which is ascertainable by inferential valid cognition is necessarily an existent (a phenomenon); and phenomena may be divided into two types, positive and negative.

This "other" division is subsumed within the main division, but it does not duplicate it. In the main division, the positive/negative criterion is combined with the criterion of the relationship between the sign and predicate.

Division by Way of the Probandum

A correct sign must be capable of producing inferential valid cognition of the probandum in the consciousness of the opponent. That which is ascertained by inferential valid cognition is necessarily a hidden phenomenon, one that the opponent cannot initially ascertain by direct perception. (If the predicate of the probandum is not a hidden phenomenon, there is no need of proof for the opponent in question.) Objects of comprehension of inferential valid cognition are said to be either very hidden phenomena or slightly hidden phenomena, but within slightly hidden phenomena a distinction is made between those that are terminological suitabilities and those that are not—giving us three types of signs in this division. These can be ascertained in three ways:

- A slightly hidden phenomenon through a correct sign by the power of the fact.
- A terminological suitability through a correct sign of renown.
- A very hidden phenomenon through a correct sign of belief.

Study of this division "by way of the probandum" leads the student to consider three types of cognition: inferential valid cognition by the power of the fact, inferential valid cognition of renown, and inferential valid cognition of belief. Each type has a separate object of comprehension; the first ascertains a slightly hidden phenomenon, the second a terminological suitability, and the third a very hidden phenomenon. Generation of any of these types of inference depends on a correct sign.

This division of correct signs is presented in a way that brings home to the student the fact that hidden phenomena are of different types, differently ascertained. The first step is to analyze the two types of slightly hidden phenomena.

Slightly Hidden Phenomena

Correct Sign by the Power of the Fact

In the syllogism, "The subject, sound, is impermanent because of being a product," product is a sign proving a hidden phenomenon (sound's impermanence). Impermanence is not something attributed to sound by convention, as a name might be. Sound is by its very nature impermanent; impermanence is a quality of sound. The quality of impermanence is found to be there by the power of the thing itself, or "by the power of the fact."

Correct Sign of Renown

In contrast, the name "sound" (or the word for any phenomenon in any language) is arbitrary; it does not inhere in the object. An example might be: "The subject, a fragrant flower with many petals, is suitable to be expressed by the term 'rose' because of existing among objects of thought." The *suitability* of calling a certain flower by a certain name is proved though a "sign of renown."

Such terminological suitabilities (if they need proof at all) are slightly hidden phenomena. What is hidden for one person may not be hidden for another. It can be proved by valid cognition "by the power of renown" that it is suitable to call x anything at all. The introductory logic manuals do not dwell on the relationship between terms and the phenomena they refer to, but the topic is introduced here, if only lightly.

Studying these two types of slightly hidden phenomena, the student learns to differentiate between phenomena that are established (proved) through realizing something fundamental about their very

nature and phenomena that are proved through renown. The impermanence of sound is one example of slightly hidden phenomena ascertainable by reasoning. Another is the fact that fire exists on a smoky
mountain pass. The fire is hidden in that context—is not ascertainable
by direct perception. If the opponent is wondering about it, a correct
sign by the power of the fact can prove that the fire is there: "The subject, on a smoky pass, fire exists because smoke exists."

Very Hidden Phenomena

Correct Sign of Belief

Very hidden phenomena are not ascertained in the same way as
slightly hidden phenomena and terminological suitabilities, but
through correct signs of belief. This does not mean that one can acquire
valid knowledge concerning very hidden phenomena by simply accepting what one hears from teachers and reads in scriptures—through
mere worldly renown; *that* only works with terminological suitabilities.
One must investigate these phenomena carefully and develop one's
own inferential valid cognition of belief in regard to them.

An example of very hidden phenomena is the specific cause-and-
effect of actions. Buddhist scripture teaches that specific results arise
from specific actions: through being generous one acquires good resources (wealth), and through engaging in ethics one achieves a good
rebirth. These teachings on specific causes and effects of actions are
considered to be very hidden phenomena. Students cannot confirm
their truth either through direct perception or through inference by
the power of the fact. They must rely on inferential valid cognition of
belief, which is produced through a correct sign of belief.

Practically speaking, this involves studying all of a scripture's
teachings and ascertaining that they are accurate when they touch on
manifest phenomena (ascertainable by direct perception) and on
slightly hidden phenomena (impermanence and emptiness, for example—ascertainable by inferential valid cognition by the power of the
fact). Then, if there is no internal contradiction when the scripture
touches on very hidden phenomena, one can develop inferential valid
cognition of belief in regard to them.

Division by Way of the Mode of Proof

This division focuses on the explicit predicate of the probandum—
whether it is a definition, a definiendum, or both. Not every correct

sign is included in this division, for not every valid reasoning will contain a predicate that is either a definition or a definiendum. Study of this way of dividing signs introduces beginners to the relationship between definition and definiendum and how they are ascertained. Detailed study of these issues is beyond the scope of beginners in logic, but they are introduced.

Ge-luk-pa scholars apparently agree that ascertainment of a definition must precede ascertainment of its definiendum. In other words, a specific order of ascertainment is recognized: knowing the name of an object without knowing the meaning is useless and cannot be called knowledge at all. One cannot be said to have understood "thing," for example, until one has ascertained its definition ("that which is able to perform a function") and has attached that meaning to the definiendum "thing." Thus, ascertainment of the meaning is said to necessarily precede ascertainment of the object defined. To understand the expression "impermanent" (the definiendum), one must first understand its meaning, "momentary" (the definition). Furthermore, realization of "impermanent" must be accompanied by realization of "momentary," but realization of "momentary" *need not* be accompanied by realization of "impermanent."

Pur-bu-jok describes three types of correct signs, when divided by way of the mode of proof, though some Ge-luk-pa scholars disagree with the third type.[a]

Correct Signs Proving Only a Definition

In "The subject, sound, is momentary because of being a product," the sign is proving "momentary," the explicit predicate of the probandum. As the definition of impermanent, momentary must be ascertained first. When momentary is newly ascertained by inferential valid cognition by means of a correct sign, product, the opponent has not yet ascertained impermanent. With this opponent, therefore, product is a correct sign proving only one phenomenon, momentary. That which is being proved explicitly for this opponent is a definition.

Correct Signs Proving Only a Definiendum

In "The subject, sound, is impermanent because of being momentary,"

[a] Pur-bu-jok posits five types, discussed in chapter eight. According to some Ge-luk-pa scholars, these are more clearly understandable if condensed into three; I have done that here for the sake of clarity

376 Essentials of Reasoning

the sign (momentary) is being used as proof of sound's impermanence. A correct opponent in this case is someone who, having ascertained that sound is momentary, is wondering whether it is impermanent. With such an opponent, momentary is a correct sign proving only a definiendum.

Correct Signs Proving Both

In Pur-bu-jok's view, when a definiendum is ascertained, its definition is also explicitly ascertained at the same time. Thus, in "The subject, sound, is impermanent because of being a product," if the opponent has not already ascertained sound's momentariness, then the sign, product, is at the same time proving *both* the impermanence and the momentariness of sound.

If momentary has already been ascertained, then this proof is newly proving only impermanent (because there is no need to prove momentary; and the explicit predicate in any proof is that which is being explicitly proved newly to the opponent). But an opponent who has *not* already ascertained momentary will need to ascertain both momentary and impermanent in reliance on this proof. Thus, according to Pur-bu-jok, for that opponent, the explicit predicate includes both a definition and a definiendum (both are being ascertained newly; both need to be proved; there is no way for the opponent to ascertain impermanent without also ascertaining momentary).

Not all Ge-luk-pa scholars agree with this, but Pur-bu-jok holds that in this proof and for this opponent there are two explicit predicates of the probandum; the sign is proving *both* a definiendum and a definition, because when the expression "impermanent" is understood, the meaning ("momentary") is also understood.

Thus, Pur-bu-jok's division of correct signs by way of the probandum is introducing students to such questions as: Once one has ascertained the meaning of impermanent—then, when "momentary" appears to one's mind, does "impermanent" automatically appear at the same time?

Division by Way of the Sign's Relationship to the Similar Class

From this point of view, there are two types of correct signs, those that pervade the similar class and those that do not. This analysis highlights certain aspects of the relationship between the sign and the predicate in a valid proof. (A valid proof is one in which the three modes have been established.) In order for the pervasions to be established, the sign and the predicate must be in a very specific relationship, which is discussed, in the study of *Signs and Reasonings*, in terms of the relationship between the sign and the similar and dissimilar classes. The sign must be existent in *only* the similar class and *just* nonexistent in the dissimilar class.

This means that the sign is pervaded by the similar class. For example, in "The subject, sound, is impermanent because of being a product," the sign (product) is necessarily pervaded by the similar class (impermanent). If there were any instances of the sign (that is, any products) that were *not* impermanent, then product would not be pervaded by impermanent and would not be a correct sign in that proof. In a correct proof, the similar class (the predicate) necessarily pervades the sign, while the sign may or *may not* pervade the similar class.

If the sign pervades the predicate, the sign and the similar class are categories of the same size; they are mutually inclusive. In the example syllogism, impermanent and product are mutually pervasive; whatever is a product is necessarily impermanent and whatever is impermanent is necessarily a product.

But the similar class and the sign in a correct proof need not be mutually inclusive; the sign does not always pervade the similar class. The sign must be completely contained within the similar class, but the similar class may be a broader category than the sign. A syllogism in which this is the case is, "The subject, the sound of a conch, is impermanent because of being arisen from [a person's] exertion." Arisen from exertion is pervaded by impermanent, but impermanent is not pervaded by arisen from exertion. The similar class is a broader category than the sign. Whatever is arisen from exertion is necessarily impermanent, but whatever is impermanent is not necessarily arisen from a person's exertion: a rock, lightning, a mountain—these are impermanent but not arisen from exertion. In this case, the sign is said to "relate to the similar class in two ways," because whatever is impermanent (1) is not necessarily arisen from exertion and (2) is not necessarily not arisen from exertion.

Study of this division of signs draws one's attention to the fact that, while the sign must exist in the similar class (and must not exist at all in the dissimilar class), the sign need not exist in all members of the similar class in order to function as a correct sign. Pervasion need not go both ways for a sign to be valid; to think so would be to eliminate a great many correct signs. This study thus enhances the students' awareness that relationships are something to be examined thorough-ly.

Division by Way of the Opponent

Pur-bu-jok's final "other division" depends on whether the reasoning is being employed to bring understanding to another person (that is, in the context of debate) or to bring understanding to oneself (that is, in the context of solitary analysis or meditation). Whether a person is us-ing a sign for the benefit of another or for his or her own benefit, it is a correct sign (the reasoning is valid) if it is able to produce new under-standing of the thesis in the mind of the "opponent."

The term "opponent" (*rgol ba*), used to describe the person for whom a reasoning is employed, implies an exchange between two people, but it is important to note that the principles of logic are not limited to use in the context of debate. A very important purpose of reasoning is to overcome mistaken ideas in one's own mind through the use of correct signs. In either case, debate or meditation, there must be a correct opponent, a prepared opponent who can benefit from the reasoning: someone for whom the sign will serve as proof of the thesis.

Summation

Beginners learn the principles of logic by studying this and other texts, listening to their teachers, thinking, and debating; these are their tools. The lively sessions of challenge and response in the debate courtyard provide an intense reciprocal reinforcement of the study of *Signs and Reasonings*, as they look for complications and contradictions. Both the curriculum and the activities of the monastic community are geared to helping the students develop a strong path of reasoning; the deepest purpose is that they shall know for themselves how to cultivate spiri-tual paths.

It is fundamental to Ge-luk-pa thought that true knowledge is prac-tical, useful, and ultimately transforming and liberating. Such know-ledge is hidden—far from obvious—but it can be attained through cor-rect reasoning. In his presentation, Pur-bu-jok emphasizes:

- The importance of understanding the concepts of cause and effect, impermanence, and emptiness. To achieve the good qualities of kindness, compassion, *bodhicitta*, and omniscience, one must culti-vate their causes; to eliminate that which is invalid and harmful (for example, mistaken conceptions), one must cultivate their anti-dotes.

- The importance of understanding that one's perception and judgment of others can easily be mistaken. Here, logic strengthens the students' efforts to develop *bodhicitta*; how can this deep and spontaneous compassionate concern for all beings be achieved if one is jumping to conclusions about people on the basis of one's limited perceptions?

Thus logic is an important tool, a part of the spiritual path, leading ultimately to complete self-transformation. Pur-bu-jok writes:

> In dependence on nonperverse realization—by way of reasons—of what to adopt and what to discard and practicing such, one easily enters the path progressing to liberation and omniscience.[600]

PART TWO: *Annotated Translation*

Pur-bu-jok Jam-pa-gya-tso's
THE TOPIC OF SIGNS AND REASONINGS FROM THE "GREAT PATH OF REASONING"
in the *Magic Key to the Path of Reasoning,*
Explanation of the Collected Topics
Revealing the Meaning of the Texts on Prime Cognition

Commentary added to facilitate understanding is either indented or put in square brackets interpolated into the text.

DM = Den-ma Lo-chö Rin-po-che
GL = Ge-shay Ge-dün-lo-drö
LR = Lati Rin-po-che

1. Signs

Homage to the Lama and the Protector Mañjughoṣa.

Here I will explain the presentation of *Signs and Reasonings* from within the Great Path of Reasoning, in the *Magic Key to the Path of Reasoning, Explanation of the Collected Topics* opening the door to reasoning.

Dignāga's *Compilation of Prime Cognition* says:

> Homage to the one
> Who has become valid,
> Who has assumed the task of helping transmigrators,
> The Teacher, Sugata and Protector.

This passage indicates that our teacher is a reliable teacher, superior to those who are not Buddhists. The words "has assumed the task of helping transmigrators" indicate that [a Buddha] comes into being in dependence on his causes, the fulfillment of contemplation and application.

What qualities does our teacher possess? The expression "Sugata and Protector" indicates that he is an unsurpassed protector because of possessing both the fulfillment of abandonment for one's own welfare and the fulfillment of realization for others' welfare. This is because Dharmakīrti's *Commentary on (Dignāga's) Compilation of Prime Cognition* says, "He has cleared away the net of conceptuality." Thus, through the eight categories of logic our teacher is established as valid, his verbal and cognitive teachings as pure, the valid cognitions set forth in his scriptures—the two, direct perceptions and inferential consciousnesses—as the pure valid cognitions to be entered into [by yogis seeking liberation], and the causes—the fulfillment of contemplation and application—as the pure paths to be practiced.

> The eight categories of logic are: correct direct perceptions and quasi-direct perceptions, correct inferential cognitions and quasi-inferential cognitions, correct proof statements and quasi-proof statements, correct refutations and quasi-refutations.[GL]

Therefore, [a wise person] who maintains the teaching of the Conqueror through skill in the presentation of proof and refutation is the foremost of those who maintain it. This is because Sa-kya Paṇḍita's (*sa skya paṇḍita*) *Treasury of Reasoning* says:

> A wise person, who knows the system
> Of reasoning consisting of proof

And refutation, is a maintainer
Of the teaching of the perfect Buddha.

Hence, here with respect to explaining the presentation of proof and refutation, Dharmakīrti says, "The property of the subject is the sign that pervades the predicate of the probandum."

The explanation of reasonings as set forth in this passage has three parts: definitions of signs, divisions of signs, and explanation of the faults and good qualities of the three—sign, example, and position (*phyogs, pakṣa*).

DEFINITIONS OF SIGNS

The definition of a sign is:

that which is set as a sign.

The definition of a sign in the proof of something is:

that which is set as a sign in the proof of that [that is, in the proof of any given probandum].

Whatever is either an existent or a nonexistent is necessarily a sign in the proof of something because whatever is either an existent or a nonexistent is necessarily set as a sign in the proof of that. This is because horn of a rabbit is set as the sign in "such-and-such a subject is impermanent because of being the horn of a rabbit."

The definition of a sign in the proof of sound as impermanent is:

that which is set as a sign in the proof of sound as impermanent.

The definition of a sign in the proof of sound as impermanent by the sign, product, is:

that which is set as a sign in the proof of sound as impermanent by the sign, product.

The mode of application is similar with respect to other [proofs]. [For example, the definition of a sign in the proof of fire as existing on a smoky pass is: that which is set as a sign in the proof of fire as existing on a smoky pass; the definition of a sign in the proof of fire as existing on a smoky pass by the sign, smoke, is: that which is set as a sign in the proof of fire as existing on a smoky pass by the sign, smoke.]

2. Bases of Relation of Correct Signs

When signs are divided, there are two types: correct signs and their opposites, quasi-signs. The presentation of correct signs has three parts: bases of relation, definitions, and divisions, the first of which has two parts: (1) the basis of relation of the property of the subject, that is, the subject [about which something is] sought to be known [hereafter referred to as the subject sought to be known], and (2) the basis of relation of the pervasion, that is, the similar and dissimilar classes.

BASIS OF RELATION OF THE PROPERTY OF THE SUBJECT

This section has three parts: definition of a subject sought to be known, an illustration, and ancillarily, identification of the predicate of the probandum.

DEFINITION OF A SUBJECT SOUGHT TO BE KNOWN

The definition of something's being a flawless subject sought to be known in the proof of sound as impermanent by the sign, product, is:

> that observed as a common locus of (1) being held as a basis of debate in the proof of sound as impermanent by the sign, product, and of (2) there existing a person who, having ascertained that it [sound] is a product, is engaged in wanting to know whether or not it is impermanent.

ILLUSTRATION OF A SUBJECT SOUGHT TO BE KNOWN

Sound is the subject sought to be known in the proof of sound as impermanent by the sign, product. Whatever is the subject sought to be known in the proof of sound as impermanent by the sign, product, is necessarily one with sound.

> In the proof of sound as impermanent, the following are equivalent:
> (1) the subject sought to be known (*shes 'dod chos can*)
> (2) the flawless subject sought to be known (*shes 'dod chos can skyon med*)
> (3) the basis of debate (*rtsod gzhi*)
> (4) the basis of inference (*dpag gzhi*).GL

IDENTIFICATION OF THE PREDICATE OF THE PROBANDUM

The definition of a predicate of the probandum is:

> that which is held as the predicate of the probandum.

Whatever is selfless is necessarily a predicate of the probandum because whatever is selfless is necessarily the predicate of the probandum in the proof of sound as it. [For example, horn of a rabbit is necessarily the predicate of the probandum in the proof of sound as the horn of a rabbit.] Therefore, whatever is a predicate of a probandum (*sādhyadharma*) is not necessarily a phenomenon (*dharma*). [Anything can be stated as a predicate of a probandum. In the proof of sound as impermanent, impermanent is the predicate of the probandum and is also a phenomenon (because it exists). In the proof of sound as the horn of a rabbit, horn of a rabbit is the predicate of the probandum but is not a phenomenon (because it does not exist).]

The definition of the predicate of the probandum in the proof of sound as impermanent is:

> that held as the predicate of the probandum in the proof of sound as impermanent.

If the predicates of the probandum in the proof of sound as impermanent are divided, they are of two types: the explicit and implicit predicates of the probandum in the proof of sound as impermanent.

The definition of the explicit predicate of the probandum in the proof of sound as impermanent is:

> that held as the explicit predicate of the probandum in the proof of sound as impermanent.

The impermanent is an illustration [of an explicit predicate of the probandum, as in "sound is impermanent because of being a product"].

The definition of the implicit predicate of the probandum in the proof of sound as impermanent is:

> that held as the implicit predicate of the probandum in the proof of sound as impermanent.

Opposite from not being impermanent is an illustration [of an implicit predicate of the probandum, as in "sound is impermanent because of being a product." Here, it is implicitly understood that sound is opposite from not being impermanent.]

Furthermore, [in the syllogism, "The subject, sound, is impermanent because of being a product," two explicit and two implicit predicates of the probandum are posited]. The two, impermanent and [its definition] momentary, are each the explicit predicate of the probandum in the proof of sound as impermanent by the sign, product. The two, opposite from not being impermanent and opposite from not being momentary, are each the implicit predicate of the probandum in the proof of sound as impermanent by the sign, product.

In the statement, "The subject, sound, is impermanent because of being a product,"

(1) The basis of debate in the proof of that is: sound.
(2) The predicate of the probandum in the proof of that is: the impermanent.
(3) The probandum [that which is to be proved] is: that sound is impermanent.
(4) The correct sign is: product.
(5) The predicate of the negandum is: the permanent.
(6) The negandum [that which is to be negated] in the proof of that is: that sound is permanent.

Extend this to other [examples].

Proofs

The subject, impermanent, is the explicit predicate of the probandum in the proof of sound as impermanent because of being that which is held as the explicit predicate of the probandum in the proof of sound as impermanent.

The subject, momentary, is not the explicit predicate of the probandum in the proof of sound as impermanent because of being a correct sign in that proof.

> Momentary is an explicit predicate of the probandum in the proof of sound as impermanent by the sign, product, but is not such in the proof of sound as impermanent. If the sign (for example, product) is not specified, then because momentary is a correct sign in the proof of sound as impermanent, it cannot also be the predicate of the probandum in that proof.
>
> Whether something is a correct sign or not in a certain proof depends on the specific opponent involved. For someone who has not realized that sound is a momentary, momentary is not a correct sign in the proof of sound as impermanent. For someone who has realized that sound is a momentary, momentary is a correct sign in that proof.DM

BASIS OF RELATION OF THE PERVASION, THAT IS, THE SIMILAR AND
DISSIMILAR CLASSES

This section has two parts: the actual explanation and, ancillarily, the
explanation of similar and dissimilar examples.

THE ACTUAL EXPLANATION OF THE BASIS OF RELATION OF THE
PERVASION

This section has four parts: definitions, divisions, enumeration of the
four possibilities between the etymology and the actual usage, and
analysis of whether or not similar and dissimilar classes are explicitly
contradictory.

Definition of Similar Class

The definition of the similar class in the proof of sound as impermanent
is:

> that which is not empty of impermanence, in accordance with
> the mode of proof, in the proof of sound as impermanent.
>> There are two modes of proof, an "is" (that is, copular) proof
>> and an "exists" (that is, ontological) proof. The similar class
>> must accord with whatever mode of proof is present in a syllog-
>> ism; for example, in the syllogism, "The subject, sound, *is* im-
>> permanent because of being a product," the mode of proof is an
>> "is" proof. An "exists" proof would be, "The subject, sound, *ex-
>> ists* among the impermanent because of being a product."
>> In the case of an "is" proof, all phenomena that are imper-
>> manent accord with the mode of proof and are thus the similar
>> class [that is, members of the similar class].[a]
>> In the case of the "exists" proof, however, all phenomena
>> that exist among the impermanent comprise the similar class.
>> Thus, the qualification "in accordance with the mode of proof"
>> is made in order to eliminate from the similar class those phe-
>> nomena that exist among the impermanent but are not them-
>> selves impermanent; for example, object of knowledge.[GL]

---

[a] Pur-bu-jok makes it clear that "similar class" (*mthun phyogs*) includes two categories
of phenomena: (1) those that *are* the similar class (*mthun phyogs*) and (2) those that *exist*
in the similar class (*mthun phyogs la yod pa*). In order to make this distinction, I refer to
the first category, those that are the similar class, as "members of the similar class."

Impermanent and similar class in the proof of sound as impermanent are mutually inclusive.

> If someone says, "It follows that the subject, sound, is not [a member of] the similar class in the proof of sound as impermanent because of being the basis of debate in that proof," the response is, "Although the reason is true, it does not entail that sound is not a member of the similar class in that proof."
>
> In the proof of sound as impermanent, there are three possibilities between [a] being the basis of debate and [b] being a member of the similar class:
> (1) Sound is both the basis of debate and a member of the similar class in that proof.
> (2) Whatever is the basis of debate in that proof is necessarily a member of the similar class, but whatever is a member of the similar class in that proof is not necessarily the basis of debate. For instance, a pot.
> (3) Permanent is neither the basis of debate nor a member of the similar class in that proof.
>
> In the proof of sound as impermanent, there are four possibilities between [a] being a correct sign and [b] being a member of the similar class:
> (1) Product is both a correct sign and a member of the similar class in that proof.
> (2) Sound is a member of the similar class, but not a correct sign.
> (3) Particularity of product is a correct sign, but not a member of the similar class. (Particularity of product exists in the similar class because whatever is a particularity of product is necessarily impermanent. However, particularity of product (*byas pa'i bye brag*) itself is permanent and thus not a member of the similar class.)
> (4) Uncompounded space is neither a member of the similar class nor a correct sign.[GL]

Definition of Dissimilar Class

The definition of dissimilar class in the proof of sound as impermanent is:

> that which is empty of impermanence in accordance with the mode of proof in the proof of sound as impermanent. [For example, nonproduct, particularity of thing, object of knowledge,

the permanent, etc.]

The nonimpermanent and dissimilar class in the proof of sound as impermanent are mutually inclusive.

Divisions of Dissimilar Classes

There are three types of dissimilar classes:

(1) [A member of] the dissimilar class that is a nonexistent in the proof of sound as impermanent. [For instance,] horn of a rabbit.
(2) [A member of] the dissimilar class that is other [than the impermanent] in the proof of sound as impermanent. [For instance,] object of knowledge.
(3) [A member of] the dissimilar class that is contradictory [with the impermanent] in the proof of sound as impermanent. [For instance,] the permanent.

Enumeration of the Four Possibilities between the Etymology and Actual Usage

First Question: Does whatever is [a member of] the similar class in the proof of something necessarily exist in accordance with the etymological explanation of similar class in the proof of that?

Answer: No. There are three possibilities between being [a member of] the similar class in the proof of something and existing in accordance with the etymological explanation of similar class in the proof of that.

> It is correct to say that there exist three possibilities between being a member of the similar class in the proof of something and existing in accordance with the etymological explanation of similar class in the proof of that because this is a general statement, without reference to any specific proof.
>
> When one does consider a specific proof, however, there are not three possibilities. For example, there are not three possibilities between being a member of the similar class and existing in accordance with the etymological explanation of similar class in the proof of sound as impermanent.
>
> There are three possibilities only from the point of view of considering two proofs: both the proof of sound as impermanent and the proof of sound as permanent. Thus, in the following enumeration of the three possibilities, the first applies to

the proof of sound as permanent and the other two apply to the proof of sound as impermanent.ᴳᴸ

(1) The possibility of being [a member of] the similar class in the proof of something but not existing in accordance with the etymological explanation of similar class in the proof of that [can be posited. For example,] uncompounded space is [a member of] the similar class in the proof of sound as permanent but does not exist in accordance with the etymological explanation of similar class in the proof of sound as permanent.

The proof of this example is: The subject, uncompounded space, is [a member of] the similar class in the proof of sound as permanent because of being permanent. It does not exist in accordance with the etymological explanation of similar class in the proof of sound as permanent because uncompounded space and sound are not qualitatively similar in being permanent. [This is because uncompounded space is permanent and sound is impermanent.]

(2) The possibility of both being [a member of] the similar class in the proof of something and existing in accordance with the etymological explanation of similar class in the proof of that [can be posited. For example,] pot both is [a member of] the similar class in the proof of sound as impermanent and exists in accordance with the etymological explanation of similar class in the proof of sound as impermanent.

The proof of this example is: The subject, pot, is [a member of] the similar class in the proof of sound as impermanent because of being impermanent. The subject, pot, exists in accordance with the etymological explanation of similar class in the proof of sound as impermanent because the two, pot and sound, are qualitatively similar in being impermanent. This is because it [pot] is impermanent and sound is impermanent.

(3) The possibility of neither being [a member of] the similar class in the proof of something nor existing in accordance with the etymological explanation of similar class in the proof of that [can be posited. For example,] uncompounded space neither is [a member of] the similar class in the proof of sound as impermanent nor exists in accordance with the etymological explanation of similar class in the proof of sound as impermanent.

The proof of this example is: The subject, uncompounded space, is not [a member of] the similar class in the proof of sound as impermanent because of not being impermanent. The subject, uncompounded space, does not exist in accordance with the etymological explanation of similar class in the proof of sound as impermanent because the two, it [uncompounded space] and sound, are not qualitatively similar in being impermanent. This is because it [uncompounded space] is permanent and sound is impermanent.

[*Second Question:* Can something exist in accordance with the etymological explanation of similar class in the proof of something, but not be a member of the similar class in the proof of that?

Answer: No.] A possibility of existing in accordance with the etymological explanation of similar class in the proof of something, but not being [a member of] the similar class in the proof of that does not exist. This is because whatever exists in accordance with the etymological explanation of similar class in the proof of something must be [a member of] the similar class in the proof of that.

[*Third Question:* If something is the class in the expression "similar class in the proof of something," is it necessarily the predicate of the probandum in the proof of that?

Answer: No.] Whatever is the class in the expression "similar class in the proof of something" is not necessarily the predicate of the probandum in the proof of that. This is because the two, (a) class in "similar class [or member of the similar class] in the proof of sound as impermanent" and (b) class in "exists in the similar class in the proof of sound as impermanent," must be posited as dissimilar. The proof of this pervasion is easy.

> The Tibetan, *mthun phyogs la yod pa*, means "exists in the similar class." That which exists in the similar class intersects the similar class in various ways without necessarily being found only in the similar class. In other words, that which exists in the similar class is not necessarily a member of the similar class.
>
> Class in "exists in the similar class in the proof of sound as impermanent" refers to the predicate of the probandum, impermanent itself, and nothing else, not even things that are impermanent.
>
> There are three ways a phenomenon can exist in a similar class:
>
> (1) Pot exists in the similar class in the proof of sound as impermanent because pot is impermanent.
> (2) Object of knowledge exists in the similar class in the proof of sound as impermanent because impermanent is an object of knowledge. However, object of knowledge is not a member of the similar class, for it is a member of the dissimilar class because of being permanent.

(3) Particularity of product, even though it itself is permanent, exists in the similar class in the proof of sound as impermanent because whatever is a particularity of product is necessarily impermanent.

However, class in "similar class in the proof of sound as impermanent" can refer not only to the general-isolate of impermanent, that is, impermanent itself, but also to phenomena that are impermanent, such as a pot, or even to others that are synonymous with impermanent, such as product.[LR]

The two, (a) class in "similar class in the proof of sound as impermanent," and (b) class in "exists in the similar class in the proof of sound as impermanent," must be posited as dissimilar because there are three usages of, or objects to be inferred by, the term *pakṣa* [translated according to context as class, position, or subject] in the proof of sound as impermanent.

(1) In "property of the subject (*pakṣadharma*) in the proof of sound as impermanent," subject (*pakṣa*) refers to the subject sought to be known in the proof of sound as impermanent [and, therefore, in this text *pakṣadharma* has been translated as property of the subject for the sake of convenience. When one says, "The subject, sound, is impermanent because of being a product," sound is the subject sought to be known. This is because sound is the basis of debate in the proof of that and also because there exists a person, who, having ascertained that sound is a product, is engaged in wanting to know whether or not it is impermanent.]

(2) The two—(a) class (*pakṣa*) in "exists or does not exist in the similar class in the proof of sound as impermanent" and (b) position [or predicate] (*pakṣa*) that is the object of relation of the pervasion in the proof of that—both refer to the general-isolate of impermanent [that is to say, impermanent itself], the predicate of the probandum in the proof of sound as impermanent.

(3) Class (*pakṣa*) in "similar class in the proof of sound as impermanent" must be posited as the general-isolate of impermanent and as all basis-isolates of impermanent [that is to say, all phenomena that are impermanent].

Fourth Question: Is whatever exists in accordance with the etymological explanation of dissimilar class in the proof of something necessarily [a member of] the dissimilar class in the proof of that?

Answer: No, there are three possibilities.

In general, "dissimilar class in the proof of that" does not exist because whatever is selfless is necessarily a similar class.

However, there are said to be three possibilities between being a member of a dissimilar class and existing in accordance with the etymological explanation of dissimilar class. This is true from the point of view of considering both the proof of sound as impermanent and the proof of sound as permanent.[GL]

(1) Uncompounded space exists in accordance with the etymological explanation of dissimilar class in the proof of sound as permanent without being a member of the dissimilar class in the proof of sound as permanent.

Uncompounded space exists in accordance with the etymological explanation of dissimilar class in the proof of sound as permanent because uncompounded space and sound are qualitatively dissimilar in being permanent. This is because uncompounded space is permanent but sound is impermanent.

Uncompounded space is not a member of the dissimilar class in the proof of sound as permanent because, being permanent, it is a member of the similar class in the proof of that.[LR]

(2) Pot neither [exists in accordance with the etymological explanation of dissimilar class nor is a member of the dissimilar class] in the proof of sound as impermanent.

Pot does not exist in accordance with the etymological explanation of dissimilar class in the proof of sound as impermanent because it exists in accordance with the etymological explanation of similar class in the proof of sound as impermanent. This is because pot and sound are qualitatively similar in being impermanent.

Pot is not a member of the dissimilar class in the proof of sound as impermanent because of being a member of the similar class in the proof of sound as impermanent. This is because sound is impermanent.[LR]

(3) Uncompounded space exists in accordance with the etymological explanation of dissimilar class in the proof of sound as impermanent and is also [a member of] the dissimilar class in the proof of sound as impermanent. [This is because uncompounded space is permanent but sound is impermanent.]

There is no possibility of being [a member of] the dissimilar class in the proof of something but not existing in accordance with the etymological explanation of dissimilar class in the proof of that. This is because whatever is [a member of] the dissimilar class in the proof of something necessarily exists in accordance with the etymological explanation of dissimilar class in the proof of that.

Analysis of Whether or Not Similar and Dissimilar Classes Are Explicitly Contradictory

Although similar class is explicitly contradictory with dissimilar class, dissimilar class is not explicitly contradictory with similar class because dissimilar class does not exist. This is because whatever is an established base is necessarily [a member of] a similar class because whatever is an established base is necessarily [a member of] a similar class of a correct sign. This is because whatever is an established base is necessarily [a member of] the similar class of the correct sign in the proof of sound as an object of knowledge. [This, in turn, is because whatever is an established base is an object of knowledge.]

Objection: It follows that dissimilar class does exist because a dissimilar class in the proof of sound as impermanent exists, and because a correct statement of proof using a qualitative dissimilarity [between the subject and the example] also exists.

> Statements of proof are of two types: those using a qualitative similarity and those using a qualitative dissimilarity between the subject and the example. The similarity or dissimilarity refers to whether the example given is similar or dissimilar to the basis of debate [the subject], this difference being in terms of the predicate of the probandum.
>
> In the syllogism, "The subject, sound, is impermanent because of being a product," the basis of debate is sound.
>
> (1) A statement of proof using a qualitative similarity between the subject and the example is, "Whatever is a product is necessarily impermanent, as is the case with pot; sound also is a product." The conclusion, that sound is impermanent, is considered to be implicit and therefore is not stated. Here, pot and sound are similar in having the qualities of being a product [the sign] and being impermanent [the predicate of the probandum].
>
> (2) A statement of proof using a qualitative dissimilarity between the subject and the example is, "Whatever is not impermanent is necessarily not a product, as is the case with uncompounded space; sound, however, is a product." Again, the conclusion, that sound is impermanent, is not explicitly stated.[LR]

Answer to the objection: [Although the reason is true,] it does not entail [that dissimilar class exists].

Similar and Dissimilar Examples

The definition of a similar example is:

> that held as a similar example. [Whatever someone posits as a similar example, whether it be right or wrong, is a similar example.]

Whatever is selfless is necessarily a similar example because whatever is an established base is necessarily a similar example and also whatever is not an established base is necessarily a similar example.

> It follows that whatever is an established base is necessarily a similar example because pot is a similar example and [all other established bases] are the same.

> It follows that whatever is not an established base is necessarily a similar example because horn of a rabbit is a similar example and [all other nonestablished bases] are the same.

> It follows that the subject, horn of a rabbit, is a similar example because of being held as a similar example in the proof of sound as impermanent. This is because there exists a syllogism, "The subject, sound, is impermanent because of being a product, as is the case with it [horn of a rabbit]," and there also exists a proof statement, "Whatever is a product is necessarily impermanent, as is the case with it [horns of a rabbit]."

The definition of a similar example in the proof of sound as impermanent is:

> that held as a similar example in the proof of sound as impermanent.
> > The similar example is that basis with respect to which, prior to realizing that sound is impermanent, one realizes the pervasion, "whatever is a product is necessarily impermanent."DM

Whatever is selfless is necessarily a similar example in the proof of sound as impermanent. Extend the reasoning [in the same way as above, adding "in the proof of sound as impermanent"]: Whatever is an established base [is necessarily a similar example in the proof of sound as impermanent and whatever is not an established base is necessarily a similar example in the proof of sound as impermanent. It follows that whatever is an established base is necessarily a similar example in the proof of sound as impermanent because pot is a similar example and all other established bases are the same. And so forth, through the rest of the subproofs].

This [mode of progression] is also to be applied with respect to the sign, product.

> In other words, whatever is an established base is necessarily a similar example in the proof of sound as impermanent by the sign, product, and whatever is not an established base is necessarily a similar example in the proof of sound as impermanent by the sign, product, etc.[GL]

That held as a dissimilar example is not the definition of dissimilar example. This is because dissimilar example does not exist, since whatever is an established base is necessarily a correct similar example. However, that there exists a correct dissimilar example in the proof of sound as impermanent has already been proven above. [In any specific proof, a dissimilar example does exist.]

3. Correct Sign

The definition of a correct sign is:

> that which is the three modes.

What are the three modes? They are the three—the property of the subject, the forward pervasion, and the counterpervasion. Each of the three modes has its own definition, illustration, and mode of proving [the illustration].

DEFINITION OF THE THREE MODES

The definition of property of the subject in the proof of something is:

> that ascertained by valid cognition as only existing, in accordance with the mode of statement, with the flawless subject sought to be known in the proof of that. [For example, product is the property of the subject in the proof of sound as impermanent by the sign, product.]

The definition of forward pervasion in the proof of something is:

> that ascertained by valid cognition as existing in only the similar class in accordance with the mode of statement in the proof of that. [For example, product is the forward pervasion in the proof of sound as impermanent by the sign, product.]

The definition of counterpervasion in the proof of something is:

> that ascertained by valid cognition as only nonexistent in the dissimilar class, in accordance with the mode of statement, in the proof of that by the power of [the sign's] relation with the meaning-isolate of the explicit predicate of the probandum in the proof of that.
>
> For example, in the proof of sound as impermanent by the sign, product, the explicit predicate of the probandum is impermanent. The meaning-isolate of impermanent is its definition, momentary. Product and momentary are related because they are equivalent; whatever is a product is necessarily momentary and whatever is momentary is necessarily a product. A product cannot be permanent, and, therefore, product is only

nonexistent in the dissimilar class in the proof of sound as impermanent.LR

However, these three definitions are formulated mainly for the sake of understanding; there is no definiteness with regard to them.

Stating the definition in this general way leaves one open to the following debate. It has already been stated that whatever is an existent is necessarily a sign in the proof of something. Furthermore, whatever is an existent is necessarily a correct sign. Therefore, these absurd consequences can be put forth:

It follows that the subject, the subject sought to be known in the proof of something, is a correct sign in the proof of that.

If that is so, then it follows that the subject, the subject sought to be known in the proof of that, is the property of the subject in the proof of that.

It follows, then, that the subject, the subject sought to be known in the proof of that, is ascertained by valid cognition as only existing, in accordance with the mode of statement, with the flawless subject sought to be known in the proof of that.

If that is so, then the subject sought to be known in the proof of that must be different from itself. This cannot be, because whatever is an established base must be one with itself.LR

[There is no definiteness with regard to these definitions] because although sound fulfills those three definitions in the proof of sound as impermanent, [sound] is individually not their definiendum.

Let us, in relation to a particular base, state the definitions at length [without entailing any of those faults]: The definition of something's being the property of the subject in the proof of sound as impermanent is:

sound is the flawless subject sought to be known in the proof of sound as impermanent by the sign, x [that is, any correct sign]; and x is ascertained by valid cognition as only existing, in accordance with the mode of statement, with sound in the manner of a mutual difference with sound. [The qualification, "in the manner of a mutual difference with sound," is added in order to prevent one from stating "sound" itself as the reason.]

The definition of something's being the forward pervasion in the proof of sound as impermanent is:

(1) there exists a correct similar example that possesses the

two, the sign and the predicate of the probandum, in the proof of sound as impermanent by the sign, x; (2) x is related with impermanent; and (3) x is ascertained by valid cognition as just existing, in accordance with the mode of statement, in only the similar class in the proof of sound as impermanent. [The qualification, "x is related with impermanent," is stated in order to prevent one from stating "impermanent" itself as the reason.]

The definition of something's being the counterpervasion in the proof of sound as impermanent is:

(1) there exists a correct dissimilar example that does not possess the two, the sign and the predicate of the probandum, in the proof of sound as impermanent by the sign, x; (2) x is related with impermanent; and (3) x is ascertained by valid cognition as only nonexistent in the dissimilar class in the proof of sound as impermanent.

ILLUSTRATION

Product is the property of the subject, as well as the forward pervasion and counterpervasion in the proof of sound as impermanent by the sign, product.

Methods of Proof

Product Is the Property of the Subject

Reasoning proving that product is the property of the subject in the proof of sound as impermanent:

It follows that the subject, product, is the property of the subject in the proof of sound as impermanent because of being that definition, [that is, because (1) sound is the flawless subject sought to be known in the proof of sound as impermanent by the sign, product, and (2) product is ascertained by valid cognition as only existing, in accordance with the mode of statement, with sound in the manner of mutual difference with sound].

If someone says that the *first root reason* is not established, [then the response is,] "It follows that the subject, sound, is the flawless subject sought to be known in the proof of sound as impermanent by the sign, product, because it [sound] is held as the basis of debate in the proof of sound as impermanent by the sign, product, and because there exists a person who, having ascertained it [sound] by valid cognition as a product, is engaged in wanting to know whether or not it is impermanent." It follows [that the subject, sound, is held as the basis of debate in the proof of sound as impermanent by the sign, product,] because there exists the syllogism, "The subject, sound, is impermanent because of being a product." It follows [that there exists a person who, having ascertained by valid cognition that sound is a product, is engaged in wanting to know whether or not it is impermanent] because there exists a person who has not ascertained by valid cognition that sound is impermanent.

If someone says that the *second root reason* is not established, [then the response is,] "It follows that the subject, product, is ascertained by valid cognition as only existing, in accordance with the mode of statement, with sound in the manner of mutual difference with sound because it [product] is mutually different from sound and it [product] is ascertained by valid cognition as only existing, in accordance with the mode of statement, with sound. That [product is mutually different from sound] is easy [to prove because product is different from sound and sound is different from product]. It follows that the subject, product, is ascertained by valid cognition as only existing, in accordance with the mode of statement, with sound because (1) the mode of statement in the proof of that by the sign of it is an "is" statement [rather than an "exists" statement], (2) sound is it [product], and (3) it [product] is with the subject, sound [that is, product is a quality of sound]. These reasons are easy [to prove].

Product Is the Forward Pervasion

Reasoning proving that product is the forward pervasion in the proof of sound as impermanent:

> It follows with respect to the subject, product, that it is the forward pervasion in the proof of sound as impermanent because of being that definition, [that is, because (1) there exists a correct similar example that possesses the two, the sign and the predicate of the probandum, in the proof of sound as impermanent by the sign of it [product]; (2) it [product] is related with impermanent; and (3) it [product] is ascertained by valid cognition as existing, in accordance with the mode of statement, in only the similar class in the proof of sound as impermanent].

The *first root reason* [number (1) above] follows because pot is a correct similar example that possesses the two, the sign and the predicate of the probandum, in the proof of sound as impermanent by the sign of it [product]. If someone says that this reason is not established, [then the response is:] "It follows with respect to the subject, pot, that it is a correct similar example that possesses the two, the sign and the predicate of the probandum in the proof of that by the sign, product, because (a) it is held as a similar example in the proof of that by the sign, product, and (b) there exists a correct opponent in the proof of that who, prior to ascertaining by valid cognition that whatever is a product is necessarily impermanent in terms of sound, ascertains by valid cognition that whatever is a product is necessarily impermanent in terms of it [pot]. This is because it [pot] is a particularity of product.

[If someone says that the first reason (a) is not established then the response is:] "It follows with respect to the subject, pot, that it is held as a similar example in the proof of that by the sign, product, because there exists the syllogism, 'The subject, sound, is impermanent because of being a product, as is the case with pot.'"

If someone says that the second reason [b] is not established, [that is, if someone says that there does not exist a correct opponent in the proof of that who, prior to ascertaining by valid cognition that whatever is a product is necessarily impermanent in terms of pot, then the response is:] "It follows with respect to the subject, object of knowledge, that there exists such a correct opponent because there exists a correct opponent in the proof of that who, prior to ascertaining by valid cognition that sound is impermanent, ascertains by valid cognition that pot is impermanent. This is because there exists a correct opponent in the proof of sound as impermanent. This, [in turn,] is because a correct opponent in the proof of sound as impermanent is [a correct opponent in the proof of sound as impermanent who, prior to ascertaining by valid cognition that sound is impermanent, has ascertained by valid cognition that pot is impermanent].

And, this is because the correct opponent in the proof of that is a person who has not ascertained by valid cognition that sound is impermanent, but has ascertained by valid cognition that a pot is impermanent. These two signs are proven by the subject. [That a correct opponent has not ascertained by valid cognition that sound is impermanent, but has ascertained by valid cognition that pot is impermanent, is established by the mere fact that he is a correct opponent in the proof of that.]

The *second root reason* [that product is related with impermanent] follows because it [product] is related as one entity with impermanent.

The *third root reason* follows [that is, it follows that product is ascertained by valid cognition as existing, in accordance with the mode of statement, in only the similar class in the proof of sound as impermanent] because (a) the mode of statement in the proof of sound as impermanent by the sign of it [product] is an "is" statement, (b) the mode of proof is an "is" proof, (c) [product] is impermanent, and (d) whatever is it [product] is necessarily impermanent.

The first reason (a) is easy [to understand because the statement is, "The subject, sound, *is* impermanent because of being a product."]

The second reason (b) follows because the mode of proof in the proof of sound as impermanent by the sign, product, is either an "is" proof or an "exists" proof and it is not the latter. It follows [that the mode of proof is either an "is" or an "exists" proof] because it is set as a sign in the proof of that. If someone says that the second reason is not established [meaning that the mode of proof in the proof of sound as impermanent by the sign, product, is an "exists" proof; that is, the subject, sound, exists among the impermanent because of being a product,] then the response is, "It follows [from that view] that product is a sign that relates as pervader to the similar class in the proof of sound as existing among the impermanent because, [according to you,] there exists a sign that relates to the similar class in the proof of that as a pervader." If that is accepted, then it [absurdly] follows that the subject, object of knowledge, is a product because of existing among the impermanent.

The last two consequences are false; they follow from a mistaken view. If the mode of proof in the proof of sound as impermanent by the sign, product, were an "exists" proof, then it would follow that the sign, product, relates to the similar class as pervader in the proof of that. That a sign relates to the similar class in the proof of something as a pervader means that whatever is a member of the similar class in the proof of that is necessarily that sign.

Thus, if one asserts that product relates to the similar class as a pervader in the proof of sound as existing among the impermanent, then it follows that whatever exists among the impermanent is necessarily a product. This is mistaken because something can be posited that exists among the impermanent but is not a product. For example, object of knowledge exists among the impermanent because the impermanent are objects of knowledge; however, object of knowledge is not impermanent because of being permanent.[LR]

With respect to the third reason (c), it follows [that product is imper-manent] because of being a product. The fourth reason (d), [that is, whatever is a product is necessarily impermanent] is set aside [because it should be obvious].

Product Is the Counterpervasion

Reasoning proving that product is the counterpervasion in the proof of sound as impermanent:

> It follows that the subject, product, is the counterpervasion in the proof of sound as impermanent because of being that defi-nition [that is, because (1) there exists a dissimilar example that does not possess the two, the sign and the predicate of the probandum, in the proof of sound as impermanent by the sign, product, (2) it (product) is related with impermanent, and (3) it is ascertained by valid cognition as only nonexistent in the dis-similar class in the proof of that].

The *first root reason* is established because uncompounded space is [a dissimilar example that does not possess the sign or the predicate of the probandum in the proof of sound as impermanent by the sign, product]. The *second root reason* has already been established [in the proof of product as the forward pervasion]. The *third root reason* [that product is ascertained by valid cognition as only nonexistent in the dis-similar class in the proof of sound as impermanent by the sign, prod-uct] is established because product does not exist among the nonim-permanent.

4. Effect Signs

DIVISIONS OF CORRECT SIGNS

The divisions of correct signs are of six types: divisions by way of (1) the entity, (2) the predicate of the probandum, (3) the mode of proof, (4) the probandum, (5) relating to the similar class, and (6) the opponent.

DIVISIONS OF CORRECT SIGNS BY WAY OF THE ENTITY

These are divided into three parts: correct effect signs, correct nature signs, and correct nonobservation signs.

Correct Effect Signs

The presentation of correct effect signs has four parts: definitions, divisions, explanation of the valid cognition ascertaining the definition in terms of an illustration, and identification of the sign, predicate of the probandum, and basis of debate.[a]

Definitions of Correct Effect Signs

The definition of something's being a correct effect sign in the proof of that is:

> It is a correct sign of a positive phenomenon in the proof of that [that is, the predicate of the probandum is a positive phenomenon] and there exists a common locus of (1) being that which is held as the explicit predicate of the probandum in the proof of that by the sign of it and (2) being its [the sign's] cause.

When debating, the definition of correct effect sign is:

> that which is the three effect modes.

"Correct effect sign" and "caused phenomenon" are synonymous.
The definition of correct effect sign in the proof of something is:

> that which is the three effect modes in the proof of that.

From the point of view of understanding, the definition of its being a

---

[a] *Chos,* which usually means "subject," here refers to "predicate of the probandum." *Don,* usually "object" or "meaning," means "basis of debate" in this context.

correct effect sign in the proof of something is:

> (1) it is a correct sign in the proof of that and (2) there exists a common locus of (a) being the main object held as the explicit predicate of the probandum in the proof of that by the sign of it and (b) being its cause.

Divisions of Correct Effect Signs

This section has five parts: correct effect signs proving an actual cause, a preceding cause, a general cause, and a particular cause, and correct effect signs that are means of inferring causal attributes.

Correct Effect Signs Proving an Actual Cause

Illustration of a correct effect sign proving an actual cause: One can state, "With respect to the subject, on a smoky pass, fire exists because smoke exists." In that, "smoke" is a correct effect sign proving an actual cause in the proof of fire as existing on a smoky pass.

Correct Effect Signs Proving a Preceding Cause

Illustration of a correct effect sign proving a preceding cause: One can state, "The subject, the bluish rising smoke in the intermediate space, is preceded by its own former cause, fire, because of being smoke." In that, "smoke" is a correct effect sign proving a preceding cause in the proof of the bluish rising smoke in the intermediate space as having been preceded by its own former cause, fire.

Correct Effect Signs Proving a General Cause

Illustration of a correct effect sign proving a general cause: One can state, "The subjects, the appropriated aggregates, have their own causes because of being occasionally produced things." In that, "occasionally produced things" is a correct effect sign proving the general cause (or the self-isolate of the cause) in the proof of the appropriated aggregates as having their own causes.

Correct Effect Signs Proving a Particular Cause

Illustration of a correct effect sign proving a particular cause: One can state, "The subject, a sense consciousness perceiving blue, has its own observed object condition because of being a thing that is not produced without the existence of its observed object condition." In that, "thing that is not produced without the existence of its observed object condition" is a correct effect sign proving a particular cause in the proof of a sense consciousness perceiving blue as having its own observed object condition.

Correct Effect Signs That Are Means of Inferring Causal Attributes

Illustration of a correct effect sign that is a means of inferring causal attributes: One can state, "With respect to the subject, with the lump of molasses in the mouth, there exists the capacity of the former taste of molasses to generate the later form of molasses because the present taste of molasses exists." In that, "the present taste of molasses" is a correct effect sign that is a means of inferring causal attributes in the proof that the capacity for generating the later form of molasses by the former taste of molasses exists with the lump of molasses in the mouth.

> In dependence on a correct effect sign that is a means of inferring causal attributes two different types of inferential consciousnesses are produced. Thus, when one states, "The subject, with the lump of molasses in the mouth, the capacity of the former taste of molasses to generate the later form of molasses exists because the present form of molasses exists," "the present form of molasses exists" is a correct effect sign that produces two inferential consciousnesses: one that realizes the existence of the capacity of the former taste of molasses to produce the present form of molasses, and another that realizes the existence of the present form of molasses.[LR]

In another way, when correct effect signs are divided, there are two. This is because smoke is a correct effect sign that relates to the similar class as a pervader in the proof of the existence of the direct cause of the smoke on a smoky pass, and smoke is an effect sign that relates to the similar class in two ways in the proof of the existence of fire on a smoky pass. The fact that [smoke] relates to the similar class as a pervader in the proof of [the existence of the direct cause of the smoke on a smoky pass] means that wherever the direct cause of smoke exists smoke necessarily exists. That [smoke] relates to the similar class in two ways in the proof of the existence of fire on a smoky pass means that wherever fire exists smoke does not necessarily exist [and also wherever fire exists smoke does not necessarily not exist].

Proofs/Explanation of the Valid Cognition Ascertaining the Definition in Terms of an Illustration

With respect to the subject, smoke, it is an effect sign in the proof of fire as existing on a smoky pass because (1) it [smoke] is a correct sign in the proof of that and (2) it [smoke] is an effect of fire. This is just [one] illustration.

Identification of the Sign, Predicate of the Probandum, and Basis of Debate

[Sign]

Smoke is a correct sign in the proof of fire as existing on a smoky pass, and is both the stated sign and the sign that appears to the mind in the proof of that, and is also a correct sign [in the proof of fire as existing on a smoky pass] by the sign, smoke.

Although the existence of smoke is a correct sign and the stated sign in the proof of fire as existing on a smoky pass, it [the existence of smoke] is not the sign that appears to the mind in the proof of that and is not a correct sign [in the proof of that] by the sign, smoke.

> The existence of smoke is not the sign that appears to the mind in the proof of fire as existing on a smoky pass, because the existence of smoke is not what appears to the mind of the opponent. With respect to the statement, "On a smoky pass, fire exists because smoke exists," the sign that appears to the mind of the opponent is just "smoke" and not "the existence of smoke."

> The existence of smoke is not a correct sign in the proof of fire as existing on a smoky pass by the sign, smoke, because in that syllogism "smoke" rather than "the existence of smoke" is the effect sign. This is because "smoke" rather than "the existence of smoke" is the effect of fire. The existence of smoke is not the effect of fire because the existence of smoke is permanent.[LR]

[Predicate]

Fire is the predicate of the probandum and the stated predicate of the probandum as well as the predicate of the probandum that appears to the mind in the proof of [fire as existing on a smoky pass] by the sign, smoke.

The existence of fire is the predicate of the probandum and the stated predicate of the probandum in the proof of [fire as existing on a smoky pass] as well as the predicate of the probandum in the proof of that by the sign, smoke. It is not, however, the predicate of the probandum that appears to the mind in the proof of that.

[Basis of Debate]

Fire as observed by valid cognition [the definition of existence of fire] and the hot and burning [the definition of fire] are not, individually, that which is held as the explicit predicate of the probandum in the proof of fire as existing on a smoky pass because of being correct signs in the proof of that. However, those two are, individually, that which is held as the explicit predicate of the probandum in the proof of that by the sign, smoke. This is because there exists a common locus of (1) being that which is held as the explicit predicate of the probandum in the proof of that and (2) being a definition.

According to Ge-shay Ge-dün-lo-drö, "fire as observed by valid cognition" and "hot and burning" are explicit predicates of the probandum in the proof of fire as existent on a smoky pass by the sign, smoke. However, according to Lati Rin-po chay, "fire as observed by valid cognition" is the explicit predicate of the probandum only in the proof of fire as observed by valid cognition and, similarly, "hot and burning" is the explicit predicate of the probandum only in the proof of hot and burning as existent on a smoky pass.

5. Nature Signs

This section has three parts: definitions, divisions, and illustrations.

DEFINITIONS OF CORRECT NATURE SIGNS

The definition of a correct nature sign is:

> that which is the three nature modes.

The definition of a correct nature sign in the proof of something is:

> that which is the three nature modes in the proof of that.

In another way, the definition of its being a correct nature sign in the proof of something is:

> (1) it is a correct sign in the proof of that and (2) it is posited from the point of view that whatever is held as the explicit predicate of the probandum in the proof of that by such-and-such a sign must be of one nature with that sign.
>
> > The words "posited from the point of view" indicate that there are exceptions. In other words, whatever sign is of one nature with that held as the explicit predicate of the probandum in the proof of something is not necessarily a correct nature sign in the proof of that. For example, one can state, "The subject, sound, is empty of being permanent because of being a product." In that, the sign—product—is of one nature with the explicit predicate of the probandum—empty of being permanent—but is not a correct nature sign; instead, it is a correct nonobservation sign in the proof of that. This is because the predicate of the probandum is a negative phenomenon.[GL]

DIVISIONS OF CORRECT NATURE SIGNS

[There are two ways of dividing correct nature signs: (1) according to whether they involve a qualification and (2) according to the relation to the similar class.]

Division of Correct Nature Signs according to Whether They Involve a Qualification

Correct nature signs are of two types: correct nature signs involving a qualification in the proof of something and those that are free of qualification in the proof of something.

Correct Nature Signs Involving a Qualification

Definition. The definition of a correct nature sign involving a qualification in the proof of something is:

> a correct nature in the proof of that which is posited from the point of view that the term expressing it indicates its own agent.

Divisions. Correct nature signs involving a qualification are of two types: those that explicitly indicate their agent and those that implicitly indicate their agent.

Illustrations. [One can state, "The subject, the sound of a conch, is impermanent because of being arisen from exertion," and "The subject, the sound of a conch, is impermanent because of being a created phenomenon." In those,] arisen from exertion and created phenomenon are [correct nature signs that explicitly indicate their own agent] in the proof of the sound of a conch as impermanent.

[One can state, "The subject, sound, is impermanent because of being a product." In that,] product is [a correct nature sign that implicitly indicates its own agent] in the proof of sound as impermanent.

Correct Nature Signs Free of Qualification

Definition. The definition of a correct nature sign that is free of qualification in the proof of something is:

> a correct nature sign in the proof of that which is posited from the point of view that the term expressing it does not indicate its own agent.

Illustration. [One can state, "The subject, sound, is impermanent because of being a thing." In that,] thing is a correct nature sign that is free of qualification in the proof of sound as impermanent.

Division of Correct Nature Signs according to the Relation to the Similar Class

In another way, correct nature signs in the proof of sound as impermanent are of two types:

1. Correct nature sign in the proof of [sound as impermanent] that relates to the similar class as a pervader in the proof of that. An illustration of this is product.
2. Correct nature sign in the proof of [sound as impermanent] that relates to the similar class in two ways in the proof of that. An illustration of this is particularity of product.

    Particularity of product relates to the similar class in two ways in the proof of sound as impermanent because:
    (1) whatever is impermanent is not necessarily a particularity of product; for example, product is impermanent but is not a particularity of product because whatever is a particularity of product must be different from product; and
    (2) whatever is impermanent is not necessarily not a particularity of product; for example, a pot is both impermanent and a particularity of product.[LR]

Proof of the Illustrations

"Product" is [a correct nature sign in the proof of sound as impermanent that relates to the similar class in the proof of that as a pervader of it] because that [product] is a correct nature sign in the proof of that and whatever is an impermanent phenomenon is necessarily that [product].

"Particularity of product" is [a correct nature sign in the proof of sound as impermanent that relates to the similar class in the proof of that in two ways] because that [particularity of product] is a correct nature sign in the proof of that and whatever is impermanent is not necessarily that [particularity of product].

6. Nonobservation Signs

CORRECT NONOBSERVATION SIGNS

This section has three parts: definition, divisions, and explanation of the ascertainment of the definitions in terms of illustrations.

DEFINITION OF CORRECT NONOBSERVATION SIGN

The definition of something's being a correct nonobservation sign in the proof of that is:

> (1) it is a correct sign in the proof of that and (2) there occurs a common locus of (a) being what is held as the explicit predicate of the probandum in the proof of that by such-and-such a sign and (b) being a negative phenomenon.

DIVISIONS OF CORRECT NONOBSERVATION SIGNS

This section has two parts: correct nonobservation signs of the nonappearing and correct nonobservation signs of the suitable to appear.

Correct Nonobservation Signs of the Nonappearing

Sūtra says: "A person cannot estimate the measure of [another] person. [If one does so,] one will degenerate." By the mere fact of their not appearing to oneself, it is not reasonable to say that another does not have such-and-such good qualities.

> This is directed primarily at the Nihilists, who assert that there is no liberation or omniscience or relationship of cause and effect of actions because they do not perceive them. The presentation of correct nonobservation signs concerning the nonappearing is set forth mainly in order to refute such views.[LR]

To indicate this meaning, Dharmakīrti's *Commentary on (Dignāga's) "Compilation of Prime Cognition"* says: "When a valid cognition is nonoperating and nonexistent, then it has as effect the nonoperation of a subsequent cognition."

> A valid cognition is a cause; its effect is a subsequent cognition. When a valid cognition does not operate, there is also no operation of a factually concordant subsequent cognition.[DM]

Definition of Nonobservation Sign of the Nonappearing

The definition of something's being a correct nonobservation sign of the nonappearing in the proof of that is:

> (1) it is a correct nonobservation sign in the proof of that and (2) although, in general, the object that is designated as the predicate of the negandum in the proof of that by such-and-such a sign does exist, it does not appear to a valid cognition of the person for whom it has become the property of the subject in the proof of that.

Divisions of Nonobservation Signs of the Nonappearing

Correct nonobservation signs of the nonappearing are of two types: correct signs of the nonappearing that are a nonobservation of a related object in the proof of that and correct signs of the nonappearing that are an observation of a contradictory object in the proof of that.

Definitions of Nonobservation Signs of the Nonappearing

The definition of a correct sign of the nonappearing that is a nonobservation of a related object in the proof of something is:

> that which is a common locus of (1) being a correct nonobservation sign of the nonappearing in the proof of that and (2) being a nonaffirming negative phenomenon.

The definition of a correct sign of the nonappearing that is an observation of a contradictory object in the proof of something is:

> that which is a common locus of (1) being a correct nonobservation sign of the nonappearing in the proof of that and (2) being either an affirming negative phenomenon or a positive phenomenon.

Correct Signs of the Nonappearing That Are a Nonobservation of a Related Object in the Proof of That

Divisions of Correct Signs of the Nonappearing That Are a Nonobservation of a Related Object in the Proof of That

When correct signs of the nonappearing that are a nonobservation of a related object are divided, there are three types: correct signs of the nonappearing that are a nonobservation of a cause,[a] a pervader, and a nature.

Illustration of a Correct Sign of the Nonappearing That Is a Nonobservation of a Cause

[One can state, "With respect to the subject, here in this place in front, there does not exist a factually concordant subsequent cognition (that ascertains a flesh-eater) in the continuum of a person for whom a flesh-eater is a supersensory object because there does not exist a prime cognition (that observes a flesh-eater) in the continuum of a person for whom a flesh-eater is a supersensory object."] In that, "the nonexistence of a prime cognition (that observes a flesh-eater) in the continuum of a person for whom a flesh-eater is a supersensory object" is a correct sign of the nonappearing that is a nonobservation of a cause in the proof that, here in this place in front, there does not exist a factually concordant subsequent cognition (that ascertains a flesh-eater) in the continuum of a person for whom a flesh-eater is a supersensory object.

> In this proof, the predicate of the negandum is "a factually concordant subsequent cognition (that ascertains a flesh-eater) in the continuum of a person for whom a flesh-eater is a supersensory object." If that subsequent cognition were existent, its cause would be "a valid cognition (that observes a flesh-eater) in the continuum of a person for whom a flesh-eater is a supersensory object." When the nonexistence of that cause is stated as the sign, it is a correct sign of the nonappearing that is a nonobservation of a cause.[GL]

Illustration of a Correct Sign of the Nonappearing That Is a Nonobservation of a Pervader

[One can state, "With respect to the subject, here in this place in front, it is unsuitable for a person (for whom a flesh-eater is a supersensory object) to posit the existence of a flesh-eater because of the nonobservation by valid cognition of the existence of a flesh-eater by a person for whom the existence of a flesh-eater is a supersensory object."] In that, "the nonobservation by valid cognition of the existence of a flesh-eater by a person for whom the existence of a flesh-eater is a

---

[a] Later in the text Pur-bu-jok refers to this type as a correct sign of the nonappearing which is a nonobservation of a related cause.

supersensory object" is a correct sign of the nonappearing that is a nonobservation of a pervader in the proof that it is unsuitable for a person (for whom a flesh-eater is a supersensory object) to posit the existence of a flesh-eater with respect to this place in front.

> In this proof, the predicate of the negandum—"the suitability of a person for whom a flesh-eater is a supersensory object to posit the existence of a flesh-eater"—is the object pervaded. The pervader is "the observation by valid cognition of the existence of a flesh-eater by a person for whom the existence of a flesh-eater is a supersensory object." In other words, the observation by valid cognition of the existence of a flesh-eater is a necessary condition for the suitability of a person to posit the existence of a flesh-eater.

> In this proof, the nonobservation of the pervader is stated as the sign, thus it is a correct sign of the nonappearing that is a nonobservation of a pervader.^{GL}

Illustration of a Correct Sign of the Nonappearing That Is a Nonobservation of a Nature

[One can state, "With respect to the subject, here in this place in front, there does not exist a factually concordant subsequent cognition (that ascertains a flesh-eater) in the continuum of a person for whom a flesh-eater is a supersensory object because of the nonobservation by valid cognition of a factually concordant subsequent cognition (that ascertains a flesh-eater) in the continuum of a person for whom a flesh-eater is a supersensory object."] In that, "the nonobservation by valid cognition of a factually concordant subsequent cognition (that ascertains a flesh-eater) in the continuum of a person for whom a flesh-eater is a supersensory object" is a correct sign of the nonappearing that is a nonobservation of a nature in the proof of the nonexistence of a factually concordant subsequent cognition (that ascertains a flesh-eater in this place in front) in the continuum of such a person.

> Here, the predicate of the negandum and the reverse of the sign, if existent, would be of one nature. The predicate of the negandum is "the existence of a factually concordant subsequent cognition (that ascertains a flesh-eater) in the continuum of a person for whom a flesh-eater is a supersensory object." This is of one nature with the reverse of the sign, "the observation by valid cognition of a factually concordant subsequent cognition (that ascertains a flesh-eater) in the continuum of

such a person." This is because "that which is observed by valid cognition" is the definition of "existent."

In this proof, the nonobservation of such a factually concordant subsequent cognition is stated as the sign; thus, it is a correct sign of the nonappearing that is a nonobservation of a nature.ᴳᴸ

Purpose of Positing Nonobservation Signs of the Nonappearing

It is unsuitable for a person—for whom [the two] an intermediate being [who will be] a god [in the next lifetime] and a flesh-eater are supersensory objects from the viewpoint of his doubting whether or not they exist in front of him—to decide whether or not those two exist in that place. Taking this as an example, the purpose [of positing nonobservation signs of the nonappearing] is to understand the unsuitability of reifying or deprecating any person's faults or good qualities when one has not ascertained [the presence or absence of faults and virtues] by valid cognition.

> In general, ordinary beings cannot ascertain by valid cognition another person's faults and virtues. One could be positing existence to faults that do not exist or denying the existence of virtues that do actually exist.ᴸᴿ

Whatever is an object designated as the predicate of the negandum in the proof of something is not necessarily the predicate of the negandum on the proof of that [and is not necessarily not the predicate of the negandum in the proof of that]. This is because:

(1) "The existence of a factually concordant subsequent cognition (that ascertains the existence of a flesh-eater) in the continuum of a person for whom a flesh-eater is a supersensory object with respect to this place in front" is both an object designated as the predicate of the negandum in the proof of the nonexistence of such a factually concordant subsequent cognition and the predicate of the negandum in that.

(2) However, a flesh-eater and a factually concordant subsequent cognition that ascertains it are, individually, objects designated as the predicate of the negandum in the proof of that but are not the predicate of the negandum in the proof of that.

The *first part of the reason* is easy [to prove]. If someone says that the *second part of the reason* is not established, then the response is that [a flesh-eater and a subsequent cognition that ascertains it are both, individually, objects designated as the predicate of the negandum in the proof of that] because an opponent in the proof of that doubts whether or not a flesh-eater exists in this place in front and because such [an opponent] doubts whether or not a factually concordant subsequent cognition exists. The two, [a flesh-eater and a factually concordant subsequent cognition that ascertains it] are not, individually, the predicate of the negandum in the proof of that. This is because, in general, flesh-eaters exist and also because, for example, smoke is not the predicate of the negandum in the proof of the nonexistence of smoke on a lake at night.

> In this example, the predicate of the negandum is not smoke, but rather the existence of smoke. This is because the second party does not have doubts about smoke in general but rather about the existence of smoke when it cannot be seen, such as on a lake at night.[LR]

Correct Signs of the Nonappearing That Are an Observation of a Contradictory Object in the Proof of That

Illustration of a correct sign of the nonappearing that is an observation of a contradictory object: [One can state, "With respect to the subject, here in this place in front, there does not exist a factually concordant subsequent cognition (which ascertains a flesh-eater) in the continuum of a person for whom a flesh-eater is a supersensory object because (the place in front) exists."] In that, "exists" is a correct sign of the nonappearing that is an observation of a contradictory object in the proof that there does not exist a factually concordant subsequent cognition (which ascertains a flesh-eater in this place in front) in the continuum of a person for whom a flesh-eater is a supersensory object.

> Here, the predicate of the negandum is "the existence of a factually concordant subsequent cognition (which ascertains a flesh-eater in this place in front) in the continuum of a person for whom a flesh-eater is a supersensory object." The existence of that factually concordant subsequent cognition does not exist in fact and, thus, is contradictory with existence. Because the sign—"exists"—is contradictory with the predicate of the negandum, it is a correct sign concerning the nonappearing that is an observation of a contradictory object.[GL]

In general, there are three types of objects that are supersensory in terms of the mind. These three are the supersensory objects of place, time, and entity.

Objects that are supersensory by way of place are, for example, the specifics of environments and beings that are very far away from one-self. Objects that are supersensory by way of time are, for example, the specifics of past and future aeons. Although these [objects] are not su-persensory in general, they are supersensory in terms of one's mind. Objects that are supersensory by way of entity are objects that are beyond one's ken even when nearby, due to their subtle entities; for example, a flesh-eater or an intermediate being of a god that is right in front [of oneself], or the aggregates of those beings.

Correct Nonobservation Signs of the Suitable to Appear

This section has two parts: definition and divisions.

Definition

The definition of a correct sign that is a nonobservation of the suitable to appear in the proof of something is:

> a common locus of (1) being a correct nonobservation sign in the proof of that and (2) its being true that the object designat-ed as the predicate of the negandum in the proof of that is not a supersensory object for the person for whom [the sign] has be-come the property of the subject in the proof of that.

Divisions

When correct signs that are a nonobservation of the suitable to appear are divided, there are two types: correct signs that are a nonobserva-tion of a related object suitable to appear and correct signs that are an observation of a contradictory object suitable to appear.

Nonobservation of a Related Object Suitable to Appear

This section has three parts: a definition, divisions, and illustrations.

Definition

The definition of a correct sign that is a nonobservation of a related object suitable to appear is:

> that which is a common locus of (1) being a correct nonobser-vation sign of the suitable to appear and of (2) being a nonaf-firming negative phenomenon.

Divisions

This section has four parts: correct signs that are a nonobservation of (1) a cause suitable to appear, (2) a pervader suitable to appear, (3) a nature suitable to appear, and (4) a direct effect suitable to appear.

Nonobservation of a Cause Suitable to Appear

The definition of a correct sign that is a nonobservation of a cause suitable to appear is:

> that which is the three modes of the nonobservation of a cause suitable to appear.

This form applies to the others. [That is, the definition of a correct sign that is a nonobservation of a pervader suitable to appear is: that which is the three modes of the nonobservation of a pervader suitable to appear, etc.]

Illustration of a correct sign that is a nonobservation of a cause suitable to appear: [One can state, "With respect to the subject, on a lake at night, smoke does not exist because of the nonexistence of fire." In that,] "the nonexistence of fire" is a correct sign that is a nonobservation of a cause suitable to appear in the proof of smoke as nonexistent on a lake at night.

> In this proof, the object designated as the predicate of the negandum is "smoke," which is the effect of fire. Because the nonexistence of fire is set as the sign, it is a correct sign that is a nonobservation of a cause suitable to appear.[GL]

Nonobservation of a Pervader Suitable to Appear

Illustration of a correct sign that is a nonobservation of a pervader suitable to appear: [One can state, "With respect to the subject, on a craggy cliff where trees are not observed by valid cognition, an *aśoka* (a kind of tree) does not exist because of the nonexistence of trees." In that,] "the nonexistence of trees" is a correct sign that is a nonobservation of a pervader suitable to appear in the proof of the nonexistence of an *aśoka* on a craggy cliff where trees are not observed by valid cognition.

> Here, the object designated as the predicate of the negandum is "*aśoka*" that is pervaded by "trees." Because the nonobservation of trees is set as the sign, it is a correct sign that is a nonobservation of a pervader suitable to appear.[GL]

Nonobservation of a Nature Suitable to Appear

Illustration of a correct sign that is a nonobservation of a nature suitable to appear: [One can state, "With respect to the subject, on a place where pot is not observed by valid cognition, pot does not exist because of the nonobservation of pot by valid cognition. In that,] "the nonobservation of pot by valid cognition" is a correct sign that is a nonobservation of a nature suitable to appear in the proof of the nonexistence of pot on a place where pot is not observed by valid cognition.

> In this proof the object designated as the predicate of the negandum is "pot," which is of one nature with the observation of pot by valid cognition. Because the nonobservation of pot by valid cognition is set as the sign, it is a correct sign that is a nonobservation of a nature suitable to appear.^{GL}

Nonobservation of a Direct Effect Suitable to Appear

Illustration of a correct sign that is a nonobservation of a direct effect suitable to appear: [One can state, "With respect to the subject, in a walled circle devoid of smoke, the direct cause of smoke does not exist because of the nonexistence of the direct effect, smoke." In that,] "the nonexistence of the direct effect, smoke," is a correct sign that is a nonobservation of a direct effect suitable to appear in the proof of the nonexistence of the direct cause of smoke in a walled circle devoid of smoke.

> Here, the object designated as the predicate of the negandum is "the direct cause of smoke," the direct effect of which is "smoke." Because the nonexistence of the direct effect of smoke is set as the sign, it is a correct sign that is a nonobservation of a direct effect suitable to appear.

> In all four illustrations, the object designated as the predicate of the negandum is something that is not suitable to appear to the opponent under the given circumstances. The nonexistence of that which is designated as the predicate of the negandum is established by a sign that is a nonobservation of something that *is* indeed suitable to appear in the given situation.^{GL}

Someone says that "fireless" is [an illustration of] the first [a correct sign that is a nonobservation of a cause suitable to appear] and that "treeless" is [an illustration of] the second [a correct sign that is a nonobservation of a pervader suitable to appear]. The response to that is: "It [absurdly] follows with respect to the subject, horn of a rabbit, that smoke does not exist because of being fireless; and it follows with respect to the subject, horn of a rabbit, that an *aśoka* does not exist because of being treeless. You have accepted the pervasions." Both signs are established because the subject [horn of a rabbit] is not an established base. Since smoke is the direct effect of fire, one cannot assert that smoke does not exist; and since *aśoka* is an object of pervasion by tree, one cannot assert that an *aśoka* does not exist.

Observation of a Contradictory Object Suitable to Appear

This section has two parts: a definition and divisions.

Definition

The definition of a correct sign that is an observation of a contradictory object suitable to appear is:

> that which is a common locus of (1) being a correct nonobservation sign of the suitable to appear in the proof of that and of (2) being either an affirming negative phenomenon or a positive phenomenon.

Divisions

When divided, correct signs that are an observation of a contradictory object are of two types: (1) correct signs that are an observation of an object suitable to appear that is contradictory in the sense of not abiding together [with the predicate of the negandum] and (2) correct signs that are an observation of an object suitable to appear that is contradictory in the sense of mutual exclusion.

Correct Signs That Are an Observation of an Object Suitable to Appear That Is Contradictory in the Sense of Not Abiding Together

This section has two parts: a definition and divisions.

Definition

The definition of correct sign that is an observation of an object suitable to appear that is contradictory in the sense of not abiding together in the proof that the continuous tangible object, cold, does not exist on a place in the east covered by a large powerful fire is:

that which is a common locus of (1) being a correct sign that is an observation of a contradictory object in the proof that the continuous tangible object, cold, does not exist on a place in the east covered by a large powerful fire and of (2) being contradictory with the continuous tangible object, cold, in the sense of not abiding together with it.

Divisions

This section has three parts: correct signs that are an observation of an object that is contradictory (1) in the sense of material phenomena not abiding together, (2) in the sense of consciousnesses not abiding together, and (3) in the sense of nonassociated compositional factors not abiding together.

Correct Signs That Are an Observation of an Object That Is Contradictory in the Sense of Material Phenomena Not Abiding Together

This section has five parts: correct signs that are an observation of (1) a nature that is contradictory with the nature [of the designated predicate of the negandum], (2) a nature that is contradictory with a cause [of the designated predicate of the negandum], (3) a nature that is contradictory with a pervader [of the designated predicate of the negandum], (4) an effect that is contradictory with the nature [of the designated predicate of the negandum], (5) an effect that is contradictory with a cause [of the designated predicate of the negandum].

A Nature Contradictory with the Nature

Illustration of a correct sign that is an observation of a nature contradictory with the nature of the designated predicate of the negandum: [One can state, "With respect to the subject, on a place in the east covered by a large powerful fire, the continuous tangible object, cold, does not exist because of being a place covered by a large powerful fire." In that,] "a place covered by a large powerful fire" is a correct sign that is an observation of a nature contradictory with the nature [of the designated predicate of the negandum] in the proof that the continuous tangible object, cold, does not exist on a place in the east covered by a large powerful fire.

> The object designated as the predicate of the negandum is "the continuous tangible object, cold," that is of one nature with the

tangible object, cold. Fire is contradictory with the tangible object, cold; and a place covered by a large powerful fire is of one nature with fire. Thus, in the proof given, "a place covered by a large powerful fire" is a correct sign that is an observation of a nature (fire) contradictory with the nature (the tangible object, cold) of the designated predicate of the negandum.ᴳᴸ

A Nature Contradictory with a Cause

Illustration of a correct sign that is an observation of a nature contradictory with a cause of the designated predicate of the negandum: [One can state, "With respect to the subject, on a place in the east covered by a large powerful fire, continuous goose bumps that are an effect of the cold do not exist because of being a place covered by a large powerful fire." In that,] "a place covered by a large powerful fire" is a correct sign that is an observation of a nature that is contradictory with a cause [of the designated predicate of the negandum] in the proof that continuous goose bumps that are an effect of cold do not exist on a place in the east covered by a large powerful fire.

> The object designated as the predicate of the negandum is "continuous goose bumps" that are caused by the cold. Fire is contradictory with the cold and is of one nature with a place covered by a large powerful fire. Therefore, in the proof given, "a place covered by a large powerful fire" is a correct sign that is an observation of a nature (fire) contradictory with a cause (cold) of the designated predicate of the negandum (goose bumps).ᴳᴸ

A Nature Contradictory with a Pervader

Illustration of a correct sign that is an observation of a nature contradictory with a pervader of the designated predicate of the negandum: [One can state, "With respect to the subject, on a place in the east covered by a large powerful fire, the continuous tangible object, snow, does not exist because of being a place covered by a large powerful fire." In that,] "a place covered by a large powerful fire" is a correct sign that is an observation of a nature contradictory with the pervader [of the designated predicate of the negandum] in the proof that the continuous tangible object, snow, does not exist on a place in the east covered by a large powerful fire.

> The object designated as the predicate of the negandum is "the continuous tangible object, snow," which is pervaded by the

tangible object, cold. Fire is contradictory with the tangible object, cold, and is of one nature with a place covered by a large powerful fire. Therefore, in the proof given, "a place covered by a large powerful fire" is a correct sign that is an observation of a nature (fire) contradictory with a pervader (the tangible object, cold) of the designated predicate of the negandum (the tangible object, snow).[GL]

An Effect Contradictory with the Nature

Illustration of a correct sign that is an observation of an effect contradictory with the nature of the designated predicate of the negandum: [One can state, "With respect to the subject, on a place in the east covered by strongly billowing smoke, the continuous tangible object, cold, does not exist because of being a place covered by strongly billowing smoke." In that,] "a place covered by strongly billowing smoke" is a correct sign that is an observation of an effect contradictory with the nature of the designated predicate of the negandum in the proof that the continuous tangible object, cold, does not exist on a place in the east covered by strongly billowing smoke.

> The object designated as the predicate of the negandum is "the continuous tangible object, cold"; the nature of that is cold. Fire, the cause of smoke, is contradictory with the tangible object, cold, and "a place covered by strongly billowing smoke" is of one nature with fire. Therefore, in the proof given, "a place covered by strongly billowing smoke" is a correct sign that is an observation of an effect (smoke) contradictory with the nature (cold) of the designated predicate of the negandum.[GL]

An Effect Contradictory with a Cause

Illustration of a correct sign that is an observation of an effect contradictory with a cause of the designated predicate of the negandum: [One can state, "With respect to the subject, on a place in the east covered by strongly billowing smoke, continuous goose bumps that are an effect of cold do not exist because of being a place covered by strongly billowing smoke." In that,] "a place covered by strongly billowing smoke" is a correct sign that is an observation of an effect contradictory with a cause of the designated predicate of the negandum in the proof that continuous goose bumps that are an effect of cold do not exist on a place covered by strongly billowing smoke.

> The object designated as the predicate of the negandum is

"continuous goose bumps that are an effect of cold." The cold in turn is contradictory with fire, which is the cause of smoke. Thus, in the proof given, "a place covered by strongly billowing smoke" is a correct sign that is an observation of an effect (smoke) contradictory with a cause (cold) of the designated predicate of the negandum (goose bumps).^{GL}

Correct Signs That Are an Observation of an Object That Is Contradictory in the Sense of Consciousnesses Not Abiding Together

One can state, "The subject, a noninterrupted path of a Hearer path of meditation that is an actual antidote to the conception of a self of persons, does not abide harmlessly together with the conception of a self of persons because of being an actual antidote to the conception of a self of persons." [In that, "an actual antidote to the conception of a self of persons" is a correct sign that is an observation of a contradictory object in the sense of consciousnesses not abiding together.]

The object designated as the predicate of the negandum is "the conception of a self of persons," which is contradictory—in the sense of not abiding together—with an actual antidote to the conception of a self of persons. Thus, that which is set as the sign—"an actual antidote to the conception of a self of persons"—is a correct sign that is an observation of a contradictory object in the sense of consciousnesses not abiding together.^{GL}

Correct Signs That Are an Observation of an Object That Is Contradictory in the Sense of Nonassociated Compositional Factors Not Abiding Together

One can state, "The subject, a crow in the east, does not abide harmlessly together with an owl because of being a crow." [In that, "crow" is such a sign.]

The object designated as the predicate of the negandum is "owl," which is contradictory—in the sense of not abiding together—with a crow. Thus, "crow" is a correct sign that is an observation of a contradictory object in the sense of compositional factors not abiding together. Crows, being persons (*gang zag*), are compositional factors.^{GL}

Correct Signs That Are an Observation of an Object Suitable to Appear That Is Contradictory in the Sense of Mutual Exclusion

Definitions

The definition of a correct sign that is an observation of an object suitable to appear that is contradictory in the sense of mutual exclusion in the proof of sound as not permanent is:

> that which is a common locus of (1) being a correct sign that is an observation of a contradictory object in the proof that sound is not permanent and of (2) not being contradictory with permanent in the sense of not abiding together [with it].

An illustration of such a sign is "product" [as in, "The subject, sound, is not permanent because of being a product."]

> The object designated as the predicate of the negandum is "permanent," which is mutually contradictory with product. Thus, in the proof that sound is not permanent, "product" is a correct sign that is an observation of a contradictory object in the sense of mutual exclusion.[GL]

The definition of a correct sign that is an observation of objects contradictory in the sense of mutual exclusion in the proof that a horned mass in front [of oneself] is not a horse is:

> that which is a common locus of (1) being a correct sign that is an observation of a contradictory object in the proof that a horned mass in front [of oneself] is not a horse and of (2) not being contradictory with horse in the sense of not abiding together [with it].

[When one states, "The subject, the horned mass in front of oneself is not a horse because of being horned,"] "horned" is such a sign.

> The object designated as the predicate of the negandum, horse, is mutually contradictory with being horned. Thus, in the proof that the horned mass in front of oneself is not a horse, "being horned" is a correct sign that is an observation of an object suitable to appear that is contradictory in the sense of mutual exclusion.[GL]

Divisions

This section has two parts, (1) correct signs that, through dependence, refute definiteness and (2) correct signs that, through definiteness, refute dependence.

Correct Signs That, through Dependence, Refute Definiteness

Illustration: One can state, "The subject, white cloth, is not definite in possessing a dyed color from its mere establishment because its becoming that which has dyed color must depend on causes arising later than itself." In that, "its becoming that which has dyed color must depend on causes arising later than itself" is a correct sign in the proof of that, which, through dependence, refutes definiteness.

Correct Signs That, through Definiteness, Refute Dependence

Illustration: One can state, "With respect to the subject, product, its disintegration does not depend on other causes and conditions arising later than itself because of being definite to disintegrate from its mere establishment." In that, [the reason given] is a correct sign in the proof of that, which, through definiteness, refutes dependence.

The statement, "It follows that impermanent is not a correct sign in the proof of sound as a product because product is a correct sign in the proof of sound as impermanent," is refuted in dependence on this reasoning [for if the pervasion were true, then one could state,] "It [absurdly] follows with respect to the subject, object of knowledge, that [being] definite to disintegrate from its mere establishment is not a correct sign in the proof that product does not depend for its own disintegration on other causes arising later than itself because a thing that does not depend for its own disintegration on other causes arising later than itself is a correct sign in the proof of product as definite to disintegrate from its mere establishment.

With regard to this, someone says, "It follows that the subject, that which possesses horns, is a correct sign that is an observation of a contradictory object in the sense of not abiding together in the proof that the horned mass in front [of oneself] is not a horse because of being a correct sign that is an observation of a contradictory object in the proof of that and because of being a different entity from horse." [In response to that, one would state that] the predicate does not necessarily follow from the reason.

> "That which possesses horns" is a correct sign that is an observation of a contradictory object in the proof that the horned mass in front of oneself is not a horse and is also a different substantial entity from horse. Thus, the opponent's reason is established in the proof of that; this does not entail, however,

that "that which possesses horns" is a correct sign that is an observation of a contradictory object in the sense of not abiding together in the proof of that. For, that which possesses horns and a horse can abide together peacefully; they do not fight each other as do a crow and an owl, and thus are not contradictories in the sense of not abiding together, but rather, in the sense of mutual exclusion.LR

[One can counter with a consequence of this view,] "It [absurdly] follows with respect to the subject, object of knowledge, that whatever are different substantial entities must be contradictories in the sense of not abiding together because of your assertion."

If the opponent accepts this, [then one can state the consequence,] "It follows that the subject, the two, fire and smoke, are contradictories in the sense of not abiding together because of your assertion." If this is accepted, [one can say,] "It [absurdly] follows that the subject, the two, fire and smoke, are object harmed and harmer because of your assertion." This cannot be accepted because they are assister and object assisted. This, in turn, is because [fire and smoke] are cause and effect.

ASCERTAINMENT OF THE DEFINITIONS IN TERMS OF ILLUSTRATIONS

Correct Sign of the Nonappearing

Nonobservation of a Related Cause

The first explanation is of a correct sign of the nonappearing that is a nonobservation of a related cause. This is presented in four stages.

The illustration is: "With respect to the subject, here in the place in front, there does not exist a factually concordant subsequent cognition (that ascertains a flesh-eater) in the continuum of a person for whom a flesh-eater is a supersensory object because there does not exist a prime cognition—that observes a flesh-eater in the place in front—in the continuum of a person for whom a flesh-eater is a supersensory object. The reason given in the illustration is shown to be all four:

(1) A correct nonobservation sign.
(2) A correct nonobservation sign of the nonappearing.
(3) A correct sign of the nonappearing that is a nonobservation of a related object.
(4) A correct sign of the nonappearing that is a nonobservation of a related cause.

(1) The subject, the nonexistence of a prime cognition (that

observes a flesh-eater) in the continuum of a person for whom a flesh-eater is a supersensory object, is a correct nonobservation sign in the proof that there does not exist a factually concordant subsequent cognition (that ascertains a flesh-eater in the place in front) in the continuum of a person for whom a flesh-eater is a supersensory object because (a) it is a correct sign in the proof of that and (b) the nonexistence of a factually concordant subsequent cognition (that ascertains a flesh-eater in the place in front) in the continuum of a person for whom a flesh-eater is a supersensory object is a negative phenomenon.

(2) The subject, the nonexistence of a prime cognition (that observes a flesh-eater) in the continuum of a person for whom a flesh-eater is a supersensory object, is a correct nonobservation sign of the nonappearing in the proof of that because (a) of being a correct nonobservation sign in the proof of that and (b) a flesh-eater is a supersensory object for a person for whom it [the sign] has become the property of the subject in the proof of that.

If someone says that the latter part of the reason is not established, then it follows with respect to the subject, a person for whom a flesh-eater is a supersensory object with respect to the place in front, that a flesh-eater is a supersensory object for him because it is the subject.

(3) The subject, the nonexistence of a prime cognition (that observes a flesh-eater) in the continuum of a person for whom a flesh-eater is a supersensory object, is a correct sign of the nonappearing that is a nonobservation of a related object in the proof that there does not exist a factually concordant subsequent cognition (that ascertains a flesh-eater in the place in front) in the continuum of a person for whom a flesh-eater is a supersensory object because of (a) being a correct nonobservation sign of the nonappearing in the proof of that and (b) being a nonaffirming negative phenomenon.

(4) It follows with respect to the subject, object of knowledge, that the nonexistence of a prime cognition (that observes a flesh-eater) in the continuum of a person for whom a flesh-eater is a supersensory object is a correct sign of the nonappearing that is a nonobservation of a related cause in the proof that there does not exist a factually concordant subsequent cognition (that ascertains a flesh-eater in the place in front) in the continuum of a person for whom a flesh-eater is a supersensory object because (a) of being a correct sign of the nonappearing that is a nonobservation of a related object in the proof of that and (b) a prime cognition that observes a flesh-eater is the cause of a factually concordant subsequent cognition that ascertains a flesh-eater.

Extend this to the other [two: correct signs of the nonappearing that are an observation of a pervader and those that are an observation of a nature].

Observation of a Contradictory Object

The subject, existent, is a correct sign that is an observation of a contradictory object in the proof that there does not exist a factually concordant subsequent cognition [that ascertains a flesh-eater in the place in front] in the continuum of a person for whom a flesh-eater is a supersensory object because existent is a correct nonobservation sign in the proof of that and is either an affirming negative phenomenon or a positive phenomenon. [The latter reason is established] because [existent] is a positive phenomenon.

> In another way, for the sake of understanding the meaning: The subject, existent, is a correct sign that is an observation of a contradictory object in the proof of that because the object imputed as the predicate of the negandum—a subsequent cognition (that ascertains a flesh-eater in the place in front) in the continuum of a person for whom a flesh-eater is a supersensory object—is contradictory with "existent" that is set as the sign in the proof of that.GL

Nonobservation of the Suitable to Appear

The subject, product, is a correct nonobservation sign of the suitable to appear in the proof that sound is not permanent because (1) of being a correct nonobservation sign in the proof of that and (2) permanent is not a supersensory object for a person for whom it has become the property of the subject in the proof of that. The first reason is easy [to prove].

> The subject, product, is a correct nonobservation sign in the proof of that because (1) it is a correct sign in the proof of that and (2) there occurs a common locus of (a) being what is held as the explicit predicate of the probandum in the proof of that by such-and-such a sign and (b) being a negative phenomenon.GL

[If someone says that the latter reason is not established, then the response is,] "The latter reason is established because it follows with respect to the subject, a person for whom product has become the property of the subject in the proof that sound is not permanent, that permanent is not a supersensory object for that person because it [the subject] is that subject."

> The permanent—the object designated as the predicate of the

negandum in the proof that sound is not permanent—is not a supersensory object for the person for whom product has become the property of the subject in the proof of that because the permanent can be realized by that person.[DM]

Nonobservation of a Related Object Suitable to Appear

The subject, the nonexistence of fire, is a correct sign that is a nonobservation of a related object suitable to appear in the proof of smoke as nonexistent on a lake at night because of (1) being a correct nonobservation sign of the suitable to appear in the proof of that and (2) being a nonaffirming negative phenomenon.

> The object designated as the predicate of the negandum in the proof of that is "smoke," which is an object related to fire. "The nonexistence of fire" is set as the sign in the proof of that and, thus, is a correct sign that is a nonobservation of a related object suitable to appear.[GL]

Nonobservation of a Cause Suitable to Appear

With respect to the subject, object of knowledge, the nonexistence of fire is a correct sign that is a nonobservation of a cause suitable to appear in the proof of smoke as nonexistent on a lake at night because it [the nonexistence of fire] is a correct nonobservation sign of the suitable to appear in the proof of that and (2) fire is the cause of smoke.

Extend this reasoning to the [three] others, [correct signs that are a nonobservation of (1) a pervader suitable to appear, (2) a nature suitable to appear, and (3) a direct effect suitable to appear].

Observation of a Contradictory Object Suitable to Appear

The subject, product, is a correct sign that is an observation of a contradictory object suitable to appear, in the proof that sound is not permanent because of (1) being a correct nonobservation sign of the suitable to appear in the proof of that and (2) being either an affirming negative or a positive phenomenon. This is because [product] is a positive phenomenon.

> Another way of carrying out this proof is: With respect to the subject, product, it is a correct sign that is an observation of a contradictory object suitable to appear in the proof that sound is not permanent because (1) it is a correct nonobservation sign of the suitable to appear in the proof of that and (2) the object

designated as the predicate of the negandum in the proof of that by the sign of it is "permanent," which is contradictory with product. Since the observation of it (product) is set as the sign, it is a correct sign that is an observation of a contradictory object suitable to appear.^{GL}

Observation of an Object Suitable to Appear That Is Contradictory in the Sense of Not Abiding Together

With respect to the subject, object of knowledge, a place covered by a large powerful fire is a correct sign that is an observation of a contradictory object in the sense of not abiding together in the proof that the continuous tangible object, cold, does not exist on a place in the east covered by a large powerful fire because (1) of being a correct sign that is an observation of a contradictory object in the proof of that and (2) that place covered by a large powerful fire is a contradictory object that does not abide together with the continuous tangible object, cold.

> In another way: With respect to the subject, object of knowledge, a place covered by a large powerful fire is a correct sign that is an observation of a contradictory object in the sense of not abiding together in the proof of that because (1) it is a correct sign that is a nonobservation of a contradictory object in the proof of that and (2) the object designated as the predicate of the negandum in the proof of that by the sign of it is the continuous tangible object, cold, which does not abide together with a place covered by a large powerful fire. Since it (a place covered by a large powerful fire) is set as the sign, it is a correct sign that is an observation of a contradictory object in the sense of not abiding together.^{GL}

Correct Sign That Is an Observation of an Object Suitable to Appear That Is Contradictory in the Sense of Mutual Exclusion

With respect to the subject, product, it [product] is a correct sign that is an observation of a contradictory object in the sense of mutual exclusion in the proof that sound is not permanent because (1) it [product] is a correct sign that is an observation of a contradictory object in the proof of that and (2) it [product] is not contradictory with the permanent in the sense of not abiding together. This is because it [product] is not of a substantial entity different from the permanent.

In another way: With respect to the subject, product, it is a correct sign that is an observation of a contradictory object in the sense of mutual exclusion in the proof that sound is not permanent because (1) it (product) is a correct sign that is an observation of a contradictory object in the proof of that and (2) the object designated as the predicate of the negandum in the proof of that by the sign of it is "the permanent," which is contradictory with product in the sense of mutual exclusion. Since it (product) is set as the sign, it is a correct sign that is an observation of a contradictory object in the sense of mutual exclusion.GL

IDENTIFICATION OF THE SIGN, PREDICATE OF THE PROBANDUM, AND BASIS OF DEBATE

This section involves the positing of theses and the stating of probans. The nonexistence of fire is the reason in the proof of smoke as nonexistent on a lake at night by the sign, nonexistence of fire. Fireless is not the reason in the proof of smoke as nonexistent on a lake at night by the sign, nonexistence of fire. The nonexistence of smoke is both (1) the predicate of the probandum in the proof of smoke as nonexistent on a lake at night by the sign, nonexistence of fire, and (2) that held as the explicit predicate of the probandum in the proof of that. Smokeless is not either of those. The same reasoning [applies] to treeless and so forth.

> The nonexistence of trees is the reason in the proof that an *aśoka* tree does not exist on a craggy cliff where trees are not observed by valid cognition by the sign, nonexistence of trees. Treeless is not the reason in the proof of that by the sign, nonexistence of trees. The nonexistence of an *aśoka* tree is both (1) the predicate of the probandum in the proof of that by the sign, nonexistence of trees, and (2) that held as the explicit predicate of the probandum in the proof of that. *Aśoka*-treeless is not either of those.LR

The nonobservation of pot by valid cognition is the reason in the proof that a pot does not exist on a place where pot is not observed by valid cognition. The nonexistence of pot is both (1) the explicit predicate of the probandum in the proof that pot does not exist on a place where pot is not observed by valid cognition, and (2) that held as the explicit predicate of the probandum in the proof of that. Extend this to others of similar types.

Flesh-eater is an object designated as the predicate of the negandum in the proof that there does not exist a factually concordant subsequent cognition (that ascertains a flesh-eater in the place in front) in the continuum of a person for whom a flesh-eater is a supersensory object. However, flesh-eater is not the predicate of the negandum in the proof of that.

The existence of a factually concordant subsequent cognition (that ascertains a flesh-eater) in the continuum of a person for whom a flesh-eater is a supersensory object is both the predicate of the negandum in the proof of that and an object designated as the predicate of the negandum in the proof of that.

Smoke is an object designated as the predicate of the negandum in the proof of smoke as nonexistent on a lake at night, but is not the predicate of the negandum in the proof of that. The existence of smoke there is both an object designated as the predicate of the negandum in the proof of smoke as nonexistent on a lake at night and the predicate of the negandum in the proof of that.

Permanent [is both an object designated as the predicate of the negandum and the predicate of the negandum in the proof that sound is not permanent. Not being impermanent] is an object designated as the predicate of the negandum in the proof that sound is not permanent but is not the predicate of the negandum in the proof of that.

7. Other Divisions of Correct Signs

This section has two parts: correct signs of a positive phenomenon and correct signs of a negative phenomenon.

CORRECT SIGNS OF A POSITIVE PHENOMENON

Definition

The definition of a correct sign of a positive phenomenon is:

> (1) it is a correct sign in the proof of that and (2) there exists a common locus of being that held as the explicit predicate of the probandum in the proof of that by the sign of it and of being a positive phenomenon.

Divisions

Correct signs of a positive phenomenon are of two types: correct effect signs and correct nature signs. Whatever is either a correct effect sign or a correct nature sign is necessarily a correct sign of a positive phenomenon.

CORRECT SIGNS OF A NEGATIVE PHENOMENON

Definition

The definition of a correct sign of a negative phenomenon is:

> (1) it is a correct sign in the proof of that and (2) there exists a common locus of being that held as the explicit predicate of the probandum in the proof of that by the sign of it and of being a negative phenomenon.

The two—(a) correct sign of a negative phenomenon and (b) correct nonobservation sign—are equivalent. Although correct sign of a negative phenomenon in the proof of that and correct sign of a positive phenomenon in the proof of that are contradictory, correct sign of a negative phenomenon and correct sign of a positive phenomenon are not contradictory. This is because product is both [a correct sign of a negative phenomenon and a correct sign of a positive phenomenon].

This [in turn] is because it [product] is both a correct sign of a negative phenomenon in the proof that sound is not permanent and a correct sign of a positive phenomenon in the proof that sound is impermanent.

DIVISION BY WAY OF THE MODES OF PROOF

Divisions of correct signs by way of the modes of proof are of five types: correct signs proving (1) the meaning, (2) the expression, (3) only the meaning, (4) only the expression, and (5) both the meaning and the expression. This section has three parts: definitions, illustrations, and reasons proving [the illustrations].

DEFINITIONS

(1) The definition of something's being a correct sign proving the meaning in the proof of that is:

> (a) it is a correct sign in the proof of that and (b) there exists a common locus of being that held as the explicit predicate of the probandum in the proof of that by the sign of it and of being a definition.

(2) The definition of something's being a correct sign proving the expression in the proof of that is:

> (a) it is a correct sign in the proof of that and (b) there exists a common locus of being that held as the explicit predicate of the probandum in the proof of that by the sign of it and of being a definiendum.

(3) The definition of something's being a correct sign proving only the meaning in the proof of that is:

> (a) it is a correct sign in the proof of that and (b) there does not exist a common locus of being that held as the explicit predicate of the probandum in the proof of that by the sign of it and of being a definiendum, but (c) there does exist a common locus of [being that held as the explicit predicate of the probandum in the proof of that by the sign of it] and of being a definition.

(4) The definition of something's being a correct sign proving only the expression in the proof of that is:

> (a) it is a correct sign in the proof of that and (b) there does not exist a common locus of being that held as the explicit

predicate of the probandum in the proof of that by the sign of it and of being a definition, but (c) there does exist a common locus of being [that held as the explicit predicate of the probandum in the proof of that by the sign of it] and of being a definiendum.

(5) The definition of something's being a correct sign proving both the meaning and the expression in the proof of that is:

> (a) it is a correct sign in the proof of that and (b) there exists a common locus of being that held as the explicit predicate of the probandum in the proof of that by the sign of it and of being a definition and (c) there exists a common locus of being [that held as the explicit predicate of the probandum in the proof of that by the sign of it] and of being a definiendum.

ILLUSTRATIONS AND REASONS PROVING THEM

[When one states, "The subject, sound, is impermanent because of being momentary,"] momentary is a correct sign proving only the expression in the proof of sound as impermanent. However, [momentary] is not a correct sign proving sound as impermanent by the sign, product. This is because whatever is a correct sign in the proof of sound as impermanent by the sign, product, must be one with product.

Product is a correct sign proving only the expression in the proof of sound as impermanent for a correct opponent who has already established by valid cognition that sound is momentary. However, in general [product] is a correct sign proving both the meaning and the expression in the proof of sound as impermanent. This is because [product] is a correct sign proving both the meaning and the expression for an opponent who has not ascertained by valid cognition that sound is momentary.

> (1) One can state, "The subject, sound, is momentary because of being a product." In that, product is a correct sign proving the meaning because product is a correct sign in the proof of that and there occurs a common locus of being that held as the explicit predicate of the probandum in the proof of that by the sign of it and of being a definition. Momentary, the definition of impermanent, is posited as that common locus.
> (2) One can state, "The subject, sound, is impermanent because of being a product." In that, product is a correct sign proving the expression because (a) product is a correct sign in the proof

of that and (b) there occurs a common locus of being that held as the explicit predicate of the probandum in the proof of that by the sign of it and of being a definiendum. Impermanent, the definiendum of momentary, is posited as that common locus.

(3) One can state, "The subject, sound, is momentary because of being a product." In that, product is a correct sign proving only the meaning because (a) product is a correct sign in the proof of that and (b) there does not occur a common locus of being that held as the explicit predicate of the probandum in the proof of that by the sign of it and of being a definiendum, but (c) there does exist a common locus (momentary, the definition of impermanent) of being that held as the explicit predicate of the probandum in the proof of that by the sign of it and of being a definition.

(4) One can state, "The subject, sound, is impermanent because of being momentary." In that, momentary is a correct sign proving only the expression because (a) momentary is a correct sign in the proof of that by the sign of it and (b) there does not occur a common locus of being that held as the explicit predicate of the probandum in the proof of that by the sign of it and of being a definition, but (c) there does exist a common locus (impermanent, the definiendum of momentary) of being that held as the explicit predicate of the probandum and of being a definiendum.

(5) One can state, "The subject, sound, is impermanent because of being a product." In that, product is a correct sign proving both the meaning and the expression because (a) product is a correct sign in the proof of that and (b) there occurs a common locus (momentary) of being that held as the explicit predicate of the probandum in the proof of that by the sign of it, and (c) there occurs a common locus (impermanent) of being that held as the explicit predicate of the probandum and of being a definiendum.[GL]

DIVISION BY WAY OF THE PROBANDUM

This section has three parts: correct signs through the power of the thing, correct signs of belief, and correct signs of renown.

CORRECT SIGNS THROUGH THE POWER OF THE THING

[This section has three parts: a definition, divisions, and illustrations.]

Definition

The definition of a correct sign through the power of the thing [in the proof of that] is:

> that which is a correct sign in the proof of that and is a producer of an inferential valid cognition—through the power of the thing—of the probandum in the proof of that.

Divisions

Correct signs through the power of the thing are of three types: correct effect, nature, and nonobservation signs [through the power of the thing].

Illustrations

[One can state, "With respect to the subject, on a smoky pass, fire exists because smoke exists." In that,] smoke is a correct effect sign through the power of the thing in the proof of fire as existent on a smoky pass.

[One can state, "The subject, sound, is impermanent because of being a product." In that,] product is a correct nature sign through the power of the thing in the proof of sound as impermanent.

[One can state, "With respect to the subject, on a lake at night, smoke does not exist because fire does not exist. In that,] the nonexistence of fire is a correct nonobservation sign through the power of the thing in the proof of smoke as nonexistent on a lake at night.

CORRECT SIGNS OF BELIEF

This section has three parts: a definition, divisions, and illustrations.

Definition

The definition of a correct sign of belief [in the proof of that] is:

> that which is a correct sign in the proof of that and is a producer of an inferential valid cognition—of belief—of the probandum in the proof of that.

Divisions

Correct signs of belief are of three types: correct effect, nature, and nonobservation signs of belief.

Illustration of Correct Effect Sign of Belief

[One can state, "The subject, the scripture, 'Through giving, resources; through ethics, happy migrations,' is preceded by a valid cognition that realizes the meaning that is its object of indication because of being a scripture that is devoid of the three contradictions." In that,] "scripture that is devoid of the three contradictions" is a correct effect sign of belief in the proof that the scripture, "Through giving, resources; through ethics, happy migrations," is incontrovertible with respect to the meaning that is its object of indication.

Illustration of Correct Nature Sign of Belief

[One can state, "The subject, the scripture, 'Through giving, resources; through ethics, happy migrations,' is incontrovertible with respect to the meaning that is its object of indication because of being a scripture that is devoid of the three contradictions." In that,] "scripture that is devoid of the three contradictions" is a correct nature sign of belief in the proof that the scripture, "Through giving, resources; through ethics, happy migrations," is incontrovertible with respect to the meaning that is its object of indication.

Illustration of Correct Nonobservation Sign of Belief

[One can state, "The subject, the scripture, 'Through giving, resources; through ethics, happy migrations,' is not controvertible with respect to the meaning that is its object of indication because of being a scripture that is devoid of the three contradictions." In that,] "scripture that is devoid of the three contradictions" is a correct nonobservation sign of belief in the proof that the scripture, "Through giving, resources; through ethics, happy migrations," is not controvertible with respect to the meaning that is its object of indication.

> There are three valid cognitions: direct valid cognition, inferential cognitions through the power of the thing, and inferential cognitions of belief. There are also three types of objects of comprehension: manifest, slightly hidden, and very hidden. In order for a scripture to be pure by way of the three analyses, and thus devoid of the three contradictions, the following three conditions must prevail with regard to that scripture:
> 1) If it contains teachings of manifest phenomena, then these must not be damaged when analyzed by direct valid cognition.

2) If it contains teachings of slightly hidden phenomena, then these must not be damaged when analyzed by inference through the power of the fact.
3) If it contains teachings of very hidden phenomena, then these must be free of inner contradictions of assertion when analyzed by inference of belief.[LR]

CORRECT SIGNS OF RENOWN

Definition

The definition of a correct sign of renown [in the proof of that] is:

> that which is a correct sign in the proof of that and is a producer of an inferential valid cognition—of renown—of the probandum in the proof of that.

Divisions

Correct signs of renown are of two types: [correct nature signs of renown and correct nonobservation signs of renown].

Illustration of Correct Nature Sign of Renown

[One can state: "The subject, rabbit-bearer, is suitable to be expressed by the term 'moon' because of existing among objects of thought." In that,] "existing among objects of thought" is a correct nature sign of renown in the proof of rabbit-bearer as suitable to be expressed by the term "moon."

Illustration of Correct Nonobservation Sign of Renown

[One can state: "The subject, rabbit-bearer, is not suitable to be expressed by the term 'moon' through the power of the thing because of existing among objects of thought." In that,] "existing among objects of thought" is a correct nonobservation sign of renown in the proof of rabbit-bearer as not suitable to be expressed by the term "moon" through the power of the thing.

DIVISION BY WAY OF THE MODE OF RELATING TO THE SIMILAR CLASS

This section has two parts: correct sign that relates to the similar class as pervader and correct sign that relates to the similar class in two ways.

CORRECT SIGN THAT RELATES TO THE SIMILAR CLASS AS PERVADER

Definition

The definition of a correct sign that relates to the similar class as pervader is:

> that which is the three modes and relates to the similar class as pervader in the proof of sound as impermanent.

Illustration

Product [is a correct sign that relates to the similar class as pervader in the proof of sound as impermanent by the sign, product. This is because whatever is impermanent is necessarily a product.]

CORRECT SIGN THAT RELATES TO THE SIMILAR CLASS IN TWO WAYS

Definition

The definition of a correct sign that relates to the similar class in two ways is:

> that which is the three modes and relates to the similar class in two ways in the proof of sound as impermanent.

Illustration

Particularity of product [is a correct sign that relates to the similar class in two ways in the proof of sound as impermanent by the sign, particularity of product].

DIVISION BY WAY OF THE PARTY

This section has two parts: correct sign on the occasion of one's own purpose and correct sign on the occasion of another's purpose.

CORRECT SIGN ON THE OCCASION OF ONE'S OWN PURPOSE

Definition

The definition of a correct sign on the occasion of one's own purpose is:

It is a common locus of (1) being a correct sign in the proof of sound as impermanent and (2) there not existing a correct second party [or "latter opponent"] in the proof of that by the sign of it.

Illustration

The first party states to himself that product is a sign in the proof of sound as impermanent. At the time of that proof, product is a correct sign on the occasion of one's own purpose in the proof of sound as impermanent.

CORRECT SIGN ON THE OCCASION OF ANOTHER'S PURPOSE

Definition

The definition of a correct sign on the occasion of another's purpose is:

It is a common locus of (1) being a correct sign in the proof of that and (2) there existing a correct second party in the proof of that by the sign of it.

Illustration

[One can state to the second party, "The subject, sound, is impermanent because of being a product." In that,] "product" is a correct sign on the occasion of another's purpose in the proof of sound as impermanent.

Someone says: "Product is both a correct sign on the occasion of one's own purpose in the proof of sound as impermanent and a correct sign on the occasion of another's purpose in the proof of sound as impermanent."

> Pur-bu-jok presents this as a false view; however, there are different opinions on this point. According to Ge-shay Ge-dün-lo-drö, product is indeed both a correct sign on the occasion of one's own purpose and a correct sign on the occasion of another's purpose in the proof of sound as impermanent. This is because (1) when product becomes a correct sign on the occasion of another's purpose, it (product) is a correct sign on the occasion of another's purpose; and (2) when product becomes a correct sign on the occasion of one's own purpose, it (product) is a correct sign on the occasion of one's own purpose.

[*Response:*] "It [absurdly] follows that with respect to the subject, product, there does not exist a correct second party in the proof of sound as impermanent by the sign, product, because it [product] is a correct sign on the occasion of one's own purpose in the proof of sound as impermanent." If this is accepted, then [one states]: "With respect to the subject, product, there does exist a correct second party in the proof of sound as impermanent by the sign, product, because it [product] is a correct sign on the occasion of another's purpose in the proof of sound as impermanent."

Furthermore, if someone says: "A correct sign on the occasion of one's own purpose does not exist," [the response is,] "That is not correct, because when product becomes a correct sign on the occasion of one's own purpose in the proof of sound as impermanent, product is a correct sign on the occasion of one's own purpose in the proof of sound as impermanent."

Further, a correct sign on the occasion of one's own purpose exists because there exists a correct sign on the occasion of one's own purpose in the proof of sound as impermanent. If someone says that the reason is not established, [then the response is:] "It [absurdly] follows that with respect to the subject, object of knowledge, whatever is a correct sign in the proof of sound as impermanent is necessarily not a correct sign on the occasion of one's own purpose in the proof of that because [according to you] that reason is not established. If this is accepted, then it [absurdly] follows that when product becomes a correct sign on the occasion of one's own purpose in the proof of sound as impermanent, the subject, product, is not a correct sign on the occasion of one's own purpose in the proof of that because of being a correct sign in the proof of that. [You have accepted the] three spheres.

The three spheres are:

1) The opposite of the consequence: that when product becomes a correct sign on the occasion of one's own purpose in the proof of sound as impermanent, the subject, product, is a correct sign on the occasion of one's own purpose in the proof of that.

2) The reason: that product is a correct sign in the proof of sound as impermanent.

3) The pervasion: that whatever is a correct sign in the proof of sound as impermanent is necessarily not a correct sign on the occasion of one's own purpose in the proof of that.

Further, it follows that product is not a correct sign on the occasion of one's own purpose in the proof of sound as impermanent because that [product] is a correct sign on the occasion of another's purpose in the

451   Other Divisions of Correct Signs

proof of that. This is because the syllogism, "The subject, sound, is impermanent because of being a product," is a pure application of a correct sign on the occasion of another's purpose.

Objection: It [absurdly] follows that when there does not exist a correct second party in the proof of sound as impermanent by the sign, product, there does exist a correct second party in the proof of sound as impermanent by the sign, product, because when product has become the correct sign on the occasion of one's own purpose in the proof of sound as impermanent, product is a correct sign on the occasion of another's purpose in the proof of sound as impermanent.

Answer to the objection: The reason is not established. If it were accepted [that when there does not exist a correct second party in the proof of sound as impermanent by the sign, product, there does exist a correct second party in the proof of sound as impermanent by the sign, product,] then it would [absurdly] follow that when product is nonexistent, product exists because when a correct second party in the proof of sound as impermanent by the sign, product, does not exist, a correct second party in the proof of sound as impermanent by the sign, product, exists. You have accepted the reason.

Someone says: "Although correct sign on the occasion of one's own purpose does not exist, when product has become a correct sign on the occasion of one's own purpose in the proof of sound as impermanent, product is a correct sign on the occasion of one's own purpose in the proof of sound as impermanent."

[*Response:*] "That is not correct. It [absurdly] follows that a correct sign on the occasion of one's own purpose exists because a correct sign on the occasion of one's own purpose in the proof of sound as impermanent exists. This [in turn] is because (1) when product has become a correct sign on the occasion of one's own purpose in the proof of sound as impermanent, product exists and (2) when product has become a correct sign on the occasion of one's own purpose in the proof of sound as impermanent, product is a correct sign on the occasion of one's own purpose in the proof of sound as impermanent. The reason has been accepted."

Further, it [absurdly] follows that a correct sign on the occasion of one's own purpose in the proof of sound as impermanent exists because there exists a product that has become a correct sign on the occasion of one's own purpose in the proof of sound as impermanent. [This is] because there exists a person for whom product has become a correct sign on the occasion of one's own purpose in the proof of that. This [in turn] is because there exists a person for whom smoke has become a correct sign on the occasion of one's own purpose in the proof of fire as existent on a smoky pass.

SYLLOGISMS PROVING THE EXISTENCE OF FORMER AND LATER LIVES

With respect to the subject, the last moment of the mind of a common being who is just about to die, there exists a later knower that is its substantial effect because it is a knower [of one] who has a continuum involved with attachment. An example is the present mind.

The subject, the mind of one who has just been born, is preceded by a mind of similar type because of being a knower, as is the case, for example, with the mind of an old person.

8. Contradictory Reasons

The explanation of the opposite of correct signs, quasi-reasons, has two parts: definitions and divisions.

DEFINITIONS OF CONTRADICTORY REASONS

This section also has two parts: refutation of another's view and presentation of our own system.

REFUTATION OF ANOTHER'S VIEW

In accordance with another's system, someone says: "The definition of a quasi-reason is: that which is not the three modes." That is not correct, because a quasi-reason does not exist. This is because whatever is an established base [that is, whatever exists] is necessarily a correct sign. In our own system, the definition of a quasi-reason is:

> that which is not the three modes in the proof of that.

Although in general quasi-reasons do not exist, in application to specific instances, there are three types: contradictory reasons in the proof of that, indefinite reasons in the proof of that, and nonestablished reasons in the proof of that.

PRESENTATION OF OUR OWN SYSTEM

The explanation of contradictory reasons has four parts: a definition, divisions, illustrations, and the statement of reasonings of proof.

Definition

The definition of a contradictory reason in the proof of sound as permanent is:

> that which is a common locus of (1) being the property of the subject in the proof of sound as permanent and (2) being the forward pervasion in the proof of sound as not being permanent.

Divisions

Contradictory reasons are of two types: contradictory reason that relates to the dissimilar class as a pervader and contradictory reason that relates to the dissimilar class in two ways.

Illustrations

Product is a contradictory reason that relates to the dissimilar class as a pervader in the proof of sound as not being impermanent. [This is because whatever is impermanent is necessarily a product.] Particularity of product is a contradictory reason that relates to the dissimilar class in two ways in the proof of sound as not being impermanent.

The Stating of Proof

It follows that the subject, product, is a contradictory reason that relates to the dissimilar class as a pervader in the proof of sound as not being impermanent (1) because of being a contradictory reason in the proof of that and (2) [because] whatever is impermanent is necessarily it [product].

It follows that the subject, particularity of product, is a contradictory reason in the proof of sound as not being impermanent because of being a contradictory reason in the proof of sound as permanent. This is because of (1) being the property of the subject in the proof of that and (2) being ascertained as a perverse forward pervasion in the proof of that by the sign of it [particularity of product].

> If someone says that the second reason is not established, then the response is: "It follows that the subject, particularity of product, is ascertained as a perverse forward pervasion in the proof of sound as permanent by the sign, particularity of product, because whatever is a particularity of product is necessarily not permanent."GL

Further, it follows that the subject, particularity of product, is a contradictory reason in the proof of sound as permanent because of being a correct sign in the proof of sound as impermanent.

Objection: It follows that a contradictory reason in the proof of sound as impermanent exists because a contradictory reason in the proof of sound as permanent exists.

Answer: That does not follow from the reason. To accept the statement [that a contradictory reason in the proof of sound as impermanent exists] is incorrect because whatever is a quasi-reason in the proof of sound as impermanent must be either an indefinite reason in the proof of that or a nonestablished reason in the proof of that.

Someone says: "If there exist three modes in the proof of that, there necessarily exists a correct sign in the proof of that." [In response one would say]: "It [absurdly] follows that with respect to the subject, object of knowledge, there exists a correct sign in the proof of sound as permanent because there exist three modes in the proof of sound as permanent. You have accepted the pervasion."

If someone says that the reason is not established, [the response is:] "It follows that there exist three modes in the proof of sound as permanent because (1) there exists a property of the subject in the proof of that, (2) there exists a forward pervasion in the proof of that, and (3) there exists a counterpervasion in the proof of that."

(1) The *first reason* is established because product is the property of the subject in the proof of sound as permanent.

If someone says that the [first] reason is not established, [the response is:] "It follows that the subject, product, is the property of the subject in the proof of sound as permanent because of being a contradictory sign in the proof of that. This is because [product] is a correct sign in the proof of sound as impermanent.

(2) The *second reason* [that there exists a forward pervasion in the proof of sound as permanent] is established because a common locus of (1) being a phenomenon and (2) not being momentary is the forward pervasion in the proof of sound as permanent.

If someone says that the [second] reason is not established, [the response is:] "It follows that the subject, a common locus of (1) being a phenomenon and (2) not being momentary, is the forward pervasion in the proof of sound as permanent because:

(a) there exists a correct similar example that possesses the two, the sign and the predicate, in the proof of that by the sign of it, and
(b) it [a common locus of being a phenomenon and not being momentary] is ascertained by valid cognition as just existing, in accordance with the mode of statement, in only the similar class in the proof of sound as permanent.

The first reason (a) is established because uncompounded space is a correct similar example that possesses the two, the sign and the predicate, in the proof of that by the sign of it.

> One can state, "The subject, sound, is permanent because of not being momentary, as is the case with uncompounded space." In that, uncompounded space is a correct similar example that possesses the two, the sign and the predicate in the proof of that. This is because uncompounded space is permanent and is not momentary.[GL]

The second reason (b) is established because it [a common locus of being a phenomenon and not being momentary] exists, in accordance with the mode of statement, in only the similar class in the proof of that. This is because it is the definition of permanent.

(3) The *third reason* [that there exists a counterpervasion in the proof of sound as permanent] is established because a common locus of being a phenomenon and not being momentary is that.

If someone says that the reason is not established, [the response is:] "It follows that the subject, a common locus of being a phenomenon and not being momentary, is the counterpervasion in the proof of sound as permanent because (1) there exists a dissimilar example that does not possess the two, the sign and the predicate, in the proof of that by the sign of it and (2) it is ascertained by valid cognition as only nonexistent in the dissimilar class in the proof of that.

If the basic consequence [that there exists a correct sign in the proof of sound as permanent] is accepted, [then the response is:] "It follows with respect to the subject, sound, that there does not exist a correct sign in the proof of it [sound] as permanent because it is not permanent."

Objection: That which is the three modes in the proof of sound as permanent exists because (1) that which is the property of the subject in the proof of that exists, (2) that which is the forward pervasion in the proof of that exists, and (3) that which is the counterpervasion in the proof of that exists.

Answer to the objection: That does not follow from the reason.

> In response to the objection, one could state the absurd consequence: "It follows from your view that that which is a pillar and a pot exists because that which is a pillar exists and that which is a pot exists." This is mistaken because there does not exist a common locus of being both a pillar and a pot.^{GL}

9. Indefinite Reasons

This section has two parts: a definition and divisions.

DEFINITION

The definition of an indefinite reason in the proof of sound as permanent is:

> that which is a common locus of (1) being the property of the subject in the proof of sound as permanent, (2) not being the forward pervasion in the proof of sound as permanent, and (3) not being the forward pervasion in the proof of sound as not being permanent.

DIVISIONS

This section has two parts: uncommon indefinite reason in the proof of that and common indefinite reason in the proof of that.

UNCOMMON INDEFINITE REASON IN THE PROOF OF SOMETHING

This section has two parts: a definition and illustrations.

Definition

The definition of something's being an uncommon indefinite reason in the proof of that is:

> (1) it is an indefinite reason in the proof of that and
> (2) it is a common locus of (a) not being ascertained as existent in the similar class in the proof of that by a person for whom it has become the property of the subject in the proof of that, and (b) that person does not ascertain it as existing in the dissimilar class in the proof of that.

Illustrations

Object of hearing, opposite from nonsound, and sound-isolate are each both an uncommon indefinite reason in the proof of sound as permanent and an uncommon indefinite reason in the proof of sound as impermanent.

Object of hearing, opposite from nonsound, and sound-isolate each have a particularly close relationship with sound, which makes it impossible for a person to ascertain whether one of these is impermanent without simultaneously understanding that sound is impermanent. Thus none of these three can serve as a correct sign in the given proofs because it is not possible for a person—for whom sound has become the property of the subject—to ascertain the relationship between any one of these three and the similar and dissimilar classes in those proofs without simultaneously understanding the thesis.

In general, it is possible, and in fact necessary, to ascertain the definition of a particular phenomenon before ascertaining that phenomenon itself. However, this is not the case with sound and its definition, object of hearing, because of their unusually close relationship.^{GL}

COMMON INDEFINITE REASON

This section has two parts: a definition and divisions.

Definition

The definition of something's being a common indefinite reason in the proof of that is:

(1) it is an indefinite reason in the proof of that and
(2) it is a common locus of its being either (a) ascertained as existent in the similar class in the proof of that by a person for whom it has become the property of the subject in the proof of that or (b) its being ascertained as existent in the dissimilar class in the proof of that by that person [or both].

Divisions

This section has three parts: actual indefinite reason in the proof of that, indefinite reason having remainder in the proof of that, and indefinite reason that is not either of those in the proof of that.

Actual Indefinite Reasons

This section has three parts: a definition, divisions, [and illustrations].

Definition

The definition of something's being an actual indefinite reason in the proof of that is:

> (1) it is an indefinite reason in the proof of that and
> (2) it is ascertained as existing in both the similar and the dissimilar class by a person for whom it has become the property of the subject in the proof of that.

Divisions

When actual indefinite reasons are divided there are four types: (1) actual indefinite reason that relates to the similar class as pervader and to the dissimilar class as pervader in the proof of that, (2) actual indefinite reason that relates to the similar class as pervader and to the dissimilar class in two ways in the proof of that, (3) actual indefinite reason that relates to the dissimilar class as pervader and to the similar class in two ways in the proof of that, and (4) actual indefinite reason that relates to both the similar and dissimilar classes in two ways in the proof of that.

Illustrations of Actual Indefinite Reasons

(1) Relating to the Similar Class as Pervader

[One can state, "The subject, sound, is permanent because the horns of a rabbit do not exist." In that,] "the horns of a rabbit do not exist" is an actual indefinite reason that relates to the similar class as pervader in the proof of sound as permanent and to the dissimilar class as pervader in the proof of that.

> *Proofs:* It follows with respect to the subject, the horns of a rabbit do not exist, that it relates to the similar class as pervader in the proof of sound as permanent because the similar class in the proof of that is "permanent" and with respect to whatever is permanent the horns of a rabbit necessarily do not exist.
>
> It follows with respect to the subject, the horns of a rabbit do not exist, that it relates to the dissimilar class as pervader in the proof of sound as permanent because the dissimilar class in the proof of that is "impermanent," and with respect to whatever is impermanent the horns of a rabbit necessarily do not exist.[GL]

(2) Relating to the Similar Class as Pervader and the Dissimilar Class in Two Ways

[One can state, "The subject, the sound of a conch, is arisen from exertion because of being impermanent." In that,] impermanent is an actual indefinite reason that relates to the similar class as pervader and to the dissimilar class in two ways in the proof of the sound of a conch as arisen from exertion.

> *Proofs:* It follows that the subject, impermanent, relates to the similar class as pervader in the proof of the sound of a conch as arisen from exertion because the similar class in the proof of that is "arisen from exertion," and whatever is arisen from exertion is necessarily impermanent.
>
> It follows that the subject, impermanent, relates to the dissimilar class in two ways in the proof of the sound of a conch as arisen from exertion because the dissimilar class in the proof of that is "not arisen from exertion," and whatever is not arisen from exertion is not necessarily impermanent (for example, uncompounded space) and is not necessarily not impermanent (for example, a river).^{GL}

(3) Relating to the Dissimilar Class as Pervader and the Similar Class in Two Ways

[One can state, "The subject, the sound of a conch, is not arisen from exertion because of being impermanent." In that,] impermanent is an actual indefinite reason that relates to the dissimilar class as pervader and to the similar class in two ways in the proof of the sound of a conch as not arisen from exertion.

> *Proofs:* It follows that the subject, impermanent, relates to the dissimilar class as pervader in the proof of the sound of a conch as not arisen from exertion because the dissimilar class in the proof of that is "arisen from exertion," and whatever is arisen from exertion is necessarily impermanent.
>
> It follows that the subject, impermanent, relates to the similar class in two ways in the proof of the sound of a conch as not arisen from exertion because the similar class in the proof of that is "not arisen from exertion," and whatever is not arisen from exertion is not necessarily impermanent and is not necessarily not impermanent.^{GL}

(4) Relating to Both the Similar and Dissimilar Classes in Two Ways

[One can state, "The subject, a sense consciousness apprehending two moons, is a direct perception because of being a sense consciousness." In that,] "sense consciousness" is an actual indefinite reason that relates to both the similar class and the dissimilar class in two ways in the proof that a sense consciousness apprehending two moons is a direct perception.

> *Proofs*: It follows that the subject, sense consciousness, relates to the similar class in two ways in the proof that a sense consciousness apprehending two moons is a direct perception because the similar class in the proof of that is "direct perception," and whatever is a direct perception is not necessarily a sense consciousness (for example, a yogic direct perception) and is not necessarily not a sense consciousness (for example, a sense consciousness apprehending blue).
>
> It follows that the subject, sense consciousness, relates to the dissimilar class in two ways in the proof that a sense consciousness apprehending two moons is a direct perception because the dissimilar class in the proof of that is "not a direct perception," and whatever is not a direct perception is not necessarily a sense consciousness (for example, a pot) and is not necessarily not a sense consciousness (for example, a sense consciousness apprehending two moons).^{GL}

Indefinite Reason Having Remainder

This section has two parts: a definition and divisions.

Definition

The definition of something's being an indefinite reason having remainder is:

> (1) it is a common indefinite reason in the proof of that and (2) a person for whom it has become the property of the subject in the proof of that either, (a) having ascertained it as existing in the similar class in the proof of that, doubts whether or not it exists in the dissimilar class or, (b) having ascertained it as existing in the dissimilar class in the proof of that, doubts whether or not it exists in the similar class.

Divisions

This section has two parts: indefinite reason having correct remainder and indefinite reason having contradictory remainder.

Indefinite Reason Having Correct Remainder

Definition

The definition of something's being an indefinite reason having correct remainder in the proof of that is:

> (1) it is an indefinite reason having remainder in the proof of that and (2) a person for whom it has become the property of the subject in the proof of that, having ascertained it as existing in the similar class, doubts whether or not it exists in the dissimilar class.

Illustration

[One can state, "The subject, Devadatta who speaks speech, is not omniscient because of speaking speech." In that,] "speaking speech" is an indefinite reason having correct remainder for a person who has doubts with regard to omniscience in the proof that Devadatta, who speaks speech, is not omniscient.

Indefinite Reason Having Contradictory Remainder

Definition

The definition of something's being an indefinite reason having contradictory remainder in the proof of that is:

> (1) it is an indefinite reason having remainder in the proof of that and (2) a person for whom it has become the property of the subject in the proof of that, having ascertained it as existing in the dissimilar class, doubts whether or not it exists in the similar class.

Illustration

[One can state: "The subject, Devadatta who speaks speech, is omniscient because of speaking speech." In that,] "speaking speech" is an indefinite reason having contradictory remainder for a person who has doubts with regard to omniscience in the proof that Devadatta who speaks speech is omniscient.

Common Indefinite Reasons That Are Not Either

This section [common indefinite reasons that are not either of the two—actual indefinite reasons or indefinite reasons having remainder] has two parts: a definition and an illustration.

Definition

The definition of something's being a common indefinite reason that is not either of the two [actual indefinite reason and indefinite reason having remainder] is:

> (1) it is a common indefinite reason in the proof of that and (2) a person for whom it has become the property of the subject in the proof of that either ascertains that it exists in only the similar class in the proof of that or ascertains that it is nonexistent in only the dissimilar class in the proof of that.

Illustration

[One can state: "With respect to the subject, with the lump of molasses in the mouth, the present form of molasses exists because the present taste of molasses exists." In that,] the present taste of molasses is an illustration of a common indefinite reason that is not either of those two in the proof that the present form of molasses exists with the lump of molasses in the mouth.

> If "the present taste of molasses" were a correct sign in the proof that the present form of molasses exists with the lump of molasses in the mouth, then it would have to be either a correct effect, nature, or nonobservation sign in that proof.
>
> Because the present form and the present taste of molasses are simultaneous, there cannot be a causal relationship between them. Thus, "the present taste of molasses" cannot be a correct effect sign in that proof.
>
> If "the present taste of molasses" were a correct nature sign in that proof, it would have to be of one nature with the present form of molasses, the predicate of the probandum in that proof. However, the present taste and form of molasses are not of one nature because of being separate substantial entities.
>
> Further, "the present taste of molasses" is not a correct nonobservation sign in the given proof because the predicate of

the probandum is a positive phenomenon.[GL]

10. Nonestablished Reasons

The explanation of nonestablished reasons in the proof of that has two parts: a definition and divisions.

DEFINITION

The definition of a nonestablished reason in the proof of that is:

> (1) it is stated as a sign in the proof of that and (2) it is not the property of the subject in the proof of that.

DIVISIONS

When divided, nonestablished reasons are of three types: nonestablished reasons in relation to the fact, nonestablished reasons in relation to a mind, and nonestablished reasons in relation to an opponent.

NONESTABLISHED REASONS IN RELATION TO THE FACT

Divisions

This section has seven parts: nonestablished reason due to (1) the non-existence of the entity of the sign, (2) the nonexistence of the entity of the subject, (3) the nondifference of the sign and the predicate of the probandum, (4) the nondifference of the basis of debate and the sign, (5) the nondifference of the basis of debate and the predicate of the probandum, (6) the nonexistence of the sign, in accordance with the mode of statement, with the subject sought to be known, and (7) the nonexistence in the subject sought to be known of a portion of the reason. [For the sake of understanding, this seventh type should be called: a nonestablished reason due to the nonexistence in the reason of a portion of the subject sought to be known.]

Illustrations

(1) One can state: "The subject, a being, is miserable because of being pierced by the horn of a rabbit." In that, ["pierced by the horn of a rabbit" is a nonestablished reason due to the nonexistence of the entity of the sign in the proof of a being as miserable].

(2) One can state, "The subject, the horn of a rabbit, is impermanent because of being a product." In that, ["product" is a

nonestablished reason due to the nonexistence of the entity of the subject in the proof of the horn of a rabbit as impermanent].

(3) One can state, "The subject, sound, is impermanent because of being impermanent." In that, ["impermanent" is a nonestablished reason due to the nondifference of the sign and the predicate of the probandum in the proof of sound as impermanent].

(4) One can state, "The subject, sound, is impermanent because of being a sound." In that, ["sound" is a nonestablished reason due to the nondifference of the basis of debate and the sign in the proof of sound as sound].

(5) One can state: "The subject, sound, is sound because of being a product." In that, ["product" is a nonestablished reason due to the nondifference of the basis of debate and the predicate of the probandum in the proof of sound as sound].

(6) One can state: "The subject, sound, is impermanent because of being the object of apprehension by an eye consciousness." In that, ["object of apprehension by an eye consciousness" is a nonestablished reason due to the nonexistence of the sign, in accordance with the mode of statement, with the subject sought to be known in the proof of sound as impermanent].

> Object of apprehension by an eye consciousness does not exist, in accordance with the mode of statement, with sound because (1) the mode of statement is an "is" statement and (2) sound is not an object of apprehension by an eye consciousness. Sound is not an object of apprehension by an eye consciousness because of being an object of apprehension by an ear consciousness.[LR]

(7) One can state: "The subject, a tree, is sentient because of sleeping at night with curled leaves." In that, ["sleeping at night with curled leaves" is a nonestablished reason due to the nonexistence in the reason of a portion of the subject sought to be known].

> "Sleeping at night with curled leaves" is a nonestablished reason due to the nonexistence in the reason of a portion of the subject sought to be known because whatever is a tree (the subject sought to be known) does not necessarily sleep at night with curled leaves, for example, an oak tree.[GL]

Nonestablished Reasons in Relation to a Mind

Divisions

This section has four parts: nonestablished reasons due to (1) doubt with regard to the entity of the sign, (2) doubt with regard to the entity of the subject, (3) doubt with regard to the relationship of the basis of debate and the sign, and (4) the nonexistence of the subject sought to be known.

Illustrations

(1) One can state: "The subject, sound, is impermanent because of being an object of comprehension of the valid cognition [in the continuum] of a flesh-eater." For a person for whom flesh-eater is a supersensory object, [object of comprehension of the valid cognition in the continuum of a flesh-eater is a nonestablished reason due to doubt with regard to the entity of the sign in the proof of sound as impermanent].

(2) One can state: "The subject, the song of an odor-eater, is impermanent because of being a product." For a person for whom an odor-eater is a supersensory object [product is a nonestablished reason due to doubt with regard to the entity of the subject in the proof of the song of an odor-eater as impermanent].

(3) One can state: "With respect to the subject, in the middle of three mountain ridges, a peacock exists because the call of a peacock exists." For a person who does not know where the peacock exists [the call of a peacock is a nonestablished reason due to doubt with regard to the relationship of the basis of debate and the sign in the proof of a peacock as existing in the middle of three mountain ridges].

> A person, having heard the call of a peacock, knows that a peacock exists somewhere on the three mountain ridges. However, hearing the peacock's call is not a sufficient reason for establishing the peacock as existing in the middle of the three mountain ridges.^{DM}

(4) One can state: "The subject, sound, is impermanent because of being a product." For the glorious Dharmakīrti, [product is a nonestablished reason due to the nonexistence of the subject sought to be known in the proof of sound as impermanent].

> The glorious Dharmakīrti has already ascertained by valid cognition that sound is impermanent. Thus, for him, sound does not exist as a subject sought to be known in the proof of sound as impermanent.^{LR}

NONESTABLISHED REASONS IN RELATION TO AN OPPONENT

Divisions

There are three types of nonestablished reasons in relation to a party [or opponent]: nonestablished reason in relation to (1) the former opponent [that is, the person who states the reason], (2) the latter opponent [that is, the person to whom the reason is stated], and (3) both former and latter opponents.

Illustrations

(1) When a Sāṃkhya states to a Buddhist: "The subject, awareness (*buddhi*), is mindless because of having production and disintegration," [having production and disintegration is a nonestablished reason in relation to the former opponent in the proof of awareness as mindless].

> That awareness has production and disintegration is established for a Buddhist but not for a Sāṃkhya. Thus, having production and disintegration is a nonestablished reason in terms of the former opponent—a Sāṃkhya—in the proof of awareness as being mindless.[LR]

(2) When a Nirgrantha states to a Buddhist: "The subject, a tree, has mind because of dying when the bark is peeled," [dying when the bark is peeled is a nonestablished reason in relation to the latter opponent in the proof of a tree as having mind].

> From the point of view of the Buddhist, when the tree's bark is peeled the tree dries but does not die. Thus, dying when the bark is peeled is a nonestablished reason in terms of the latter opponent—the Buddhist—in the proof of a tree as having mind.[LR]

(3) When a Sāṃkhya states to an Ayata [Nihilist]: "The subject, sound, is impermanent because of being an object of apprehension by an eye consciousness," [object of apprehension by an eye consciousness is a nonestablished reason in relation to both the former and latter opponents in the proof of sound as impermanent].

> For neither the Sāṃkhya nor the Nihilist is sound established as an object of apprehension by an eye consciousness.[LR]

11. Important Subsidiary Topics

This section has two parts: explanation of proof statements and explanation of other ancillary topics.

EXPLANATION OF PROOF STATEMENTS

This section has two parts: correct [proof statements] and quasi-[proof statements]. Proof statements are of three types: effect, nature, and nonobservation proof statements.

EFFECT PROOF STATEMENTS

This section has two parts: correct proof statements using a qualitative similarity [between the subject and the example] and using a qualitative dissimilarity.

Illustration of a Correct Proof Statement Using a Qualitative Similarity between the Subject and the Example

After stating the syllogism, ["With respect to the subject, on a smoky pass, fire exists because smoke exists"] one can state [a proof statement using a qualitative similarity between the subject and the example,] "Wherever smoke exists fire necessarily exists, as is the case with a kitchen; smoke also exists on a smoky pass." [The two, "kitchen" and "smoky pass," are qualitatively similar with regard to the existence of fire.]

Illustration of a Correct Proof Statement Using a Qualitative Dissimilarity between the Subject and the Example

[After stating the syllogism, "With respect to the subject, on a smoky pass, fire exists because smoke exists,"] one can state [a correct proof statement using a qualitative dissimilarity between the subject and the example,] "Wherever fire does not exist, smoke necessarily does not exist, as is the case with a river; smoke, however, exists on a smoky pass." [The two, "river" and "smoky pass," are qualitatively dissimilar with respect to the existence of fire because fire exists on a smoky pass but not in a river.]

NATURE PROOF STATEMENTS

[Nature proof statements are of two types:] correct proof statement using a qualitative similarity [between the subject and the example] and correct proof statement using a qualitative dissimilarity.

Illustration of a Correct Proof Statement Using a Qualitative Similarity [between the Subject and the Example]

[After stating the syllogism, "The subject, sound, is impermanent because of being a product"] one can state [a correct proof statement using a qualitative similarity between the subject and the example,] "Whatever is a product is necessarily impermanent, as is the case with pot; sound also is a product." [The two, pot and sound, are qualitatively similar in being impermanent.]

Illustration of a Correct Proof Statement Using a Qualitative Dissimilarity [between the Subject and the Example]

[With regard to the same syllogism, one can state a correct proof statement using a qualitative dissimilarity between the subject and the example,] "Whatever is permanent is necessarily not a product, as is the case with uncompounded space; sound, however, is a product." [The two, uncompounded space and sound, are qualitatively dissimilar in being impermanent. This is because sound is impermanent but uncompounded space is not.]

NONOBSERVATION PROOF STATEMENTS

[Nonobservation proof statements are of two types:] those using a qualitative similarity between the subject and the example and those using a qualitative dissimilarity.

Illustration of a Correct Proof Statement Using a Qualitative Similarity [between the Subject and the Example]

[One can state the syllogism, "With respect to the subject, on a craggy cliff where trees are not observed, a juniper does not exist because trees do not exist."] The statement, "Wherever trees do not exist, a juniper necessarily does not exist, as is the case with a treeless plain; on a craggy cliff where trees are not observed, trees also do not exist," is a correct proof statement using a qualitative similarity between the subject and the example. [The two, treeless plain and craggy cliff where trees are not observed, are qualitatively similar with respect to the nonexistence of trees.]

Illustration of a Correct Proof Statement Using a Qualitative Dissimilarity [between the Subject and the Example]

The statement, "Wherever a juniper exists, tree necessarily exists, as is the case with a forest; on a craggy cliff where trees are not observed, however, tree does not exist," is a correct proof statement using a qualitative dissimilarity between the subject and the example. [The two, forest and craggy cliff where trees are not observed, are qualitatively dissimilar with respect to the nonexistence of trees because trees exist in a forest but not on a craggy cliff where trees are not observed.]

In general, a correct proof statement must indicate the three modes as well as an example, without anything extra or anything missing. To give a mere illustration of this, having stated, "The subject, sound, is impermanent because of being a product," one states, "Whatever is a product is necessarily impermanent, as is the case with pot; sound also is a product." [In that statement, the words] "whatever is a product is necessarily impermanent," explicitly express the forward pervasion and implicitly imply the counterpervasion. [The words] "sound also is a product" explicitly express the property of the subject [that is, position] in the sense of subject. [The words] "as is the case with pot" explicitly express a similar example.

With respect to explicitly expressing the property of the subject and the counterpervasion and implicitly indicating the forward pervasion, [there is, for instance,] the statement, "Whatever is permanent is necessarily not a product, as is the case with space; sound, however, is a product."

However, the two, "whatever is a product is necessarily impermanent" and "whatever is permanent is necessarily not a product," are
not the forward pervasion and the counterpervasion of the syllogism
["The subject, sound, is impermanent because of being a product."] On
the contrary, product alone is the forward pervasion, the counterpervasion, and the property of the subject of that [syllogism] because of
being the three modes in that.

OTHER EXTENSIONS OF THE MEANING

Someone asks, "Does there exist a correct sign in a syllogism in which
something nonestablished is held as the subject? If such exists, how
would the predicate of the probandum be established? If it does not
exist, then how could [the statement,] 'The subject, the horn of a rabbit,
is selfless because of being either an existent or a nonexistent' be a correct syllogism?"

Although there are differing assertions with regard to this, Gyel-
tsap Rin-bo-chay explains that among signs of a positive phenomenon
there does not exist a correct sign of that which is held to be a nonestablished basis of debate, but that among signs of a negative phenomenon, [such] does exist. Although there is much to be examined, let us
leave it.

Someone asks: "Are signs of dependent-arising, of possessing parts,
of the lack of being one or many, and signs refuting the four extremes
of production—in the Madhyamaka system—not included among the
three signs that were explained earlier?"

Response: "In general, all correct signs are included among the
three: effect, nature, and nonobservation signs; however, the two, effect and nature signs, are mainly signs of a positive phenomenon and
nonobservation signs are mainly signs of a negative phenomenon. Still,
whatever is a sign of a negative phenomenon in the proof of that is not
necessarily a negative phenomenon. This is because although product
is a positive phenomenon, [product] is a correct nature sign in the
proof of sound as impermanent and is a correct nonobservation sign in
the proof of sound as empty of permanence."

The latter reason is established [that is, product is a correct nonobservation sign in the proof of sound as empty of permanence] because
[product] is a correct sign that is an observation of a contradictory object in the proof of that. This is because it is such when one states, "The
subject, sound, is empty of permanence because of being a product."

With regard to the sign of dependent-arising in the Madhyamaka system, the Foremost Tsong-kha-pa explains that, in that system, dependent-arising is a sign that is an observation of a contradictory object in the proof of thing as not truly existent. The sign of possessing parts is the same kind.

In the Madhyamaka system, all correct signs proving nontrue existence are [signs that are an] observation of a contradictory object in the proof of that;[a] they are mainly nonobservation signs of the suitable to appear. This is to be understood through application to other [syllogisms]; for example,

- One can state, "The subject, pot, is not truly existent because of not being observed as true [that is, truly existent] by valid cognition." The sign in that is a nonobservation of a nature.
- One can also state, "With respect to the subject, on a place that is devoid of pots, golden pot does not exist because pot does not exist." In that, the sign is a nonobservation of a pervader.
- One can also state, "With respect to the subject, in a walled, fireless place, fire does not exist because smoke does not exist." The sign in that is a nonobservation of a cause.
- One can state, "The subject, a sprout, is empty of true existence because of being a dependent-arising." The sign in that is a correct sign that is an observation of a contradictory object.

In terms of one basis the three signs are contradictory, but in terms of different established bases they are not contradictory. This is because, for instance, created phenomenon is a correct effect sign in the proof of sprout as arisen from causes and conditions, but is a correct nature sign in the proof of sprout as impermanent and is a correct nonobservation sign in the proof of sprout as without a self of person.

The three—the sign, predicate of the probandum, and basis of debate—in the proof of sound as impermanent by the sign, product, are generally characterized phenomena merely designated by thought; however, whatever is any of the three—the sign, predicate of the probandum, and basis of debate in the proof of that—must be a specifically

---

[a] Ge-shay Ge-dün-lo-drö explained that in the Madhyamaka system, the two, (1) signs which are a nonobservation of a related object and (2) signs which are an observation of a contradictory object, are not contradictory; on the contrary, a common locus of these two exists. For example, in the syllogism "The subject, pot, is not truly existent because of not being observed as truly existent by valid cognition," "not being observed as truly existent by valid cognition" is a correct sign proving only the expression in that proof and is both (1) a correct sign which is a nonobservation of a related object, and (2) a correct sign which is an observation of a contradictory object.

characterized phenomenon. This is because whatever is [any of those three] must be a thing. This in turn is because whatever is the basis of debate in the proof of that must be sound, for (1) whatever is the basis of debate in the proof of that must be one with sound; (2) whatever is the explicit predicate of the probandum must be impermanent; and (3) the sign must be just product.

Therefore, it is said that the three—the sign, predicate of the probandum, and basis of debate in the proof of that—are not the three: the sign, predicate of the probandum, and basis of debate in the proof of that. One should understand this through applying it to other [syllogisms] in the same way.

APPLICATION OF CONNECTION

This section [on the application of connection between illustration, definiendum, and definition] has two parts: refutation of others' systems and presentation of our own.

Refutation of Others' Systems

Someone says: "Cypress pillar is the illustration [and] is exemplified as being a pillar [through] being that which is able to perform the function of supporting beams; this application of connection [between an illustration (cypress pillar), a definiendum (pillar), and a definition (that which is able to perform the function of supporting beams)] is a proper one."

Response: "It follows that that is not correct because there does not exist a person who, having ascertained cypress pillar by valid cognition, does not ascertain pillar by valid cognition [and thus cypress pillar cannot be an illustration of pillar]."

If someone says that the reason is not established, [then the response is,] "It follows that [such a person] does not exist because any person who has ascertained cypress pillar by valid cognition must be a person who has ascertained cypress pillar as pillar by valid cognition."

If someone says that the reason is not established, [then the response is, "Any person who has ascertained cypress pillar by valid cognition must be a person who has ascertained cypress pillar as pillar by valid cognition] because any person who has ascertained cypress pillar by valid cognition must be a person who has ascertained cypress pillar as cypress pillar by valid cognition."

Someone says: "Golden pot is the illustration [and] is exemplified as being a pot [through] being that which is bulbous, flat based, and able to perform the function of holding water." This application of connection [between an illustration (golden pot), a definiendum (pot), and a definition (that which is bulbous, flat based, and able to perform the function of holding water)] is a proper one."

Response: "It follows that that is not correct because there does not exist a person who, having ascertained golden pot by valid cognition, has not ascertained pot by valid cognition." Extend the reasoning and mode of proof.

> There does not exist a person who, having ascertained golden pot by valid cognition, has not ascertained pot by valid cognition because any person who has ascertained golden pot by valid cognition must be a person who has ascertained golden pot as pot by valid cognition. This is because any person who has ascertained golden pot by valid cognition must be a person who has ascertained golden pot as golden pot by valid cognition.ᴅᴹ

Someone says: "Golden pot is the illustration [and] is exemplified as being a pot [through] being bulbous. This application of connection [between an illustration (golden pot), a definiendum (pot), and a definition (bulbous)] is a proper one."

Response: "It follows that that is not correct because bulbous is not the definition of pot." If someone says that the reason is not established, [then the response is,] "It [absurdly] follows that whatever is bulbous must be a pot because [according to you] bulbous is the definition of pot. You have accepted the reason."

If the consequence [that whatever is bulbous must be a pot] is accepted, then it [absurdly] follows that the subject, bottomless pot, is a pot because of being bulbous. If someone says that the reason is not established, [then the response is, "It (absurdly) follows that the subject, a bottomless pot,] is bulbous because of being directly established as being bulbous."

If the consequence [that a bottomless pot is a pot] is accepted, then it follows that the statement of "able to perform the function of holding water" is not necessary as part of the definition of pot because a bottomless pot is a pot. The consequence cannot be accepted.

Presentation of Our Own System

Golden thing that is bulbous, flat based, and able to perform the function of holding water is the illustration [and] is exemplified as being a pot [through] being that which is bulbous, flat based, and able to perform the function of holding water. Such an application of connection [between an illustration, a definiendum, and a definition] is a proper one.

For someone to whom an object appears to mind but who does not know what verbal convention to designate to that [object], one must make a terminological connection and cause it to become known, [saying,] "The verbal designation for this type of object is such-and-such." For example, there is a person who, although having already ascertained in mind that which is able to perform the function of supporting beams, does not know to apply the convention "pillar" to it. When that person is told, "That which is able to perform the function of supporting beams is the definition or meaning of pillar," he will be able to understand the relationship between the name and the meaning— thinking, "That which is able to perform the function of supporting beams is a pillar." Thus, between the two, definition and definiendum, the definition is easier to understand and the definiendum must be more difficult to understand in relation to that.

Furthermore, [the following] are also proper applications of connection [between illustration, definiendum, and definition]:

(1) The application of the connection: sound is the illustration [and] is exemplified as being impermanent [through] being momentary.
(2) The application of the connection: pot is the illustration [and] is exemplified as being a thing [through] being able to perform a function.
(3) The application of the connection: the first moment of a sense direct perception apprehending blue is the illustration [and] is exemplified as being a valid cognition [through] being a new, incontrovertible knower.

Others are to be understood through extension of this reasoning.

> A correct syllogism and a proper application of connection between illustration, definiendum, and definition can be very similar. For example, the syllogism, "The subject, sound, is impermanent because of being momentary," is similar to the application of connection: sound is the illustration (and) is exemplified as being impermanent (through) being momentary. They differ, however, in that the syllogism directly expresses a reason whereas the application of connection merely expresses the relationship between an illustration, a definiendum, and a definition without directly expressing a reason.[GL]

With respect to the subjects, the explanation of the presentations of correct signs, quasi-signs, and ancillarily, the application of connections, there exists a purpose. This is because in dependence on nonperverse realization, by way of reasons, of what to adopt and what to discard and practicing [such], one easily enters the path progressing to liberation and omniscience.

May the meaning of the thought of the Subduer's texts be illuminated by means of this lamp of unerring explanation—with few words and clear meaning—of reasoning, in accordance with the texts of Dignāga and Dharmakīrti, beautifying the world.

This explanation—of the presentation of the two, the small and middling paths of reasoning, and the greater, ranging from consequences through awareness [and knowledge] and signs [and reasonings][a] in the *Magic Key to the Path of Reasoning, the Explanation of the Collected Topics Revealing the Meaning of the Texts on Prime Cognition*—was written by Purbu-jok when the supreme great all-knower and perceiver, the holy refuge and protector, the king of kings [the Thirteenth Dalai Lama], was maintaining the kindness of listening to tenets.

---

[a] The work translated here is the last part, that is, on *Signs and Reasonings.*

Glossary

English	Tibetan	Sanskrit
A		
actual cause	dngos rgyu	sākṣāt-kāraṇa
actual indefinite reason	dngos kyi ma nge pa'i gtan tshigs	
affirming negative phenomenon	ma yin dgag	paryudāsa-pratiṣedha
another's purpose	gzhan don	parārtha
application of connection	mtshon sbyor	
ascertain/ascertainment	nges pa	niścaya
awareness	blo	buddhi
B		
basis-isolate	gzhi ldog	
basis of debate	rtsod gzhi	
basis of inference	dpag gzhi	*anumāna-āśraya
basis of relation	ltos gzhi	
belief	mos pa	adhimokṣa
C		
causal relationship/ relationship of provenance	de byung 'brel	tadutpatti-saṃbandha
cause	rgyu	hetu/kārana
class	phyogs	pakṣa
common indefinite reason	mthun mong pa'i ma nges pa'i gtan tshigs	
common locus	gzhi mthun pa	samāna-adhikaraṇa
condition	rkyen	pratyaya
consciousness	shes pa	jñāna/vijñāna
consequence	thal 'gyur	prasaṅga
contradictory	'gal ba	virodha
contradictory in the sense of mutually exclusive	phan tshun spang 'gal	*anyonya-parihāra-virodha
contradictory in the sense of not abiding together	lhan cig mi gnas 'gal	*sahana-vastha-virodha
contradictory object	'gal zla	
contradictory reason	'gal ba'i gtan tshigs	viruddha-hetu

English	Tibetan	Sanskrit
correct opponent	phyi rgol yang dag	*samyak-purva-pakṣa
correct sign	rtags yang dag	*samyak-liṅga
correct similar example	mthun pa'i yang dag	*samyak sadṛṣṭānta
counterpervasion	ldog khyab	vyatireka-vyāpti
created phenomenon	skyes pa	utpanna
D		
definiendum	mtshon bya	lakṣya
definite/definiteness	nges pa	niścaya
definition	mtshan nyid	lakṣaṇa
dependence	ltos pa	
dependent-arising	rten 'byung	pratītyasamutpāda
direct effect	dngos 'bras	*sākṣāt-phala
direct perception	mngon sum	pratyakṣa
dissimilar class	mi mthun phyogs	vipakṣa
dissimilar example	mi mthun dpe	*vidṛṣṭānta
E		
effect contradictory with a cause	rang bzhin tang 'gal ba'i 'bras bu	*hetu-viruddha-kārya
effect contradictory with the nature	rgyu tang 'gal ba'i 'bras bu	*svabhāva-viruddha-kārya
effect sign	'bras rtags	kārya-hetu
emptiness	stong pa nyid	śunyatā
empty	stong pa	śūnya
entity	ngo bo	vastu
established base	gzhi grub	
etymology	sgra bshad	
example	dpe	dṛṣṭānta
existent	yod pa	sat
existing in the similar class	mthun phyogs la yod pa	sapakṣa-sattva
explicit/actual	dngos	sākṣāt
explicit predicate of the probandum	dngos kyi bsgrub bya'i chos	sākṣāt-sādhyo-dharma
explicitly contradictory	dngos 'gal	sākṣāt-virodha
F		
fact	don	artha

English	Tibetan	Sanskrit
factually concordant subsequent cognition	bcad shes don mthun	*anvartha-paricchinna-jñāna
flawless subject sought to be known	shes 'dod chos can skyon med	
former party/former opponent	snga rgol	uttara-pakṣa
forward pervasion	rjes khyab	anvaya-vyāpti
free of qualification	khyad par dag pa	
G		
general cause	rgyu spyi	*sāmānya-hetu
general-isolate	spyi ldog	
generally characterized phenomenon	spyi mtshan	sāmānya-lakṣaṇa
H		
having remainder	lhag ldan	
hidden phenomenon	lkog gyur	parokṣa
I		
impermanent	mi rtag pa	anitya dharma
implicit predicate of the probandum	shugs kyi bsgrub bya'i chos	
indefinite reason	ma nges pa'i gtan tshigs	anaikāntika-hetu
indefinite reason having remainder	lhag ldan gyi ma nges pa'i gtan tshigs	
inference/inferential cognition	rjes dpag	anumāna
inference of causal attributes	rgyu chos rjes dpog	
inference through renown	grags pa'i rjes dpag	*prasiddha-anumāna
inference through the power of the fact	dngos stobs rjes dpag	*vastu-bala-anumāna
inferential cognition of belief	yid ches rjes dpag	*āpta-anumāna
inherent existence	rang bzhin gyis grub pa	svabhāvasiddhi
involving a qualification	khyad por ltos pa	
isolate	ldog pa	vyatireka
K		
knowledge	rig	saṃvedana

English	Tibetan	Sanskrit
L		
latter opponent/second party	phyi rgol	pūrva-pakṣa
logic	rtog ge	tarka
M		
manifest phenomenon	mngon gyur	abhimukhī
material phenomenon	bem po	kanthā
meaning/fact, object, welfare, purpose	don	artha
meaning generality	don spyi	artha-sāmānya
meaning isolate	don ldog	*artha-vyatireka
mind	sems	citta
mode	tshul	rūpa
mode of statement	'god tshul	
momentary	skad cig ma	kṣaṇika
mutual exclusion	phan tshun spang 'gal	*anyonya-parihāra
N		
nature contradictory with a cause	rgyu tang 'gal pa'i rang bzhin	*hetu-viruddha-svabhāva
nature contradictory with a pervader	khyab byed tang 'gal ba'i rang bzhin	*vyāpaka-viruddha-svabhāva
nature sign	rang bzhin gyi rtags	svabhāva-hetu
negandum/object of negation	dgag bya	pratiṣedhya
negative/negative phenomenon	dgag pa	pratiṣedha
nonaffirming negative phenomenon	med dgag	prasajya-pratiṣedha
nonassociated compositional factor	ldan min 'du byed	viprayukta-saṃskāra
nonestablished reason	ma grub pa'i gtan tshigs	asiddha-hetu
nonexistent	med pa	asat
nonobservation of a cause	rgyu ma dmigs pa	kāraṇa-anupalabdhi
nonobservation of a direct effect	dngos 'bras ma dmigs pa	*sākṣāt-kārya-anupalabdhi
nonobservation of a nature	rang bzhin ma dmigs pa	svabhāva-anupalabdhi
nonobservation of a pervader	khyab byed ma dmigs pa	vyāpaka-anupalabdhi

English	Tibetan	Sanskrit
nonobservation of an effect	'bras ma dmigs pa	kārya-anupalabdhi
nonobservation sign	ma dmigs pa'i rtags	anupalabdhi-hetu
nonobservation sign of the nonappearing	mi snang ba ma dmigs pa'i rtags	*apratibhāsa-anupalabdhi
nonobservation sign of the suitable to appear	snang rung ma dmigs pa'i rtags	
not abiding together	lhan cig mi gnas 'gal	*sahāna-vasthā-virodha
O		
object	yul/don	viṣaya/artha
object of apprehension	gzung bya/bzung bya	
object of comprehension	gzhal bya	prameya
object of indication	bstan bya	
object of knowledge	shes bya	jñeya
object of relation	'brel yul	*sambandha-viṣaya
object of thought	rtog yul	*kalpanā-viṣaya
object pervaded	khyab bya	vyāpya
object to be inferred	rjes su dpag bya	anumeya
one's own purpose	rang don	svārtha
opponent/party	rgol ba	pakṣa
P		
particular cause	rgyu khyad par	asādhāraṇa-kāraṇa
particularity	bye brag	viśeṣa
party/opponent	rgol ba	pakṣa
permanent phenomenon	rtag pa	nitya
pervader	khyab byed	vyāpaka
perverse forward pervasion	khyab pa phyin ci log	
phenomenon/attribute	chos	dharma
place/object	yul	viṣaya
position/class, subject, party	phyogs	pakṣa
positive/positive phenomenon	sgrub pa	vidhi
possibility	mu	
preceding cause	rgyu sngon song	*samanantara-hetu
predicate of the negandum	dgag bya'i chos	*pratiṣedhya-dharma

English	Tibetan	Sanskrit
predicate of the probandum	bsgrub bya'i chos	sādhyadharma
probandum	bsgrub bya	sādhya
probans	bsgrub byed	sādhana
product	byas pa	kṛta
proof statement	sgrub ngag	sādhana-vākya
proof statement using a qualitative dissimilarity	chos mi mthun sbyor gyi sgrub ngag	*vaidharmya-prayoga-sādhana-vākya
proof statement using a qualitative similarity	chos mthun sbyor gyi sgrub ngag	*sādharmya-prayoga-sādhana-vākya
property of the subject	phyogs chos	pakṣadharma
Q		
qualification	khyad par	viśeṣa
quasi-reason	gtan tshigs ltar snang	hetu-ābhāsa
R		
reason	gtan tshigs	hetu
reasoning	rigs	nyāya
related object	'brel zla	
relationship	'brel ba	sambandha
relationship of provenance		tadutpatti-sambandha
relationship of sameness of nature	bdag gcig 'brel	tādātmya-sambandha
renown	grags pa	prasiddha
S		
second party/latter opponent	phyi rgol	pūrva-pakṣa
self-isolate	rang ldog	
selfless	bdag med	nairātmya
sign	rtags	liṅga
sign of belief	yid ches kyi rtags	*āpta-liṅga
sign of renown	grags pa'i rtags	*prasiddha-liṅga
sign proving the expression	tha snyad sgrub kyi rtags	
sign proving the meaning	ton sgrub kyi rtags	
sign that appears to the mind	song tshod kyi rtags	

English	Tibetan	Sanskrit
sign through the power of the fact	dngos stobs kyi rtags	*vastu-bala-liṅga
similar class	mthun phyogs	sapakṣa
similar example	mthun dpe	*sadṛṣṭānta
slightly hidden phenomenon	cung zad lkog gyur	*kiṃcid-parokṣa
sound	sgra	śabda
specifically characterized phenomenon	rang mtshan	svalakṣaṇa
stated sign	bkod tshod gyi rtags	
subject	chos can	dharma
subject sought to be known	shes 'dod chos can	
subsequent cognition	bcad shes	*paricchinna-jñāna
substantial entity	rdzas	dravya
supersensory object	skal don	adṛśya-anupalabdhi
syllogism	sbyor ba	prayoga
T		
tangible object	reg bya	spraṣṭavya
terminological suitability	sgra byung grags pa	
thesis	dam bca'	pratijñā
thing/actual, explicit	dngos po	bhāva
thought	rtog pa	kalpanā
three modes	tshul gsum	trirūpa
time	dus	kāla
U		
uncommon indefinite reason	thun mong ma yin pa'i ma nges pa'i gtan tshigs	
V		
valid cognition	tshad ma	pramāṇa
very hidden phenomenon	shin tu lkog gyur	*atyarta-parokṣa

Detailed Outline

Part Two: *Annotated Translation* Pur-bu-jok Jam-pa-gya-tso's *The Topic of Signs and Reasonings from the "Great Path of Reasoning"* 381

List of Abbreviations

DM = Den-ma Lo-chö Rin-po-che
GL = Ge-shay Ge-dün-lo-drö
LR = Lati Rin-po-che
"P," standing for "Peking edition," refers to the *Tibetan Tripiṭaka*
 (Tokyo-Kyoto: Tibetan Tripiṭaka Research Foundation, 1955-1962).

Bibliography

Entries found in the Peking Edition of the *Tibetan Tripiṭaka* (Tokyo-Kyoto: Tibetan Research Foundation, 1956) are designated by the letter "P," followed by the entry number and the volume number.

Barker, Stephen. *The Elements of Logic.* New York: McGraw-Hill Book Company, 1980.

Ba-so Chö-gyi-gyel-tsen (*ba so chos kyi rgyal mtshan*). *Dbu ma'i lta khrid chen mo of Ba-so Chö-gyi-gyel-tsen.* New Delhi: Lha-mkhar Yoṅs-'dzin Bstan-pa-rgyal-mtshan, 1973. (Madhyamika Text Series, vol. 7.)

Den-ma-lo-chö Rin-po-che. Unpublished transcripts on the topic of *Signs and Reasonings.*

Dharmakīrti (*chos kyi grags pa*). *Analysis of Relations* (*sambandhaparīkṣāvṛtti, 'brel pa brtag pa'i rab tu byed pa*). P5713, vol. 130.

_____. *Ascertainment of Prime Cognition* (*pramāṇaviniścaya, tshad ma rnam par nges pa*). P5710, vol. 130.

_____. *Commentary on (Dignāga's) "Compilation of Prime Cognition"* (*pramāṇavarttikakārikā, tshad ma rnam 'grel gyi tshig le'ur byas pa*). P5709, vol. 130.

_____. *Drop of Reasoning* (*nyāyabinduprakaraṇa, rigs pa'i thigs pa zhes bya ba'i rab tu byed pa*). P5711, vol. 130.

_____. *Drop of Reasons* (*hetubindunāmaprakaraṇa, gtan tshigs kyi thigs pa zhes bya ba'i rab tu byed pa*). P5712, vol. 130.

_____. *Proof of Other Continuums* (*saṃtānāntarasiddhināmaprakaraṇa, rgyud gzhan grub pa zhes bya ba'i rab tu byed pa*). P5716, vol. 130.

_____. *Reasoning for Debate* (*vādanyāyanāmaprakaraṇa, rtsod pa'i rigs pa zhes bya ba'i rab tu byed pa*). P5715, vol. 130.

Dignāga (*phyogs glang*, 5th century). *Compilation of Prime Cognition* (*pramāṇasamuccaya, tshad ma kun las btus pa*). P5700, vol. 130.

Ge-dün-drup-pa (*dge 'dun grub pa*, First Dalai Lama). *Ornament of Reasoning on Prime Cognition* (*tshad ma'i bstan bcos chen po rigs pa'i rgyan*). Mundgod, South India: Drepung Loseling Press, 1984.

Ge-dün-lo-drö, Ge-shay. Unpublished transcripts of instruction on the topic of *Signs and Reasonings,* Charlottesville, Virginia, 1979.

Gyel-tsap (*rgyal tshab*). *Complete Explanation of the Stanzas of the Commentary on Prime Cognition, the Faultless Revealer of the Path of Liberation* (*tshad ma rnam 'grel gyi tshig le'ur byas pa'i rnam bshad thar lam phyin ci ma log par gsal bar byed pa*), vol. 1. Varanasi: Geluk-pa Press, 1974.

_____. *Treasure of the Essence of Good Sayings, Commentary on (Dharmakīrti's Treatise) on Prime Cognition, the Drop of Reasoning* (*tshad ma rigs thigs kyi 'grel pa legs bshad snying po'i gter*). Collected Works, 8. Delhi: Guru Deva.

Hattori, Masaaki. *Dignāga, On Perception, Being the Pratyakṣapariccheda of Dignāga's "Pramāṇasamuccaya" from the Sanskrit Fragments and the Tibetan Versions.* Cambridge, Massachusetts: Harvard University Press, 1968.

Hopkins, Jeffrey. *Meditation on Emptiness.* London: Wisdom Publications, 1983.

Jam-pel-sam-pel, Ge-shay ('jam dpal bsam 'phel, dge bshes). *Presentation of Awareness and Knowledge, Composite of All the Important Points, Opener of the Eye of New Intelligence* (*blo rig gi rnam bzhag nyer mkho kun 'dus blo gsar mig 'byed*). Modern blockprint, n.p., n.d.

Jam-yang-chok-hla-ö-ser (*'jam dbyangs phyogs lha 'od zer*). *Ra-tö Collected Topics* (*rva stod bsdus grva*). Dharamsala, India: Damchoe Sangpo, 1980.

Jam-yang-shay-pa (*'jam dbyangs bzhad pa*). *Presentation of Signs and Reasonings* (*rtags rigs kyi rnam bzhag*). The Collected Works of 'Jam-dbyaṅ-bzhad-pa'i-rdo-rje, vol. 15. New Delhi: Ngawang Gelek Demo, 1973.

Kajiyama, Yuichi. *An Introduction to Buddhist Philosophy: An Annotated Translation of the Tarkabhāṣā of Mokṣākaragupta.* Kyoto: Kyoto University, 1966.

Kön-chok-tse-ring, Ge-shay. Unpublished transcripts of individual instruction on the topic of *Signs and Reasonings,* Charlottesville, Virginia, 1989.

Lati Rin-po-che. *Mind in Tibetan Buddhism.* Trans. and ed., with an introduction by Elizabeth Napper. London: Rider, 1980; Ithaca, New York: Snow Lion Publications, 1980.

_____. Unpublished lectures on the topic of *Signs and Reasonings,* Charlottesville, Virginia, 1976-1977.

Lob-sang-gya-tso, Ge-shay. Unpublished transcripts of individual instruction on the topic of *Signs and Reasonings,* Mundgod, India, 1984.

Miller, David, ed. *Popper Selections.* Princeton, New Jersey: Princeton University Press, 1985.

Mookerji, S. and H. Nagasaki. *The Pramāṇavārttikam of Dharmakīrti.* Nalanda, India: Nālandā Mahāvihāra, 1964.

Nāgārjuna (*klu sgrub*). *Precious Garland of Advice for the King* (*rājaparikathāratnāvalī, rgyal po la gtam bya ba rin po che'i phreng ba*). P5658, vol. 129. English translation: Jeffrey Hopkins. *Nāgārjuna's Precious Garland: Buddhist Advice for Living and Liberation.* Ithaca, New York: Snow Lion, 1998.

Napper, Elizabeth. *Dependent-Arising and Emptiness.* London: Wisdom Publications, 1989.

Paṇ-chen Sö-nam-drak-pa (*pan chen bsod nams grags pa*). *Illumination of the Thought, Commentary on the Difficult Points of (Dharmakīrti's) "Commentary on (Dignāga's) 'Compilation of Prime Cognition.'"* Mundgod, India: Drepung Loseling Printing Press, 1989.

Pel-den-drak-pa, Ge-shay. Unpublished transcripts of individual instruction on the topic of *Signs and Reasonings,* Delhi, India, 1984.

Perdue, Daniel. *Debate in Tibetan Buddhism.* Ithaca, New York: Snow Lion Publications, 1992.

Pur-bu-jok Jam-pa-gya-tso (*phur bu lcog byams ba rgya mtsho*). "The Greater Path of Reasoning" (*rigs lam che ba*). In *The Presentation of Collected Topics Revealing the Meaning of the Texts on Prime Cognition, the Magic Key to the Path of Reasoning* (*tshad ma'i gzhung don 'byed pa'i bsdus grva'i rnam bzhag rigs lam 'phrul gyi lde mig*). Buxa, India: n.p., 1965.

_____. "The Introductory Path of Reasoning" (*rigs lam chung ngu*). In *The Presentation of Collected Topics Revealing the Meaning of the Texts on Prime Cognition, the Magic Key to the Path of Reasoning* (*tshad ma'i gzhung don 'byed pa'i bsdus grva'i rnam bzhag rigs lam 'phrul gyi lde mig*). Buxa, India: n.p., 1965.

_____. "The Middling Path of Reasoning" (*rigs lam 'bring*). In *The Presentation of Collected Topics Revealing the Meaning of the Texts on Prime Cognition, the Magic Key to the Path of Reasoning* (*tshad ma'i gzhung don 'byed pa'i bsdus grva'i rnam bzhag rigs lam 'phrul gyi lde mig*). Buxa, India: n.p., 1965.

_____. *The Topic of Signs and Reasonings from the "Great Path of Reasoning" in the Magic Key to the Path of Reasoning, Explanation of the Collected Topics Revealing the Meaning of the Texts on Prime Cognition* (*tshad ma'i gzhung don 'byed pa'i bsdus grva'i rnam par bshad pa rigs lam 'phrul gyi lde'u mig las rigs lam che ba rtags rigs kyi skor*). Buxa, 1965.

Sa-kya Paṇḍita (*sa skya paṇḍita*). *Treasury of Reasoning on Valid Cognition* (*tshad ma rigs pa'i gter*). In *The Complete Works of the Great Masters of the Sa-skya Sect of the Tibetan Buddhism*, vol. 5, 155.1.1-167.2.1. Tokyo: Toyo Bunko, 1968.

Sang-gyay-sam-drup, Ge-shay (Professor Georges Dreyfus). Unpublished transcripts of commentary on Gyel-tsap's *Revealer of the Path of Liberation*, Dharamsala, India, 1983.

Sopa, Ge-shay Lhundup. *Lectures on Tibetan Religious Culture*. An unpublished textbook of intermediate Tibetan prepared for the Department of Indian Studies, University of Wisconsin, 1972.

Ten-dar-hla-ram-pa (*bstan dar lha ram pa*). *Notes Helping with the Difficult Points in Signs and Reasonings, Clear Sunlight of New Explanation* (*rtags rigs kyi dka' ba'i gnas la phan pa'i zin bris gsar bshad nyi ma'i 'od zer*). Collected Works of Bstan-dar Lha-ram of A-lag-sha, vol. 1. New Delhi: Lama Guru Deva, 1971.

Tillemans, T. "On a Recent Work on Tibetan Buddhist Epistemology." *Asiatische Studien*, 38 1 (1984), 59-66.

_____. "On Scriptural Authority." In *Felicitation Volume for Professor A. Uno Tetsugaku*, 1986, 31-47.

_____. "Formal and Semantic Aspects of Tibetan Buddhist Debate Logic." *Journal of Indian Philosophy* 17 (1989), 265-297.

Tsong-kha-pa (*tsong kha pa*). *Great Exposition of the Stages of the Path* (*lam rim chen mo*). P6001, vol. 152. Also: Dharamsala: Shes rig par khans, 1964. English translation: Lamrim Chenmo Translation Committee. *The Great Treatise on the Stages of the Path to Enlightenment*. 3 vols. Joshua W.C. Cutler, editor-in-chief, Guy Newland, editor. Ithaca, New York: Snow Lion Publications, 2000-2004.

Tsül-trim-nam-gyel, Ge-shay (*tshul khrims rnam rgyal, dge bshes*). *The Presentation of Signs and Reasonings, a Mirror Illuminating All Phenomena* (*rtags rigs kyi rnam bzhag chos kun gsal ba'i me long*). In: *The First Magic Key Opening a Hundred Doors to the Path of Reasoning* (*rigs lam sgo brgya 'byed pa'i 'phrul gyi lde mig dang po*). Mundgod, India: Drepung Loseling Library, 1979.

Ye-shay-tup-ten, Ken-sur. Unpublished transcripts of individual instruction on the topic of *Signs and Reasonings*, Charlottesville, Virginia, 1981.

ENDNOTES

[1] See "A Standard System of Tibetan Transcription," *Harvard Journal of Asian Studies*, vol. 22 (1959), pp. 261-267.

[2] Gyel-tsap (*rgyal tshab*, 1364-1432), *Complete Explanation of the Stanzas of the Compilation of Prime Cognition, Faultless Revealer of the Path of Liberation*, vol. 1 (Varanasi: Ge-luk-pa Press, 1974).

[3] The First Dalai Lama, Ge-dün-drup-pa (*dge 'dun grub pa*, 1391-1474), *Ornament of Reasoning on Prime Cognition* (Mundgod: Drepung Loseling Printing Press, 1984).

[4] Paṇ-chen Sö-nam-drak-pa (*paṇ chen bsod nams grags pa*, 1478-1554), *Illumination of the Thought, Commentary on the Difficult Points of (Dharmakīrti's) "Commentary on (Dignāga's) 'Compilation of Prime Cognition'"* (Mundgod: Drepung Loseling Printing Press, 1989).

[5] Ge-shay Tsül-trim-nam-gyel, *The Presentation of Signs and Reasonings, Mirror Illuminating All Phenomena* (Mundgod, India: Drepung Loseling Library, 1979).

[6] Jam-yang-shay-pa (*'jam dbyangs bzhad pa*, 1648-1721), *Presentation of Signs and Reasonings*, in the Collected Works of 'Jam-dbyaṅ-bzhad-pa'i-rdo-rje, vol. 15 (New Delhi: Ngawang Gelek Demo, 1973).

[7] Ge-shay Jam-pel-sam-pel, *Presentation of Awareness and Knowledge, Composite of All the Important Points, Opener of the Eye of New Intelligence*, modern block-print, n.p., n.d.

[8] Sa-kya Paṇḍita Jam-yang-kün-ga-gyel-tsen (1182-1251), *Treasury of Reasoning on Valid Cognition*, in *The Complete Works of the Great Masters of the Sa-skya Sect of Tibetan Buddhism*, vol. 5, 155.1.1-167.1.1 (Tokyo: Tokyo Bunko, 1968).

[9] Jam-yang-chok-hla-ö-ser (*'jam dbyangs phyogs lha 'od zer*, 1429-1500), *Ra-tö Collected Topics* (Dharamsala: Damchoe Sangpo, 1980).

[10] Mokṣākaragupta's work, the *Tarkabhāṣā*, is found in Kajiyama's *An Introduction to Buddhist Philosophy* (Kyoto: Memoirs of the Faculty of Letters 10, 1966).

[11] Pur-bu-jok, *Signs and Reasonings*, p. 8b.6-7.

[12] Unpublished commentary on *Signs and Reasonings*, vol. 1, p. 49.

[13] Ibid., vol. 2, p. 20.

[14] *Signs and Reasonings*, p. 15a.4.

[15] Commentary on *Signs and Reasonings*, vol. 3, p. 15.

[16] *Ornament of Reasoning on Prime Cognition*, p. 159.

[17] See Daniel Perdue's *Debate in Tibetan Buddhism* for a detailed study of "The Introductory Path of Reasoning" from Pur-bu-jok's *Collected Topics*.

[18] Robert Thurman, "Buddhist Hermeneutics," *Journal of the American Academy of Religion*, 46 (1978), 38, provides Sanskrit from Shāntarakṣita's *Compendium of Principles (Tattvasaṃgraha)* (D. Shastri, ed., Varanasi: Bauddha Bharati, 1968).

[19] *Signs and Reasonings*, p. 1a. 3-4.

[20] Ibid., p. 2a.4.

[21] Commentary on *Signs and Reasonings*, vol. 1, p. 4.

[22] *Signs and Reasonings*, p. 2.5-2b.1.

[23] Ibid., p. 5b.1.

[24] David Miller, ed. *Popper Selections* (Princeton, New Jersey: Princeton University Press, 1985), p. 91.

[25] Stephen Barker, *The Elements of Logic* (New York: McGraw-Hill Book Company, 1980), p. 20.

[26] Pur-bu-jok, *Signs and Reasonings*, p. 5b.5-6.

[27] Ibid., p. 6a.2.

[28] Lati Rin-po-che, commentary on *Signs and Reasonings*, vol. 1, 1977, p. 29.

[29] *Signs and Reasonings*, p. 2b.4-6.

[30] Ibid., p. 3b.6-7.

[31] Ibid., p. 6a.3-4.

[32] Ibid., p. 6a.4-5.

[33] Ibid., p. 6a.5.

[34] Commentary on *Signs and Reasonings*, vol. 1, p. 3.

[35] Commentary on *Signs and Reasonings,* vol. 5, pp. 18-19.

[36] Commentary on *Signs and Reasonings,* vol. 2, Nov. 15, 1976, pp. 3-4.

[37] Ibid., vol. 1, p. 20.

[38] Ibid., vol. 2, Feb. 2, p 2.

[39] Ibid., vol. 1, Feb. 2, 1977, pp. 1-2.

[40] *Signs and Reasonings,* p. 5b.1.

[41] Ibid., p. 5b.5-6.

[42] Ibid., p. 5b.2.

[43] Ibid., p. 5b.4.

[44] Ibid., p. 5b.4-5.

[45] Commentary on *Signs and Reasonings,* vol. 1, p. 30.

[46] *Signs and Reasonings,* p. 6a.2-3.

[47] Ibid., p. 6a.5-7.

[48] Ibid., p. 6a.6-7.

[49] Commentary on *Signs and Reasonings,* vol. 2, p. 2.

[50] Ibid., vol. 2, p. 31.

[51] The discussion of these possibilities is based on commentary from Ge-shay Lob-sang-gya-tso (unpublished transcripts of oral commentary on *Signs and Reasonings,* vol. 2, pp. 4-5).

[52] Commentary on *Signs and Reasonings,* vol. 1, p. 32.

[53] Ibid., vol. 2, Feb. 2, 1977, p. 1.

[54] Ibid., vol. 2, Feb. 14, 1977, p. 4.

[55] Ibid., vol. 2, Feb. 9, 1977, p. 5.

[56] Kajiyama, *An Introduction to Buddhist Philosophy,* pp. 65-67.

[57] Commentary on *Signs and Reasonings,* vol. 1, p. 30.

[58] *Signs and Reasonings,* p. 4a. 2-3.

[59] *Signs and Reasonings,* p. 6a.6-7.

[60] Commentary on *Signs and Reasonings,* vol. 2, p. 2.

[61] *Signs and Reasonings,* pp. 4a.3-4b.1.

[62] Commentary on *Signs and Reasonings,* vol. 1, p. 30.

[63] *Signs and Reasonings,* p. 4b.1-3.

[64] Ibid., p. 4b.3.

[65] Commentary on *Signs and Reasonings,* vol.1, pp. 32-33.

[66] *Signs and Reasonings,* pp. 2b.7-3a.1.

[67] Commentary on *Signs and Reasonings,* vol. 1, p. 19.

[68] *Signs and Reasonings,* p. 3a.1-4.

[69] Commentary on *Signs and Reasonings,* vol. 1, p. 19.

[70] *Signs and Reasonings,* p. 3a.4-5.

[71] Commentary on *Signs and Reasonings,* vol. 2, Jan. 28, 1977, p. 6.

[72] Ibid., vol. 2, Jan. 28, 1977, p. 6.

[73] *Signs and Reasonings,* p. 3a.5-6.

[74] Ibid., p. 3a.6-7.

[75] Commentary on *Signs and Reasonings,* vol. 2, Feb. 2, 1977, p. 2.

[76] Commentary on *Signs and Reasonings,* vol. 2, p. 2.

[77] This explanation is offered by Ge-shay Pel-den-drak-pa, commentary on *Signs and Reasonings,* vol. 2, p. 2.

[78] Commentary on *Signs and Reasonings,* vol. 2, Feb. 4, 1977, pp. 11-12.

[79] Ibid., vol. 2, Feb. 4, 1977, pp. 12-13.

[80] This phrase was discussed above in the subsection "only exist."

[81] Commentary on *Signs and Reasonings,* vol. 2, p. 4.

[82] Ibid., p. 5.

[83] Ibid., vol. 2, p. 4.

[84] *Signs and Reasonings,* p. 5b.2.

[85] Commentary on *Signs and Reasonings,* vol. 2, Feb. 9, 1977, p. 2.

[86] Commentary on *Signs and Reasonings,* vol. 2, p. 11.

[87] *Signs and Reasonings,* p. 2a.3.

[88] Commentary on *Signs and Reasonings,* vol. 1, p. 10.

[89] *Signs and Reasonings,* p. 24a.4-7.

[90] Ibid., p. 5b.6-6a.2.

[91] Ibid., p. 3b.2-3.

[92] Commentary on *Signs and Reasonings,* vol. l, p. 9.

93 Pur-bu-jok, *Signs and Reasonings*, pp. 6b.7-7a.1.

94 Commentary on *Signs and Reasonings*, vol.1, p 23.

95 *Signs and Reasonings*, p.3b.5.

96 Commentary on *Signs and Reasonings*, section 3, 1979, pp. 1-2.

97 *Signs and Reasonings*, pp. 3b. 5-7.

98 Ibid., pp. 3b.7-4a.5.

99 Ibid, p. 3b.3.

100 Commentary on *Signs and Reasonings*, vol. 1, Feb. 2, p. 6.

101 Commentary on *Signs and Reasonings*, section 3, p. 2.

102 Ibid., section 3, pp. 2-3.

103 *Signs and Reasonings*, p. 4a.5.

104 Commentary on *Signs and Reasonings*, vol. 1, p. 23.

105 Ibid., vol. 2, Feb. 2, 1977, p. 4.

106 Ibid., vol. 1, p.35.

107 *Signs and Reasonings*, p. 4b.1-2.

108 Commentary on *Signs and Reasonings*, vol. 2, Feb. 2, 1977, pp. 7-8.

109 *Signs and Reasonings*, p. 4b.2.

110 Ibid., p. 3b.3.

111 Commentary on *Signs and Reasonings*, vol. 1, p. 9.

112 *Signs and Reasonings*, p. 3b.3-4.

113 Ibid., p. 3b. 4-5.

114 Commentary on *Signs and Reasonings*, vol. 1, p. 12.

115 Ibid., vol. 1, p. 12.

116 Ibid., vol. 1, p. 9.

117 Ibid., vol. 1, p. 9.

118 *Signs and Reasonings*, p. 4b.2-4.

119 Commentary on *Signs and Reasonings*, vol. 2, Feb. 4, 1977, p. 1.

120 *Signs and Reasonings*, p. 4b.4.

121 Commentary on *Signs and Reasonings*, vol. 2, Feb. 4, 1977, pp. 1-2.

122 *Signs and Reasonings*, p. 4b.4-5.

123 Commentary on *Signs and Reasonings*, vol. 2,

Feb. 4, 1977, p. 2.

124 *Signs and Reasonings*, p. 4b. 5-6.

125 Commentary on *Signs and Reasonings*, section 3, p. 3.

126 *Signs and Reasonings*, pp. 4b.6-5a.1.

127 Commentary on *Signs and Reasonings*, section 3, p. 5.

128 *Signs and Reasonings*, pp. 4b.6-5a. 2.

129 Ibid., p. 5a.2-3.

130 Ibid., p. 5a.3-5.

131 Commentary on *Signs and Reasonings*, vol. 1, p. 14.

132 *Signs and Reasonings*, p. 6a.7.

133 Commentary on *Signs and Reasonings*, vol. 2, p. 7.

134 Commentary on *Signs and Reasonings*, vol. 2, p. 12.

135 *Signs and Reasonings*, p. 6b.3.

136 Ibid., pp. 6b.3-6.

137 Commentary on *Signs and Reasonings*, vol. 1, p. 13.

138 *Signs and Reasonings*, p. 6b.6.

139 Commentary on *Signs and Reasonings*, vol. 2, Feb. 14, 1977, p. 1.

140 Ibid., vol. 2, Feb. 2, 1977, pp. 6-7.

141 Ibid., p. 7.

142 *Signs and Reasonings*, p. 7a.3-4.

143 This explanation is based on Lati Rin-po-che's commentary on *Signs and Reasonings*, vol. 1, p. 40.

144 Commentary on *Signs and Reasonings*, vol.1, p. 23.

145 *Signs and Reasonings*, p. 5b.1.

146 Commentary on *Signs and Reasonings*, vol. 1, p. 43.

147 Ibid., vol. 1, p. 43.

148 *Signs and Reasonings*, p. 7a.3.

149 Ibid., p. 7a.3-4.

150 Commentary on *Signs and Reasonings*, vol. 1, pp. 12-13.

151 *Signs and Reasonings*, p. 7a.4.

152 Ibid., p. 7a.4.

7

[153] Commentary on *Signs and Reasonings*, vol. 1, pp. 45-46.

[154] Ibid., vol. 1, p. 47.

[155] *Signs and Reasonings*, p. 5b.1.

[156] Commentary on *Signs and Reasonings*, vol. 1, p. 48.

[157] *Signs and Reasonings*, p. 5b.4.

[158] Kajiyama, *An Introduction to Buddhist Philosophy*, p. 93.

[159] Ibid., p. 94.

[160] Ge-shay Sang-gyay-sam-drup, commentary on Gyel-tsap's *Revealer of the Path of Liberation*, vol. 1, p. 10.

[161] Gyel-tsap, *Revealer of the Path of Liberation*, p. 39.15-18.

[162] Ge-shay Sang-gyay-sam-drup, commentary on *Revealer of the Path of Liberation*, vol. 1, May 23, 1983, pp. 2-3.

[163] Ibid., commentary on *Revealer of the Path of Liberation*, vol. 1, May 25, 1983, p. 4.

[164] Ibid., vol. 1, May 24, 1983, p. 2.

[165] Commentary on *Signs and Reasonings*, vol. 2, p. 17.

[166] This explanation is from Ge-shay Sang-gyay-sam-drup, commentary on *Revealer of the Path of Liberation*, vol. 2, p. 1.

[167] This analysis is based on the explanation by Ge-shay Sang-gyay-sam-drup (commentary on *Revealer of the Path of Liberation*, vol. 2, pp. 5-7).

[168] *Signs and Reasonings*, p. 23a.1-4.

[169] Ibid., p. 23a.4-6.

[170] *Revealer of the Path of Liberation*, p. 47.14-15.

[171] Commentary on *Revealer of the Path of Liberation*, vol. 2, p. 6.

[172] Ibid., vol. 1, June 3, 1983, pp. 2-3.

[173] Commentary on *Signs and Reasonings*, p. 12.

[174] Commentary on *Revealer of the Path of Liberation*, vol. 2, p. 5.

[175] Ibid., vol. 1, May 27, 1983, p. 4.

[176] Ibid., p. 6.

[177] Ibid., vol. 1, May 27, 1983, p. 8.

[178] Commentary on *Signs and Reasonings*, vol. 1, p. 12.

[179] Commentary on *Signs and Reasonings*, vol. 2, p. 14.

[180] Ge-shay Lob-sang-gya-tso, commentary on *Signs and Reasonings*, vol. 2, p. 15.

[181] Ibid., vol. 2, p. 16.

[182] Ibid., vol. 2, p. 16.

[183] *Signs and Reasonings*, p. 7a.4-5.

[184] Pur-bu-jok posits this division in *Signs and Reasonings*, p. 7a5-6.

[185] Commentary on *Signs and Reasonings*, vol. 1, p. 49.

[186] Commentary on *Signs and Reasonings*, vol. 2, p. 20.

[187] Ibid.

[188] Ibid., vol. 3, p.11.

[189] *Signs and Reasonings*, p. 24a.2-4.

[190] Commentary on *Signs and Reasonings*, vol. 1, p. 58.

[191] Ibid., vol. 1, p. 50.

[192] Lati Rin-po-che, commentary on *Signs and Reasonings*, vol. 1, p. 58.

[193] Commentary on *Signs and Reasonings*, vol. 1, p. 58.

[194] *Signs and Reasonings*, pp. 7a.7-7b.1.

[195] Ibid., 7b.1-3.

[196] Commentary on *Signs and Reasonings*, vol. 3, p. 12.

[197] *Ornament of Reasoning on Prime Cognition*, p. 149.

[198] *Signs and Reasonings*, p. 7b.3-4.

[199] Ibid., p. 7b.4-5.

[200] Commentary on *Signs and Reasonings*, vol. 3, pp. 13-14.

[201] Commentary on *Signs and Reasonings*, vol. 1, p. 53.

[202] Kajiyama, *Introduction to Buddhist Philosophy*, p. 74.

[203] Ibid., p. 74.

[204] Ibid, p. 113.

[205] *Signs and Reasonings*, p. 7b.5-6.

[206] Commentary on *Signs and Reasonings*, vol. 1, p. 55.

[207] *Signs and Reasonings*, p. 7b.6-7.

[208] Commentary on *Signs and Reasonings*, vol. 1, p. 56.

[209] Commentary on *Signs and Reasonings*, vol. 3, p. 2.

[210] Commentary on *Signs and Reasonings*, vol. 1, p. 56.

[211] *Signs and Reasonings*, pp. 7b.7-8a.2.

[212] Commentary on *Signs and Reasonings*, vol. 2, Apr. 15, 1977, p. 2.

[213] Commentary on *Signs and Reasonings*, vol. 3, p. 13.

[214] *Signs and Reasonings*, p. 7a.1-2.

[215] Commentary on *Signs and Reasonings*, vol. 2, Apr. 15, 1977, p. 2.

[216] Ibid, vol. 2, Feb. 9, 1977, p. 5.

[217] Ibid, vol. 2, Apr. 15, 1977, p. 4.

[218] Kajiyama, *Introduction to Buddhist Philosophy*, p. 74.

[219] Commentary on *Signs and Reasonings*, vol. 3, p. 3.

[220] Ibid., vol. 2, p. 3.

[221] Ibid., vol. 3, p. 6.

[222] Ibid., vol. 3, p. 5.

[223] Ibid., vol. 3, p. 6.

[224] Commentary on *Signs and Reasonings*, vol. 2, Apr. 15, 1977, p. 3.

[225] Ibid., vol. 2, Apr. 15, 1977, p. 3.

[226] Commentary on *Signs and Reasonings*, vol. 3, p. 3.

[227] Kajiyama, *Introduction to Buddhist Philosophy*, p. 74.

[228] Commentary on *Signs and Reasonings*, vol. 1, p. 57.

[229] Kajiyama, *Introduction to Buddhist Philosophy*, pp. 74-75.

[230] *Signs and Reasonings*, p. 8a.4-5.

[231] Ibid., p. 8a.5-6.

[232] Commentary on *Signs and Reasonings*, vol. 1, p. 102.

[233] *Signs and Reasonings*, p 8a.6-7.

[234] Ibid., p. 8a.7-8b.1.

[235] Commentary on *Signs and Reasonings*, vol. 3, p. 2.

[236] *Signs and Reasonings*, p. 8b.1-3.

[237] Commentary on *Signs and Reasonings*, vol. 3, p. 2.

[238] Ibid., vol. 3, p. 2.

[239] Ibid., vol. 3, p. 3.

[240] *Signs and Reasonings*, p. 7b.1-3.

[241] Ibid., p. 8b.3-5.

[242] Lati Rin-po-che, commentary on *Signs and Reasonings*, vol. 2, Apr. 15, 1977, p. 6.

[243] *Signs and Reasonings*, p. 3a.4.

[244] Commentary on *Signs and Reasonings*, vol. 3, p. 15.

[245] Ibid.

[246] *Signs and Reasonings*, p. 15a.4.

[247] Ibid., p. 15a.3.

[248] Commentary on *Signs and Reasonings*, vol. 3, p. 15.

[249] Commentary on *Signs and Reasonings*, vol. 2, Apr. 15, 1977, p. 7.

[250] *Ornament of Reasoning on Prime Cognition*, p. 159.

[251] Commentary on *Signs and Reasonings*, vol. 1, p. 59.

[252] *Signs and Reasonings*, p. 9a.1-2.

[253] Lati Rin-po-che, commentary on *Signs and Reasonings*, vol. 1, p. 58.

[254] *Signs and Reasonings*, p. 9a.2-3.

[255] Commentary on *Signs and Reasonings*, vol. 1, p. 60.

[256] *Signs and Reasonings*, p. 9a.3.

[257] Commentary on *Signs and Reasonings*, vol. 3, p. 14.

[258] *Signs and Reasonings*, p. 9a.3-4.

[259] Commentary on *Signs and Reasonings*, vol. 3, p. 11.

[260] Ibid., vol. 3, p. 11.

[261] Commentary on *Signs and Reasonings*, vol. 3, p. 14.

[262] Commentary on *Signs and Reasonings*, vol. 1, p. 61.

263 Commentary on *Signs and Reasonings,* vol. 3, p. 11.

264 Ibid., vol. 3, p. 10.

265 *Signs and Reasonings,* p. 9a.4-5.

266 Ibid., p. 9a.5-6.

267 Commentary on *Signs and Reasonings,* vol. 2, Apr. 18, 1977, p. 2.

268 Kajiyama, *An Introduction to Buddhist Philosophy,* p. 76.

269 Commentary on *Signs and Reasonings,* vol. 1, p. 62.

270 Commentary on *Signs and Reasonings,* vol. 4, p. 8.

271 Ibid., vol. 4, p. 4.

272 Commentary on *Signs and Reasonings,* vol. 1, p. 63.

273 Ibid.

274 Ibid., vol. 4, p. 14.

275 Ibid., vol. 4, p. 5.

276 Ibid., vol. 5, p. 3.

277 Ibid., vol. 4, p. 11.

278 *Signs and Reasonings,* p. 9b.3-5.

279 Commentary on *Signs and Reasonings,* vol. 4, p. 4.

280 *Signs and Reasonings,* p. 9b.2-3.

281 Ibid., p. 9b.5.

282 Ibid., p. 9b.6.

283 Ibid., p. 9b.7.

284 Ibid., p. 10a. 1-3.

285 Commentary on *Signs and Reasonings,* section 6, p. 3.

286 *Signs and Reasonings,* pp. 13a.4-b.5.

287 Ibid., p. 13a.4-6.

288 Ibid., p. 13a.6-13b.1

289 Commentary on *Signs and Reasonings,* vol. 5, p. 14.

290 Ibid., vol. 5, pp. 13-15.

291 *Signs and Reasonings,* p. 13b.1-3.

292 Ibid., p. 13b.3-5.

293 Commentary on *Signs and Reasonings,* vol. 1, p. 65.

294 *Signs and Reasonings,* p. 10a.6-b.2.

295 Ibid., p. 10b.2.

296 Commentary on *Signs and Reasonings,* vol. 1, p. 67.

297 Ibid., vol. 4, p. 1.

298 Ibid., vol. 4, p. 6.

299 *Signs and Reasonings,* pp. 10b.2-4.

300 Commentary on *Signs and Reasonings,* vol. 4, p. 6.

301 Ibid., vol. 4, pp. 13-14.

302 Commentary on *Signs and Reasonings,* vol. 2, Apr. 18, 1977, p. 6.

303 *Signs and Reasonings,* p. 10a.3-4.

304 Commentary on *Signs and Reasonings,* section 6, p. 4.

305 Commentary on *Signs and Reasonings,* p. 67.

306 Commentary on *Signs and Reasonings,* vol. 4, p. 5.

307 Ge-shay Lob-sang-gya-tso, commentary on *Signs and Reasonings,* vol. 4, p. 7.

308 *Signs and Reasonings,* p 10a.4-5.

309 Commentary on *Signs and Reasonings,* section 6, p. 5.

310 *Signs and Reasonings,* p. 9b.6-7.

311 Ibid., p. 10b.4-5.

312 Ibid., p. 13b.5-6.

313 Commentary on *Signs and Reasonings,* p. 12.

314 *Signs and Reasonings,* p, 10a.5-6.

315 Commentary on *Signs and Reasonings,* vol. 4, p. 7.

316 Commentary on *Signs and Reasonings,* vol. 2, Apr. 18, 1977, p. 5.

317 *Signs and Reasonings,* p. 11a.1-2.

318 Commentary on *Signs and Reasonings,* vol. 1, p. 70.

319 Commentary on *Signs and Reasonings,* vol. 4, p. 19.

320 Ibid., vol. 4, p. 19.

321 *Signs and Reasonings,* p. 11a.5.

322 Ge-shay Ge-dün-lo-drö, commentary on *Signs and Reasonings,* section 7, p. 2.

323 Commentary on *Signs and Reasonings,* vol. 1,

p. 71.

324 Commentary on *Signs and Reasonings,* section 7, p. 2.

325 Commentary on *Signs and Reasonings,* vol. 5, pp. 4-5.

326 Ibid., vol. 5, p. 2.

327 Ibid., vol. 5, p. 3.

328 Commentary on *Signs and Reasonings,* vol. 4, p. 14.

329 Ge-shay Lob-sang-gya-tso, commentary on *Signs and Reasonings,* vol. 4, p. 15.

330 Commentary on *Signs and Reasonings,* vol. 1, p. 71.

331 Commentary on *Signs and Reasonings,* vol. 5, p. 1.

332 Ibid., vol. 5, pp. 1-2.

333 Ibid., vol. 5, p. 2.

334 *Signs and Reasonings,* p. 11a.6.

335 Ibid., p. 11a.6-7.

336 Ge-shay Ge-dün-lo-drö, commentary on *Signs and Reasonings,* section 7, p. 6.

337 Commentary on *Signs and Reasonings,* vol. 1, p. 72.

338 Ibid., vol. 1, p. 73.

339 Correct effect signs are discussed in chapter four.

340 Commentary on *Signs and Reasonings,* vol. 5, pp. 6-7. The ge-shay adds, "In this case, the related object is smoke."

341 Ibid., vol. 5 p. 7.

342 Commentary on *Signs and Reasonings,* vol. 1, p. 73.

343 *Signs and Reasonings,* pp. 11a.6-11b.1.

344 Commentary on *Signs and Reasonings,* section 7, p. 7.

345 Commentary on *Signs and Reasonings,* vol. 5, p. 11.

346 Ibid.

347 *Signs and Reasonings,* p. 11a.3-4.

348 Ibid., p. 11b.1-3.

349 Ibid., p. 11 b.3-5.

350 Ibid., p. 12a.4-5.

351 Ibid., p. 11b.5-6.

352 Ibid., p. 11b.7.

353 Ibid., pp. 11b.7-12 a. 1.

354 Ge-shay Ge-dün-lo-drö, commentary on *Signs and Reasonings,* section 7, p. 8.

355 *Signs and Reasonings,* p. 12a.1-2.

356 Ge-shay Ge-dün-lo-drö, commentary on *Signs and Reasonings,* section 7, p. 8.

357 Ge-shay Tsül-trim-nam-gyel, *Signs and Reasonings,* p. 11b.1.

358 *Signs and Reasonings,* p. 12a.2-3.

359 Commentary on *Signs and Reasonings,* section 7, p. 8.

360 *Signs and Reasonings,* p. 12a.3-4.

361 Ge-shay Ge-dün-lo-drö, commentary on *Signs and Reasonings,* section 7, p. 8.

362 Lati Rin-po-che, commentary on *Signs and Reasonings,* vol. 1, p. 82.

363 Ibid., vol. 1, p. 79.

364 *Signs and Reasonings,* p. 12a.6-7.

365 Commentary on *Signs and Reasonings,* section 8, p. 2.

366 This explanation is based on instructions by Lati Rin-po-che (commentary on *Signs and Reasonings,* vol. 1, p. 82).

367 Commentary on *Signs and Reasonings,* vol. 1, p. 82.

368 Commentary on *Signs and Reasonings,* section 8, p. 2.

369 Commentary on *Signs and Reasonings,* vol. 5, p. 12.

370 Ibid., vol. 5, p. 10.

371 Commentary on *Signs and Reasonings,* section 8, p. 2.

372 Commentary on *Signs and Reasonings,* vol. 5, p. 12.

373 *Signs and Reasonings,* p. 12b.1-3.

374 Ibid., p. 12b.3-5.

375 Commentary on *Signs and Reasonings,* vol. 2, Apr. 25, 1977, p. 2.

376 *Signs and Reasonings,* p. 12b.5-6.

377 Commentary on *Signs and Reasonings,* section 8, p. 3.

378 *Signs and Reasonings,* p. 12b.6-13a.1.

[379] Commentary on *Signs and Reasonings,* vol. 2, Apr. 25, 1977, p. 2.

[380] *Signs and Reasonings,* p. 13a.1-2.

[381] Commentary on *Signs and Reasonings,* vol. 2, Apr. 25, 1977, p. 3.

[382] *Signs and Reasonings,* p. 13a.2-4.

[383] Ibid., pp. 13b.6-14a.1.

[384] Commentary on *Signs and Reasonings,* section 8, p. 3.

[385] *Signs and Reasonings,* p. 14a.1.

[386] Commentary on *Signs and Reasonings,* vol. 5, p. 14.

[387] Commentary on *Signs and Reasonings,* vol. 2, Apr. 25, 1977, p. 6.

[388] *Signs and Reasonings,* p. 14a1-2.

[389] Commentary on *Signs and Reasonings,* section 8, p. 3.

[390] *Signs and Reasonings,* p. 14a.2-4.

[391] Ibid., p. 14a.4-5.

[392] Commentary on *Signs and Reasonings,* section 8, p. 4.

[393] *Signs and Reasonings,* p. 14a.5-7.

[394] Commentary on *Signs and Reasonings,* section 8, p. 5.

[395] *Signs and Reasonings,* p. 14a.7-14b.1.

[396] Ibid., p. 14b.1-3.

[397] Ibid., p. 14b.3-5.

[398] Ibid., pp. 14b.7-15a.1.

[399] Commentary on *Signs and Reasonings,* vol. 2, Apr. 18, 1977, p. 6.

[400] Commentary on *Signs and Reasonings,* Apr. 30, section 10, pp. 1-2.

[401] Ibid., section 10, p. 2.

[402] *Signs and Reasonings,* p. 15a.1-2.

[403] Commentary on *Signs and Reasonings,* vol. 5, p. 15.

[404] Commentary on *Signs and Reasonings,* section 9, p. 1.

[405] Ibid., p. 5.

[406] Kajiyama, *Introduction to Buddhist Philosophy,* p. 77.

[407] Ibid., pp. 81-82.

[408] Ibid., pp. 82-85.

[409] Ibid., p. 85.

[410] Ibid.

[411] Pur-bu-jok, "The Greater Path of Reasoning" in *Collected Topics,* p.40a.2-3.

[412] Ibid., p. 40a.4-5.

[413] *Signs and Reasonings,* p.15a.2-3.

[414] Ibid., *Signs and Reasonings,* p. 12b.1.

[415] Commentary on *Signs and Reasonings,* vol. 6, p. 1.

[416] *Signs and Reasonings,* p.15a.3-4.

[417] Ibid., p.15a.4-5.

[418] Ibid., pp. 9a.7-9b.1.

[419] Ibid., p. 15a.5-6.

[420] Ibid., p. 15a.6-7.

[421] Commentary on *Signs and Reasonings,* vol. 5, p. 9.

[422] Commentary on *Signs and Reasonings,* vol. 6, p. 1.

[423] Commentary on *Signs and Reasonings,* vol. 5, p. 9.

[424] Commentary on *Signs and Reasonings,* vol. 1, April 21, 1977, p. 96.

[425] Ge-shay Tsül-trim-nam-gyel discusses these two types of signs in his *Signs and Reasonings,* pp. 12b.2-14a.2.

[426] *Signs and Reasonings,* p. 15a.7-b.1.

[427] Ibid., p. 3a.3.

[428] Ibid., p. 15b.2-3.

[429] Ibid., p. 15b.3-4.

[430] Ibid., p. 15b.4-5.

[431] *Signs and Reasonings,* p. 13b.4.

[432] *Signs and Reasonings,* p. 15b.5-6.

[433] Commentary on *Signs and Reasonings,* vol. 1, p. 88.

[434] *Signs and Reasonings,* p. 15b.6-7.

[435] Ibid., p. 16a.1-3.

[436] Commentary on *Signs and Reasonings,* vol. 6, p. 3.

[437] *Signs and Reasonings,* p. 25a.5-6.

[438] Ibid., pp. 24a.7-24b.2.

439 Ibid., p. 24b.2.

440 Ibid., p. 24b.2-3.

441 Ibid., p. 24b.23-5.

442 This analysis of Pur-bu-jok's reasoning was provided by Den-ma Lo-chö Rin-po-che in individual instruction on *Signs and Reasonings*.

443 *Signs and Reasonings*, p. 24b.5-6.

444 Ibid., pp. 24b.6-25a.1.

445 Ibid., p. 25a.1-2.

446 Ibid., p. 25a.2-5.

447 Ibid., p. 25a.5-7.

448 Commentary on *Signs and Reasonings*, section 17, pp. 1-2.

449 Ibid., section 17, p. 2.

450 Ibid.

451 Commentary on *Signs and Reasonings*, vol. 6, p. 2.

452 Commentary on *Signs and Reasonings*, vol. 2, March 28, 1977, p. 2.

453 Pur-bu-jok posits this division on p. 16a.3 of *Signs and Reasonings*.

454 *Signs and Reasonings*, p. 16a.3-4.

455 Commentary on *Signs and Reasonings*, vol. 1, p. 99.

456 Commentary on *Signs and Reasonings*, vol. 6, pp. 4-5.

457 *Signs and Reasonings*, p. 16a.5-7.

458 Commentary on *Signs and Reasonings*, vol. 6, pp. 5-6.

459 *Signs and Reasonings*, p. 16a.4-5.

460 Commentary on *Signs and Reasonings*, vol. 1, p. 97.

461 Commentary on *Signs and Reasonings*, vol. 6, pp. 6-7.

462 See Lati Rin-po-che's discussion of this topic in *Mind in Tibetan Buddhism*, p. 82.

463 Commentary on *Signs and Reasonings*, vol. 6, p. 7.

464 *Signs and Reasonings*, p. 16b.2-3.

465 Commentary on *Signs and Reasonings*, vol. 5, p. 18.

466 *Signs and Reasonings*, p. 16b.3-4.

467 Commentary on *Signs and Reasonings*, vol. 5, p. 18.

468 *Signs and Reasonings*, p. 16a.4.

469 Ibid., p. 16a.7-16b.1.

470 Lati Rin-po-che, *Mind in Tibetan Buddhism*, p. 78.

471 Commentary on *Signs and Reasonings*, vol. 1, p. 93.

472 Commentary on *Signs and Reasonings*, vol. 5, p. 17.

473 Commentary on *Signs and Reasonings*, vol. 1, p. 94.

474 Ibid., vol. 1, p. 94.

475 *Signs and Reasonings*, p. 16a.7-b.1.

476 Commentary on *Signs and Reasonings*, vol.1, p. 95.

477 *Signs and Reasonings*, p. 26b.1.

478 Commentary on *Signs and Reasonings*, vol. 5, p. 17.

479 Ibid., vol. 5, pp. 17-18.

480 *Signs and Reasonings*, p. 16b.1-2.

481 Ibid., p. 16b.4-6.

482 Commentary on *Signs and Reasonings*, vol. 5, p. 12.

483 Commentary on *Signs and Reasonings*, vol. 1, p. 102.

484 Ibid., p. 106.

485 *Signs and Reasonings*, p. 16b.6.

486 Commentary on *Signs and Reasonings*, vol. 5, p. 20.

487 Commentary on *Signs and Reasonings*, vol. 1, p. 103.

488 Ibid., vol. 1, p. 104.

489 Ibid., vol. 1, pp. 104-105.

490 Ibid., vol. 1, p. 105.

491 Ibid., vol. 1, p. 104.

492 Commentary on *Signs and Reasonings*, vol. 5, p. 20.

493 Ge-shay Lob-sang-gya-tso, commentary on *Signs and Reasonings*, vol. 5, p. 15.

494 *Signs and Reasonings*, pp. 16b.7-17a.1.

495 Ibid., p.17a.2.

[496] Commentary on *Signs and Reasonings*, April 30, p. 7.

[497] Quasi-signs (or "quasi-reasons") are discussed in chapter nine.

[498] *Signs and Reasonings*, p. 17a.2-3.

[499] Commentary on *Signs and Reasonings*, section 10, pp. 14-15.

[500] Commentary on *Signs and Reasonings*, vol. 6, p. 8.

[501] *Signs and Reasonings*, p. 17a.4.

[502] Ibid., p. 17a.4-6.

[503] Ibid., p. 17a.6-7.

[504] Commentary on *Signs and Reasonings*, vol. 6, pp. 8-9.

[505] *Signs and Reasonings*, pp. 17a.7-17b.2.

[506] Ibid., p. 17b.2-3.

[507] Ibid., p. 17b.3.

[508] Ibid., p. 17b.3-4.

[509] Ibid., p. 17b.4-5.

[510] Ibid., pp. 17b.5-18a.2.

[511] Commentary on *Signs and Reasonings*, section 10, p. 15.

[512] *Signs and Reasonings*, p. 18a.4-6.

[513] Commentary on *Signs and Reasonings*, vol. 2, Feb 4, p. 10.

[514] *Signs and Reasonings*, p. 18a.6-7.

[515] Ibid., p. 18a.7.

[516] Ibid., p. 18a.7-18b.1.

[517] *Signs and Reasonings*, p. 16a.4.

[518] Commentary on *Signs and Reasonings*, section 12, p. 3.

[519] *Signs and Reasonings*, p. 18b.1-2.

[520] Ibid., p. 18b.2-3.

[521] Ibid., p. 18b.3-4.

[522] Commentary on *Signs and Reasonings*, section 12, p. 3.

[523] *Signs and Reasonings*, p. 18b.4-5.

[524] Commentary on *Signs and Reasonings*, section 12, p. 3.

[525] *Signs and Reasonings*, p. 18b.5-6.

[526] Ibid., p. 18b.6-7.

[527] Commentary on *Signs and Reasonings*, section 12, p. 4.

[528] Lati Rin-po-che, commentary on *Signs and Reasonings*, vol. 1, p. 106.

[529] *Signs and Reasonings*, pp. 18b.7-19a.1.

[530] Ibid., p. 19a.1-3.

[531] Ibid., p. 19a.3-4.

[532] Ibid., p. 19a.4-5.

[533] Commentary on *Signs and Reasonings*, section 12, p. 4.

[534] *Signs and Reasonings*, p. 19a.5-6.

[535] Ibid., p. 19a.6-7.

[536] Ibid., pp. 19a.7-19b.1.

[537] Ibid., p. 19b.1-2.

[538] Commentary on *Signs and Reasonings*, section 12, p. 5.

[539] *Signs and Reasonings*, p. 19b.2-3.

[540] Ibid., p. 19b.4-6.

[541] Ibid., p. 19b.6-7.

[542] Commentary on *Signs and Reasonings*, section 12, p. 5.

[543] Commentary on *Signs and Reasonings*, vol. 6, p. 10.

[544] Commentary on *Signs and Reasonings*, vol. 5, p. 17.

[545] *Signs and Reasonings*, pp. 19b.7-20a.2.

[546] Commentary on *Signs and Reasonings*, vol. 1, p. 113.

[547] Ibid., vol. 1, p. 113.

[548] *Signs and Reasonings*, p. 20a.2-3.

[549] Ibid., p. 20a.3-4.

[550] Commentary on *Signs and Reasonings*, vol. 1, p. 115.

[551] *Signs and Reasonings*, p.20a.5-7.

[552] Ibid., p. 20a.7.

[553] Commentary on *Signs and Reasonings*, section 12, p. 6.

[554] *Signs and Reasonings*, pp. 20a.7-20b.1.

[555] Commentary on *Signs and Reasonings*, section 12, p. 6.

[556] *Signs and Reasonings*, p. 20b.1-2.

[557] Commentary on *Signs and Reasonings*, section

12, p. 7.

558 *Signs and Reasonings,* p. 20b.2-3.

559 Commentary on *Signs and Reasonings,* section 12, p. 7.

560 *Signs and Reasonings,* p. 20b.3-5.

561 Ibid., p. 20a.6-7.

562 Commentary on *Signs and Reasonings,* vol. 6, p. 15.

563 Ibid., vol. 6, p. 16.

564 *Signs and Reasonings,* p. 21a.2.

565 Commentary on *Signs and Reasonings,* vol. 6, p. 16.

566 Ibid.

567 *Signs and Reasonings,* pp. 20b.7-21a.2.

568 Ibid., p. 21a.3.

569 Ge-shay Tsül-trim-nam-gyel, *Signs and Reasonings,* p. 19b.1-3.

570 Commentary on *Signs and Reasonings,* section 13, pp. 1-3.

571 Commentary on *Signs and Reasonings,* section 2, p. 1.

572 Ibid., section 2, p. 2.

573 *Signs and Reasonings,* pp. 21a.6-21b.1.

574 Ibid., p. 21b.1-4.

575 Ibid., p. 21b.4.

576 Ibid., p. 21b.5.

577 Ibid., p. 21b.5-6.

578 Ibid., p. 6a.7.

579 Commentary on *Signs and Reasonings,* vol. 2, p. 2.

580 *Signs and Reasonings,* p. 21b.6.

581 Ibid., p. 21b.6-7.

582 Commentary on *Signs and Reasonings,* vol. 1, p. 30.

583 *Signs and Reasonings,* p. 21b.7.

584 Commentary on *Signs and Reasonings,* section 13, p. 9.

585 *Signs and Reasonings,* pp. 21b.7-22a.2.

586 Ibid., p. 22a.2-3.

587 Ibid., p. 22a.3-4.

588 Ibid., p. 22a.4.

589 Individual instruction on *Signs and Reasonings.*

590 *Signs and Reasonings,* p. 22a.5.

591 Commentary on *Signs and Reasonings,* vol. 2, April 8, 1977, p. 7.

592 *Signs and Reasonings,* p. 22a.6-7.

593 Commentary on *Signs and Reasonings,* vol. 2, April 8, 1977, p. 7.

594 *Signs and Reasonings,* pp. 22a.7-22b.1.

595 Commentary on *Signs and Reasonings,* vol. 2, April 8, 1977, p. 7.

596 *Signs and Reasonings,* p. 22b.1-2.

597 Lati Rin-po-che, commentary on *Signs and Reasonings,* vol. 1, p. 122.

598 *Signs and Reasonings,* p. 9b.2-3.

599 Ibid., p. 23b. 6-24a.2.

600 Ibid., p. 25b. 1-2.

INDEX

(See also the Detailed Outline, pp. 487ff.)